Praise for *My Promised Land*

"If Ari Shavit is not actually the angel in the minefield he certainly writes like one. Not a page of *My Promised Land* goes past without a smart provocation . . . or a perfectly focused vision. . . . Shavit conducts this orchestration of the senses like a maestro, even when his subject encompasses hatred, slaughter and (less inevitably) taking ecstasy in Tel Aviv. His accomplishment is so unlikely, so total . . . that it makes you believe anything is possible, even, God help us, peace in the Middle East. [The] book is not just enthralling, but morally dignified. . . . And it is just because Shavit's pages are so full of unresolved conflicts, personal anguish and humane compassion for both suffering peoples, along with a brilliant gift for capturing the high voltage creative exuberance of an Israel living on the edge, that his book is, by some light years, the best thing to have been written on the subject. . . . It helps that Shavit . . . is one of the most dazzling nonfiction writers alive. . . . Even if you've had it up to here with the Jews and the Arabs, this book will sweep you up in its narrative force and not let go of you until it is done. It is a reminder that if the first obligation of history is self-criticism, the second is philosophically enriched storytelling—and how very rarely this goal is achieved. . . . Shavit has produced a historical narrative pitched to our restless times, and cinematic in its widescreen pathos . . . [a] scrupulously just, wisely impassioned book. . . . He is committed to a redefinition of his nation, 'a new Jewish Israeli narrative.' If that does come to pass, Ari Shavit will be recognized as having written its inaugural text."

—Simon Schama, *Financial Times*

"Spellbinding . . . Mr. Shavit subtly builds his stories with a mix of individual portraits, historical detail and personal memoir. [He] is that rare person who can listen as intensely as he can think. Although he is a columnist for the left-leaning Israeli daily *Haaretz*, he transcends tribal politics. Sympathetic but unflinching, he finds things to chastise—and admire—on every side. In a place with too much history and too much certainty, a 'lonely rock in a stormy ocean,' he manages to reach conclusions without lapsing into narrow judgments, and finds truth without asserting that it is the only truth. . . . In this divided, fought-over shard of land splintered from the Middle East barely seventy years ago, Mr. Shavit's prophetic voice carries lessons that all sides need to hear."

—*The Economist*

"Israel is not a proposition, it is a country. Its facticity is one of the great accomplishments of the Jews' history. . . . It is one of the achievements of Ari Shavit's important and powerful book to recover [that] feeling . . . and to revel in it, to restore the grandeur of the simple fact in full view of the complicated facts. *My Promised Land* startles in many ways, not least in its relative lack of interest in providing its readers with a handy politics. Shavit . . . has an undoctrinaire mind. He comes not to praise or to blame, though along the way he does both, with erudition and with eloquence; he comes instead to observe and to reflect. This is the least tendentious book about Israel I have ever read. It is a Zionist book unblinkered by Zionism. It is about the entirety of the Israeli experience. Shavit is immersed in all of the history of his country. While some of it offends him, none of it is alien to him. His extraordinary chapter on the charismatic and corrupt Aryeh Deri, and the rise of Sephardic religious politics in Israel, richly illustrates the reach of his understanding. . . . There is love in *My Promised Land*, but there is no propaganda. . . . The author of *My Promised Land* is a dreamer with an addiction to reality. He holds out for affirmation without illusion. Shavit's book is an extended test of his own capacity to maintain his principles in full view of the brutality that surrounds them."

—LEON WIESELTIER, *The New York Times Book Review*

"One of the most nuanced and challenging books written on Israel in years . . . [The] book's real power: On an issue so prone to polemic, Mr. Shavit offers candor."

—OREN KESSLER, *The Wall Street Journal*

"I can think of no better time for a good book about Israel—the real Israel, not the fantasy, do-no-wrong Israel peddled by its most besotted supporters or the do-no-right colonial monster portrayed by its most savage critics. Ari Shavit, the popular *Haaretz* columnist, has come out with just such a book. . . . Shavit is one of a handful of experts whom I've relied upon to understand Israel ever since I reported there in the 1980s. What do all my Israeli analytical sources have in common? They all share a way of thinking about Israel—which is expressed with deep insight, compassion and originality in Shavit's must-read book—that to understand Israel today requires keeping several truths in tension in your head at the same time. . . . The uniqueness of Shavit's book is that when you're done with it you can understand, respect or love Israel—but not in a dogmatic or unthinking way, and not a fake or contrived Israel. Shavit celebrates the Zionist man-made miracle—from its start-ups to its gay bars—while remaining affectionate, critical, realistic and morally anchored. . . . His book is a real contribution to changing the conversation about Israel and building a healthier relationship with it. Before their next ninety-minute phone call, both Barack and Bibi should read it."

—THOMAS L. FRIEDMAN, *The New York Times*

"A searingly honest, descriptively lush, painful and riveting story of the creation of Zionism in Israel and [Shavit's] own personal voyage."

—SALLY QUINN, *The Washington Post*

"A tour de force. Written in lyrical prose by a distinguished journalist who listens attentively when he interviews, Shavit engages his subjects and also the land of Israel. . . . *My Promised Land* is a work without peer. No single work depicts the complexity, vitality and achievements of Israel society as well. And no other work also depicts Israel's failings and its challenges so poignantly, so lovingly and so soberly."

—MICHAEL BERENBAUM, *Jewish Journal*

"Required reading for both the left and the right . . . Shavit is a master storyteller. [His] retelling of history jars us out of our familiar retrospections, reminds us (and we do need reminders) that there are historical reasons why Israel is a country on the edge."

—JEROME A. CHANES, *The Jewish Week*

"A virtue of Shavit's virtuous book is that it exhumes the dream of Zionism—and also its success."

—RICHARD COHEN, *The Washington Post*

"This book [is] the most extraordinary book that I've read on [Israel] since Amos Elon's book called *The Israelis* and that was published in the late sixties."

—DAVID REMNICK on *Charlie Rose*

"[A] valuable new book ... Its success indicates something intriguing: a significant audience for a serious discussion about Israel, rooted in reality and without polemic. Shavit's book provides an in-depth portrait of contemporary Israeli society in a way that few recent books have—or have even attempted. From the founders' dilemmas and romantic yearnings for statehood to a contemporary Israel whose politics lunges between crisis and petty intrigue and whose landscape encapsulates the fast-paced, even hedonistic dynamism of Tel Aviv, Shavit tells a tale that gets the reader inside daily reality."

—JO-ANN MORT, *Dissent*

"With the heart of a storyteller and the mind of a historian, Ari Shavit has written a powerful and compelling book about the making of modern Israel. No country is more emotionally connected to the United States, and no country's fate matters more to many Americans. And yet until Shavit's *My Promised Land*, it has been growing more difficult to sense the character of Israel through all the caricatures. This book is vital reading for Americans who care about the future, not only of the United States but of the world."

—JON MEACHAM

"A beautiful, mesmerizing, morally serious, and vexing book. I've been waiting most of my adult life for an Israeli to plumb the deepest mysteries of his country's existence and share his discoveries, and Ari Shavit does so brilliantly, writing simultaneously like a poet and a prophet. *My Promised Land* is a remarkable achievement."

—JEFFREY GOLDBERG, national correspondent, *The Atlantic*

"Ari Shavit's *My Promised Land* takes readers on a moving and, in many ways, heart-rending ride on the emotional roller coaster that is an essential element of Israel's very existence. Shavit, a true Israeli patriot, poignantly describes his cherished homeland while courageously baring his own certainties and doubts about the Zionist enterprise and drawing us into the intimate relationship Israelis have with their nation, with one another, and with the Jewish people. With all of the challenges Israel faces from within and without, Israelis like Ari Shavit want to see Israel continue to succeed and flourish. This book gives all of us reason to want to be a part of that success."

—ABRAHAM FOXMAN, national director, Anti-Defamation League

"My Promised Land is an Israeli book like no other. Not since Amos Elon's *The Israelis,* Amos Oz's *In the Land of Israel,* and Thomas L. Friedman's *From Beirut to Jerusalem* has there been such a powerful and comprehensive book written about the Jewish state and the Israeli-Palestinian conflict. Ari Shavit is one of Israel's leading columnists and writers. Yet the story he tells describes with great empathy the Palestinian tragedy and the century-long struggle between Jews and Arabs over the Holy Land. While Shavit is being brutally honest regarding the Zionist enterprise, he is also insightful, sensitive, and attentive to the dramatic life stories of his fascinating heroes and heroines. The result is a unique nonfiction book that has the qualities of fine literature. It brings to life epic history without being a conventional history book. It deepens contemporary political understanding without being a one-sided political polemic. It is painful and provocative yet colorful, emotional, life-loving, and inspiring. *My Promised Land* is the ultimate personal odyssey of a humanist exploring the startling biography of his tormented homeland, which is at the very center of global interest."

—EHUD BARAK, former prime minister and defense minister of Israel

"Ari Shavit's *My Promised Land* is without question one of the most important books about Israel and Zionism that I have ever read. Both movingly inspiring and at times heartbreakingly painful, *My Promised Land* tells the story of the Jewish state as it has never been told before, capturing both the triumph and the torment of Israel's experience and soul. This is the book that has the capacity to reinvent and reshape the long-overdue conversation about how Israel's complex past ought to shape its still uncertain future."

—DANIEL GORDIS, author of *Saving Israel* and
Koret Distinguished Fellow at Shalem College, Jerusalem

"With deeply engaging personal narratives and morally nuanced portraits, Ari Shavit takes us way beneath the headlines to the very heart of Israel's dilemmas in his brilliant new work. His expertise as a reporter comes through in the interviews, while his lyricism brings the writing—and the people—to life. Shavit also challenges Israelis and Diaspora Jewry to be bold in imagining the next chapter for Israel, a challenge that will no doubt be informed by this important book."

—RICK JACOBS, president, Union for Reform Judaism

"*My Promised Land* is a passionate yet fair-minded account of how the Israel of today came into being. Whether or not you agree with its premises and assumptions, you will find this book hard to put down for its sheer narrative force. Both lyrically personal and rigorously reported, Ari Shavit's book will undoubtedly shape the conversation about a country we all talk about but few of us know well for years to come."

—DAPHNE MERKIN, author of *Dreaming of Hitler* and *Enchantment*

"This is the epic history that Israel deserves—beautifully written, dramatically rendered, full of moral complexity. Ari Shavit has made a storied career by explaining Israel to Israelis; now he shares his mind-blowing, trustworthy insights with the rest of us. It is the best book on the subject to arrive in many years."

—FRANKLIN FOER, editor of *The New Republic*

MY PROMISED LAND

MY PROMISED LAND

THE TRIUMPH AND TRAGEDY OF ISRAEL

ARI SHAVIT

SPIEGEL & GRAU
NEW YORK

Published in the United States by Spiegel & Grau, an imprint of
Random House, a division of Penguin Random House LLC, New York.

Spiegel & Grau and Design is a registered
trademark of Penguin Random House LLC.

Originally published in the United States in hardcover and in slightly different
form in 2013 and subsequently in trade paperback in 2015 by Spiegel & Grau,
an imprint of Random House, a division of Penguin Random House LLC.

Portions of this work were originally published in different form
in *Haaretz* and *The New York Review of Books*.

All credits for permission to reproduce photographs can be found on page 481.

Library of Congress Cataloging-in-Publication Data
Shavit, Ari.
My promised land / Ari Shavit.
p.   cm.
ISBN 978-0-385-52171-0
eBook ISBN 978-0-8129-8464-4
1. Arab-Israeli conflict.   2. Israel—Politics and government.   I. Title.
DS119.7.S381877   2013
956.05'4—dc23   20120466122

Printed in the United States of America on acid-free paper

randomhousebooks.com
spiegelandgrau.com

8 9

Book design by Susan Turner

To my love, Timna

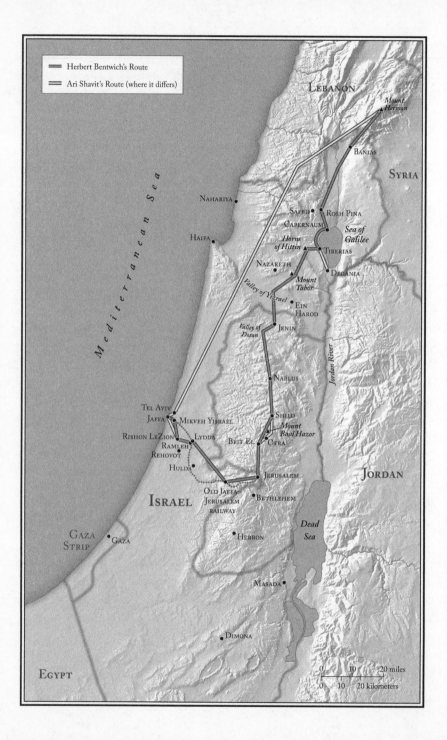

CONTENTS

For as long as I can remember, I remember fear. Existential fear. The Israel I grew up in—the Israel of the mid-1960s—was energetic, exuberant, and hopeful. But I always felt that beyond the well-to-do houses and upper-middle-class lawns of my hometown lay a dark ocean. One day, I dreaded, that dark ocean would rise and drown us all. A mythological tsunami would strike our shores and sweep my Israel away. It would become another Atlantis, lost in the depths of the sea.

One morning in June 1967, when I was nine years old, I came upon my father shaving in the bathroom. I asked him if the Arabs were going to win. Would the Arabs conquer our Israel? Would they really throw us all into the sea? A few days later the Six Day War began.

In October 1973, the sirens of imminent disaster began to wail. I was in bed with the flu in the late noon of that silent Yom Kippur as F-4 jets tore through the sky. They were flying 500 feet above our roof en route to the Suez Canal to fend off the invading Egyptian forces that took Israel by surprise. Many of them never returned. I was sixteen years old, and I was petrified as the news came in of the collapse of our defenses in the Sinai desert and the Golan Heights. For ten terrifying days it seemed that my primordial fears were justified. Israel was in peril. The walls of the third Jewish temple were shaking.

In January 1991, the first Gulf War broke out. Tel Aviv was bombarded by Iraqi SCUD missiles. There was some concern regarding a possible chemical weapons attack. For weeks, Israelis carried their gas mask kits with them everywhere they went. Occasionally, when a warning sounded that a warhead was on its way, we shut ourselves in sealed rooms with the masks on our faces. Although it turned out that the threat was not real, there was something horrific about this surreal ritual. I listened closely to the sounds of sirens and looked with dismay at the terrified eyes of my loved ones locked in German-made gas masks.

In March 2002, a wave of terror rattled Israel. Hundreds died as Palestinian suicide bombers attacked buses, nightclubs, and shopping malls. As I was writing in my Jerusalem study one night, I heard a loud boom. It had to be our neighborhood pub, I realized. I grabbed my writing pad and ran up the street. Three handsome young men were sitting at the bar in front of their half-full beer mugs—dead. A petite young woman was lying in a corner—lifeless. Those who were only wounded were screaming and crying. As I looked at the hell around me in the glowing lights of the blown-up pub, the journalist I now was asked, What will be? How long can we sustain this lunacy? Will there come a time when the vitality we Israelis are known for will surrender to the forces of death attempting to annihilate us?

The decisive victory in the 1967 war dissipated the prewar fears. The recovery of the 1970s and 1980s healed the deep wound of 1973. The peace process of the 1990s mended the trauma of 1991. The prosperity of the late 2000s glossed over the horror of 2002. Precisely because we are shrouded in uncertainty, we Israelis insist on believing in ourselves, in our nation-state, and in our future. But throughout the years, my own muted fear never went away. To discuss or express this fear was taboo, yet it was with me wherever I went. Our cities seemed to be built on shifting sand. Our houses never seemed quite stable. Even as my nation grew stronger and wealthier, I felt it was profoundly vulnerable. I realized how exposed we are, how constantly intimidated. Yes, our life continues to be intense and rich and in many ways happy. Israel projects a sense of security that emanates from its physical, economic, and military success. The vitality of our daily life is astonishing. And yet there is always the fear that one day daily life will freeze like Pompeii's.

My beloved homeland will crumble as enormous Arab masses or mighty Islamic forces overcome its defenses and eradicate its existence.

For as long as I can remember, I remember occupation. Only a week after I asked my father whether the Arab nations were going to conquer Israel, Israel conquered the Arab-populated regions of the West Bank and Gaza. A month later, my parents, my brother, and I embarked on a first family tour of the occupied cities of Ramallah, Bethlehem, and Hebron. Wherever we went, there were remains of burned Jordanian jeeps, trucks, and military vehicles. White flags of surrender hung over most houses. Some streets were blocked with the mangled, blackened carcasses of fancy Mercedes automobiles that had been run over by the treads of Israeli tanks. Palestinian children my age and younger had fear in their eyes. Their parents appeared devastated and humiliated. Within a few weeks the mighty Arabs were transformed into victims, while the endangered Israelis became conquerors. The Jewish state was now triumphant and proud and drunk with a heady sense of power.

When I was a teenager, everything was still fine. The common wisdom was that ours was a benevolent military occupation. Modern Israel brought progress and prosperity to the Palestinian regions. Now our backward neighbors had the electricity and running water and health care they never had before. They had to realize that they had never had it so good. They were surely grateful for all that we bestowed upon them. And when peace came, we would hand back most of the occupied territories. But for the time being, all was well in the Land of Israel. Arab and Jew coexisted throughout the country, enjoying calm and plenty.

Only when I was a soldier did I grasp that something was wrong. Six months after joining the elite paratrooper brigade of the IDF, I was posted in the very same occupied cities that I had toured as a child ten years earlier. Now I was assigned to do the dirty work: checkpoint duties, house arrests, violent dispersal of demonstrations. What traumatized me most was breaking into homes and taking young men from their warm beds to midnight interrogations. What the hell was going on, I asked myself. Why was I defending my homeland by tyrannizing civilians who were deprived of their rights and freedom? Why was my Israel occupying and oppressing another people?

So I became a peacenik. First as a young activist and then as a journalist, I fought occupation with a passion. In the 1980s I opposed establishing settlements in the Palestinian territories. In the 1990s I supported the establishment of a PLO-led Palestinian state. In the first decade of the twenty-first century I endorsed Israel's unilateral retreat from the Gaza Strip. But almost all the antioccupation campaigns I was involved with ultimately failed. Almost half a century after my family first toured the occupied West Bank, the West Bank is still occupied. As malignant as it is, occupation has become an integral part of the Jewish state's being. It has also become an integral part of my life as an Israeli. Although I oppose occupation, I am responsible for occupation. I cannot deny the fact or escape the fact that my nation has become an occupying nation.

Only a few years ago did it suddenly dawn on me that my existential fear regarding my nation's future and my moral outrage regarding my nation's occupation policy are not unconnected. On the one hand, Israel is the only nation in the West that is occupying another people. On the other hand, Israel is the only nation in the West that is existentially threatened. Both occupation and intimidation make the Israeli condition unique. Intimidation and occupation have become the two pillars of our condition.

Most observers and analysts deny this duality. The ones on the left address occupation and overlook intimidation, while the ones on the right address intimidation and dismiss occupation. But the truth is that without incorporating both elements into one worldview, one cannot grasp Israel or the Israeli-Palestinian conflict. Any school of thought that does not relate seriously to these two fundamentals is bound to be flawed and futile. Only a third approach that internalizes both intimidation and occupation can be realistic and moral and get the Israel story right.

I was born in 1957 in the university town of Rehovot. My father was a scientist, my mother an artist, and some of my ancestors were among the founders of the Zionist enterprise. Conscripted to the army at eighteen, like most Israelis, I served as a paratrooper, and upon completion of my service I studied philosophy at the Hebrew University in Jerusalem, where I joined the peace movement and later the human rights movement. Since 1995, I have been writing for Israel's leading liberal newspaper, *Haaretz*. Although I always stood for peace and supported the two-state solution, I gradually became aware of the flaws and biases of the peace movement. My understanding of both occupation and intimidation made my voice somewhat different from those of others in the media. And as a columnist, I challenge both right-wing and left-wing dogmas. I have learned that there are no simple answers in the Middle East and no quick-fix solutions to the Israeli-Palestinian conflict. I have realized that the Israeli condition is extremely complex, perhaps even tragic.

In the first decade of the twenty-first century Israel did well. Terror subsided, high tech boomed, everyday life was vibrant. Economically, Israel proved to be a tiger. Existentially, it proved to be a powerhouse of vitality, creativity, and sensuality. But under the glow of an extraordinary success story, anxiety was simmering. People started asking aloud the questions that I have been asking myself all my life. It was not just Left-Right politics anymore. It was not just secular versus religious. Something deeper was taking place. Many Israelis were not at ease with the new Israel that was emerging. They were asking themselves if they still belonged to the Jewish state. They had lost their belief in Israel's ability to endure. Some obtained foreign passports; some sent their young to study abroad. The elite saw to it that alongside the Israeli option they would have an alternative one. Although most Israelis still loved their homeland and celebrated its blessings, many lost their unshaken faith in its future.

As the second decade of the twenty-first century has begun to unfold, five different apprehensions cast a shadow on Israel's voracious appetite for life: the notion that the Israeli-Palestinian conflict might not end in the foreseeable future; the concern that Israel's regional strategic hegemony is being challenged; the fear that the very legitimacy of the Jewish state is eroding; the concern that a deeply transformed Israeli society is now divided and polarized, its liberal-democratic foundation crumbling; and the realization that the dysfunctional governments of

Israel cannot deal seriously with such crucial challenges as occupation and social disintegration. Each one of these five apprehensions contains a significant threat, but their combined effect makes the overall threat dramatic. If peace is not feasible, how will we withstand a generation-long conflict as our strategic superiority is endangered and our legitimacy is fading and our democratic identity is fractured and our internal fissures tear us apart? While Israel remains innovative, seductive, and energetic, it has become a nation in doubt. Angst hovers above the land like the enormous shadow of an ominous volcano.

This is why I embarked on this journey. Sixty-five years after its founding, Israel has returned to its core questions. One hundred and sixteen years after it was launched, Zionism is confronted with its core contradictions. Now the challenge goes far beyond that of occupation, and much deeper than the issue of peace. What we all face is the three-fold Israel question: Why Israel? What is Israel? Will Israel?

The Israel question cannot be answered with polemics. As complex as it is, it will not submit itself to arguments and counterarguments. The only way to wrestle with it is to tell the Israel story. That is what I have tried to do in this book. In my own idiosyncratic way and through my own prism I have tried to address our existence as a whole, as I understand it. This book is the personal odyssey of one Israeli who is bewildered by the historic drama engulfing his homeland. It is the journey in space and time of an Israeli-born individual exploring the wider narrative of his nation. Through family history, personal history, and in-depth interviews, I will try to tackle the larger Israel story and the deeper Israel question. What has happened in my homeland for over a century that has brought us to where we are now? What was achieved here and what went wrong here, and where are we heading? Is my deep sense of anxiety well founded? Is the Jewish state in real jeopardy? Are we Israelis caught in a hopeless tragedy, or might we yet revive ourselves and save ourselves and salvage the land we so love?

MY PROMISED LAND

ONE

At First Sight, 1897

ON THE NIGHT OF APRIL 15, 1897, A SMALL, ELEGANT STEAMER IS EN route from Egypt's Port Said to Jaffa. Thirty passengers are on board, twenty-one of them Zionist pilgrims who have come from London via Paris, Marseille, and Alexandria. Leading the pilgrims is the Rt. Honorable Herbert Bentwich, my great-grandfather.

Bentwich is an unusual Zionist. At the end of the nineteenth century, most Zionists are Eastern European; Bentwich is a British subject. Most Zionists are poor; he is a gentleman of independent means. Most Zionists are secular, whereas he is a believer. For most Zionists of this time, Zionism is the only choice, but my great-grandfather chooses Zionism of his own free will. In the early 1890s, Herbert Bentwich makes up his mind that the Jews must settle again in their ancient homeland, Judea.

This pilgrimage is unusual, too. It is the first such journey of upper-middle-class British Jews to the Land of Israel. This is why the founder of political Zionism, Theodor Herzl, attributes such importance to these twenty-one travelers. He expects Bentwich and his colleagues to write a comprehensive report about the Land. Herzl is especially interested in the inhabitants of Palestine and the prospects for colonizing it. He expects the report to be presented at the end of the summer to the first Zionist Congress that is to be held in Basel. But my great-grandfather is somewhat less ambitious. His Zionism, which preceded Herzl's, is essentially romantic. Yet he, too, was carried away by the English translation of Herzl's prophetic manifesto *Der Judenstaat*, or *The State of the Jews*. He personally invited Herzl to appear at his prestigious London club, and he was bowled over by the charisma of the visionary leader. Like Herzl, he believes that Jews must return to Palestine. But as the flat-bottomed steamer *Oxus* carves the black water of the Mediterranean, Bentwich is still an innocent. My great-grandfather does not wish to take a country and to establish a state; he wishes to face God.

I remain on deck for a moment. I want to understand why the *Oxus* is making its way across the sea. Who exactly is this ancestor of mine, and why has he come here?

As the twentieth century is about to begin there are more than 11 million Jews in the world, of whom nearly 7 million live in Eastern Europe, 2 million live in Central and Western Europe, and 1.5 million live in North America. Asian, North African, and Middle Eastern Jewry total less than one million.

Only in North America and Western Europe are Jews emancipated. In Russia they are persecuted. In Poland they are discriminated against. In Islamic countries they are a "protected people" living as second-class citizens. Even in the United States, France, and Britain, emancipation is merely a legality. Anti-Semitism is on the rise. In 1897, Christendom is not yet at peace with its ultimate other. Many find it difficult to address Jews as free, proud, and equal.

In the eastern parts of Europe, Jewish distress is acute. A new breed of ethnic-based anti-Semitism is superseding the old religious-based anti-Semitism. Waves of pogroms befall Jewish towns and townships in Russia, Belarus, Moldova, Romania, and Poland. Most shtetl Jews realize that there is no future for the shtetl. Hundreds of thousands sail to Ellis Island. The Jewish Diaspora experiences once again the cataclysmic phenomenon of mass migration.

Worse than the past is what the future holds. In the next half century, a third of all Jews will be murdered. Two-thirds of European Jewry will be wiped out. The worst catastrophe in the history of the Jewish people is about to occur. So as the *Oxus* approaches the shores of the Holy Land, the need to give Palestine to the Jews feels almost palpable. If the Jews won't disembark here, they will have no future. This emerging coastline may be their only salvation.

There is another need. In the millennium preceding 1897, Jewish survival was guaranteed by the two great g's: God and ghetto. What enabled Jews to maintain their identity and their civilization was their closeness to God and their detachment from the surrounding non-Jewish world. Jews had no territory and no kingdom. They had no liberty and no sovereignty. What held them together as a people were religious belief, religious practice, and a powerful religious narrative, as well as the high walls of isolation built around them by gentiles. But in the hundred years prior to 1897, God drifted away and the ghetto walls collapsed. Secularization and emancipation—limited as they were—eroded the old formula of Jewish survival. There was nothing to maintain the Jewish people as a people living among others. Even if Jews were not to be slaughtered by Russian Cossacks or to be persecuted by French anti-Semites, they were faced with collective mortal danger. Their ability to maintain a non-Orthodox Jewish civilization in the Diaspora was now in question.

There was a need for revolution. If it was to survive, the Jewish people had to be transformed from a people of the Diaspora to a people of sovereignty. In this sense the Zionism that emerges in 1897 is a stroke of genius. Its founders, led by Dr. Herzl, are both prophetic and heroic. All in all, the nineteenth century was the golden age of Western Europe's Jewry. Yet the Herzl Zionists see what is coming. True, they do not know that the twentieth century will conjure up such places as Auschwitz and Treblinka. But in their own way they act in the 1890s in order to preempt the 1940s. They realize they are faced with a radical problem: the coming extinction of the Jews. And they realize that a radical problem calls for a radical solution: the transformation of the Jews, a transformation that can take place only in Palestine, the Jews' ancient homeland.

Herbert Bentwich does not see things as lucidly as Theodor Herzl does. He doesn't know that the century about to begin will be the most dramatic in Jewish history. But his intuition tells him that it's time for radical action. He knows that the distress in Eastern Europe is intolerable and that in the West, assimilation is unavoidable; in the East, Jews are in danger, while in the West, Judaism is in trouble. My great-grandfather understands that the Jewish people desperately need a new place, a new beginning, a new mode of existence. If they are to survive, the Jewish people need the Holy Land.

Bentwich was born in 1856 in the Whitechapel district of London. His father was a Russian-Jewish immigrant who made his living as a traveling salesman, peddling jewelry in Birmingham and Cambridge. But the salesman wanted more for his beloved son. He sent Herbert to fine grammar schools where the boy did well. Knowing that all his parents' hopes were invested in him, the disciplined youngster worked hard to prove himself. In his thirties he was already a successful solicitor living in St. John's Wood.

Before traveling to Palestine, my great-grandfather was a leading figure in the Anglo-Jewish community. His professional expertise was copyright law. In his social life he was one of the founders of the prominent dining and debating Maccabean Club. In his private life he was married to a beautiful, artistic wife who was raising nine children in their magisterial Avenue Road home. Another two would be born in the coming years.

A self-made man, Herbert Bentwich is rigid and pedantic. His dominant traits are arrogance, determination, self-assurance, self-reliance, and nonconformity. Yet he is very much a romantic, with a soft spot for mysticism. Bentwich is a Victorian. He feels deeply indebted to the British Empire for opening its gates to the immigrant's son he once was. When Bentwich was two years old, the first Jew was elected to British Parliament. When he was fifteen, the first Jew was admitted to Oxford. When he turned twenty-nine, the first Jew entered the House of Lords.

For Bentwich these milestones are wonders. He does not look upon emancipation as a belated fulfillment of a natural right but as an act of grace carried out by Queen Victoria's Great Britain.

In his physical appearance Bentwich resembles the Prince of Wales. He has steely blue eyes, a full, well-trimmed beard, a strong jaw. His manner is also that of a nobleman. Although poor at birth, Herbert Bentwich vigorously embraced the values and customs of the empire that ruled the seas. Like a true gentleman he loves travel, poetry, and theater. He knows his Shakespeare and he is at home in the Lake District. Yet he does not compromise his Judaism. With his wife, Susan, he nurtures a family home that is all Anglo-Jewish harmony: morning prayers and chamber music, Tennyson and Maimonides, Shabbat rituals and an Oxbridge education. Bentwich believes that just as imperial Britain has a mission in this world, so do the Jewish people. He feels it is the duty of the emancipated Jews of the West to look after the persecuted Jews of the East. My great-grandfather is absolutely certain that just as the British Empire saved him, it will save his brethren. His loyalty to the Crown and his loyalty to the Jewish vocation are intertwined. They push him toward Palestine. They lead him to head this unique Anglo-Jewish delegation traveling to the shores of the Holy Land.

Had I met Herbert Bentwich, I probably wouldn't have liked him. If I were his son, I am sure I would have rebelled against him. His world—royalist, religious, patriarchal, and imperial—is eras away from my world. But as I study him from a distance—more than a century of distance—I cannot deny the similarities between us. I am surprised to find how much I identify with my eccentric great-grandfather.

So I ask again: Why is he here? Why does he find himself on this steamer? He is in no personal danger. His life in London is prosperous, fulfilling. Why sail all the way to Jaffa?

One answer is romanticism. In 1897, Palestine is not yet British, but it is on the British horizon. In the second half of the nineteenth century, the yearning for Zion is as English as it is Jewish. George Eliot's Daniel Deronda has paved the way; Laurence Oliphant has taken it further. The fascination with Zion is now at the heart of the English Romanticism of the colonial era. For my great-grandfather, a romantic, a Jew, and a Victorian gentleman, the temptation is irresistible. The yearning for Zion has become an integral part of his constitution. It defines his identity.

The second answer is more important and more relevant. Herbert Bentwich is way ahead of his time. The journey he took from Whitechapel to St. John's Wood in the late nineteenth century is analogous to the journey taken by many Jews from the Lower East Side to the Upper West Side in the twentieth century. As 1900 approaches, my great-grandfather is faced with the challenge that will face American Jewry in the twenty-first century: how to maintain a Jewish identity in an open world, how to preserve a Judaism not shielded by the walls of a ghetto, how to prevent the dispersion of the Jews into the liberty and prosperity of the modern West.

Yes, Herbert Bentwich takes the trip from Charing Cross to Jaffa because he is committed to ending Jewish misery in the East, but his main reason for taking this journey is his understanding of the futility of Jewish life in the West. Because he was blessed with a privileged life, he already sees the challenge that will follow the challenge of anti-Semitism. He sees the calamity that will follow the Holocaust. He realizes that his own world of Anglo-Jewish harmony is a world in eclipse. That's why he crosses the Mediterranean.

He arrives on April 16 at the mouth of the ancient port of Jaffa. I watch him as he awakens at 5:00 A.M. in his first-class compartment. I watch him as he walks up the stairs to the *Oxus*'s wooden deck in a light suit and a cork hat. I watch him as he looks from the deck. The sun is about to rise over the archways and turrets of Jaffa. And the land my great-grandfather sees is just as he hoped it would appear: illuminated by the gentle dawn and shrouded by the frail light of promise.

Do I want him to disembark? I don't yet know.

I have an obsession with all things British. Like Bentwich, I love Land's End and Snowdon and the Lake District. I love the English cottage and the English pub and the English countryside. I love the breakfast ritual and the tea ritual and Devon's clotted cream. I am mesmerized by the Hebrides and the Scottish Highlands and the soft green hills of Dorset. I admire the deep certainty of English identity. I am drawn to the quiet of an island that has not been conquered for eight hundred years, to the continuity of its way of life. To the civilized manner in which it conducts its affairs.

If Herbert Bentwich disembarks, he will bid farewell to all that. He will uproot himself and his children and grandchildren and great-grandchildren from the deep English green in order to settle us all—for generations—in the wild Middle East. Isn't it foolish to do so? Isn't it mad?

But it's not that simple. The British Isles are not really ours. We are only passersby, for the road we travel is much longer and far more tormented. The English green provided us with only an elegant and temporary refuge, a respite along the way. The demography tells a clear story: In the second half of the twentieth century, which Herbert Bentwich will not live to see, the Anglo-Jewish community will shrink by a third. Between 1950 and 2000 the number of Jews in the British Isles will drop from over 400,000 to approximately 300,000. Jewish schools and synagogues will close. The communities of such cities as Brighton and Bournemouth will dwindle. The rate of intermarriage will increase to well over 50 percent. Young non-Orthodox Jews will wonder why they should be Jewish. What's the point?

A similar process will take place in other Western European countries. The non-Orthodox Jewish communities of Denmark, Holland, and Belgium will almost disappear. After playing a crucial role in the shaping of modern Europe for more than two hundred years—think of Mendelssohn, Marx, Freud, Mahler, Kafka, Einstein—Jews will gradually leave center stage. The golden era of European Jewry will be over. The very existence of a viable, vital, and creative European Jewry will be questioned. What was shall not be again.

Fifty years later, this same malaise will hit even the powerful and prosperous American-Jewish community. The ratio of Jews to non-Jews in American society will shrink dramatically. Intermarriage will be rampant. The old Jewish establishment will fossilize, and fewer non-Orthodox Jews will be affiliated or active in Jewish life. American Jewry will still be far more vibrant than Europe's. But looking across the ocean at their European and British cousins, American Jews will be able to see what the twenty-first century holds, and it is not a pretty sight.

So should my great-grandfather disembark? If he doesn't, my personal life in England will be rich and rewarding. I won't have to do military services; I'll face no immediate danger and no gnawing moral dilemmas. Weekends will be spent at the family's thatched-roof cottage in Dorset, summers in the Scottish Highlands.

Yet if my great-grandfather does not disembark, chances are that my children will be only half Jewish. Perhaps they will not be Jewish at all. Britain will muffle our Jewish identity. In the green meadows of Old England, and in the thick woods of New England, secular Jewish civilization might evaporate. On both coasts of the Atlantic, the non-Orthodox Jewish people might gradually disappear.

So smooth is the Mediterranean as the Bentwich delegation disembarks that it appears to be a lake. Arab stevedores ferry the *Oxus* passengers ashore in rough wooden boats. The Jaffa port proves to be less traumatic than expected. But in the city of Jaffa it is market day. Some of the European travelers are shocked by the hanging animal carcasses, the smelly fish, the rotting vegetables. They notice the infected eyes of the village women, the scrawny children. And the hustling, the noise, the filth. The sixteen gentlemen, four ladies, and one maid make their way to the downtown hotel, and the elegant Thomas Cook carriages arrive promptly. As soon as they are out of the chaos of Arab Jaffa, the Europeans are in good spirits once again. They smell the sweet scent of the April orange groves and are uplifted by the sight of the blazing red and timid purple fields of wildflowers.

The twenty-one travelers are greeted by my other great-grandfather, Dr. Hillel Yoffe, who makes a positive impression on them. In the six years since he, too, disembarked at the Jaffa port, carried ashore by the very same Arab stevedores, he has accomplished a great deal. His medical work—trying to eradicate malaria—is now well known. His public work—as chairman of the Zionist Committee in Palestine—is outstanding. Like the British pilgrims, he is committed to the idea that the privileged Jews of the West must assist the impoverished Jews of the East. It's not only a matter of saving them from benighted Cossacks but a moral duty to introduce them to science and the Enlightenment. In the harsh conditions of this remote Ottoman province, Dr. Yoffe is the champion of progress. His mission is to heal both his patients and his people.

Led by Dr. Yoffe, the Bentwich convoy reaches the French agricultural school of Mikveh Yisrael. The students are away for the Passover holiday, but the teachers and staff are impressive. Mikveh Yisrael is an oasis of progress. Its fine staff trains the young Jews of Palestine to toil the land in modern ways; its mission is to produce the agronomists and vine growers of the next century. The French-style agriculture it teaches will eventually spread throughout Palestine and make its deserts bloom. The visitors are ecstatic. They feel they are watching the seeds of the future sprouting. And it is indeed the very future they want to see.

From the Mikveh Yisrael school they travel to the colony of Rishon LeZion. Baron Edmond de Rothschild is the colony's sponsor and benefactor. The local governor, representing the baron, hosts the esteemed pilgrims in his colonial home. The Brits take to the Frenchman. They are relieved to find such architecture and such a household and such fine food in this backwater. Yet what delights the European travelers most is the formidable, advanced winery established by the baron at the center of the fifteen-year-old colony. They are amazed at the notion of turning Palestine into the Provence of the Orient. They can hardly believe the sight of the red-roofed colonial houses, the deep-green vineyards, or the heady smell of the first Hebrew wine in the Jewish homeland after eighteen hundred years.

By noon, when they arrive in Ramleh, it is clear to them. Seven hours after landing in Palestine, most of the Bentwich pilgrims have no doubts: Judea is the place where the persecuted Jewish masses of Russia, Poland, and Romania should be settled. Palestine is to be a Jewish home that will ensure Jewish salvation. Soon the delegation will get on the train from Lydda to Jerusalem. But a man like Herbert Bentwich will not waste a valuable half hour. His fellow travelers are exhausted. They rest, mulling over their many impressions and emotions. But my great-grandfather is restless. In his white suit and his white cork hat he climbs up the white tower rising like a beacon from the center of Ramleh. And from the grand white tower my great-grandfather sees the Land.

Looking out over the vacant territory of 1897, Bentwich sees the quiet, the emptiness, the promise. Here is the stage upon which the drama will play out, all that was and all that shall be: the carpets of wildflowers, the groves of ancient olive trees, the light purple silhouette of the Judean hills. And over there, Jerusalem. By pure chance, my great-grandfather is at the epicenter of the drama. And at this juncture a choice must be made: This way or the other. Move forward or pull back. Choose Palestine or reject it.

My great-grandfather is not really fit to make such a decision. He does not see the Land as it is. Riding in the elegant carriage from Jaffa to Mikveh Yisrael, he did not see the Palestinian village of Abu Kabir. Traveling from Mikveh Yisrael to Rishon LeZion, he did not see the Palestinian village of Yazur. On his way from Rishon LeZion to Ramleh he did not see the Palestinian village of Sarafand. And in Ramleh he does not really see that Ramleh is a Palestinian town. Now, standing atop the white tower, he does not see the nearby Palestinian town of Lydda. He does not see the Palestinian village of Haditha, the Palestinian village of Gimzu, or the Palestinian village of El-Kubbab. My great-grandfather does not see, on the shoulder of Mount Gezer, the Palestinian village of Abu Shusha.

How can this be, I ask myself in another millennium. How is it possible that my great-grandfather does not see?

There are more than half a million Arabs, Bedouins, and Druze in Palestine in 1897. There are twenty cities and towns, and hundreds of villages. So how can the pedantic Bentwich not notice them? How can the hawkeyed Bentwich not see from the tower of Ramleh that the Land is taken? That there is another people now occupying the land of his ancestors?

I am not critical or judgmental. On the contrary, I realize that the Land of Israel on his mind is a vast hundred thousand square kilometers, which includes today's Kingdom of Jordan. And in this vast land there are fewer than a million inhabitants. There is enough room there for the Jewish survivors of anti-Semitic Europe. Greater Palestine can be home to both Jew and Arab.

I also realize that the land Bentwich observes is populated by many

Bedouin nomads. Most of the others who live there are serfs with no property rights. The vast majority of the Palestinians of 1897 live in humble villages and hamlets. Their houses are nothing but dirt huts. Bowed by poverty and disease, they are hardly noticeable to a Victorian gentleman.

It is also likely that Herbert Bentwich, a white man of the Victorian era, cannot see nonwhites as equals. He might easily persuade himself that the Jews who will come from Europe will only better the lives of the local population, that European Jews will cure the natives, educate them, cultivate them. That they will live side by side with them in an honorable and dignified manner.

But there is a far stronger argument: In April 1897 there is no Palestinian people. There is no real sense of Palestinian self-determination, and there is no Palestinian national movement to speak of. Arab nationalism is awakening at a distance: in Damascus, in Beirut, in the Arabian Peninsula. But in Palestine there is no cogent national identity. There is no mature political culture. In these distant parts of the Ottoman Empire, there is no self-rule and no Palestinian autonomy. If one is a proud subject of the British Empire, it is quite understandable that one would see the land as a no-man's-land. As a land the Jews may legitimately inherit.

Yet I still ask myself why he does not see. After all, Arab stevedores woke him at dawn and carried him ashore in the rough wooden boat. Arab peddlers passed him in the Jaffa market. Arab staff attended to him in the Jaffa hotel. He saw Arab villagers from the carriages along the way. And the Arab residents of Ramleh and Lydda. The Arabs in his own Thomas Cook convoy: the guides, the horsemen, the servants. The Baedeker guide to Palestine states emphatically that the city of Ramleh is a city built by Arabs, and that the white tower of Ramleh is an Arab tower.

As I observe the blindness of Herbert Bentwich as he surveys the Land from the top of the tower, I understand him perfectly. My great-grandfather does not see because he is motivated by the need not to see. He does not see because if he does see, he will have to turn back. But my great-grandfather cannot turn back. So that he can carry on, my great-grandfather chooses not to see.

• • •

He does carry on. He gathers his fellow pilgrims and they board the train to Jerusalem. The Jaffa–Jerusalem railway was laid down by a French company only a few years earlier, and the engine is a modern steam engine carrying modern cars with comfortably upholstered seats. But as thrilled as he is by the signs of progress he sees embodied by the new train, he is even more impressed by the landscape. Through the wide windows of the French-made cars he sees the remains of the ancient Hebrew city of Gezer (but he does not see the adjacent Palestinian village of Abu Shusha). He sees the tombs of the heroic Maccabeans in Modi'in (but not the Palestinian village of Midia). He sees Samson's Tsora (but not Artouf). He does not see Dir-el-Hawa, and he does not see Ein Karem. My great-grandfather sees the ancient glory of the twisting gorge leading to Jerusalem, but he does not see the Palestinian peasants tilling the craggy terraces of the Jerusalem hills.

Two things drive Herbert Bentwich: a vivid historical memory coupled with a belief in progress, and a longing for the glory of the past that gives rise to determination to pave the way for modernization. Yes, he is committed to Russian Jewry groaning under the tsar's tyranny. He never forgets the victims of the 1881–82 pogroms in the Ukraine and the victims of the recent Romanian persecutions. But what really captivates him is the Bible and Modernity. His real passions are to revive the prophets and to put up telegraph lines. Between the mythological past and the technological future there is no present for him. Between memory and dream there is no here and now. In my great-grandfather's consciousness, there is no place for the Land as it is. There is no place for the Palestinian peasants who stand by their olive and fig trees and wave hello to the British gentleman dressed in fine linen who is absorbed by the biblical landscape he sees through the train windows.

As I follow the train on its climb up to Jerusalem, I think of Ferdinand-Marie de Lesseps, the French consul general in Egypt who devised a detailed plan to connect the Mediterranean and the Indian Ocean with an artificial waterway. He then raised the money to carry out his vision by founding a general stock company. Within ten years the Suez Canal was dug, at a horrendous human cost, and Lesseps proved to the nineteenth century that there were no limits, that in this age of reason any

problem could be solved. No mountain was too high for rational progress.

Herbert Bentwich is not French but British, and though his person-
ality is not Cartesian but Tory, the de Lesseps spirit affects him, too. He
believes there must be a rational answer to the Jewish question. For
him, Theodor Herzl is the de Lesseps of the Jewish question. Herzl
would get the charter, draw up the plan, raise the money by founding a
general stock company. Herzl would erect the great artificial nation-
state that would connect East to West and would link the past to the
future and would turn this wasteland into an arena of momentous events
and great deeds.

My great-grandfather's fellow travelers are excited, too. They have seen
so much since dawn: Jaffa, Mikveh Yisrael, Rishon LeZion, Ramleh, the
plains of Judea, the Judean hills, the gorge en route to Jerusalem. The
locomotive travels slowly, and the Thomas Cook tourists make good
use of the time by reading their various guide and reference books: Baedeker, Smith, Thompson, Oliphant, Condor. As they pass the Valley of
Ayalon, they reconstruct the great biblical battles that occurred there;
astonished, they recognize the site of the heroic victory of the Hasmoneans at Beth Horon. They feel they are traveling back in time, making
their way between the epochs of the remarkable history of the sons of
Israel.

I take a close look at them. There are sixteen men and five women.
Sixteen Brits, three Americans, and two Continental Europeans. All
but three are Jewish. All but one are well off. Almost all are well read,
well-to-do, emancipated Jews of the modern era. And although they are
a bit outlandish in their dress, and although they are naïve, there is no
malice in them. What brought them here is desperation, and desperation breeds resolve. They are unaware of the huge forces coursing
through them—imperialism, capitalism, science, technology—that will
transform the land. And when imperialism, capitalism, science, and
technology breed with their determination, nothing can stand in the
way. These forces will flatten mountains and bury villages. They will
replace one people with another. So as the train moves on with its
Baedeker-reading passengers, change becomes inevitable.

• • •

Of the twenty-one travelers, only one is not naïve at all. Israel Zangwill is a well-known author whose novel *Children of the Ghetto* is an international bestseller. Zangwill is sharp-tongued, sharp-minded, and merciless. He doesn't share my great-grandfather's benevolent conservatism and humane romanticism. There is no need for him to deceive himself, no need to see and yet not see. All that Herbert Bentwich doesn't see, Israel Zangwill sees. He sees the Palestinian cities of Jaffa, Lydda, and Ramleh, the Palestinian villages of Abu Kabir, Sarafand, Haditta, and Abu Shusha. He sees all the humble villages and miserable hamlets en route to Jerusalem. He sees the farmers who toil the land wave at the passing French train.

In seven years' time, all that Zangwill sees now will pour out of him. In a landmark speech in New York, the world-renowned writer will shock his audience by stating that Palestine is populated. In the district of Jerusalem, Zangwill will argue, population density is double that of the United States. But the provocative Zionist will not only spout subversive demographic data; he will also claim that no populated country was ever won without the use of force. Zangwill will conclude that because others occupy the Land of Israel, the sons of Israel should be ready to take tough action: "To drive out by sword the tribes in possession, as our forefathers did."

Zangwill's speech will be perceived by the Zionist movement as scandalous heresy. In 1897, and even in 1904, no Zionist but Zangwill articulates such a blunt analysis of reality and reaches such cruel conclusions. After his speech, the nonconformist writer will be driven out of the movement, but he will return some years later, and on his return, in the second decade of the twentieth century, he will proclaim in public what no Zionist dared whisper to himself: "There is no particular reason for the Arabs to cling to these few kilometers. 'To fold their tents and silently steal away' is their proverbial habit: let them exemplify it now. . . . We must gently persuade them to trek."

But all that will take place much later. It is still the early days. In the late afternoon of Friday, April 16, 1897, after a long and exciting train ride, the Bentwich pilgrims get off the train in Jerusalem's newly built stone station. My great-grandfather is thrilled. They have reached Jerusalem.

Time is short. Their arrival coincides with Passover. In a few hours the holiday of freedom will begin, and Jews will celebrate a previous exodus. So after the pilgrims are greeted at the station by the notables of Jerusalem's old Jewish community, they are rushed to the Old City. Once again they are confronted with the misery of the Orient: dark, crooked alleyways, filthy markets, hungry masses. The impoverished Arabs and the pre-Zionist Jews who have been residing in the Holy City for generations, living on charity and prayer, are a wretched sight. But when they reach—at last—the Wailing Wall, they are overwhelmed by the devotion of the worshippers there. They are moved by the genuine grief of elderly, bearded Jews as they stand by the only remnant of the temple and lament the eighteen-hundred-year-long catastrophe of their history.

The British ladies and gentlemen, along with their American and European counterparts, are surprised to find that they, too, are flooded by longing and lament. They deposit their scribbled yearnings in the cracks of the Wall. But as they are short on time, Bentwich hurries the breathless pilgrims onward, through the dark, crooked alleyways, to the Kaminitz Hotel, where the seder is to be held. Then on to David's Citadel and David's Tomb the following morning. And then to the breathtaking Mount of Olives. And yet wherever the pilgrims go, the contrast is striking: venues of the glorious past coexist with present-day squalor. In the breathtaking beauty of the ancient city of Jerusalem, both Arab and Jew are stricken with poverty. Young boys look like old men. Disease and despair are everywhere.

The day after Passover the pilgrims head north. Now it is time for the Thomas Cook brothers to display their outstanding skills. For the forty-four guineas it has charged each traveler, the prestigious tourism agency now delivers a hundred horses and mules, with free English saddles and covered sidesaddles for the women. They provide top-quality white Indian tents. No fewer than forty-eight servants arrive, including a butcher, a chef, and a staff of trained waiters. An English breakfast will be laid out every morning; lunch will be packed in handwoven picnic baskets; and in the evening, a gourmet repast will be served: warm soup, two kinds of meat or poultry, three different desserts.

Between April 20 and April 27, 1897, Herbert Bentwich leads a convivial colonial convoy through the land. They travel from Jerusalem to Beit El, from Beit El to Shilo, from Shilo to Nablus, from Nablus to Jenin via the Valley of Dotan. From Jenin they journey on to Mount Tabor via the Valley of Yizrael. From Mount Tabor they go to Tiberias via the Horns of Hittin. And after two days on the shores of the Sea of Galilee, they travel by boat to Capernaum. And from Capernaum to Rosh Pina. From Rosh Pina along the river Jordan to its sources. Then on to Mount Hermon, Damascus, Beirut.

Is this colonialism? If it looks like a duck and walks like a duck and quacks like a duck, it probably is a duck. The photographs are incriminating: white safari suits, cork hats, Thomas Cook tents. The language that my great-grandfather uses in his diary is incriminating, too. There is no ambiguity, no beating about the bush. His aim and that of his London circle is to colonize Palestine. The Herzl Zionists seek imperial backing for their endeavor. They are persistently courting Britain, Germany, Austria, and the Ottoman Empire. They want a major European power to use its might to impose the Zionist project on the Land. They want the West to tame this part of the Orient. They want this Arab land to be confiscated by Europe so that a European problem will be solved outside the boundaries of Europe.

And yet the Bentwich delegation seeks to acquire another part of the planet not for the glory of Britain, but to save persecuted masses. They don't really represent an empire but a deprived people seeking the help of empires. They do not intend to oppress but to liberate. They do not want to exploit the land, but to invest in it. Apart from Israel Zangwill, no member of the delegation considers their mission as a form of conquest, dispossession, or expulsion.

So as I observe the gentlemen sitting on their fine English saddles and the ladies teetering on their sidesaddles, I see no evil. I do not see a condescending attempt to take the poor man's lamb. For although the setting is colonial and the customs are colonial, these pilgrims are not agents of a colonial power. Although their appearance, thinking, and manners are European, these pilgrims do not represent Europe. On the contrary. They are Europe's victims. And they are here on behalf of Europe's ultimate victims.

It is a dire story. Herbert Bentwich's generation is one of emancipated Jews who fell in love with Europe and tied their fate to Europe. After breaking free from the ghetto in which they had been imprisoned for centuries, they went forth and embraced enlightened Europe—enriching the Continent and enriching themselves. Yet as the nineteenth century draws to a close, these Jews realize that as much as they care for Europe, Europe does not care for them. For these newly emancipated European Jews, Europe is like a surrogate mother. They look up to her, they worship her, they give her all they have. Then, suddenly, these devoted sons of Europe notice that Europe won't have them. Europe thinks they smell. Overnight there is a new, strange look in Mother Europe's eyes. She is about to go insane. They see the insanity dancing in her eyes, and they understand that they must run for their lives.

That is why Theodor Herzl is going to convene a congress in the late summer, and why Herbert Bentwich and the Bentwich delegation are riding now through the ancient land of Israel. Because just as Europe's progress and enlightenment have reached a peak, the Jews must escape Europe. This desolate land is where they will find refuge from Europe's Medean insanity.

Herbert Bentwich's journal stops abruptly after the visit to Jerusalem. Perhaps fatigue has taken its toll, perhaps too much excitement. One witness claims that Bentwich fell into a local prickly pear cactus whose tiny thorns tormented him and deprived him of his peace of mind. But notes taken by other pilgrims tell me that what impressed Bentwich most of all was the sight of Jerusalem at dusk, as he saw it from Mount Scopus just before departure. The next day it was the eerie, ancient quiet surrounding the Sebastian ruins that enchanted the chief pilgrim. He was moved by the biblical views of Samaria: terraced hills, olive groves, sleepy valleys. He found Mount Gilboa magical. Yet what left the strongest impression on him was the sight of the Sea of Galilee at sunset, surrounded by glowing red mountains, and the experience of taking an early morning sail in the lake's silence.

I watch my great-grandfather lead a hundred-horse convoy as it climbs from the Sea of Galilee to the Lake of Hula over the Valley of

Ginosar. And I watch him as the hundred-horse convoy climbs from the Lake of Hula to the springs of the Banias, the snow-covered summit of Mount Hermon hovering above. The twentieth century is also hovering above. My great-grandfather doesn't know it yet, but the next half century is going to be the worst ever in the history of the Jews. After that will come another half century in which, at horrendous cost, the Jews will regain their sovereignty. But for the time being, all is quiet. The land is at peace. One can hear the hoofs of the horses as they climb the slopes of the Hermon. One can hear the musings of the gentlemen, the silence of the ladies. And when my great-grandfather looks back, he sees for the very last time a land not yet affected by his future enterprise, a land not yet transformed by the need and despair of the Jews. He observes the serenity of Galilee, the magic of the lake, the staggering omen of the Horns of Hittin.

Herbert Bentwich will not make it to the first Zionist Congress in Basel. Though he will attend future Zionist conventions, he will not be there to present the report that Dr. Herzl was counting on at the historic 1897 gathering. But once back in London, he will talk and write about his experiences. Wherever he goes, my great-grandfather will be adamant. "Palestine has never yet adopted another population," he will claim. Arguing with the critics of Zion, he will insist that Palestine is absolutely suitable for "the teeming millions who are in distress in the East of Europe for whom a home might have to be found with a minimum of difficulty and a maximum of hope."

In the future debate, my great-grandfather will have the upper hand. Along with his friends and colleagues he will establish a sound Zionist power base in Europe's foremost capital. Exactly twenty years after his pilgrimage to Palestine, Herbert Bentwich will attend the first meetings between the Zionist leadership and the British Crown regarding Palestine. By that time, the aging, dignified solicitor will be a relic of times past, but as a matter of honor and courtesy, he will be given the right to participate in the early stages of the dramatic negotiations. Half a year later, on November 2, 1917, the negotiations will produce a famous seventy-word commitment, included in a letter, that will be sent by Foreign Secretary Lord Balfour to Lord Rothschild:

Foreign Office
November 2nd, 1917

Dear Lord Rothschild,

I have much pleasure in conveying to you, on behalf of His Majesty's
Government, the following declaration of sympathy with Jewish Zi-
onist aspirations which has been submitted to, and approved by, the
Cabinet.

His Majesty's Government views with favour the establishment
in Palestine of a national home for the Jewish people, and will use
their best endeavours to facilitate the achievement of this object, it
being clearly understood that nothing shall be done which may prej-
udice the civil and religious rights of existing non-Jewish communities in Palestine, or the rights and political status enjoyed by Jews in
any other country.

I should be grateful if you would bring this declaration to the
knowledge of the Zionist Federation.

Yours sincerely,
Arthur James Balfour

The Bentwich journey to Palestine was short and hurried and somewhat
absurd. Yet it transformed the life of my great-grandfather. On his return to England, he would not be able to resume his Victorian gentleman's routine. He would not settle for practicing law, playing chamber
music, reading Shakespeare, and raising his nine daughters and two
sons to be British gentlemen and gentlewomen. The twelve days Bentwich spent in the Land of Israel would make it difficult for him to enjoy
the comforts of his privileged life on the family's estate in Birchington-
by-the-Sea. For beyond the Kent coastline he would now see a lighthouse. The Bentwiches would now live in constant dialogue with that
beacon.

The enigmatic attraction to Palestine would inhabit the souls of all
members of the family. In 1913, Herbert Bentwich's daughter and son-
in-law would build a fine mansion in the wine-producing colony of Zi-
chron Ya'acov. In 1920 Herbert Bentwich's son would be appointed the
first attorney general of the British Mandate in Palestine, the British

rule over Palestine authorized by the League of Nations in 1922. In 1923, Herbert Bentwich himself would establish the first Anglo-Jewish colony on the shoulder of Tel Gezer and within the Palestinian village of Abu Shusha. In 1929, the elderly Bentwich would finally settle in the Land of Israel, where he would die three years later. The patriarch would be buried on the western slopes of Mount Scopus, by the newly built Hebrew University, not far from the spot from which he viewed that unforgettable sight of Jerusalem at dusk in April 1897.

But now the steamer carrying the Bentwich delegation back from Palestine to London is crossing the dark sea on its way to Constantinople. The May night is hot. My great-grandfather is on deck, watching the white foam and the black waves. He only vaguely understands what he has just done, only vaguely envisions the transformation that will take place in the Land of Israel. His understanding of the Land is so very limited. But he does know that an era has come to a close and that a new era is set to begin. Something both grand and terrible occurred when the *Oxus* made its appearance at the Jaffa port and laid on its shore all that it carried on board.

TWO

Into the Valley, 1921

I am bound north. From Tel Aviv to Hadera it is all asphalt, gas stations, and shopping malls. Crowded graceless cities appear and disappear, and it is difficult to tell them apart. Coastal Israel is dense, intense, consumerist, and sweaty. But when I turn east and pass the Arab-Israeli villages of Bartoa and Umm el-Fahem, and reach the Valley of Yizrael, which Bentwich crossed in 1897, I see a fertile basin of plowed brown fields. And when I continue eastward, surrounded by the scent of heavy soil, I arrive at one of my favorite Israeli vantage points. Just after the kibbutz named Yizrael, the landscape suddenly opens up. Before me are the Valley of Harod and the rocky ridges of Mount Gilboa, and I can see the gentle green slopes of the Isaschar heights, with its numerous kibbutzim. It's so quiet here. The spell of another era still hangs over the Valley of Harod.

In the dilapidated archives of Ein Harod, the first kibbutz of the valley, I pore over maps, plans, protocols, articles, letters, and personal journals. I look at the black-and-white photographs from the 1920s: our very beginning in the valley. Before me is the genesis of the Zionist adventure.

· · ·

Harod Valley is a long, narrow strip of land locked between the dramatic mountain ridge to its south and the gentle heights to its north. To the east is the city of Beit Shean; to the west, the watershed line. In the 1920s there were three Palestinian villages and two Palestinian hamlets in the valley. These thirty thousand dunams* were owned by the Sarsouk family of Alexandria. Most local inhabitants were their serfs.

Local history is ancient and bloody. On the mountaintop of Gilboa, King Saul and his son Jonathan were killed when the army of Israel was crushed by the Philistines. The bodies of the king and prince were violated. Under Gilboa burbles the water source to which Gideon brought his warriors before defeating the Midianites. And by the spring of Harod, Gideon divided the brave from the timid, separating those fit to serve their nation from those unfit.

In 1904 the Turkish Empire laid down a German-planned railway in the midst of the long strip of land. Yet the valley's torpor proved to be stronger than progress. Twice a day the steam train whistled through the silence, but the silence prevailed. As late as 1920, the valley was first and foremost a patchwork of wild fields scarred by boulders and stubborn bushes that prevent cultivation. Scattered among the fields were deadly marshes in which Anopheles mosquitoes bred, infecting most of the local Palestinians with malaria. Yet on the paths descending from the spring of Harod, barefoot village girls walked in their long black dresses, carrying clay jars full of water on their heads. Skinny young shepherds roamed with their herds of gaunt sheep. On both sides of the Turkish-German railway, native life meandered as it had for hundreds of years. Still, death was in the air. It lurked low in the poison-green marshes of Palestine, and it hovered above the endangered Jews of Europe.

In April 1903 an Easter pogrom took place in Moldova's capital, Kishinev. Forty-nine Jews were murdered, hundreds brutally injured. World Jewry was in turmoil. Theodor Herzl was personally shocked. Deeply

---

*A dunam is a traditional unit of land measurement representing the area that could be plowed in a day. It is approximately equivalent to a quarter of an acre.

affected by Kishinev, he considered buying the property of the Sarsouk family in Palestine in order to relocate the victims of European anti-Semitism there. He had the proposal reviewed by a consultant, who concluded that the land in the Valley of Harod was exquisite, but to evacuate the serfs from the estate would require the use of force.

Herzl's Zionism of 1903 found the use of force unacceptable. But seventeen years later, Zionism was no longer so fastidious. The Great War and the Great Revolution had hardened hearts. So when the Sarsouk transaction was finally signed, in the summer of 1920, it was clear to all concerned what was required: decisive, rapid action. Action to be carried out by a new breed of Jew.

In the decade following the Kishinev pogrom, some one million Jews fled Eastern Europe, while fewer than thirty-five thousand immigrated to Palestine. The choice was clear: the masses who wanted a life went to America. The few who wanted utopia made *aliyah* to the Land of Israel. Unlike the traditional farmers my great-grandfather met in the colonies of 1897, the post-Kishinev immigrants were secular and utopian. They were Tolstoyan idealists who traveled to Palestine in order to find salvation, both for the nation and the individual, by adopting a humane and environmentally friendly socialism.

The great creation of the utopians was the commune. In 1909 they established Degania, the first small, intimate commune, with the aim of respecting individual needs and freedom. Degania survived, but the utopians failed. Many felt lonely in the harsh, barren land. Some sank into depression. A few committed suicide. Most gave up and left for America.

Meanwhile, in Europe, big events were occurring. The First World War was perceived by many Jews as Armageddon. Lenin's October Revolution was considered a messianic event. But despite war, revolution, and postrevolution civil war, persecution was worse than ever. Pogroms were everywhere.

The failure of the socialist utopians in Palestine and the acute distress of Jews in Eastern Europe forced Zionism to look for new modes of action. The new idea was to colonize Palestine by establishing communist colonies that would not be small, intimate, and utopian like Degania, but large, rigid, and almost Bolshevik. The idea now was to win the land by forming a tough, determined, semimilitary Labor Brigade.

In the summer of 1920 the Labor Brigade was founded. A year later it was hundreds of comrades strong. They felt and spoke as if they were the avant-garde of the Jewish people. They acted as if they were the revolutionary elite marching ahead of the masses they were about to liberate. No job was unworthy, no mission impossible. They would do whatever needed to be done in the name of the Zionist revolution.

I look closely at their photographs. The young men I see are indeed new Jews. They are strong, buff, beaming with certainty. It is hard to believe that the parents they left behind in Eastern Europe were shtetl merchants or ghetto scholars. Within a short period of time, the transformation among these youngsters was beyond comprehension. Now they wear egalitarian berets and caps, khakis and sleeveless shirts, khakis and no shirts at all. And their fine torsos are proudly on display. They are tanned and muscular; they look like models of revolutionary potency. From the recesses of previous generations' humiliation, manly energy is now bursting.

The girls are surprisingly provocative. Some still wear the vestiges of trendy European fashion. Had they not landed on the Palestine shore, they would be dancing the Charleston to the music of the Roaring Twenties. But even those clad in spartan khaki are tantalizing. As there is no God and no father in Palestine, all is free. As there is no religion and no family, all is open. Under these empty blue skies there is no mercy, but there are also no limits. There is nothing to stop the most ambitious and audacious of all twentieth-century revolutions.

It is the summer of 1921, and all is quiet in the valley. Apart from the railway, what is here now is what has been here for hundreds of years. What the American traveler John Ridgway described in the last quarter of the previous century can still be seen in the first quarter of the new century: "The valley full of harvesters, pickers and packers. Donkeys heavily laden with sacks of grain are walking by while women are busy picking whatever is left in the field. Often one hears the singing of harvesters as they bend over the stalks of grain, their bodies swaying to the rhythm of age-old chants."

Below the mountainside village of Nuris stand the stone houses built by the Sarsouk family for its Ein Jaloud serfs. And where Kibbutz Yizrael will be built sits the quiet village of Zarin. On one of the hills slump the mud huts of Tel Fir. Down below are hidden the scattered homes of Shatta. And over on the northern heights, the village of Komay overlooks the valley it commands.

The waters flow slowly from the lively spring of Harod to the pools of Sahneh via the old mills, as they have for a thousand years. Every so often, water trickles into the ditches that the peasants dig in order to nourish their meager crops. But these waters create the boggy marshes from which rise the poisonous vapors of malaria that have turned the old village of Rihanyah into a ghost village. Everything here, by the grave of Sheikh Hassan and around the Spring of Hassan, is idle— the torpor of an ancient land deep in ancient slumber.

And yet there are forces about to be unleashed on the quiet valley. The energy generated by Kishinev and the Great War and the Great Revolution and the pogroms. The opportunity produced by the Balfour Declaration and the British Mandate and the Sarsouk transaction. The acute distress of Eastern European Jews that compels them to flee to the valley. And the new identity of the new Jews that allows them to enter the valley—to build and transform themselves in a valley inhabited by others.

On September 21, 1921, a bizarre convoy penetrates the Valley of Harod: two cars, four horses, and a number of country wagons. The dozens of Labor Brigade pioneers in the convoy are highly excited, very much aware that they are about to tilt history. In his personal journal, one of the youngsters writes:

> No road and no path. Walking along the railway, Z. is riding ahead of us, followed by two cars and wagons and the entire platoon. The heat is unbearable. It's already past noon and we hardly advance. Stop. Advance. . . .

Now we must turn right toward Mount Gilboa. At the foot of the mountain-ridge flows the spring of Harod. The spring is the valley's water source. We must conquer it. The spring is the key to the conquest of the valley and we are about to capture that key. Z. is still ahead, riding his noble Arab horse to the spring. Between water ponds and dank marshes we follow him until we arrive at the slopes of Gilboa. Here it is: the mouth to the cave from which the water burst: the spring of Harod.

The time is half past four. Like our forefathers who followed Gideon to save Israel, we kneel by the water, drinking happily. East of the spring is the small hamlet of Jaloud. We set up camp right next to it, west of the spring. We raise thirty-five tents. We pound iron poles into the soil and surround the camp with barbed wire. We dig combat trenches. Within hours we have a camp with all the facilities. Like an army regiment we have all we need. There is a field-kitchen now and the girl-comrades cook supper. By sunset we finish our first day of labor in Ein Harod. We break bread and bless the valley with its first pioneers' hora dance.

The community of Ein Harod is imprinted on every Israeli's psyche. In a sense it is our Source, our point of departure. But for me Ein Harod has personal significance, too. I have family here. Throughout my childhood I used to come here for the summer holidays. I was always attached to the aura of this mythological kibbutz. I loved to walk its shady pathways and enjoyed the languor of the serene afternoons of the archetypical commune. I would stand on the porch of the communal dining room and look down at the verdant valley, across the imposing Mount Gilboa.

Now I am sitting in Ein Harod's dilapidated archives. And as I go over the records of that first day the pioneers arrived, I find all the formative elements: the heat, the spring, the Arabs, the tents, the barbed wire. The awareness of the founding fathers that what they are about to do may require violence. Their determination to conquer the valley—come what may.

I am no judge. I am an observer. And at this critical point I choose not to zoom in on the single dimension of Jew and Arab, us and them,

Israel and its other. Rather, I widen my scope of vision and see how the different dimensions of the Zionist tale interplay in the Valley of Harod.

By 1921 it is clear that nonsocialist Zionism will not be able to colonize Palestine. The bourgeois Rothschild colonies, like the one Herbert Bentwich visited in 1897, are done with. They are based on liberal values, a middle-class way of life, and market forces that are not up to the task. Utopian communes like Degania will not do, either. Liberty, intimacy, and individualism are incompatible with the mission. If Zionism is to prevail, there is a need now for a well-organized, disciplined socialist structure. The twenty-nine thousand dunams bought from the Sarsouk family provide the territorial base for such a structure. For the very first time, Zionism overtakes a substantial chunk of the land by building upon it a large communist colony. A kibbutz.

Kibbutz socialism is now essential for several reasons. Without group effort, Zionist colonizers will not be able to endure the hardships involved in the colonizing process. Without the idealism of kibbutz socialism, Zionism will not have the sense of moral superiority that is essential for the colonization process to succeed. Without the communal aspect of kibbutz, socialist Zionism will lack legitimacy and will be perceived as an unjust colonialist movement. Only kibbutz socialism can give Zionism the social cohesion, the mental determination, and the moral imperative needed at this revolutionary stage. And only the Labor Brigade ethos of kibbutz socialism will enable Zionism to take the valley and to take the Land.

The move is not only brilliant, it is brave. The young Labor Brigade comrades settling in the Valley of Harod do not ask themselves how the eighty thousand Jews living in Palestine in 1921 will deal with more than six hundred thousand Arabs. They do not ask themselves how a tiny avant-garde of Palestine socialists will lead the fifteen million of the Jewish Diaspora on an audacious historical adventure. Like Herbert Bentwich, the seventy-four Ein Harod pioneers are blessed and cursed with convenient blindness. They see the Arabs but they don't. They see the marshes but they ignore them. They know that historic circumstances are unfavorable but they believe they will overcome them. Their ethos is one of steely defiance. Against all odds they set up camp in the valley and create Ein Harod.

They are rebels, of course. But their revolution is at least sixfold.

The seventy-four twenty-year-olds launching Ein Harod rebel against the daunting Jewish past of persecution and wandering. They rebel against the moldering Jewish past of a people living an unproductive life, at the mercy of others. They rebel against Christian Europe. They rebel against the capitalist world order. They rebel against Palestine's marshes and boulders. They rebel against Palestine's indigenous population. The Labor Brigade pioneers rebel against all forces that are jeopardizing Jewish existence in the twentieth century as they pitch their tents by the spring of Harod.

I watch the encampment grow. First it is located by the spring, so that it will have absolute control over the valley's water source. Weeks later, when the serfs of the Ein Jaloud hamlet give up and leave, the encampment is transplanted to the mountain slope, right next to the deserted stone houses. By now there are 150 comrades in the Labor Brigade kibbutz of Ein Harod. They occupy seventy cone-shaped white tents.

At the center of each tent is a red iron pole from which hangs a kerosene lamp. Three metal beds covered with gray-brown military blankets surround the pole. There are no desks or chairs, but by each bed stands an improvised cupboard made of old wooden fruit boxes in which each pioneer places his or her few personal belongings. There is also one rifle in every tent, along with some ammunition. The barren soil is covered with white gravel, and a deep trench is dug around each tent to protect it from the rains soon to fall. Metal pegs secure each tent to the ground with taut military ropes.

The young founders of Ein Harod are ecstatic. "It's all astounding," writes one of them. "I cannot but think of the sons of Israel in their tents in the desert. But this is our last stop. Here our wandering ends." The excitement is not only personal but collective. The brigade builds the land shoulder to shoulder, male and female. The collective also dances and sings. At night, young legs are thrust up in the air. Young hands are bound together. Faces glow, eyes glitter. They dance in circles around a bonfire, as if dance is prayer. They dance as if the act of settling in the valley is of biblical significance. Shots of celebration pierce the air.

The pitch-black night is now reddened by fire. The downtrodden villagers wonder who are these newcomers singing, dancing, shooting in the air. The astonished valley wonders where these nomads came from to pitch tents and dance wildly into the night, to awaken the dormant valley from its thousand-year sleep. Yet the gaiety of the dancing is misleading. The exhausted young pioneers who retire to their tents and collapse onto their metal beds are all orphans. They have cut themselves off from their roots and have turned their backs on their parents. Now they are fatherless, motherless, and godless. Their camp on the slopes of the Gilboa is very much an orphanage.

After all, Zionism was an orphans' movement, a desperate crusade of Europe's orphans. As the unwanted sons and daughters of the Christian Continent fled the hatred of their surrogate mother, they discovered they were all alone in the world. Godless, parentless, and homeless, they had to survive. Having lost one civilization, they had to construct another. Having lost their homeland, they had to invent another. That is why they came to Palestine, and why they now cling to the land with such desperate determination.

But in Ein Harod the sense of orphanhood is even deeper. It occupies the hearts and dreams of every pioneer. "When immigrating to this land," writes one of the youngsters,

we were on our own. We left the past behind. We have cut ourselves off from all we were. We have distanced ourselves from our previous identity and from those dearest to us. Overnight we were uprooted from the rich soil of our parents' culture that was enriched with thousands of years of history. Then, after being uprooted we were thrown forcefully by a supreme hand onto this barren land. In parched, sunstruck fields we are now faced with naked rocks, exposed to the fire above. Face to face with the elements, face to face with brutal existence, no protection at all. And here, in this desolate valley, we must sculpt our lives. From these rocks we must carve our new foundation. In the Ein Harod valley we must dig, dig deep, to find the hidden spring that will nourish—and inspire—our new lives.

• • •

Yet orphanhood does not weaken the orphans. On the contrary. What's extraordinary about Ein Harod is that it transforms its comrades' loneliness and despair into a unique generator of remarkable energy. As there is no father, there is no boundary and no restraint. As there is no mother, there is no ease and no comfort. As there is no God, there is no mercy. No second chance. No hope of a miracle.

From the very outset Ein Harod is brutally realistic. The exhausted pioneers now sleeping in their white tents know that there is no shelter for them. No shade to rest under, no tree to hide behind. All is exposed to an extremely cruel history. And the test ahead is an ultimate one. Life or death. All depends on these weary boys and girls. Are they up to the task? Do they have the necessary stamina and persistence?

As Jewish Europe has no more hope, Jewish youth is all there is. It is the Jewish people's last resort. And this specific avant-garde of Jewish youth is at history's forefront. There is hardly any time left. In only twenty years, European Jewry will be wiped out. That's why the Ein Harod imperative is absolute. There is no compassion in this just-born kibbutz. There is no indulgence, no tolerance, no self-pity. There is no place for individual rights and individual needs and individual wants. Every single person is on trial. And although remote and desolate, this valley will witness the events that determine whether the Jews can establish a new secular civilization in their ancient homeland. Here it will be revealed whether the ambitious avant-garde is indeed leading its impoverished people to a promised land and a new horizon, or whether this encampment is just another hopeless bridgehead with no masses and no reserves to reinforce it, a bridgehead to yet another valley of death.

As the sun rises, the sight is breathtaking. Row after row of white tents dot the dramatic mountain ridge. One of the awakening pioneers describes the tents as a flock of birds from a distant land that came down to rest and restore their powers on the rocky slopes of a remote island.

The pioneers themselves can hardly believe the audacity of what they are doing. It is as if a new Old Testament is being written. But there is no time for contemplation. Three obsolete American tractors arrive, sent from Tel Aviv by the Labor Movement. A dozen strong, pedigreed

Hungarian horses arrive—bought from somewhere in the Galilee. So now the youngsters can begin their work. First, they clear the fields of boulders and rocks. Then they plant the first forests (eucalyptus, pine). Then they lay a gravel path connecting the kibbutz with the local railway station. The girls plant a small vegetable garden. In the abandoned stone buildings of Ein Jaloud, the boys set up a carpentry shop, a shoe-making shop, a welding shop, and a tannery. A clinic is erected for the first victims of malaria. A communal dining hall is built that will serve all. A village bakery and a provisional library are constructed. From somewhere, somehow, a piano appears.

A few weeks later the day arrives that everyone has been waiting for. At first light there is a commotion at the new dining hall. The early risers gather, drinking hot chocolate and eating thick slices of bread spread with olive oil or jam. Once breakfast is over, the men march into the fields. They march in military rhythm, in one line, singing.

The fields have already been cleared of rocks, wild bushes, and thorny native plants, and now the grand spectacle begins. Two pairs of Hungarian horses, harnessed to a modern iron plow, lead the procession. Behind them follow four pairs of Arab mules harnessed to local plows. As the convoy slowly advances into the fields, the iron blades pierce the ground and create furrow after furrow. The blades of the sun catch the blades of the plows as they turn the valley's soil, penetrating the crust of the ancient valley's deep earth. And as the plows begin to do their work, the Jews return to history and regain their masculinity: as they take on the physical labor of tilling the earth, they transform themselves from object to subject, from passive to active, from victims to sovereigns.

A few days later it's time to sow. There is great excitement among the youth. Half-sacks full of seeds are hoisted up on the shoulders of a half dozen sowers who spread out through the field. They take a step, slip a large hand into the sack, bring forth a fistful of seed, and in a wide arc scatter the seed over the tilled field. Step after step, they sow wheat and barley, and when they return to the encampment at the end of the day, everyone gathers around them in glee. After eighteen hundred years, the Jews have returned to sow the valley. In the communal dining hall, they sing joyfully. They dance through the night, into the light of dawn.

Progress is fast. Within a few months the Ein Harod pioneers plow 1,900 dunams and sow 900 dunams of land. They clear more and more fields. They blast open a mountain quarry. There are milking cows in their dairy and egg-laying hens in their coops. The number of comrades in the six-month-old kibbutz keeps rising: 180, 200, 220. But what is even more striking is that these comrades now wear kibbutz-made shoes and enjoy kibbutz-baked bread and drink rich kibbutz milk and eat kibbutz-laid eggs. They celebrate the very first kibbutz tomatoes.

As one of the leaders looks around him, he is astonished at what is being achieved. He feels that his comrades resemble Robinson Crusoe, who was swept ashore after his boat was lost. He feels that like Crusoe, he and his comrades never wept, never lamented their wretched fate. Like Crusoe, they looked around their desolate island and wondered what could be done. Like Crusoe, they made the most of whatever they found. They were practical, imaginative, and innovative. They were brave. And like Crusoe, they created a surreal, man-made miracle.

The winter of 1921 is vicious. The valley winds whip through the encampment and sow destruction. The mountain rain falls down the slopes in cascades. The white tents are thrown to the ground time after time. There is no refuge in this improvised refugee camp, no sense of home for the homeless.

Tragedy strikes, too. Only five months after Ein Harod is founded, one of its founders cannot take it anymore. He is twenty-four when he takes his life with a shotgun. A month later the morning quiet is torn once again by the hollow sound of three more shots. A blond twenty-year-old beauty is found dead in a pool of her own blood. Lying by her side is her handsome twenty-five-year-old lifeless lover. Lust, despair, and jealousy are all at work in the camp. As conditions are extreme, so are emotions.

One of the more introspective pioneers tries to define the problem. "We stand naked in the universe," he writes.

> We are totally exposed. And within this explosive situation, we try to shape a new way of life. But our life, too, is exposed and harsh. We don't have the subtleness of previous generations. We don't have the

merciful ambiguity of dusk. It's either day or night here. Hard labor at the noon of day and ideological debates into the night. A loving family, the soft caress of a mother's hand, the stern but encouraging look of a loving father—all the things that make life bearable—are not here. Even the intimate touch between a young man and a young woman is there for all to see, matter-of-fact, obvious, almost gruff. And so we must face ourselves revealed and exposed. Naked. Totally naked. Every spark of light we must instill in our hearts. Every drop of life we must imbibe from the wellspring of our own souls. And where shall we find the strength? How will we be able to go on, to conquer each day? Where shall we find power? Where?

Yet the kibbutz does not disintegrate. Even as rain falls and storms strike, the camp is in high spirits. Suicide and murder cast their shadow for a while, but they are overcome, denied, and almost forgotten. Loneliness bites hard, but it only forces the frontier community to close ranks and hold on to its fragile solidarity. In the long winter nights there is more singing than dancing—folk songs, revolutionary songs, Hasidic songs. There is mischief: hoaxes, practical jokes, satirical sketches. A first play is produced, more and more books are read in the library (Marx, Dostoyevsky, Kropotkin, Hamsun). Love affairs flourish, babies are born. And while they ponder their future and make love in their tents, the young pioneers of Ein Harod listen to the lonely violin of a tall, lanky violinist who plays in his tent after each long day in the quarry. By the light of a kerosene lamp, he sounds the strains of throat-choking solitude.

When Yitzhak Tabenkin joins Ein Harod in the winter of December 1921, many of the Labor Brigade comrades are taken aback. Tabenkin is older than they are—nearly thirty-four. And he already has a family—a wife and two sons. While most comrades are the anonymous rank-and-file soldiers of the Zionist revolution, Tabenkin is something of a celebrity. In the ten years since he emigrated from Poland to Palestine, he has emerged as one of the prominent leaders of the Labor Movement. While his friend and rival David Ben Gurion decides to run socialist politics from Tel Aviv, Tabenkin chooses to join the new kibbutz that is already captivating the hearts of the Jewish masses. Although he will always remain something of an outsider, by his very presence, he turns Ein Harod into the Mecca of the kibbutz movement.

Tabenkin was born in Belorussia in 1888 and was raised in Warsaw. His father turned his back on religion as a young man and embraced radical politics, and his mother was active in Poland's revolutionary intelligentsia. After doing time as a political prisoner, his father died, and his mother dedicated herself to her promising son. By the age of eighteen Tabenkin was a well-known figure in socialist Zionist circles. At the age of twenty-four he arrived at the port of Haifa, passed through the valley, and settled in Tel Aviv. Although he believed in labor and preached labor, the young Tabenkin was not very good at labor. He liked to talk more than he liked to plow. His inability to practice what he preached tormented him and often drove him to depression. At times he considered suicide.

Joining the valley's first kibbutz is something of a remedy for Tabenkin. At last he is with real workers doing real work. At last he is at the forefront of the great Zionist revolution. Although he is not analytical, eloquent, or brilliant, Tabenkin has charisma. The young, enthusiastic comrades look up to him as something of a father figure or teacher. Within a short time Tabenkin will be the kibbutz's guru, the secular rabbi of Ein Harod.

Both by temperament and conviction, Tabenkin is very much an anarchist. Deeply influenced by Kropotkin and Bakunin, he is averse to the state, detests all establishments, and is suspicious of military structures, hierarchies, and uniforms. Yet Tabenkin is no liberal or pacifist. He acknowledges the need to use force. His leadership is Bolshevik in style and his political outlook is combative. Tabenkin has no respect for the individual whatsoever. For him, every person is simply raw material for the Cause. As far as he is concerned, every member of Ein Harod must recast himself as a pioneer by foregoing all individual traits that might jeopardize the fulfillment of the socialist-Zionist vision.

And what is that vision? What is Ein Harod's dream? It is quite clear: to be a large, ever-growing kibbutz. Tabenkin and his lot reject Herzl's political Zionism. They don't want a Jewish state and they don't believe in diplomacy. Their approach is socialist, practical, and down-to-earth. They have no expectations of the Great Powers. They despise both Bentwich's Victorianism and Herzl's haut-bourgeois elitism. They want communism to colonize Palestine. If possible, they want to turn the entire country into one Zionist working-class commune.

The way to that goal begins with Ein Harod. Let Ein Harod grow as fast as it can. Let it take more and more fields, capture more and more of the valley. Allow it to diversify into the profitable areas of crafts, light industry, and heavy industry. Let it conquer every patch of land in sight, conquer every field of human activity. Subjugate the valley to an alternative socioeconomic regime, self-reliant and self-possessed and able to fulfill the needs and realize the dreams of Jewish socialism in the Land of Israel.

When spring arrives, the Ein Harod pioneers begin to drain the valleys. One evening, a quiet and earnest engineer arrives in the young kibbutz. Wearing a gray suit, he stands before the bewildered pioneers and explains what is about to be done. He shows them a map of the valley: the thick blue lines are major canals, the thin ones are minor canals. The minor canals lead to the major canals, whose purpose is to drain the bad waters out of the valley. The network of thin and thick lines is laid out across the valley like a fisherman's net. It will drain the thousand-year-old marshes and muck and malarial scourge and clear the valley for progress.

Some days later, strange men appear. Wearing khaki shorts and bizarre-looking high rubber Wellingtons, the surveyors look like prehistoric amphibious creatures. And yet these human frogs manage to walk about the cursed swamps. They hammer pegs and tie ropes along which the major canals and the minor canals will be dug. After they are done, Wellingtons, ropes, and shovels of all sorts arrive in camp. By sunrise the Labor Brigade pioneers take off into the valley's marshes. The heat is unbearable but the mosquitoes are worse. Buzzing about the ears, eyes, and private parts, they suck fresh blood from the strong young bodies. The stench of the swamp is overpowering. The tall reeds are infested with snakes. Yet the canals must be dug.

The boys work in teams of five. Each team digs one layer of mud and then moves on so that the next team will dig deeper. Standing in a two-yard-wide ditch, each bare-chested pioneer has to stick his shovel between the dripping walls of the canal and lift the filth above him. Once the hard soil, hidden under the marsh for a millennium, is finally exposed, there is a fury of festive shouting. Now the girls walk in, bearing baskets filled with white gravel that, since morning, they have been producing with their small, efficient chisels. Only now, when the girls' gravel lines the boys' canal, may lunch be served. Canned beef and loaves of bread sate their hunger.

Only a few months ago the draining project seemed unreal—as ambitious as the Suez Canal project, as dangerous as the Panama Canal. But now, day by day, the swamps retreat. Clay pipes laid in the newly dug, well-lined canals absorb the deadly subterranean waters. The July sun does the rest. Acre after acre, the marshes give way to fertile fields. Zionist planning, Zionist know-how, and Zionist labor push back the swamps that have cursed the valley for centuries. Malaria is on a dramatic decline. Even the remaining Arab neighbors benefit from the miraculous project. The desolate Valley of Harod is gradually turning green.

In years to come, historians will try to determine which is the more dominant feature of the endeavor, socialism or nationalism. Some will argue that choosing socialism at this critical stage is Zionism's cunning way of conquering the land. Socialism gives this belated colonizing project a sense of justice and an aura of legitimacy. As the colonizers of the Valley of Harod don't resemble at all the French masters of Algeria or the British plantation owners of Rhodesia, they are in the clear. By working the land with their bare hands and by living in poverty and undertaking a daring, unprecedented social experiment, they refute any charge that they are about to seize a land that is not theirs. Yet all this idealistic socialism is just subterfuge, future critics will claim. It is the moral camouflage of an aggressive national movement whose purpose is to obscure its colonialist, expansionist nature.

True and not true. Just before May Day 1922, a young poet living in Ein Harod translates the international socialist anthem into Hebrew. The Hebrew version gives a poignant subtext to the original words that refer to the universal working class. Now the text is not only about the world's poor, it is also about the world's most oppressed people. It is about the mission Ein Harod took upon itself: to destroy an old world and build another, to unload the heavy burden from a broken back. As there is no God, no king, and no hero, we shall break through toward the light all by ourselves. We shall win the last battle of an eternal war. Yesterday, nothing; tomorrow, everything.

Tabenkin is the very incarnation of this Zionist-socialist symbiosis. In his mid-thirties, he is still an attractive man, with sensual lips and a high forehead. He is not a profound intellectual, but he has historical pathos and conviction. He doesn't write much, but he speaks passionately and at great length. There is something truly Soviet about him. Had he not been Jewish he could have stood now by Lenin or Stalin in some remote kolkhoz or at a mass gathering of the Novosiberian proletariat.

But Tabenkin is Jewish. And he believes that in the twentieth century the Jewish people are heading for disaster. Twenty years before the Holocaust he feels and breathes the Holocaust daily. That's why he is impossible to be with and impossible to live with. He believes that in Jewish youth lies the only remedy, that only Jewish youth can save the Jewish people from the approaching catastrophe. But he knows there is no time. And he feels that all that is being done is not enough. Palestine might not be ready in time. The valley might not be ours in time. That's why Tabenkin is so demanding. He is as cruel to himself as he is to others. He is preachy, stringent, chastising. He says over and over again that socialist Zionism must do more, much more. He preaches over and over again that every young pioneer must achieve more, much more. The avant-garde of Ein Harod must stretch itself beyond its capabilities. Ein Harod must accomplish its mission impossible. Tabenkin is not much of a theoretician. Unlike other revolutionaries, he does not have an overall, systematic ideology. But the Ein Harod rabbi has a powerful concept: activism.

Ideologically, activism means practicing revolutionary values in everyday life. Socially, activism is wrestling with human nature and changing the unjust order of things. Politically, activism is seizing the initiative and confronting the Arabs by force. But activism has an overall meaning that is far deeper than all that. Activism is the revolt of the Jews against the passivity of their past. It is the rebellion of the Jews against their tragic fate and against acceptance of their tragic fate. It is not a specific goal or target, but momentum. Activism is the momentum of doing, of moving forward. Activism is the last attempt of the Jews to resist oblivion. Activism is the desperate rebellion of Jewish life against Jewish death.

Like Bentwich, Tabenkin is not a gentleman whose company I would enjoy. Personally, I cannot stand Soviet-type politicians, dogmatic revolutionaries, and leaders who preach but don't practice. Yet as I go over Tabenkin's old photographs in the Ein Harod archives, I am far more forgiving. There is something fascinating about the man. He does not have Ben Gurion's political genius. He does not have the intellectual depth of some other founding fathers of Zionism. He does not have the impressive work ethic and moral rectitude of his fellow rank-and-file comrades in Ein Harod. But there is fire in his belly. More than any other Zionist leader in Palestine, he understands the Diaspora and feels for the Diaspora. More than any other local socialist-Zionist leader, he is Jewish. Even when he rails against Judaism, he does so as a Jew. Even when he rises up against religion, he rises up religiously. There is so much God in the godless Tabenkin as he assaults God and dismisses God and tries to create a God-free, godless world.

That's why, in the early 1920s, Tabenkin is the link between the events in the Valley of Harod and the events in Eastern Europe. That's why Tabenkin talks to the valley's youth on behalf of the Diaspora, and talks to the Diaspora on behalf of the valley's youth. That's why, day in and day out, Tabenkin wonders whether the work being done in the valley will be sufficient, whether the valley's youth will have enough in them to pull European Jewry from the deadly ocean in which it is drowning.

On its first anniversary, Ein Harod celebrates its success. By now the year-old kibbutz has mastered 8,390 dunams of cultivated land. Grain takes up 7,000 dunams, olive tree groves and vineyards 450 dunams, the vegetable garden 200. There are over 600 dunams of forest, with 14,000 eucalyptus trees, 2,000 pine trees, and 1,000 cypresses, which cover the inclines of Mount Gilboa with the first green shoots of hope.

There are nearly three hundred comrades in Ein Harod in the summer of 1922. Apart from Tabenkin and a few others, the age range is from nineteen to twenty-five. Two hundred white, cone-shaped tents house a young, thriving, and energetic community that is transforming the valley and the lives of its inhabitants. Four other new kibbutzim are now flourishing in the valley. Momentum is fast and strong; there is not a force in sight to stop it.

Many now come to see the wonder. As the Ein Harod experiment becomes world famous, it attracts attention in Jewish communities and progressive circles worldwide. Some compare its revolutionary ways to those being tried in the young USSR. Some see it as providing the only example of successful, democratic socialism. When one of Zionism's leading lights arrives for a day-long visit, he thinks in different terms. Deeply touched, the national moral leader says the following:

> From the nation's valley of death rose a new generation. This genera-
> tion finds life's meaning in toiling our ancestor's land and reviving our
> ancient tongue. The draining of the Harod swamps, which only cov-
> ered the land after our people were forced to go into exile, is a true
> wonder. But this wonder also symbolizes the draining of the swamp
> our nation was bogged down in during two millennia of exile. You,
> the pioneers of Harod, are the heroes of the new generation. What
> you are doing is healing the land and healing the nation. You are tak-
> ing us back to the source.

Yet the listening comrades are not heroes. What's remarkable about them is their lack of heroism. Practical and down-to-earth, they know they must do whatever must be done, but there is no self-aggrandizement about them, no sentimentality, no smugness. Caught in a drama larger than themselves, they simply carry on. Another furrow, another acre, another swamp, until the valley is truly theirs. Until the land is once again the Land of Israel.

But there is one feature of the landscape that does not yet retreat. The serfs of Ein Jaloud are gone, but the serfs of Shatta remain, living by the railway station right in the center of the valley. And the villagers of Nuris menacingly overlook Ein Harod from the mountaintop. The villagers of Zarin are actually doing quite well as the valley booms. The friendly neighbors of Tel Fir and those of Komay are multiplying now, as the anopheles mosquitoes are no longer here to take the lives of their young. The Bedouins, too, find the valley more attractive now. As summer peaks, they pitch their black tents in the northern part of the valley. Their herds of sheep foray into the fields, and their young, armed horsemen terrify the kibbutz girls. So mission is not yet accomplished. There is indeed a solid Jewish base in the valley. Five different kibbutzim have begun to establish one of the first strips of Jewish territorial continuity in the country. But the work isn't done. The Arabs of the Harod Valley still stand in the way of the Jewish liberation movement that needs to remove them from this valley.

At noon on April 17, 1926, the working day is cut short in the Valley of Harod, and the last blast is heard in the quarry. An hour later all harvesting stops in the fields. The young comrades of Ein Harod are called back to camp. So are the young comrades of the neighboring Tel Yosef, Gvat, Beit Alpha, and Hephzibah. Throughout the valley, kibbutz members are showering, shaving, and donning their white Shabbat outfits. Back in the quarry a wooden stage is set up. By four o'clock all is ready. The old piano is on the stage decorated with green palm leaves. By horse, by mule, by carriage, by wagon, and on foot, thousands of pioneers flock to the valley quarry turned amphitheater.

From day one, the rough Labor Brigade pioneers of Ein Harod have had a soft spot for all things musical. One of them has an explanation. "The playing of classical music fills the void in our lives," he writes.

> The time of music is the only time that our communal dining room resembles a place of worship. There is a reason for that. Leaving God behind caused a terrible shock to us all. It destroyed the basis of our lives as Jews. This became the tragic contradiction of our new life. We had to start from scratch and build a civilization from the very foundation. Yet we had no foundation to build on. We had no Ultimate. Above us there were blue skies and a radiant sun, but no God. That's the truth we couldn't ignore and cannot ignore for a moment. That is the void. And music for us is an attempt to fill the void. When the

sounds of violins fill our dining hall, they reacquaint us with life's other dimension. They raise the deepest, forgotten feelings buried in all of us. Our eyes close, turn inward, and an aura almost of sanctity enwraps us all.

Just a few months earlier, in the late autumn, the first quarry concert was held. Thousands gathered from all over the valley to hear the local choir and string quartet play Beethoven, Bach, and Mendelssohn. A local teacher said that on this great day the mountains of Gilboa were revived. A young girl read Ezekiel's Vision of the Valley of Dry Bones. And all were silent as the tall, lanky violinist of Ein Harod played Bach against the backdrop of the quarry's walls. But today is different. Today it is Jascha Heifetz who is about to play.

Heifetz was born in 1901 in the Lithuanian capital of Vilna. He began playing the violin at three, and by the time he was seven he played Mendelssohn's concerto brilliantly in public. At the age of twelve he was considered one of Europe's musical prodigies, and at the age of sixteen—a week before the Balfour Declaration was issued—he made his legendary American debut at New York's Carnegie Hall. Now an American citizen and star, Heifetz is to the music of the twenties what Chaplin is to comedy and Einstein to physics. An astounding talent; a rare incarnation of man's extraordinary, almost divine gift.

That's why the Harod Valley pioneers are so excited. It's not only that they appreciate music and regard it as almost sacred. It's not only that music is the one thing that allows them to let go and allows suppressed pain and longing to moisten their eyes. It's also the fact that the world's most renowned violinist recognizes the importance of their endeavor by giving a concert in their remote quarry. It's the fact that the best that secular Jewish Diaspora civilization has produced is about to pay homage to their audacious attempt to create a new secular Jewish civilization in the valley. Heifetz is Heifetz, but he is also Jascha, one of us. One who rose from the misery and despair of the Jewish past and the Jewish present and has distilled his genius from them. One who has escaped the hopelessness of Eastern Europe and chosen America. So when this brilliant cousin chooses to acknowledge his fellow young Jews who are escaping what he escaped in a very different way and in a very different place, even the toughest among the Labor Brigade comrades are beside themselves. They feel that a biblical-like spectacle is about to happen.

There are thousands and thousands of them now, packing the make-shift seats of hard, gray boulders. And when Heifetz arrives at last, I watch both the maestro and his ecstatic audience. Both the violinist and the pioneers are as old as the century. Both the violinist and the pio-neers will become the century's icons. They tell the century's Jewish tale. And when the young men and women of Harod stand up and clap and cheer, the Vilna boy, who cannot start playing until they quiet down, is truly touched. Although he is a cold, perfectionist performer, he is overwhelmed. And between the young man standing on the im-provised stage and the young masses standing in the improvised amphi-theater, there is suddenly an intimate dialogue. The two great forces, the two sorts of creative energies that erupted dramatically out of mod-ern Jewish distress and that represent the two great choices of the Jew-ish people in the twentieth century, face each other. In the quarry of the Valley of Harod, one bows to the other.

But as Heifetz stretches his arm to pull the bow across the strings, I think of all that is to happen in the valley.

In three years' time, the firstborns of Ein Harod will crouch for days in the first cement-built dairy, hiding from the gunfire of Arab neighbors.

In nine years' time, the Arab villagers of Shatta will be forced to leave their homes by the railway station, and a new kibbutz will take their place.

In ten years' time—to the day—the valley's fields will be set on fire by Arabs who suddenly realize how far the Jews have come. Watching the burning fields, the firstborns of Ein Harod will harden their hearts.

In twelve years' time, in Ein Harod, the first elite Anglo-Jewish commando unit will be founded. The unit will raid Arab villages at night, killing some of their civilian inhabitants.

A few months later, a landmark Jewish sergeants' course will be launched in Ein Harod. The course will lay the very first foundation for Israel's future army.

In twenty years' time, Ein Harod—and the forces it gave birth to—
will have real military might. In twenty-two years, that military might
will attack the villages of Nuris, Zarin, and Komay. It will drive all
Palestinian inhabitants out of the valley.

As Heifetz plays and his music reverberates in the hushed quarry, I
wonder at the incredible feat of Ein Harod. I think of the incredible
resilience of the naked as they faced a naked fate in a naked land. I think
of the astonishing determination of the orphans to make a motherland
for themselves—come hell or high water. I think of that great fire in the
belly, a fire without which the valley could not have been cultivated, the
land could not have been conquered, the State of the Jews could not
have been founded. But I know that the fire will blaze out of control. It
will burn the valley's Palestinians and it will consume itself, too. Its
smoldering remains will eventually turn Ein Harod's exclamation point
into a question mark.

I close the Heifetz file in Ein Harod's dilapidated archives and go
out into the early evening air. I have supper with my dear elderly relatives. I wander the paths of the deteriorating kibbutz. Over the last
thirty years, it has lost its way. The economic base of Ein Harod collapsed and its social fabric frayed. Most of the young have left; most of
the elderly are aging in despair. The collective dining room is empty,
the collective children's homes are closed, and the collective spirit is
gone. Just as the kibbutz rose, the kibbutz fell. So as I look out at the
spring down below and at the mountain ridge casting its shadow, I
realize it's a spring-or-mountain question: Triumphant Gideon or defeated Saul? But my question is not yet answered as the dying light caresses the darkening Valley of Harod.

THREE

Orange Grove, 1936

Oranges had been Palestine's trademark for centuries. In the 1850s, a new variety of orange was discovered in the citrus groves of Jaffa, and by 1890 the new Shamouti orange—large, oval, and juicy—had found its way to Queen Victoria's table. By 1897, when Herbert Bentwich disembarked at the remote port of Jaffa, the same grizzled stevedores who took him ashore were already loading thousands of crates of Shamouti oranges (now called Jaffa oranges) each winter onto Liverpool-bound ships. After World War I, the new awareness of the virtues of vitamin C brought about a dramatic rise in the demand for citrus fruit throughout Europe. In 1925 there were only 30,000 dunams of citrus groves in Palestine; two years later there were nearly twice as many, and two years after that, by 1929, they had multiplied yet again to 87,000 dunams. By 1935 there were 280,000 dunams of citrus groves in Palestine. Within a decade, citrus growing in Palestine had risen almost tenfold. The small province, now under the British Mandate, had become a powerhouse of citrus export, so much so that in 1935, one-third of the oranges imported to Great Britain were Jaffa oranges.

The colony of Rehovot discovered the virtues of citrus in the 1920s. Rehovot was founded in 1890 on 10,600 dunams of the Ottoman feudal estate of Duran, situated some fifteen miles southeast of Jaffa. After the barren land was purchased and the Bedouins occupying it were evicted, it was taken over by Russian and Polish Jews hoping to find peace and plenty in the land of Israel. The settlers did well. Rehovot was a place where Orthodox and secular, rich and poor, Ashkenazi and Yemenite Jews lived side by side in relative harmony. Its Jewish inhabitants lived in peace with their Arab neighbors, too. By 1935 the rapidly growing colony of Rehovot was the most prosperous Jewish colony in Palestine, leading the citrus industry, which in turn was leading the country into an unprecedented boom.

Rehovot and orange groves were a perfect match. Rehovot's loamy red *hamra* soil suited the citrus trees because its unique combination of sand, silt, and clay holds plenty of moisture but also drains well, so that sufficient air can reach the trees' delicate roots. Rehovot's moderate climate was also well suited to the trees, since it was not too warm when the trees blossomed in spring and not too cold or windy in winter, when they bore fruit. Rehovot was rich with the water that the citrus trees badly needed, and it was close to the port of Jaffa. Rehovot embraced free-market principles, thrived on private enterprise, and had a cheap and efficient labor force provided by neighboring Arab villages. Rehovot also benefited from the cutting-edge scientific knowledge of the mostly German-Jewish agronomists working in its newly established agricultural institute. Those agronomists introduced the efficient Californian method of cultivation. Rehovot was where Western know-how, Arab labor, and laissez-faire economics merged to make the Jaffa orange a world-renowned brand. So while Europe and America were still in the grip of the Great Depression, Jaffa oranges and quickening immigration to Palestine made Rehovot prosper. And while hundreds of thousands of uprooted Jews couldn't find a home in Europe or America, those who had chosen Rehovot were flourishing. In Rehovot of the early 1930s, the optimal conditions of Palestine met the benign aspirations of modern Zionism.

The particular orange grove whose story I will tell was planted in 1931. A small fortune bequeathed to the owner by his English-Jewish father-in-law enabled him to buy seventy dunams of land from the villagers of

Qubeibeh in the Valley of Dew on a hilly plot overlooking Rehovot, north of the railway. First he plowed the barren wasteland. Then he hired beret-wearing Jewish socialists and kaffiyeh-wearing Palestinian Arabs to rid the land of obstinate poisonous weeds. He commissioned one of the roaming bands of well diggers to dig a water well. But only when the excited diggers shouted that they had found water did he know that the land was indeed suitable for planting. He marked out the land meticulously with white ropes and wooden stakes. And every four meters he dug a half-meter hole, in which he planted lemon rootstock that he had brought over from a nearby nursery. He covered the plantlings with soil, which he tamped down and watered. Then he and his delicate, sun-shy, English-born wife stood in front of a weighty Kodak camera and took a picture of hope.

Several months later, the Rehovot farmer grafted Shamouti branches onto the lemon rootstock. He gently affixed the Shamouti to the lemon and tamped the soil again, and watered and fertilized and prayed that the winds would not hit, that the hail would not despoil. Only after a long year of apprehension did the orange grower see that the grafting had gone well: the Shamouti and lemon had become one, and the fragile saplings had been welcomed by the red soil. So he and his elegant English wife stood once again between the long rows of budding trees in front of the Kodak camera and took another picture, of a hesitant beginning: the young couple, he in a pressed khaki suit, she in a bias-cut silk dress, standing beside the tentative orange saplings that had risen from a bare land.

The orange grower, a native of Rehovot who had worked for years in other orange groves, was disciplined and particular. He saw that his trees were watered in a timely manner and fertilized judiciously. He made sure the pruning was spare and the weeding merciless. He sealed the well walls with cement, mounted a formidable diesel wheel pump atop the well, and built a large, open square pool to collect the water drawn from the well. He laid out a network of cement canals to carry the water and dug furrows in the sandy soil of the grove to receive the water from the canals. Around each Shamouti sapling he dug a wide sand bowl, so the trees would never want for water. Then he erected a modern rectangular packing house with square windows and a red tile roof, and he built a two-story turreted house for the Arab guardian of the grove. He positioned an impressively ornate iron gate at the entrance to the grove and then waited patiently for four years for the trees to bear fruit.

In the spring of 1935, when the orange grove is about to bear fruit, so does Zionism. Now the liberation movement of the Jewish people is no longer the wild fantasy it had been when Herbert Bentwich rode by Rehovot in April 1897. Nor is it the Spartan revolutionary endeavor it had been in the Valley of Harod in September 1921. In 1935, Zionism does not demand superhuman effort and total sacrifice of its pioneers. It already has a middle class living a life of comfort and leisure. It has cities, towns, colonies, and villages. The Jewish population of Palestine now comprises more than a quarter of the overall population of Palestine, and every year the number of Jews in Palestine rises by more than ten percent. Jerusalem already has the Hebrew University, and Haifa has the Technion. Tel Aviv, now twenty-five years old, is a bustling mini-metropolis full of theaters, restaurants, cafés, and numerous publishing houses. Yes, there is much work to be done, and the task is still Herculean. But throughout the country the signs of success are palpable; the Zionist adventure is becoming a Zionist reality. Over the verdant orange groves of Rehovot the blue skies of spring seem to carry the promise of the future.

There is a feeling not only of success but of justice. In the spring of 1935, Zionism is a just national movement. Two years after Germany chose Nazism, the need for a Jewish home becomes self-evident. Now one does not need Herzl's prophetic genius or Tabenkin's catastrophic inclinations to envision the future. Now any reasonable person can see that Europe is becoming a death trap for Jews; and it is also clear that America would not open its gates in time to save the persecuted Jews of Europe. Only a Jewish state in Palestine can save the lives of the millions who are about to die. In 1935, Zionist justice is an absolute universal justice that cannot be refuted.

At this point in time the injustice caused to native Arabs by the Zionist project is still limited. It is true that tenant Palestinian farmers had already been uprooted from their land in the Harod Valley and in

Rehovot and in dozens of other locations in Palestine. But the lives of those farmers under their Arab masters had in many cases been worse than their lives as the field hands of the Jewish colonizers. Most of them did not have a solid right of possession under their Arab masters, and when the Jews took over, many of them were compensated with cash or land. Moreover, while some Palestinians do suffer, many of them benefit considerably as Zionism advances. In Qubeibeh, Zarnuga, and the other Arab villages surrounding Rehovot, Jewish capital, Jewish technology, and Jewish medicine are a blessing to the native population, bringing progress to desperate Palestinian communities. So the Zionists of Rehovot can still believe that the clash between the two peoples is avoidable. They cannot yet anticipate the imminent, inevitable tragedy.

The first season of the young orange grove is critical. The orange grower has to start up the formidable pump that draws water from the deep well. He has to clear out the irrigation canals into which unripe fruit has fallen in winter. He has to redig the furrows and bowls, and weed, clean, and dispose of dry thorny branches. He has to make sure that all was set for the first rains of summer.

At the end of April 1935, disaster strikes in the form of a heat wave. On April 27, the mercury climbs to 35 degrees centigrade (95 degrees Fahrenheit). On April 30, it hits 38 degrees centigrade. For ten consecutive days, dry desert winds wreak havoc with the delicate white citrus blossoms. If action is not taken immediately, half of the orange crop would be lost and the citrus season of 1935–36 would be a bust. The first watering of the young Rehovot grove is therefore an act of emergency. The pump pulls the clear water to the pool, and from there the water travels down the open, cemented canals until it emerges from the circular openings of the clay grate into the sandy furrows. The Arab guardian, his pants hiked up to his knees, his bare feet covered in mud, guides the water with a hoe from tree to tree. He quickly traps the water by each tree with a tall mound of soil so that the trees would be able to withstand the deadly dry desert winds.

The heat wave brings with it a sense of panic. More water is needed quickly. They must save what can be saved. The orange grower and the

Arab guardian are joined by their families, who work beside them in the stifling heat. Still, in the midst of the panic they can hear the sounds of children's gaiety, shouting in Hebrew and in Arabic, as they run to watch the gushing water. After the children lent their small hands to the great common effort, they steal away to the square pool and jump gleefully into its cool waters. While the adults are still struggling with the heat and with the sense of approaching calamity, the youngsters discover all that is forbidden, wondrous, and fun in this man-made Garden of Eden.

After the heat wave subsides and the emergency watering effort is completed, in May, June, and July the children return time after time to the orange grove. They bathe in its pool, sail paper boats in its canals, and hide among the thickening trees. And toward the end of July they watch with dismay as long convoys of camels advance toward the grove from the distant south, jute sacks heavy with sheep dung. By the end of summer, Rehovot's rich, fertile *hamra* soil gives rise to a fine Shamouti grove, with gleaming young oranges beginning to emerge on its branches.

At the end of July 1935, Alfred Dreyfus dies. In mid-September 1935, Nazi Germany enforces the racist laws of Nuremberg. From a Zionist point of view there is a link between the two events. Dreyfus was the French Jewish army officer whose persecution made Herzl fear the nightmare that awaited the Jews of twentieth-century Europe. The racist laws of Nuremberg prove Herzl right. It is impossible to imagine that within a decade, millions of Jews would be gassed to death, yet in the summer of 1935 the Jews of Berlin are experiencing something they had not experienced in a hundred years—pogroms. The news reaching Rehovot in late summer leaves no room for doubt: the great avalanche had begun. European Jewry is about to be decimated.

At the same time, the Jews of the Holy Land have a ball. In February 1935 the new triple-decked ship the *Tel Aviv* inaugurates the Haifa–Trieste line. Luxury cruises are the fashion of the season. In March 1935, the city of Tel Aviv hosts the Purim festival of Adloyada. For three days and nights, fifty thousand people celebrate raucously in the streets of the first Hebrew city. In April 1935, the second Maccabiah Games are held. Thirteen hundred and fifty Jewish athletes from twenty-eight countries participate in the games, parading their muscle power in front of tens of thousands. In May 1935, the numbers are out regarding the record-breaking citrus season of 1934–35. The new figures show that Palestine had exported over 7 million crates of oranges, grapefruits, and lemons compared with 5.5 million crates in the previous year. In June 1935, the film *Land of Promise* is being shot in the Promised Land. A formidable team of German cinematographers documents the pioneers performing wonders in the ancient land. In July 1935, elections are held to the Zionist Congress that convenes a month later in Lucerne, Switzerland. Both the elections and the congress prove that the Zionist movement is now a mature and powerful political body, run in an orderly, civilized, and democratic manner.

The Rehovot of 1935 reflects well the overall Zionist success. When established in 1890, the colony had a population of only 280 people, yet by June 1935, 5,500 men, women, and children live there. And Rehovot continues to grow. In the coming January it would have 6,500 inhabitants. By the following summer it would have 9,000 inhabitants. Doctors, scientists, agronomists, architects, engineers, and musicians fleeing Germany arrive almost daily in the rural colony. Gradually they are transforming it, endowing it with new dimensions of higher learning, sophistication, and culture. In June 1935, the first proper branch of the Anglo-Palestine Bank opens its elegant doors. The new, modern town hall, with a retractable roof, shows two movies a week and hosts a monthly concert. By now, Rehovot also has an icehouse, a small pharmaceutical plant, and a large citrus juice factory. It has an agricultural institute and a scientific institute and a sports field where the young play soccer, tennis, and handball. Rehovot is no longer only about agriculture. It has science, finance, industry, culture, and sports. Every new year is better than the previous one.

Autumn is calm. Little by little, the people of Rehovot become aware of the full significance of the new laws that went into effect in Germany on September 15, 1935. More and more information is available regarding the thirty-seven German cities in which Jews had been assaulted. But in Palestine, weather is good. August is relatively cool, and so is September. In the early morning, heavy dew envelopes the grove. The orange grower is finally satisfied that the April heat scare is behind him. Now he has to lay down the narrow-gauge Decauville tracks that in a few months' time would carry the flat Theresienstadt-manufactured Teresina railcars from the grove to the packing house. But there is no rush now. Autumn work is slow work. It is done with a deepening confidence in the orange grove and its future.

As the orange grower sits on the terrace of his spacious Rehovot home in October 1935, he can hear the quiet ticking of the water pump in the distance as he leafs through the local weekly. The journal is bursting with illustrated ads for Ford cars and Westinghouse refrigerators and RCA radios and Maxwell House coffee and Cadbury chocolates. He is happy to notice an article about the advertising campaign launched in Britain this week for the Jaffa orange. He is pleased to read that British cinema houses and department stores now promote the Jaffa orange. It is clear that in the British market, the Jaffa orange is ahead of its Spanish and South African and Californian competitors. When the orange grower finishes reading the paper and closes his eyes to relax in his rocking chair on his terrace, he can hear the ticking of the pump working in the orange grove. No sound in the world is as sweet as the reassuring sound of the pump's continuous ticking. It is the sound of quiet and peace and plenty. It is the sound of the rest that comes at the end of a trying journey. For eighteen hundred years the Jews had never had it so good. For eighteen hundred years the Jews had not lived on their own land with such security, such abundance, such a deep sense of calm.

Yet all around Rehovot is the disquieting question of the Arabs. The orange grower is a Sabra, a native of Palestine, who knows the Arabs, their tongue, and their ways. He believes that the trick with the Arabs was to honor and be honored, to give respect and demand respect. As an experienced plantation owner he thinks he knows when one must be firm and when one must be courteous and generous. So when the villagers of Qubeibeh and Zarnuga arrive for work at the orange grove at dawn, the orange grower is very strict. He puts them in line and checks them one by one to see that their hands are not dirty so they would not spread filth among his fine trees. And he checks them to see that they had clipped their nails so that they wouldn't scratch the precious fruit. When one of the villagers is suspected of stealing a donkey, the orange grower does not disgrace the man in public but goes discreetly to the village elder, with the result that the donkey is quietly returned. When one of the villagers gets into trouble with the police, the orange grower bails him out. He provides medical and financial assistance. The Arab villagers working in the grove respect the orange grower. They admire his knowledge, they appreciate his fairness, they dread his master's authority. They regard him as serfs regard a benevolent feudal lord. At the same time, the orange grower sees his Arabs as any plantation owner on any colonial estate views his native workers. He understands that his workers are the very best: strong, resilient, and disciplined. They are committed to their work and devoted to their master. And yet the orange grower knows that one day, one day.

One Arab is different from the others: Abed. Abed is the guardian of the orange grove. He is totally loyal and enjoys the owner's total trust. This is why he was permitted to live in the orange grove with his slim, tall wife and strapping sons and beautiful young daughter. When the orange grower is away, Abed is in charge. He is the one who starts the formidable pump in the frosty mornings, the one who walks the grounds when they are still covered with dew. He waters in summer and fertilizes in autumn and scrubs the packing house as winter approaches. In a knitted white cap, billowing Oriental pantaloons, and proud black mustache he rules over his fellow workers with a stern dignity. Being even more particular than his particular boss, he sees to it that all is in good order and that the orange grove is meticulously maintained.

Like many of the other workers, Abed had been born and raised in neighboring Zarnuga, which contributes nearly half of Rehovot's workforce. The orange grower is deeply involved with the village. He is well aware of a recent trend: over the last ten years, Zarnuga's population has doubled to 2,400 residents. Over the last five years its orange groves have doubled in size to 2,555 dunams. Real estate prices have soared tenfold in a decade. Just like Rehovot, Zarnuga is galloping ahead. Because so many of Zarnuga's inhabitants work in Rehovot and spend much of their time there, they learn a lot from Rehovot. They can now drive tractors and operate well pumps and manage modern orange groves. They build modern stone houses that resemble more and more the houses of Rehovot. In Rehovot they buy Western-style jackets, Western-style furniture, pots and pans, cattle, canned goods, medicine, and baby food. So in the autumn of 1935, the orange grower can conclude that the Arab issue is not an issue. The Arabs working in the orange grove are not an issue. And Abed and his family are definitely not an issue. Even the neighboring village of Zarnuga is not an issue. As Rehovot grows, Zarnuga grows. As Rehovot prospers, Zarnuga prospers, too. When the workers from Zarnuga arrive at the gate of the orange grove each morning, it seems that all is well. And when dozens of youngsters from Zarnuga ride into Rehovot on their bicycles each day, it seems that all would be well. There is no reason to believe that Jew and Arab could not live here together in peace. No reason to believe that one day Zarnuga will cease to be and the people of Zarnuga will be gone and loyal Abed and his family will be driven out of the Rehovot paradise.

But in the far north, a great distance from the orange grove, other voices are beginning to be heard. There is nothing concrete yet, certainly nothing the orange grower could make out from his tidy terrace, but an underground movement that had begun to form years earlier is about to surface.

Izz Abd al-Kader Mustafa Yusuf ad-Din al-Kassam was born in West Syria in 1882. He studied Islam in Cairo, returned to Damascus, and became a fundamentalist revolutionary. From 1918 to 1920 he led a national-religious revolt against the French rule in Syria. After the revolt was crushed, he fled to the northern seaside town of Haifa, worked as a teacher, and became the preacher of the mosque of Istiklal. His charisma, his perceived Arab patriotism, and his devotion to the Arab poor turned him quickly into a local hero. Unlike the spoiled and corrupt Palestinian leaders, he was a man of the people, committed to the people, and loved by the people. Al-Kassam was no hypocrite. He created a compelling synthesis between jihad and the war on illiteracy and ignorance. He offered both religious radicalism and social radicalism. Like the socialist Zionists, he aimed to transform his society from within and without. He promoted a revolution that would have national, political, spiritual, and economic dimensions.

In 1925 al-Kassam forged a five-phase plan: preparing the minds for revolution; establishing clandestine revolutionary cells; assembling arms, money, and intelligence; killing Jews; and launching an overall armed struggle. By 1930 the plan was implemented and a web of secretive cells formed in northern Palestine. Each cell had five members committed to Islam, to secrecy, and to the war against Jews. At night al-Kassam trained his men in the quarries on the slopes of Mount Carmel, overlooking Haifa. He preached religion, morality, rifles, and homemade bombs. In April 1931, al-Kassam's followers killed three kibbutz members returning from the fields on a hay cart. In January 1932, they killed a farmer at his door. In March 1932, they murdered another farmer. In December 1932, they killed a farmer and his eight-year-old son by throwing a bomb into their home in the Valley of Yizrael.

When the police went after them, the clandestine cells went deep underground. Their leader continued to tell them that jihad was the way, that Jewish immigration was stealing Palestine from the Palestinians, that every Jewish immigrant was an enemy. But the time had not yet come. They had to be patient. They had to practice, prepare, wait for a sign.

On October 18, 1935, as the orange grower was preparing for his first harvest, a shipment of Belgian cement barrels arrived at the port of Jaffa. One of the barrels fell and broke, and out rolled thousands of rifle bullets. There was panic in the harbor: it was clear that the illegal ammunition was headed for the illicit Jewish defense organization, the Haganah. Within hours there was panic throughout the country. Now Palestinians felt that not only was Jewish immigration a threat but so was Jewish military buildup. After a general strike was called, al-Kassam decided the day had come for action. Some eighty miles north of the Rehovot orange grove he gave his last speech. "I taught you religion and I taught you nationhood," he said to his followers. "Now it's your duty to carry out jihad. Ho, Islamists, go out on jihad."

When the preacher ended his sermon, the crowd was in tears. Believers kissed his hands, promising to die for Allah. But only twelve men joined al-Kassam at midnight as he left Haifa for northern Samaria to ignite the great Palestinian revolt. Yet the only achievement of the revolt was the shooting of the policeman Moshe Rosenfeld on Mount Gilboa, not far from the Valley of Harod on November 7, 1935. A day later, British forces were already chasing the al-Kassam gang. They found no refuge in the village of Nuris above Ein Harod, or in the village of Zarin next to Ein Harod. So the rebels escaped to the Valley of Dotan, where a British plane detected them. The battle between the British Empire and the desperate rebels lasted three hours. Five of the Palestinians were captured, three shot dead. The first one to die, on November 20, 1935, was Izz Abd al-Kader Mustafa Yusuf ad-Din al-Kassam. So when the Arab workers arrived at the orange grove with the wooden ladders, straw baskets, and pruning shears needed for the first harvest, the Rehovot orange grower was calm once again. A week after al-Kassam's death, he does not see what David Ben Gurion sees: that al-Kassam is only the beginning. That the myth of the dead al-Kassam would be far more dangerous than the deeds of the living rebel. That al-Kassam would be the first Palestinian martyr whose Che Guevara–like tale would make him the icon of Islamic Palestinian resistance in the generations to come. For the time being, the orange grower did not comprehend the significance of the events in the north. He believed that the British had managed to uproot the poisonous weed that had suddenly appeared on Mount Gilboa, and that there was no longer reason for concern. Now was the time to concentrate on the large, juicy, oval fruits that were turning orange on the lush green branches of his citrus trees.

November is extremely wet, with thirteen days of rain. In a three-day period, 112 millimeters of rain descends on the orange grove. Night after night the orange grower paces the halls of his spacious villa, fearing hail. If a winter hailstorm followed the spring heat wave, the first season would be lost. But as the storm recedes and the skies clear, the orange grower finds that his fruit is unharmed. And when he stands by the trees, now heavy with oranges, he feels hopeful. Perhaps the blessing of the November rains would compensate for the curse of the April *hamsin*. Perhaps, against all odds, the first season of his young orange grove would be one of prosperity.

The orange grower is not the sort of man who believes that blessings are given freely. What is called for in this land is sweat, dedication, and precision. In the first weeks of December 1935, the orange grower clears the paths to and within the grove. He rids the trees of dry branches so that they wouldn't bruise the fruit during the harvest. And he opens the heavy lock of the packing house, where he had stored ladders and shears, satchels and baskets. He makes sure the ladders are sturdy, and sharpens the long blades of the shears. He lines the rough baskets with soft jute that would protect the fruit.

In late December the early picking begins. To protect the sensitive green fruit, work is done only by hand. Then in January 1936, as a golden winter sun paints the skies blue over Rehovot, the major harvest of the Shamouti begins. The Arab pickers work in pairs. One climbs a three-legged ladder up to the branches and begins to pick from above, while the other disappears into the thicket to pick from below. To pick the fruit, each takes the delicate Shamouti gently with the palm of his left hand and fastens the rounded blades of his shears on the petiole, separating the fruit from the branch. Then he places the fruit carefully in his satchel.

The orange grower stands by the working pairs, making sure the ladders do not hit the oranges and the shears do not scar their peels and the oranges land softly in the fast-filling satchels. Once the California-made satchels are full, he summons a Bedouin girl so that the workers can empty their bags gently into her straw basket. And when the straw basket is full, he makes sure that the workers help lift it onto the Bedouin girl's head. Once the full basket is on her head, he makes sure she joins the other Bedouin girls coming from other sections of the grove. The orange grower enjoys the sight of the procession of Bedouin girls walking along the citrus trees in their long black dresses with straw baskets on their heads full of bright Jaffa oranges.

As 1936 begins, the orange grower is somewhat concerned. There are rumors of unrest. The national Arab leadership and the nationalistic Arab press are inciting against the Jews. Some friends in Rehovot fear that something nasty is coming. But the local weekly journal reports that by January 12, 1936, Palestine exported 2,794,165 citrus crates. By January 19 it exported 2,923,571 crates. By January 26, 3,259,609. The orange groves yield nicely, the market conditions are favorable, and Zionism is heading in the right direction. The writer Moshe Smilansky, the leader of Rehovot's orange growers, publishes strong, decisive words in the local weekly:

> Never in history did a people enter a country as we entered our country. There are two reasons for this: We are returning to our homeland that has waited for us as wasteland, and we are not entering a new country that is not ours; we are a people of ancient culture, and in the long years of our exile we have added to that culture the great values of a new civilization. All these riches we bring with us as a gift to our ancient land, and to the people who have settled it while we were away, and to the other peoples of the surrounding Orient. . . .
>
> Never did a colonial project bring so much blessing as the blessing brought upon the country and its inhabitants by our project. Every piece of land upon which our feet have stepped turned good. We did good to us and we did good to all that are with us. This is our pride. It is the pride of an endeavor of justice. Never was a colonial endeavor a historical necessity to any country as our project is a historical necessity for this country. We shall not recover without this country and this country shall not recover without us. This historical imperative is to guarantee that no human hand will demolish our great deed. Our deed is a deed of justice, absolute justice. It is all decency and love.

A lazy midwinter rain falls on the red-tiled roof of the packing house. In the soft rain, the Bedouin girls walk into its dim, elongated hall with straw baskets on their heads. The Bedouin chief takes the baskets off the girls' heads and helps them empty them gently so that the oranges roll on the straw-matted cement floor and are then gathered into meter-high piles. In the gray February light, the orange grower can see pile after pile of oranges rise from the floor of his new, modern packing house.

The sorters go first. With sharp, discerning eyes, their hands flying over the fruit, the Yemenite sorters cull the export quality oranges from the rest. Next come the wrappers, most of them newly immigrated European Jewish men and women, who wrap each fruit with delicate tissue paper, as if it were a precious pearl.

Now it is time for the packers. In working-class berets and khaki uniforms, the packers are the elite of the packing house crew. With astounding speed and precision they fill every crate with row after row of the glowing freshness that is the pride of Palestine.

The carpenters come last and do their work on the front porch. They carefully hammer the crate lids with dull, rusted nails, chosen so that the oranges won't be bruised and will survive their long journey abroad.

Now the orange crates sit piled up one on top of the other near the packing house. Not so long ago, they would have been taken to port by camels, but today small trucks arrive to carry the crates along the gravel road to Rehovot's main thoroughfare. In the port of Jaffa, they will be loaded onto Liverpool-bound ships. From Liverpool the oranges will travel to the wholesale market of Covent Garden, in London, and from Covent Garden they will make their way to Chelsea, Belgravia, Hampstead, Primrose Hill, St. John's Wood, even Buckingham Palace.

The orange grower is not sentimental. He is a man of deeds. But as the rain falls on the packing house, he walks up and down the long hall observing the sorters, wrappers, packers, and carpenters. He sees that their lips are pursed in concentration. He notices the quiet, the order, the sense of the sacredness of the work, as if the working men and women realize that they are taking part in an event far greater than themselves. The orange grower thinks of Smilansky's words, which express his sentiments exactly. The sons and daughters of Jewish shopkeepers have become fine orange growers. They have learned to love the citrus tree and nurture it as in no other land. In one generation the Jews have totally transformed themselves, so much so that now the U.S. Department of Agriculture fears that the fast growth of the citrus industry in Palestine will destabilize the international citrus market.

Outside, the trucks' engines are roaring. On the porch, the carpenters' hammers are nailing the orange crates shut. But indoors it's all silence. Orange after orange wrapped in delicate Diphenyl paper, orange after orange carefully placed into the right space in the crate with precision, dedication, and proficiency. There is harmony here: man and woman, Yemenite and Ashkenazi, Jew and Arab. The two peoples of the land are working side by side, producing its golden fruit.

Years later, Smilansky's nephew Yizhar, who would become one of Israel's leading authors, will try to capture the magic of Rehovot of the 1930s. "No one was in a hurry," he will write.

Everyone lived in comfortable moderation, riding donkeys and horses. And all was open, really open, and wide and imbued with a good farmer's thoroughness. Although there was never a shortage of trouble and there were days of fear and tension too, to come to Rehovot was to come to a place that had form, that had some slowness and level-headedness and that had men of honor.

There was calm there, and safety, and things did not change much. As if there was a secret pact between the ways of people and the fullness of orange groves and the slow flight of the crows that landed boastfully atop the eucalyptus trees. And in the evening, the silence was utterly full and it was given over to the ticking of the water pumps and the strumming of strings of far-away instruments, and there were jackals, and in the silence one could hear even the waves of the distant sea.

Writers wrote essays into the night by the light of lanterns, roosters crowed in circles, and donkeys brayed from the depth of their bellies, saying that no matter what, there was no reason to worry, the world was in good order.

To come to Rehovot was to come to a place with a face. It had gravity, it had a shadow, it had earnestness and straightforwardness. There was someone to talk to about matters of utmost importance and matters of no importance. The orange groves were fertile and almost blue of rich green. The hedgerows of acacias were fragrant, with golden stars over the paths of gold. Camels carried heavy citrus crates, the irrigation pools were dream-like, and reckless boys swam recklessly in them. And there was a never-ending heart that beat there all the time, round and round, and water came up day and night from the depth of the sandy soil earth that was shaded by oranges.

But as I look back in time and watch the orange grower now leaving the packing house and riding his horse in the sweet, lazy afternoon hours of mid-March 1936, I see even more than that. The orange grower does not know it yet, but from the two-story stone building south of the railway that houses the new Sieff Research Institute, Israel's future scientific prowess will emerge. From the experimental farm of the Chumasch family on the grounds of the Agricultural Institute, Israel's future modern agriculture will spring forth. The talent and the knowledge of the German-Jewish scientists and agronomists who reside in the new Bauhaus homes of the Miller neighborhood will utterly transform the colony and the country. The Rehovot of 1936 is quiet and calm and harmonious, but it already has within it the seeds of a mind-boggling future.

On his way to his home in Rehovot, the orange grower's horse passes by the icehouse, the small pharmaceutical plant, the new cafés on the newly paved Herzl High Street. It passes by the Anglo-Palestine Bank, the bakeries, the hairdresser's salons, and the new bus station. It passes by the new shop of the newly arrived Austrian photographer and new shops for electrical devices. It passes by the fit youngsters who gather on the sports field for their physical exercise, and it passes the respected elderly of the local landed gentry who are gathered in the landowners' club. The horse then climbs the hill by the new maternity hospital and reaches the grand synagogue that overlooks Rehovot. In the west the orange grower can see the workers' quarters; in the east, the grand colonial houses of the wealthy orange grove owners; in the south, the Yemenites; in the north, the modern palacelike villa being built by the well-known architect Erich Mendelsohn for the Zionist leader Dr. Chaim Weizmann. For two millennia the Jews had no place. Now, in Rehovot, they have a place.

Things feel right about the Rehovot of 1936. There is a balance between the revolution of Zionism and the evolution with which it is carried out. There is a balance between the need to grow fast and the determination to grow slowly. Both the social democrats of the working class and the liberals of the landowning class agree that step-by-step development is the way to grow. Both want Zionism to be rooted in the land and to grow from it gradually and naturally. There is no talk of taking the land by force. In their different ways they all want Zionism to be a natural identity-building process. They want to merge the healing of a people with the cultivation of a land. In March 1936, there is nothing totalitarian about Rehovot. There is no Bolshevism, no fascism, no militarism. The Zionism of Rehovot is humane, pragmatic, moderate, and balanced. It is turning the seed that was planted here at the end of the nineteenth century into a living reality.

The end-of-season party is held in the orange grove in early April 1936. The orange grower is not the partying type, but his Tel Aviv friends have refused to take no for an answer. They said the current fashion was wild spring parties in the orange groves of Sharon, Judea, and Rehovot, and they have insisted that the packing house of the orange grove is just the place to hold one. They have taken it upon themselves to locate a bulky generator to generate electricity. They have hired a popular jazz band and spread the word in the Viennese-style cafés of the emerging metropolis. They have invited slim Berlin girls and mink-clad Polish society ladies. The guests have driven down from Tel Aviv's Rothschild Boulevard in a jolly convoy of luxurious American cars, arriving at the orange grove gate with horns tooting and lights blazing.

The orange grower does not really join the party. He does not drink, does not dance. Although the raucous guests honor him with a toast, he prefers to watch. Standing in the corner of his own packing house turned nightclub, he is bewildered by the young entrepreneurs of Tel Aviv and the young orange grove owners of Rehovot who are pouring drink after drink for the Yemenite beauties of Rehovot and the sophisticated urban European immigrants who now reside in Tel Aviv. He is astonished by the flashy import and export agents who lead onto the improvised dance floor the tipsy maidens in their skimpy dresses. The music played by the band becomes more and more lively. First the waltz, then the tango, then the fox-trot. What a hit, the fox-trot. After a noisy contest for the belle of the ball, and then a naughty contest for the boldest couple of the ball, some couples slip away from the light into the dark of the orange grove.

When the sun rises, the urban crowd is gone, and the orange grower is on his own again. The guardian, Abed, and his sons carry tables and chairs out of the packing house, the Zarnuga workers rake the court and wash the well house. With some dismay they collect a silky brassiere left by the irrigation pool. The orange grower turns his back on all that and walks in his high boots into the thick morning dew.

He wonders about the mysterious bond between Jews and oranges. Both arrived in Palestine around the same time. Both took root in the same coastal plain. Both needed this loamy soil, this sun, these blue skies. The moderate weather, the life by the sea. Neither Jews nor oranges could have prospered if the British had not ruled over Palestine. And now, in early April 1936, the Jews and the oranges of the Land of Israel are both flourishing.

As the orange grower walks into his grove, a flock of pheasants takes flight. A rabbit scampers away. A fox peeps from the thicket. Bees buzz as they circle above, then descend upon the flowering buds, suckling their nectar. The orange grower notices the fresh tracks of a mongoose and those of a jackal. The grove is a microcosm unto itself.

The orange grower finds all this inconceivable. Only six years have passed since he bought from the villagers of Qubeibeh these seventy dunams of once barren land in the Valley of Dew. Only five years have passed since he cleared the land of poisonous weed and planted a thousand saplings of Valencia and four thousand saplings of Shamouti. Now, as if in the blink of an eye, the five thousand saplings have turned into a forest. The gray, arid wasteland has given way to a rich habitat of flora and fauna that seems as if it has always been here. What the orange grower sees all around him is man-made nature.

The orange grower thinks about the rejuvenation of the Jews and the rejuvenation of the country. By now there are nearly 300,000 dunams of citrus groves in Palestine, more than half of them owned by Jews. Next year's exports are expected to reach ten million crates of citrus fruit, and by 1939, exports are expected to reach fifteen million crates. If disaster doesn't strike, in the 1940s Palestine is expected to export more than twenty million crates of oranges, which will make it the world's leading citrus power. What the Jews have already accomplished in the local groves has proved that there is no limit to the amount of orange gold that can be produced in this land. There is no limit to the land's bounty. And there is no limit to the ability of Palestine to absorb and save the Jews.

The orange grower reaches the summit of the grove and looks around. South of his grove are the reddish-white houses of Rehovot. To the west are the sleepy stone houses of the villages of Qubeibeh and Zarnuga that have learned to live in peace with the colony planted in their midst. North of the grove is the grandiose Oriental mansion of the Palestinian landlord who has flourished alongside the flourishing Jews and their flourishing orange groves. To the east are the tall palm trees that lead the way to Ramleh, beyond which lies the faint blue silhouette of the ridge of Jerusalem. The orange grower is not naïve. He follows the news from Germany. He is attentive to the ominous rumblings coming out of the Arab cities and villages. He is aware of the fact that the Rehovot of 1936 is threatened by the great forces buffeting European Jewry and transforming Arab Palestine. But right now, as he stands at the top of his own orange grove, he sees an orange grove to the south and an orange grove to the west and an orange grove to the north and an orange grove to the east. Wherever he looks—orange groves. And the groves are young and mature, Jewish and Arab. They are all bursting out of the land the way oil bursts out of the land in Texas. So the orange grower feels that there is a blessing in the land. There is hope in the land. And the colony of Rehovot is a living testament that the Jews were right to end their two millennia of wandering in the Plain of Judea. They were right to come here and build a home and plant a tree and put down roots. Creating something from nothing. Creating this green ocean of orange groves that whispers Peace and plenty and home.

FOUR

Masada, 1942

THE FIRST SHOTS WERE HEARD ON THE EVENING OF WEDNESDAY, APRIL 15, 1936. In the early hours of dark, approximately twenty cars were waved to a halt beside piles of rocks and tar barrels of a makeshift, unlawful checkpoint on the Tul Karem Road in the hills of Samaria. Armed men, their faces masked, demanded that every driver and passenger contribute money for rifles and ammunition for the Arab cause. But when fifty-year-old Zvi Dannenberg and seventy-year-old Israel Hazan arrived in their chicken-filled truck heading for the Tel Aviv market, the gunmen realized that they were Jews, pulled them out of the truck, and shot them. Dannenberg was killed immediately. Hazan bled to death by the idling truck.

The next day, two khaki-clad Jews arrived at a tin hut belonging to Abu Rass in the Applebaum banana plantation in the Plain of Sharon. It was almost midnight when Abu Rass heard the knocks on his door and opened it for the unexpected guests. They fired eleven pistol bullets at him and at his Egyptian roommate. Abu Rass was killed on the spot, while the Egyptian managed to crawl for a hundred yards in the pitch-black night before collapsing and dying.

The following day, Israel Hazan's funeral was held in Tel Aviv's city center. The funeral procession quickly got out of hand, becoming a

demonstration of rage. Thousands rallied in the streets, calling for revenge. Several gangs tried to lynch some Arab cartmen and shoeshine
men who were in town for a day's work. "In blood and fire Judea fell,"
the young nationalists cried out, "in blood and in fire Judea shall rise."

Two days later, a rumor swept through Jaffa that four Arabs had
been murdered in neighboring Tel Aviv. Hundreds of Arabs thronged
the streets, marching toward the city's police station and government
headquarters, demanding the bodies of those who were assumed to have
died. Then they gathered in groups on street corners, waiting for prey.
They stoned Jewish buses, Jewish taxis, and Jewish automobiles. They
chased innocent Jews passing by.

Chaim Pashigoda, twenty-three, a law clerk, was on his way to the
registrar's offices in Jaffa. Armed with stones, hammers, and knives, a
Palestinian crowd attacked and murdered him. Eliezer Bisozky, an elderly Yiddish-speaking Jew, tried to escape raging Jaffa. He almost succeeded in hopping onto a horse-drawn wagon that was heading to Tel
Aviv but fell off and into the hands of the mob, who pummeled him to
death. Chaim Kornfeld, thirty, and Victor Koopermintz, thirty-four,
were plasterers renovating a grand Arab house in the exclusive Arab
quarter of Jaballiya. The mob heading down from the citrus port beat
them to death. Yitzhak Frenkel and Yehuda Siman-Tov were murdered
in much the same way. The electrician David Shambadal was hacked to
pieces by a group of young Arab men when he arrived at a café to install
a new lighting system. Zelig Levinson was mowed down by rifle bullets
on the edge of Jaffa.

The next day seven more Jews were murdered. Within three days
Tel Aviv buried sixteen victims of Arab violence. Eighty wounded were
treated in the city's hospitals. Because of a blood shortage, the public
was urged to donate.

The following day, the national Palestinian leadership called for a
general strike. Now violence took a new form. Fires were set in Jerusalem, in Kibbutz Kfar Menachem, and in the Balfour Forest in the north.
The fields of the Valley of Harod were ablaze, and hundreds of dunams
of orange groves there were uprooted or felled.

Three weeks later, on May 13, two Jews were murdered in the Old
City of Jerusalem. On May 16, three Jews in a crowd coming out of Je-

rusalem's Edison Cinema house were picked off by snipers. On August 13, a gang broke into the house of an ultra-Orthodox family in Safed, killing the father, the sixteen-year-old son, the nine-year-old daughter, and the seven-year-old daughter in their beds. The next day Arabs ambushed four Jews who were driving to a quiet mountain retreat in the Carmel forest. A day later, a Jew was murdered in Sarafand, just a few miles from Rehovot. While the Sarafand victim's funeral was under way, a bomb was thrown from a passing train onto Tel Aviv's busy Herzl Street, wounding nineteen Jews and killing an eight-year-old Jewish boy. The following day, two young Jewish nurses were shot to death as they arrived for work at Jaffa's state hospital. Three days later, a rifle bullet penetrated the skull of a scholar as he read an ancient Islamic manuscript in the study of his humble Jerusalem home. The day after that, one female and three male Jewish workers were murdered as they returned from work in a Kfar Sabba orange grove.

The Jewish community was aghast. True, there had been violence before. In March 1920, the first Arab-Jewish confrontation erupted in the northern Galilee. In April 1920, there were riots in Jerusalem. In August 1929, there were massacres in Hebron and Safed. Yet all these incidents were short, sporadic bursts of violence. They came suddenly and passed suddenly. A British officer described them accurately as resembling the flash floods in the Negev, Palestine's southern desert. The sustained violence of 1936 was different. It created an unprecedented, all-engulfing conflict in Palestine. And because it was coupled with a Palestinian general strike and a Palestinian national institution building drive, it could not be mistaken for anything other than what it was: a collective uprising of a national Arab-Palestinian movement.

In the late spring and early summer of 1936, the Zionist response was restrained. Only in the second half of August, after four months of Arab terror, were the first Jewish acts of revenge carried out. But the eighty dead and the four hundred wounded in the summer of '36 transformed the collective psyche of the Jews. So did the scorched fields, the uprooted orange groves, the roadside ambushes, and the ongoing night shootings. The brutal events that took place between April and August 1936 pushed Zionism from a state of utopian bliss to a state of dystopian conflict. As Palestinian nationalism was asserting itself and demanding that Jewish immigration stop immediately, it was now impossible to ignore the Arabs living in the land, impossible to ignore the fact that the Arabs reviled the Zionist enterprise. The Jewish national liberation movement had to acknowledge that it was facing an Arab liberation movement that wished to disgorge the Jews from the shores they had settled on.

Day after day the papers were filled with the names of the dead in black-bordered notices and descriptions of mass funerals turned demonstrations. But there was no sense of panic or despair in the Jewish community. On the contrary. Day by day people seemed to grow more resolute. Rather than weakening their resolve, the acknowledgment of a tragic reality emboldened them. It turned the 350,000 Jews living in Palestine in 1936 into a community of combat.

In November a Royal Enquiry Commission arrived in Palestine headed by Lord Peel. Within weeks it realized that the evolving reality was intolerable. Eight months later, in July 1937, the Peel Commission handed its report to the British government recommending a partition of the land into two nation-states, Jewish and Arab. It also recommended that the Arabs residing in the Jewish state be "transferred" elsewhere, as will the Jews living in the Arab state. From this moment on, the idea of "transfer"—the removal of the Arab population—became part of mainstream Zionist thinking. What was unheard of in 1935 became acceptable in 1937. What was absolute heresy when Zionism was launched became common opinion when Zionism confronted a rival national movement face-to-face.

Berl Katznelson, spiritual leader of the Labor Movement, gave a speech in November 1937: "My conscience is absolutely clear regarding this matter. Better a distant neighbor than a close-by enemy. They will not lose by their transfer and we definitely will not lose. The bottom line shows that this reform would benefit both parties. For a while now, I have thought that it was the best solution, but during the riots I have become convinced that this must take place. But it never crossed my mind that the transfer would be to Nablus. I believed in the past and I believe now that they should be transferred to Syria and Iraq." David Ben Gurion, chairman of the Jewish Agency in Palestine, spoke in June 1938: "My approach to the solution of the question of the Arabs in the

Jewish state is their transfer to Arab countries." Later that year Ben Gurion asserted that "compulsory transfer will clear for us vast territories. I support compulsory transfer. I do not see anything immoral in it."

In December 1940, Yosef Weitz, head of the forestry division of the Jewish National Fund, wrote in his private diary, just after visiting Herbert Bentwich's estate in Tel Gezer,

Just between us, it must be clear that there is no room in the land for the two people[s]. No development will bring us to our goal to be an independent nation in this small land. If the Arabs leave, the country will be wide and spacious for us. If the Arabs remain, the land will remain narrow and poor. The only solution is the Land of Israel, at least the western Land of Israel, with no Arabs. There is no place for compromise here. The Zionist endeavor thus far . . . was all well and good . . . but it shall not give the people of Israel a state. There is no other way but to transfer the Arabs from here to the neighboring countries. To transfer all, except perhaps Bethlehem, Nazareth, Old Jerusalem. Not one village is to remain, not one tribe. The transfer should target Iraq, Syria, even Trans Jordan. For this cause, funding will be found. Much funding. Only with this transfer will the land be able to absorb millions of our brothers and the question of the Jews will have a solution. There is no other way.

In the late 1930s, the Jewish community in Palestine did not have the leverage to initiate a transfer of the Arab population. But the new idea spoke volumes about the new state of mind of the Zionist leadership. All that had been suppressed and denied since Herbert Bentwich disembarked in the port of Jaffa in 1897 now surfaced. The shocking insight of Israel Zangwill was now a part of conventional thinking. Within a year, a merciless perception of reality took root: us or them, life or death.

The change of conscience was not only that of the leadership. The Jewish community as a whole was transformed. As a consequence of the 1936 violence, the Jews of Palestine went through a metamorphosis. Gone were the innocence, the self-deception, the moral inhibitions.

With the new, merciless perception of reality came a new, merciless determination: We shall not retreat, we shall not concede. We will do all that is needed to maintain Zionism.

The pause in violence lasted from the autumn of 1936 to the autumn of 1937. But the Arab revolt erupted again in October 1937. After my grandfather's best friend, Avinoam Yalin, was shot dead outside the Board of Education office in Jerusalem, Jews took revenge by murdering an Arab passerby and an Armenian photographer. After five pioneers were ambushed in the Judean hills, where they were about to plant pine trees, Jews in Jerusalem murdered an Arab and then another Arab, and then two Arab women were burned to death when the car they were sitting in exploded by the city's bustling market. In just one month, the number of innocent Arab victims surpassed the number of innocent Jewish victims.

In 1938, the great Arab revolt reached a climax and threatened to take over large parts of the country. Police stations were burned, there was chaos in the mountain regions. The clash between the Arab liberation movement and the British Empire turned brutal. More than eighteen hundred people were killed in the course of a year. Although most were casualties of British-Arab and Arab-Arab confrontations, the number of victims of Jewish-Arab hostilities rose, too. In this dance of blood, the atrocities that Arabs visited upon the Jews and the atrocities that Jews visited upon the Arabs grew ever more grisly.

In March 1938, Arabs attacked a car en route from Haifa to Safed. They murdered six of its Jewish passengers, among them two women, a young girl, and a boy. The girl was raped, then killed and dismembered. The tide of rage triggered by the incident brought about a failed attack of Jewish extremists on an Arab bus in the Galilee. When one of the Jewish terrorists was hanged at the end of June, Jewish nationalists went mad. On July 3 and 4, several assassinations took place in Jerusalem and Tel Aviv. On July 6, Jews murdered eighteen Arabs by setting off time bombs in the Arab market of Haifa. On July 15, Jews murdered ten Arabs by setting off a time bomb in the market of Jerusalem's Old City. On July 25, Jews murdered more than thirty-five Arabs by exploding a highly powerful bomb in the crowded Haifa market. On August 26, Jews murdered twenty-four Arabs by detonating a well-hidden bomb in the market of the citrus port of Jaffa.

The Arabs were not idle, either. On June 23: an onslaught on the colony of Givat Ada (three dead). On July 5: a murderous attack on orange grove workers in the village of Ein Vered (four dead). On July 21: a well-planned attack on the poor workers' quarter of Kiryat Haroshet (five dead). On August 4: a land mine in the dirt roads of Kibbutz Ramat-Hakovesh (six dead). On August 28: an assault on Kibbutz Ein Shemer (two dead). On September 10: the lynching of electricity company workers at the Massmia junction (seven dead). On September 14: a land mine on the eastern outskirts of the Valley of Harod (three dead). On October 2: in a massacre in Tiberias, eight adults and eleven children slaughtered.

There was a significant difference between the Jewish and Arab atrocities in the first half of 1938. While the attacks on Jewish civilians were supported by the Arab national leadership and by much of the Arab public, the attacks on Arab civilians were denounced by mainstream Zionism. Most Jewish murderers were members of fringe terrorist groups who defied the policy and instructions of the elected leadership of the Jewish community in Palestine. On the other hand, some of the Jewish actions were far more lethal than the Arab ones. The summer of 1938 was different from the summer of 1936 in that the number of murdered Arab victims exceeded by far the number of murdered Jews.

The summer of carnage brought forth another dramatic turn of events. In the Valley of Harod, the iconoclastic Scottish commando warrior Col. Orde Wingate established five special night squads. The first began operating in June 1938. Formally, the squads' task had been to protect the Iraq–Haifa oil pipeline crossing the valley, but their real task was to launch an anti-insurgency campaign, to fight Arab terror by initiating Anglo-Jewish counterterror. At first the Wingate's Warriors set up ambushes in the valley and fought armed Arab gangs. Soon after, they began to raid Arab villages and terrorize their inhabitants.

There were more and more reports of looting and prisoner executions. In the autumn of 1938, the night squads' brutality accelerated. After Ein Harod's local hero, Haim Sturman, was killed when his car hit a land mine, the Anglo-Jewish guerrilla units went on a rampage in the village of Paqua on the slopes of Mount Gilboa. And after the massacre of the nineteen Jews in Tiberias, they took revenge by attacking indiscriminately on the road to Safed, in the village of Dabburiya, and in the village of Hittin. Fourteen Arabs were killed on the Safed road, fifteen were killed in Dabburiya, and scores were left dead in Hittin.

British officers were in command of Wingate's special squads. The British soldiers were in general the more ruthless warriors, but the Haganah's fighters were willing partners. As they endorsed the new combative ethos, they became the heroes of the young Hebrews of Palestine. On September 13, Wingate inaugurated a sergeants' course in the amphitheater of Kibbutz Ein Harod. The deeply religious Christian commando commander had no doubt as to the significance of the event. "We are here to found the Army of Zion," he said to the one hundred young Jews before him.

In the winter of 1938 and spring of 1939, the British suppressed the Great Arab Revolt with an iron fist. But Jewish terrorism did not abate. In February 1939, more than forty innocent Arabs were murdered when bombs went off in the Haifa train station, the Haifa market, and the Jerusalem market. On May 29, four Arab women were murdered in Bir Addas. On June 20, scores of innocent Arabs were murdered when a bomb exploded in the Arab market of Haifa. On June 29, five Arab villagers riding on a wagon into Rehovot in the early morning were shot dead. On July 20, another three Arabs were murdered in Rehovot's orange groves.

On September 19, 1939, the general staff of the Haganah was founded. Well before a Jewish state was established, a well-organized Jewish army was raised. The Arab revolt was over, but the Jewish community in Palestine made the formative decision to organize a national military structure. Twenty months later, on May 15, 1941, the Palmach Strike Force was established. In between, the arms industry of the Haganah grew and diversified. Youth movement members received paramilitary training.

For Zionism had no illusions now: it realized that the brutal civil war of 1936–39 was only the beginning. The Jewish national movement was getting ready for a new round of violence. No one knew when, no one knew under what circumstances, but no one doubted that the conflict would erupt again, and viciously. The trauma of the summer of 1936 was burned deep in the heart and the lesson was learned. Zionism would never be what it was before Chaim Pashigoda, Eliezer Bisozky,

Chaim Kornfeld, Victor Koopermintz, Yitzhak Frenkel, Yehuda Siman-Tov, David Shambadal, and Zelig Levinson were murdered in Jaffa on the morning of April 19, 1936. And yet the newly redefined Zionism was in need of a symbol and a shrine. As it redefined and transformed itself, it needed a new epicenter.

Masada is only 63 meters above sea level. But because the Dead Sea, to the east of it, is approximately 400 meters below sea level, the mesa of Masada rises to 460 meters above its heavy, salty waters. To the west is the Judean desert, to the south, Sodom, and to the north, Ein Gedi, Ein Feshcha, and Jericho. On a very clear day, the faint silhouette of Jerusalem rises in the distance.

The slopes are steep, almost vertical. The summit is flat and rhomboid, 645 meters long and 315 meters across at its widest. The desert cliff is composed of layers of sedimentary rock topped by dolomite and limestone boulders. From afar, Masada has the appearance of a lonely desert castle, inspiring majesty and awe.

The Hasmoneans were the first to erect a man-made fortress on the natural fort that is Masada. In the second century B.C., they built a castle that a hundred years later was described as the mightiest of all. But it was King Herod who turned Masada into an architectural wonder. In the years from 36 to 30 B.C. he surrounded the rock with a casemate wall, raised watchtowers and barracks, built magnificent houses and ample warehouses, carved cisterns in the stone, and capped it all with a breathtaking palace.

When the great Jewish revolt against the Roman Empire began in A.D. 66, Masada was the first fortress the rebels overtook. In A.D. 70, the Romans crushed the revolt, conquered Jerusalem, and destroyed the Temple. In the following years, a small group of Jewish zealots made Masada the last fortress of the futile revolt. In A.D. 72, the 10th Roman Legion closed in on Masada, and in the spring of A.D. 73, the legion was poised to break into the fortress. On the night before the anticipated attack, the 960 men, women, and children of Masada took their own lives rather than submit to Roman rule.

For centuries, Jewish history largely ignored Masada. The tale of its zealots was perceived as a tale of suicidal extremism, and the site of Masada was deserted for over a thousand years. The American travelers Edward Robinson and Eli Smith were the first modern men to identify Masada in 1838. In 1842, the America missionary Samuel W. Wolcott and the English painter W. Tipping were the first to climb up Masada. In 1875, the renowned English captain Claude Reignier Conder was the first to map Masada accurately. In 1932, the German scholar Adolf Schulten conducted a comprehensive archaeological dig around the ruins.

In 1923 the only historical source of the story of Masada, Flavius Josephus' *The Jewish War* (written around A.D. 75) was translated into Hebrew. In 1925, the Zionist historian Joseph Klausner wrote with great affection about the zealots of Masada. Two years later, Yitzhak Lamdan published his tragic poem "Masada." As Jewish nationalism was revived, so was interest in the remote, forgotten site and all that it embodied. High school students from Tel Aviv and Jerusalem conducted several trips to Masada in the 1920s, until one trip led to a fatal accident. And yet, until the end of the Arab revolt and the beginning of World War II in 1939, Masada did not fully capture the minds of mainstream Zionism. Only nationalistic fringe groups admired its suicidal zealots.

In January 1942, Shmaryahu Gutman is a thirty-three-year-old energetic, vigorous, and charismatic man. He is squat, but his body is agile and his movements are quick. There is no one to rival him in desert hiking and mountain climbing. Born in Glasgow, Scotland, in 1909, Gutman immigrated with his family to Palestine when he was three and settled in Merhavia, on the outskirts of the Valley of Harod. In his teens he studied at the agricultural high school Mikveh Yisrael and emerged as one of the leaders of the working-youth movement. At twenty-one he founded Kibbutz Na'an. But as he was an amateur Orientalist, geographer, historian, and archaeologist, kibbutz life was not enough for the energetic young Zionist. He walked the land and led groups of youngsters on hikes. He was a pillar of the Yediat Haaretz (knowledge of the land) movement, whose ideology was studying the land, loving the land, and becoming one with the land. At the very same time, Gutman was also working closely with the leaders of Labor Zionism Berl Katznelson and Yitzhak Tabenkin. His best friend, Israel Galili, was the strategic mastermind of the military organization the Haganah.

In the early 1940s, Gutman does not hold an official post, but in practice he is part of the inner circle of the Zionist leadership. An educator with outstanding moral authority, Gutman is privy to the innermost secrets of Zionism. He views his role as being to concentrate the minds of Hebrew youths on what lies ahead.

In January 1942, Gutman decides to take the elite of the pioneer youth movement to Masada. The trip is no ordinary excursion. Gutman, himself a zealot, wants to change the collective psyche. He wants to unify the Hebrew youth around a powerful, concrete symbol, which he recognizes in Masada. In October 1941, he led a preliminary workshop of Masada studies in Tel Aviv and then chose the forty-six youth movement leaders he would take with him to Masada in January. As he sees it, these handpicked young agents of change will be the new missionaries of Masada. They will make Masada the new locus of Zionist identity.

On Friday, January 23, 1942, Gutman and his forty-six disciples leave Jerusalem. In the early morning an Arab bus takes them to the Palestinian village of Yatta, south of Hebron. Tents, equipment, food, and water are loaded on three camels hired from local Palestinians. The guides are Palestinian Bedouins. The young men and women wear short trousers, tall boots, and rucksacks laden with rolled army blankets. Some carry walking sticks, some have tied Arab kaffiyehs around their necks, all have water canteens. When they descend the white hills into the desert of Judea, they sing loudly, with boundless enthusiasm.

Gutman is more thoughtful than the young Sabras. In fact, he is almost somber. As he is to tell me fifty years later, he knows perfectly well why the seventeen-year-olds are upbeat. Recent years have been exceptionally good for the Jews of Palestine. Since the Arab revolt was crushed and the Arab national movement disintegrated, the country has been at peace. In the early 1940s the Jewish economy has leaped forward and the Jewish organizations have gathered power and authority. A substantial industrial revolution has been taking place. ATA Ltd. is now manufacturing uniforms for the soldiers of the British army, while Elite Ltd., Liber Ltd., and Z.D. Ltd. are manufacturing chocolate bars for them. Teva is producing medicine and medical equipment for His Majesty's troops, Assis Ltd. is producing marmalade and jam, and the socialist conglomerate Solel Boneh is building bridges, railways, and military bases for the Crown in Palestine, Egypt, Iraq, and Iran. The citrus industry has fallen into crisis, but the diamond industry has replaced it as Palestine's leading exporter. So now the Land of Israel exports not only Jaffa oranges but tents, ropes, camouflage nets, parachutes, boots, water canteens, cranes, heating ovens, shaving blades, tires, measuring equipment, plastic goods, optical equipment, medical supplies, dry ice, acetone, ether, beer, furs, telephone wire, electrical wire, and land mines. The number of Jewish employees in these industries has risen threefold in just three years. Industrial production has risen fivefold in five years. Exports have doubled in two years. The ratio between Jewish industrial production and Arab industrial production in Palestine is now six to one. Since there is full employment, wages have risen dramatically and factories are working around the clock, three shifts a day. Trade-union-owned corporations and privately held enterprises are prospering. Theaters are full, cafés are bustling. While Gutman leads his youngsters into the desert, Tel Aviv holds its fourth and most successful fashion week, which is celebrated in a glittering ball in the glamorous café Piltz. This is why the Israeli-born Sabras are so self-confident. They are the sons and daughters of a fantasy that is fulfilling itself. Their life experience is that of an astounding collective success, based on self-reliance and innovation.

But Shmaryahu Gutman knows that Zionism is in trouble. Although it has fended off the Arab revolt of the 1930s and brought forth the economic miracle of the 1940s, history is closing in on the audacious Jewish national endeavor. The Arab threat has not vanished. It is clear to the Zionist leaders that when the Second World War ends, the brutal conflict over the fate of Palestine will be renewed.

Yet the Arab threat is not the only one. Rommel's Afrika Korps has just managed to pummel the British defense line not far from Benghazi, Libya. While in the summer of 1941, it seemed the Germans might attack Palestine from the north, it now looks as if they are about to invade from the south. Faced with an Arab threat and a Nazi threat, it is clear that without the use of force, Zionism will not prevail. It will go down in history as yet another movement of false messianism. This is why the youth of Israel must be prepared. Only the sons and daughters of Zion can save Zionism from utter destruction.

The Palestinian guides lose their way. The day turns to dusk. After two short stops at desert springs, the column arrives at the Bedouin camp it was supposed to have reached at noon. Some of the travelers want to stop for the night. The camels are exhausted and refuse to go on. Despite the setback, Gutman is determined to forge ahead. After all, this is the very reason he has brought these cadets to the desert: to steel them, to strengthen their resolve, to teach them not to recoil from adversity. When the sun goes down, the trek will continue by moonlight. If the camels refuse to carry the load, the young men will shoulder it themselves.

Now the journey is totally altered. The navigation mistake, the delay, and suspicions regarding the Bedouins demoralize the hikers. They have been on the road since 3:00 A.M. The previous night they had not really slept. They experience anxiety and fatigue. Their eyes can hardly see in the pitch-black night. Their throats are parched because of the shortage of water. The straps of their heavy rucksacks cut into their shoulders. The air is salty. The desert is filled with chasms and ravines. There is no plant life, no animals or birds to be seen. There are just the heavy footsteps of a column marching on.

Gutman, of course, does not know that on the previous Tuesday, January 20, 1942, fifteen representatives of the ministries of the Third Reich gathered in Berlin's Wannsee Villa to formulate the Final Solution. He does not yet know that the deportation of Jews to the east has begun, or that within six weeks, in a small redbrick building in a remote camp named Auschwitz, a first gas chamber will begin to exterminate Jews. But Gutman does know that Zionism's bleak forecast regarding the future of European Jewry is becoming reality. He knows that in every country they take, the Germans mark Jews, gather them, and concentrate them in ghettos.

Because he has a profound understanding of history, Gutman realizes that for the Jewish people the current world war is going to be far more significant than the previous one. He sees that what is happening are not the customary anti-Jewish pogroms of typical European wars. Something is happening that has never happened before. Tens of thousands of Jews have already been murdered, and their numbers might soon rise to hundreds of thousands. If the Red Army does not block the Germans in the Crimea and Leningrad, disaster is imminent. So it is not only Zionism that is at stake. For the Jewish people, the year 1942 could turn out to be the worst year since the destruction of the Second Temple. It could turn out to be the most catastrophic year in the Jews' catastrophic history.

As Gutman watches the hikers, he understands how difficult the journey is for them. They are not adept at walking in the desert as he is, and they have little experience with thirst and fatigue. The slopes of Masada are frighteningly steep, and the ascent will be difficult. The sliver of moon that has just appeared above is too weak to light their way in the menacing dark. Many are soaked with sweat, their breathing labored. Some stumble, some fall. After sixteen hours of walking, the forty-six are not far from breaking. But they are made of stronger stuff than that. Those born in Palestine's spartan twenties and shaped in Palestine's violent thirties have grown to be rock hard. Brought up on the values of strength and fortitude that define the new Hebrew culture, the cadets are tough and determined. Even when their legs betray them, they continue to march. Even when they fall, they get up again. Gutman smiles as he looks at them. As he tells me in an interview conducted in the early 1990s, he finds in their shining eyes the determination he had hoped to find.

Gutman is not naïve. Having grown up beside the malaria-infested marshes near the Valley of Harod, he has always known that Zionism is a struggle. Living under the hateful gaze of the valley's Arabs, he has always known that at its core Zionism embodies conflict. Yet he has always believed in the desperate energy of Zionism. He believes that the essence of Zionism is momentum—never to retreat, never to rest, always to push forward. The new Hebrews must push the limits of what the Jews can do, of what any people can do. They must defy fate.

But now Gutman feels that Zionism's vector of energy is about to run into a wall. The forces closing in on the audacious national movement are just too strong: the Arab front, the German front, the collapse of European Jewry. The challenge facing his cadets is unprecedented. The thought of it actually makes Gutman shiver. Twenty years after it arrived in the valley, Zionism once again demands of its followers total mobilization and sacrifice. Coming from the valleys and the orange groves and Tel Aviv, the hiking youngsters do not realize that their very existence is in peril. They are bursting with the gaiety of Zionism's decades of success. They are drunk with the experience of Hebrew renaissance and Hebrew creation and Hebrew triumph. But not long ago Gutman has heard Yitzhak Tabenkin say that "We are upon the abyss," and Berl Katznelson say that "No man of words can express the horrors of these times, the great fear that engulfs us." So Gutman knows that he has but a short time to transform these youths. It is his role to anoint them as the guardians who will stand at the gate when the time comes.

Gutman's choice of Masada has a personal dimension. At the age of sixteen, he collapsed while participating in an early Dead Sea trek and never made it to the summit. The young man made a vow to return. When he did, several years later, he nearly lost his life but managed to reach the top. The few hours he spent on Masada changed his life. He somehow felt tied to this terrible place. In the nine years that have passed, the mountainous fortress has not let him go. Often he dreams of it, and he has waking visions as well of the ancient site. He has come to believe that Masada is the true heart of the land, the crux of the Zionist story. But only in the past year has Gutman realized the opportunity to engrave Masada on the collective Jewish psyche just as it has been engraved on his own. After the early tour of October 1941, he sent an official proposition to the national leadership, and after much lobbying he raised the necessary funds. So now he can connect the different paths of his life; he can unite the educator with the historian with the amateur archaeologist. He can draw a direct line between the horrific act of A.D. 73 and the heroic challenge of 1942. He can bring Masada back to life and make it the formative site of New Zionism.

Like the shadow of a hulking, sunken ship, the shadow of the mountain appears. Fatigue is forgotten, replaced by song. Suddenly walking is no longer difficult for the youth movement's leaders as they approach the silhouette of the fortress of tragic Jewish sovereignty. A fire already dances at the foot of the mountain, lit by the front guard that arrived earlier. The rebels of the Second Temple used to signal to one another with such fires. Lamdan's Masada poem is also replete with such fires. But here are the flames of the first fire of the new Masada. When they reach the fire, the forty-six hikers take off their rucksacks, unroll their blankets, and set up camp for the night.

At dawn, Gutman warns his disciples that climbing Masada is dangerous. Some have climbed and died. From now on, each climber must take care of himself and must take care of the next climber as well. Danger lurks at every step. Gutman recites Lamdan's poignant lines about the "remnant of slaughter" that climbs the tall wall of Masada.

The youngsters standing at the foot of Masada are all too familiar with the morbid words of the canonical text now being read by their mentor. They were raised on these lines, they memorized them in school, and many still know them by heart. But now, under the mythological fortress itself, the words acquire new significance. They sound like the anthem of a desperate people coming to the desert to look for a last refuge.

For several months now, I have been studying Masada, the Masada ethos, and Gutman's Masada journey. I have read all I could find in the relevant archives and libraries; I have interviewed anyone who could still be interviewed. I reread all of my notes from my lengthy interviews with Gutman, conducted shortly before he died. I assembled this historical puzzle piece by piece. And yet, even after all my research, it all seems inconceivable. Events that took place in the fourth decade of the twentieth century, undertaken in a rational and practical manner, are already steeped in the aura of mythology. The more I learn about them, the more distant they seem to me. In an era of criticism and cynicism and self-awareness I find it difficult to truly comprehend the cadets' state of mind as they prepare to climb Masada for the very first time. Yet I realize that this paradox is exactly the essence of the Zionist Masada; it is a modern, secular icon that transcends modernity and secularism. It is an artificial symbol that transcends its artificiality. What Gutman is doing in bringing this young, idealistic group to this desert ruin is using the Hebrew past to give depth to the Hebrew present and enable it to face the Hebrew future. In order to achieve a concrete, realistic, and national goal, Gutman imbues the fortress with a man-made historically based mysticism.

• • •

The ascent begins from the east. The long column of khaki-wearing youngsters climbs up the white rampart the Romans built to strike the fortified wall of the zealots' fortress. When the column reaches the chasm between the rampart and the summit, the effort intensifies. The first five hikers strike the rock face with their picks, then hammer in pitons and tie ropes and drop them down for the others.

What makes the task especially difficult is the heavy load that must be lifted to the top: tents, blankets, canned goods, water, rucksacks, arms, and ammunition. The youngsters create a human chain that enables them to pass the load, hand to hand, to the top. Gutman finds the sight of the chain inspiring. "The chain was not broken" is a line from Lamdan's poem, and Gutman is about to establish it as the generation's motto.

Gutman instructs his cadets not to look back, not to look down. Advance, only advance. Onward and upward the forty-six go; they reach the wall, climb the wall, then at last find themselves on Masada.

It is Gutman's third time at the summit, but he is just as excited as when he first stood here nine years ago. The desert ridges and the terrifying gorge and the quiet silver wavelets of the Dead Sea stir in him a feeling of unfathomable heartache. As he recalled half a century later, Gutman is bewitched by the eight Roman compounds that surround the lonely mountain. Even after being neglected for 1,869 years, the sight feels stifling. It feels to him as if the hundred thousand Roman soldiers of the 10th Roman Legion are still besieging the one thousand defiant Jews; and he feels just as clearly that mighty historic forces are once again closing in on the Jews of Palestine.

After a few moments of looking down from the wall into the gorge, lost in thought, he shakes off his hallucination and goes back to what he must do as leader. The youngsters do not share Gutman's profound anxiety or ecstatic vision. But they are excited to see the desert hills painted pink by the setting sun and the remnants of Herod's buildings that have survived two thousand years at the summit. Gutman must see to it that this youthful joy does not get out of hand. It will be dark soon, so camp must be set up rapidly. Gutman divides his cadets into several work groups. Some gather firewood, some bring water from the wadi, some pitch tents within the fortress ruins. They improvise a table, a kitchen, a classroom. As the sun sets, the camp takes shape on Masada's flat summit. And when dark descends on the mountains of Moav, Gutman feels pride in the tent camp that has risen among the ruins. The youngsters light a campfire and sing and dance.

Then Gutman addresses the group. He tells the tale of Masada and its heroes. "Our tent, too, is pitched on the abyss," he says. When he is done speaking, he steps back into the darkness and watches the dancing begin anew. It is a rousing performance. Eyes afire, feet as light as air. The young boys and girls of Israel have returned to Masada to dance with abandon on the abyss.

Gutman is no dancer, but the spontaneous ritual is exactly what he wished for. For he knows that Zionism has no church and no theology and no mythology. He knows that Zionism is on the brink and needs a poignant symbol that will be a substitute for church and theology and mythology. In Masada he finds this symbol that will unite and inspire Zionism's followers. He finds a pillar for Zionist identity that is at once concrete, mythic, and sublime. In Masada, Gutman finds both the narrative and the image that will give the young Hebrews the depth they lack. Masada will captivate them, empower them, and galvanize them for the challenge ahead. This tragic mountain will give meaning to their struggle. In the name of Masada the dancing boys and girls will fight the cataclysmic war that will save Zionism and save the Jews.

Gutman knows that his enterprise is controversial. Even in Zionist circles, many regard the zealots of Masada as brutal extremists who robbed, murdered, and finally committed suicide. David Ben Gurion, chairman of the Jewish Agency, is apprehensive about the Masada tale because it is a tale of death and self-destruction. But Gutman begs to differ. He believes that what he is promoting is not a Masada complex but a Masada paradox: Only the young Hebrews willing to die will be able to ensure for themselves a secure and sovereign life. Only their willingness to fight to the end will prevent their end.

The youngsters sing:

A cliff we conquered and ascended
A path we carved and cleared
A trail we beat and blazed—to the abyss

Gutman walks away from the singing. Carrying a flashlight, he walks alone to the ancient southeastern living quarters that still have the remnants of a mosaic floor. He continues toward the building with the two forecourts that the German archaeologist Schulten described and enters the regal edifice to the west that Schulten mistook for Herod's palace. He goes through the square building that Schulten described as the Small Palace, then enters the giant structure at the northern end of the mountain and lingers among its many rooms. He visits the bathhouse, the tower; he walks the long corridors.

These were the soldiers' barracks, Gutman assumes. Here lived Herod's officers, here food was stored, here was the armory. Gutman is beside himself. His flashlight wanders along the thick walls. His hand feels the coarsely chiseled stones. As far as Gutman is concerned, this desert citadel is as wondrous as the pyramids of Giza. But what captures the mind of the Zionist revolutionary is not Herod's genius and ingenuity. It is the thought of the rebels seeking refuge in these deserted palaces. What the amateur archaeologist is looking for with his flashlight is the remains the zealots left behind. Perhaps shekels they coined in the four years of their great revolt, or inscriptions they carved into the stone in the final days. Perhaps clay pots to collect water, crumbling sandals, torn prayer shawls, oil lamps made of clay. But all Gutman finds in the dark are round ballista stones that the rebels prepared in order to crush the skulls of the Romans, and the ballista stones that the Romans shot from afar at the rebels' stronghold. And as he examines the stones, his thoughts are drawn to those last hours of that last night.

In his mind, Gutman reconstructs that last dreadful night of A.D. 73. Herod's casemate wall has already been breached. The rebels' improvised wooden wall has already burned down. No power in the world will stop the Romans from breaking into Masada at dawn. So Elazar Ben Yair, whom Gutman worships, decides not to surrender but to die. Here, on this very spot, Ben Yair gathers the zealots and says his last famous words, as passed down through the ages by a survivor:

It is known and written that tomorrow will come our demise, but the choice is to us to die the death of heroes, we and all those dear to us. . . . Perhaps from the beginning, when we stood to assert our liberty. . . . we should have grasped the spirit of God and realized that he has sealed the fate of the race of the Jews whom he had loved before.

We cannot save our souls. . . . So let our wives die before they are violated, let our sons die before they taste the taste of slavery. Then we shall bless one another with the blessing of heroes. How good and how great it will be when we carry our freedom to our grave.

From a distance, Gutman sees his youngsters dancing and singing around the fire. As he watches them, he contemplates what his mentor Tabenkin said recently: "In this war, we Jews are the most lonely people, the most deserted and the most just." Gutman remembers what his other mentor, Katznelson, said when the war in Europe began: "We are orphans in this world. And as the world crumbles, our orphanhood intensifies. On the weak wings of the remnants of Israel living in Palestine was placed a heavy burden, more than we can bear. It might very well be that the entire future of Jewish history depends now on what shall happen with us. Without our being asked, the most enormous task of all was set upon us." And Gutman thinks of what Katznelson had added just a few months ago: "The fate of Israel is about to be decided as it was not decided upon since the destruction of the Temple, since we lost our land and liberty. Our history has not known such a time when the fire of destruction will surround at once all of our Diasporas across the globe."

Gutman understands that these words are not empty rhetoric. Since the summer of 1940, mainstream Zionist leadership has been seriously considering the possibility of apocalypse. "If we must fall, fall we shall, here with our women and children and all that we have," said Tabenkin that summer. Since the summer of 1941, mainstream Zionist leadership has been concerned that the British will evacuate Palestine, the Germans will invade, and a Nazi-inspired Arab uprising will terminate Zionism. "I do not wish for us to die in this land," said Tabenkin. "But I do wish that we shall not depart, we shall not leave the land alive." Since November 28, 1941, when the Grand Mufti of Jerusalem, Haj Amin al-Husseini, met Adolf Hitler in Berlin, there has been an official alliance between the Arab-Palestinian movement headed by Husseini and the

Third Reich. So now, in the early winter of 1942, there is growing concern in Tel Aviv regarding the possible combination of a German invasion of the land with a pro-Nazi Arab-Palestinian assault. It now appears
that the distant past is merging with the present, that the mythical is
coupling with the real.

After midnight, the dancing subsides. The camp goes silent. Only
Gutman is awake. In his tent, by the light of his lantern, he prepares
tomorrow's curriculum. Although his mission is one of indoctrination
and reeducation, Gutman is not a one-dimensional political commissar.
Although his goal is ideological, he is not a man of simplistic propaganda. He wants his cadets to study Masada seriously. He wants them to
become familiar with its geology, history, archaeology—and to contribute to the scientific body of knowledge regarding it. In order for them
to do so, he goes over Conder's meticulous maps. He reads Schulten's
findings, some of which have been misinterpreted. He reads Flavius
Josephus and is overwhelmed by the dry and precise manner in which
Flavius described the heroic drama. Finally he reads once again Lamdan's long, melancholic poem. The immigrant poet who lost his family
in a Russian pogrom does not promise success. He does not assure the
reader that the Zionist Masada of the twentieth century will evade
the fate of the first century's zealots. All that Lamdan argues is that the
citadel is the very last chance. There is no other place for the Jews but
Palestine, no other way but the way of Masada.

Gutman spends five days and five nights with his youngsters at Masada. On the second day he shows them the casemate wall consisting of
two parallel walls and explains the details of its construction. He shows
them the remains of thirty of its towers. On the third day, Gutman
takes his cadets along the dike, to each of the eight encampments of the
Roman siege. He argues with passion that the scale of the force that the
Romans assembled around the remote, desolate Masada proves that
the mighty empire was truly challenged by the defiant rebels.

On the fourth day, Gutman selects the best and the fittest to assist
him in exploring Masada's unknown quarters. Hovering over the gorge
and literally risking their lives, the determined boys manage to discover
patches of the lost serpentine path that had escaped the notice of previous explorers and find a hitherto unknown aqueduct leading water from
the east to the mountain fortress.

On the fifth and last day, Gutman takes his cadets back to the rampart to widen it and make it suitable for thousands to climb. He sends others to pile dry wood on some of the nearby hilltops so that the nocturnal farewell ceremony will reenact the way the first-century rebels signaled each other from hill to hill.

But a storm descends that night, so the concluding ceremony is held in a cave resembling the rebels' caves. Selected chapters from ancient Flavius and contemporary Lamdan are read aloud. There is much talk about the chain that binds times past with times present. The days of Masada are not over, they say. The voice of Israel's heroes will not be silenced. No sacrifice is too dear for our freedom. We shall not be slaves again.

When it's time to eat, a Bedouin lamb is slaughtered as if it is Passover eve, the evening when the Masada wall was breached and the rebels decided to take their own lives. They read aloud Josephus' descriptions of the last deeds of Ben Yair's men on this summit:

> They hugged their women with much love and held the children to their hearts and kissed them for the very last time, tears in their eyes. . . . And all slaughtered their brethren. And each one lay down on the ground by his dead wife and sons and held them in his arms. . . . And the one left after them examined the many bodies. . . . And when he knew for certain that all were dead, he set fire to all corners of the king's palace and with all the power of his hand he thrust his sword into his own flesh and fell down dead by his slaughtered loved ones.

Gutman is hypnotized by these words. As a humanist he realizes what horror they contain. But as a Zionist Jew he also realizes what horror 1942 will contain. He is not interested in cultivating a suicidal ethos, but he feels obligated to construct an ethos of resistance. He knows that in 1942, the trial ahead is the ultimate one. But although there is a certain resemblance between Ben Yair's Masada and Gutman's Masada, Gutman wants his Masada tale to have a totally different ending. That's why his motto now is "Masada shall not fall again." That's why he tells his youngsters not to be zealots of defeat but zealots of victory. He wants to take the ancient fortress's determination and turn it on its head, transforming an ethos of devastation into one of triumph.

Late at night, when the winds are howling at the mouth of the cave, the theatrical Masada ceremony comes to an end. The cadets sign a working-youth Masada scroll and seal it in a glass bottle that they bury under a headstone they erect. They call out that the chain has not been broken. They call out that Masada calls Israel to fight for its land. They sing the socialist anthem: "Strong be the hands of our brothers building the land." They sing the national anthem: "Hope is not yet lost." Then the youngsters dismantle the tents, and pack the rucksacks, and descend the mountain, which is now engraved in their consciousness.

Is it true that, as Ben Yair wrote, God sealed the fate of the race of the Jews whom he had loved before? On the very same days in late January that Gutman's Masada graduates return to Jerusalem, Field Marshal Rommel concludes his breakthrough toward Benghazi, Libya. Four months later the Wermacht's strategic genius defeats the British at Bir al-Hakim and reaches Egypt. By June 1942, Rommel is only a hundred kilometers west of Alexandria. In Tel Aviv, Zionist leaders assume that if Alexandria falls, the British Empire will evacuate the Middle East and realign its forces in India. Some reports claim that British officers are burning secret documents in their Cairo offices. Some claim that the British are pulling elite units from Egypt. In Palestine there is much talk of Jews selling property to Arabs, preparing hideouts in monasteries, asking Christian and Muslim friends for protection. Some acquire foreign passports, others purchase poison pills.

But what is happening in Europe is far worse. On January 30, 1941, Hitler announces in the Berlin Sports Palace that the outcome of the war will be the annihilation of the Jews. In March 1942, the Auschwitz extermination camp goes active. A few days later, the Belzec and Sobibor extermination camps begin to bellow their unique smoke into Europe's spring skies. On March 17, 1942, the deportation of the Jews of Lublin to Belzec begins. On March 24 the deportation of the Jews of Slovakia to Auschwitz begins. On March 27 begins the deportation of the Jews of France to Auschwitz. On March 30, the first Paris train carrying Jews arrives in Auschwitz.

In Palestine there is little information regarding the death camps or Hitler's mass-death project. But there is a growing understanding that

Europe is experiencing a megapogrom. Similarly there is a growing understanding that if the British lose Egypt, a megapogrom will take place in Palestine. Therefore, in March 1942, the idea of establishing a modern-day Masada on Mount Carmel is seriously considered. There is no intention to commit suicide on Mount Carmel; the top-secret plan is to concentrate the Jewish population of Palestine in the mountainous region bordering the sea so that a war can be waged that might slow the Germans and convince the British not to abandon the Jews. Yet the nocturnal discussions held secretly by the Zionist leadership in the summer of 1942 on a Tel Aviv roof does not exclude the worst scenario.

In the words of Gutman's best friend, Israel Galili, there is "no place to retreat. . . . We must guarantee that we stand to the last, defend ourselves to the end, hold on even at the price of extermination."

In the words of Gutman's mentor Yitzhak Tabenkin: "These half a million Jews should not retreat. Not even one of us should survive. We must stand here to the end for the future right, the self-respect, and the historic loyalty of the Jewish people. So we are told by Masada and even before Masada. So we are told by the destruction of the Second Temple."

In the words of the former leader of Poland's Zionist movement, Yitzhak Gruenbaum: "The trouble with the Jews of the Diaspora was that they preferred the life of a beaten dog to death with honor. There is no hope for survival once the Germans invade. If, God forbid, we shall reach the moment of invasion, we must see to it that we leave a Masada legend behind us."

Tabenkin again: "We, the Jews, have no option of retreat and evacuation. Some say that women and children must be saved. There is no place to save them. There is no justice in the demand to save women and children. . . . We must have no illusions: We face annihilation. Will the Germans leave behind them the Yagur Kibbutz or the Ein Harod Kibbutz or the commune of Degania?"

As temperatures run high, Zionist policy undergoes profound changes. On May 11, 1942, in New York's Biltmore Hotel, Zionism's leaders abandon the old idea of long-term organic growth and endorse the demand to establish a Jewish commonwealth in Palestine as soon as possible. In the weeks preceding and following the Biltmore convention, the Palmach Strike Force holds its first explosives course and it exercises its first five platoons.

In June 1942, Haganah commanders are called to an emergency meeting in Tel Aviv to hear the minutes of the Masada-on-the-Carmel plan. In July, the plan is thoroughly discussed in a special gathering in the Valley of Yizrael. Initial preparations are made to stake out hiding places for arms, water, food, and shelter for a hundred thousand people in the area that lies between Haifa and the Valley. Now explicit words are spoken about turning Mount Carmel into Masada.

No wonder that between February and July 1942, Gutman's Masada ethos takes root. The youth movement's weekly publishes extensive reports of the Masada trek and seminar, and it puts Ben Yair's last speech on its March 31 cover. Other Labor publications also celebrate and glorify Masada. A press conference in which Gutman promotes Masada resonates strongly in contemporary public opinion. The forty-six youth leaders do their share to pass along the Masada message to their youth movement cadets, so that the second Masada trek, held only three months after the first, includes more than two hundred youngsters. Throughout the country, Passover youth camps and youth activities are devoted to Masada. With Rommel at the gate, with Europe's Jewry in ghettos, and with the national leadership considering extreme ideas, Gutman's gospel of Masada spreads like fire in the woods. More and more youth movements ascend Masada. Palmach squads ascend Masada. Masada overtakes the public discourse. Within a few months, the ethos of Masada becomes the formative ethos of the young nation. Masada is now at the heart of the Zionist narrative, defining its new Palestine-born generation.

By autumn, history takes yet another turn. The immediate fear of invasion subsides. On October 23, Allied Commander Field Marshal Bernard Montgomery launches a counteroffensive against Rommel, who begins his retreat from El Alamein on November 4. There is no further danger of a Nazi invasion of the Land of Israel.

But just as the Jewish community of Palestine relaxes and returns to the pleasures of an unprecedented economic boom, the news from Europe becomes grimmer. On December 17, 1942, the British foreign secretary, Anthony Eden, declares in Westminster that Nazi Germany is exterminating European Jewry. By now, it is clear that what Hitler has in mind is not a megapogrom but a holocaust. Every single day thousands are murdered. In 1942 more than a million are murdered. By the end of the war it might turn out that European Jewry has vanished completely.

As 1943 begins, hence, the ethos of Masada takes on new meaning. Now it's not only a historic legend whose purpose is to prepare the Jews for a desperate war in the Land of Israel. Now Masada is a mythical, almost metaphysical metaphor for the loneliness of the Jewish people. As always, Yitzhak Tabenkin is the one to phrase the new insight in the cruelest fashion: "Our feeling is that of ultimate loneliness. . . . There is no way to know how many Jews will remain alive. . . . There is no guarantee that the Nazis will not exterminate the entire one hundred percent. . . . Bitter is the knowledge of our solitude and the knowledge that the world is our enemy."

For spiritual leaders like Tabenkin, Katznelson, and Gutman, the significance of the Holocaust is threefold: It is a human catastrophe on a scale not seen since the Middle Ages. It is a Jewish catastrophe on a scale not experienced since the destruction of the Second Temple. And it is a Zionist catastrophe unlike any other. For Zionism, the implications of the Holocaust are devastating. Gone are the great Jewish masses that Zionism was designed to save. Gone is the great human reservoir that was to save Zionism. Gone is Zionism's raison d'être. For even if Hitler is defeated, he might still leave behind him a defeated Jewish people. With no Eastern European demographic backbone, Zionism becomes a bridgehead that no reinforcements will ever cross, protect, or hold.

But Tabenkin, Katznelson, and Gutman turn disaster into mission. All three, and many others, begin to speak out about the responsibility of Hebrew youth facing the new, disastrous circumstances. "Every Hebrew boy in the Land of Israel now weighs as ten, as we have lost Jewish communities ten times as large as the Jewish community of Palestine," writes Gutman, inspired by Tabenkin. "In the black shadow of this fact, you, the young working generation of Israel, must carry on the founders' endeavor and be a leading torch of light to the resurrection of the nation in its land."

As it turns out, 1942 is far worse than anyone could have imagined. In this year, 2.7 million Jews are murdered by the Nazis. Within twelve months, every sixth Jew in the world is exterminated and every fourth European Jew dies of disease, hunger, shooting, or gas. The Jewish people will never recover from the blow. Zionism will never overcome the loss.

But the ethos of Masada will live on. The ethos forged in Gutman's January 1942 seminar will grow stronger and stronger as the horrors of 1942 are revealed. So those who ask whether the ethos was based merely on myth ask the wrong question. It is not Ben Yair who defined Masada, it is Gutman. What matters is not the event that did or did not take place on the fringe of history in A.D. 73, but the event that does take place in the locus of history in A.D. 1942. For the Masada ethos put forth by Gutman would define the Zionism of the 1940s and would decide the fate of 1948 and would shape the future state of Israel.

The mid-nineteenth-century French physiologist Claude Bernard was the first to overturn the conventional understanding that life is an adjustment to environment. Adjustment to the surrounding environment is death, argued Bernard; the phenomenon of life is that of preserving an internal environment contrary to an outside environment. Between the summer of 1936 and the summer of 1942, Zionism reaches a similar conclusion. A sequence of blows, some of them almost deadly, teaches the outstanding movement that its surrounding environment is extremely cruel. The relevant historical circumstances are lethal. Under these conditions, adjustment is death. The only way to maintain life is resistance. From now on the decisive image of the Zionist enterprise is not that of swamps drained or of orange groves bearing fruit but that of a lonely desert fortress casting the shadow of awe on an arid land.

FIVE

Lydda, 1948

How did Zionism arrive in the Valley of Lydda? Just as it arrived in some of Palestine's other valleys and plains.

In the autumn of 1903, after the Sixth Zionist Congress, the Anglo-Palestine Bank purchased 2,330 dunams of land in the village of Haditha for 80,730 francs. Of that area, 1,946 dunams were fertile and flat, while the remaining 384 dunams were hilly and barren. Together they formed a long strip of land that stretched from the silvery olive orchards of the Arab city of Lydda to the low ridge of hills rising from the gray fields of the Lydda Valley toward Jerusalem. The Beit Arif estate became the Ben Shemen estate, one of the first plots of land purchased by Herzl's Zionist movement in Palestine.

Two years later, after exploring several other sites across the country, the civil engineer Nahum Wilbosh decided to establish his Atid (Hebrew for "future") factory in the Lydda Valley. With an investment of 150,000 francs, he bought 100 dunams from the Anglo-Palestine Bank and erected a modern plant to press oil from its orchards and manufacture fine soap from the olive refuse. In its first four years, Atid was a disappointment. The oil was murky, the soap was inferior, and expenses were high. But in its fifth, sixth, and seventh years, Atid prospered. It provided its owners with respectable profits, its workers with decent livings, and its Arab neighbors with extra income from the sale of raw materials to the new Jewish industrial enterprise. But before the Great War broke out, Atid collapsed, leaving behind in the Lydda Valley nothing but the gloomy, deserted ruins of what was meant to be.

A year after Wilbosh established his factory, a teacher named Israel Belkind built Kiryat Sefer, an agricultural school, on fifty dunams of the Ben Shemen estate, for the orphans who had survived the gruesome Kishinev pogrom three years earlier. On the top of the hill, not far from the factory, Belkind erected two-story buildings surrounding a spacious courtyard where the pogrom survivors would train to become skilled farmers. Yet after spending 43,000 francs to purchase the land and build the classrooms and dormitory, Belkind was short of funds needed to run the school, and Kiryat Sefer collapsed.

In 1908, several years after the death of Theodor Herzl, the Zionist movement decided to commemorate its founder by planting a thousand olive trees in the Valley of Lydda. Choosing the olive tree for the orchard of Herzl-Wald was both practical and symbolic. The aim was to demonstrate that the new Jews could plant olive trees that were as beautiful and deep-rooted as the ancient olive trees of the orchards of the Arabs of Lydda. As early as 1908 a nursery had been set up between the Atid factory and the Kiryat Sefer school, but an unexpected incident had taken place there: Jewish workers rallied one day and uprooted the olive trees planted by Arab workers, replanting them with their own hands in order to make a national Jewish statement. So in 1909, when Herzl-Wald was planted, all work was solely Jewish. The new Jews of Palestine planted more than twelve thousand olive trees on the gentle slope overlooking the minarets of the city of Lydda. And as the trees grew taller, it seemed that Herzl-Wald was indeed becoming a real, deep-rooted olive orchard in Palestine. But then came war, locusts, and despair. The Atid factory failed. Some of the olive trees were damaged, some perished, some were uprooted. As quickly as Herzl's olive forest had appeared in the Valley of Lydda, it disappeared.

In 1910, after a wave of immigration from Yemen reached Palestine, Boris Schatz, an art professor and the founder of Jerusalem's renowned Bezalel art academy, decided to settle Yemenite artisans skilled in silversmithing in the Lydda Valley. His intention was to establish a modest artisan colony whose residents would make a living by combining twentieth-century agriculture and traditional crafts. For that purpose he built a small neighborhood of humble homes adjacent to the Ben Shemen courtyard and the Herzl-Wald forest to which he brought twelve families of impoverished Yemenite Jews who were rich in artistic tradition. For three years the families struggled to take root in the Lydda Valley, but they were ultimately defeated by the harsh conditions, the shortage of water, and the high infant mortality rate. Like Atid, Kiryat Sefer, and the olive forest, the artisan colony vanished.

In 1909, the agronomist Yitzhak Vilkansky, who first came to Ben Shemen to work in the olive tree nursery, turned Belkind's courtyard into an exemplary agricultural enterprise. In Ben Shemen, Vilkansky established Palestine's first modern cowshed, where he bred strong German bulls with resilient Damascus cows. Vilkansky experimented in beekeeping, almond growing, and wheat harvesting. He developed new methods of irrigation and came up with the idea of mixed farming, which would enable every family of Jewish settlers in Palestine to have a homestead run on a system of rations that would make the most of every small plot of land year-round. He trained work groups of skilled farmers, one of which settled in the deserted homes of the departed Yemenites, and established a tiny but flourishing working village. For sixteen years Vilkansky performed wonders in the Lydda Valley, proving, as the Zionist leader Chaim Weizmann had said, that in the Land of Israel, Hebrew hands can perform miracles.

But in 1926 Vilkansky moved his experimental farm to the thriving orange grove colony of Rehovot. After five attempts and four failures, Zionism was faced with the questions it had faced twenty-three years earlier: how to settle the Valley of Lydda, and what to do with the strip of land descending from the rocky hills to the deserted courtyard of Ben Shemen to the ruins of Atid and the minarets rising from the Arab city of Lydda.

Siegfried Lehmann was born in Berlin in 1892. He studied medicine and served as a doctor in the German army. Although he was the son of a wealthy family of assimilated German Jews, during the Great War he rediscovered his Jewish identity and found meaning in the endeavor of rejuvenating Judaism. In 1916 he established a center for homeless Jewish children in an East Berlin slum. In 1919 he opened a shelter for Jewish war orphans in the Lithuanian city of Kovna. Inspired by his mentors Martin Buber, Gustav Landauer, Albert Einstein, and his own brother Alfred, Lehmann believed that there was no future for Jews in Germany, and that Western Jewry must renew itself by reconnecting with the masses of Eastern Jewry, with their traditions and rituals.

By 1925 the doctor turned teacher realized that a rising wave of anti-Semitism would prevent him from maintaining his Kovna children's home. There was no place to go but Palestine. First Lehmann intended to rebuild his unique institution on the very spot on which the Ein Harod white tent camp had been pitched in the Harod Valley in the late summer of 1921. But after learning that the swarms of Anopheles mosquitoes in the marshes might endanger the lives of his students, Einstein's protégé changed course. On a rainy winter day, Lehmann arrived with his wife and a dozen Kovna orphans at the courtyard built by Israel Belkind for the Kishinev orphans some twenty years earlier.

Where others had failed, Lehmann succeeded. In 1927 there were only fifteen students in Lehmann's youth village; in 1931 there were two hundred twenty; in 1946, some six hundred students. The village's ten dunams of cultivated land grew to over five hundred dunams. There was a fine cowshed now, a large sheep pen, a horse stable, an orange grove, a vegetable garden, wheat fields, chicken coops, apiaries, a vineyard. On the gentle slope descending from the courtyard of Kiryat Sefer to the ruins of the Atid factory, long red-roofed dormitories were built. A school was founded, a swimming pool dug, sports fields constructed. Flower gardens were planted along footpaths. The bright living quarters that Lehmann insisted upon for the children gave the school an air of familial warmth. Within ten years, the German-Jewish humanist succeeded in developing in the Lydda Valley one of Zionism's most endearing enterprises.

Lehmann's village was unique. For a reasonably long period of time it fulfilled the utopian values of its founder. The Berlin doctor, who was supported by Berlin's liberal Jews, was no narrow-minded Zionist. Though he dedicated his life to the salvation of homeless Jewish children, he viewed his humanitarian mission in a broad historical context. He realized that the life of the Jewish people had become unbearable. He acknowledged that the displacement and detachment they experienced threatened the Jews physically, mentally, and spiritually. But Lehmann believed that in the twentieth century, displacement and detachment were not solely a Jewish malady. He saw that a sense of rootlessness was also threatening contemporary Western civilization. Lehmann wanted Zionism to suggest a cure both for the modern Jewish people and for modern man; he wanted it to fulfill an urgent national task in a manner that would benefit all of humanity. He wanted Zionism to be a settlement movement that was not tainted by colonialism, a national movement that was not scarred by chauvinism, a progressive movement that was not distorted by urban alienation. He believed that Zionism must not establish a closed-off, condescending colony in Palestine that ignored its surroundings and native neighbors; it must not be an Occidental frontier fortress commanding the Orient. On the contrary, Lehmann believed that Zionism must plant the Jews in their ancient homeland in an organic fashion. It must respect the Orient and become a bridge between East and West. Though he never said so explicitly, Lehmann saw his Lydda Valley youth village as an example of what Zionism should be: a salvation project giving home to the homeless, providing roots to the uprooted, and restoring meaning to life. Lehmann's Ben Shemen would offer harmony to the children and to the era that had lost all harmony.

Dr. Lehmann believed that Zionism would prevail only if it was integrated into the Middle East. In July 1927, the young doctor rushed to the traumatized Arab city of Lydda to attend to the survivors of a devastating earthquake that demolished much of the old town and killed scores of its residents. In the 1930s, because of the profound impact his work had had on the community during the disaster, Lehmann made friends among Lydda's gentry and among the dignitaries of the neighboring Arab villages of Haditha, Dahariya, Gimzu, Daniyal, Deir Tarif, and Bayt Nabala. He saw to it that the villagers walking to and from Lydda in the scorching summer heat would enjoy cool water and refreshing shade at a specially designed welcome fountain that he built for them at the gate of the Zionist youth village. Lehmann instructed the youth village clinic to give medical assistance to Palestinians seeking it. He insisted that the students of Ben Shemen be taught to respect their neighbors and their neighbors' culture. Almost every weekend the youth of Ben Shemen went on trips to the villages. They also frequently visited Lydda, its market, its schools. Arab musicians and dancers were invited to participate in the youth village's festivals. An Orient fair was held, at which Arab rural civilization was studied, displayed, and celebrated.

When the Hollywood-produced film *Land* was shot in Lehmann's youth village just after World War II, the scenes it captured portrayed a humanist utopia. In black-and-white frames, the director, Helmar Lerski, and his cinematographers registered an unreal reality. Here were boys and girls who had barely escaped Germany living in a progressive, democratic educational establishment, a kind of convalescent home for the uprooted youth of an uprooted people in the land of the Bible. Here were young Hebrew shepherds herding sheep on the craggy, ancient hills between Haditha and Dahariya. Here were young weavers spinning yarn on spindles as if they were French or German villagers who had been living on the land for generations. Here was a community of orphans living a Euro-Palestinian village culture that is in peace with the land it had just descended upon. On the eve of the Sabbath, the children, wearing white shirts, gathered around white-cloth-covered tables to light candles. Although they had no parents, they had faith. Some played Bach, some sang hymns, some told Jewish legends and tales from Tolstoy. But everyone in the halls of Ben Shemen, from age eight to eighteen, took part in an exceptional ritual of secular youngsters reaching for the holy in the Holy Land.

Lydda suspected nothing. Lydda did not imagine what was about to happen. For forty-four years, it watched Zionism enter the valley: first the Atid factory, then the Kiryat Sefer school, then the olive forest, the artisan colony, the tiny workers' village, the experimental farm, and the strange youth village headed by the eccentric German doctor who was so friendly to the people of Lydda and gave medical treatment to those in need.

The city of Lydda had two mosques and a large cathedral called St. George. But though by Christian tradition, Lydda was the city of Saint George, the people of Lydda did not see that Zionism would turn into a modern-day dragon. They did not see that while Dr. Lehmann preached peace, others taught war. While Dr. Lehmann took his students to the neighboring Palestinian villages, Shmaryahu Gutman took them to Masada. While the youth village taught humanism and brotherhood, the pine forest behind it hosted military courses training Ben Shemen's youth to throw grenades, assemble submachine guns, and fire antitank PIAT shells. The people of Lydda did not see that the Zionism that came into the valley to give hope to a nation of orphans has become a movement of cruel resolve, determined to take the land by force.

In the forty-four years that Lydda watched Zionism approach, Lydda prospered. From 1922 to 1947, the population more than doubled, from eight thousand to nineteen thousand. The leap forward was not only quantitative but qualitative. Modernization was everywhere. After the devastation caused by the 1927 earthquake, many of the old clay dwellings were replaced by new solid stone houses. By the Great Mosque and the cathedral, a commercial center and a new mosque were built. On the west side of town a new modern quarter of ruler-straight streets appeared. Lydda was a central junction of Palestine's railway system, and the train company's executives resided in the new English-style garden suburb, which was the city's pride. There was electricity on some streets, running water in some houses. Two state schools and one Anglican school educated the boys and girls of Lydda separately. Two clinics, five doctors, and two pharmacies guaranteed decent medical service. The mortality rate was down to twelve out of a thousand, while the fertility rate was drastically up. A genuine social revolution had taken place in Lydda in the first half of the twentieth century.

Lydda's economy did well, too. The British Mandate, the indirect impact of Zionism, and a prime location enabled it to gallop ahead. Situated at the very center of Palestine, Lydda became a main transportation hub in the years of British rule. The train station in the south of town and the international airport in the north offered abundant employment opportunities to its residents. The cross-country roads passing nearby contributed to local commerce. And with its 3,200 dunams of orange groves, Lydda also benefited from the citrus boom. In the old town, hydraulic oil presses replaced manual ones. Three factories manufactured the oil and soap that Atid once produced. The town had a successful tannery and many spinning mills that made kaffiyehs and abbayahs. The cafés were crowded, and the stores were full of the best modern wares. On Mondays and Thursdays, thousands traveled from near and far to Lydda's famous cattle market and bazaar. Alongside the wealthy landowning class rose a flourishing commercial middle class that turned Lydda into a lively, prosperous town.

But in 1947 the question of Palestine reaches its moment of truth. In February, His Majesty's government has had enough of the conflict between the Arabs and the Jews and decides to leave the Holy Land and let the United Nations determine its fate. In June, an eleven-member UN inquiry commission arrives in Palestine and while touring the country visits Ben Shemen and the Lydda Valley. In August the committee comes to the conclusion that there is no chance that Jews and Arabs can coexist in Palestine, and therefore suggests dividing the land into two nation-states. In November, the UN General Assembly endorses the partition plan and calls for the establishment of a Jewish state and an Arab state. As the Arab League and the Arabs of Palestine reject Resolution 181, violence flares throughout the country. It is clear that Arab nationalism is about to eradicate Zionism and destroy the Jewish community in Palestine by the use of brutal force. It is clear that the Jews must defend themselves, as no one else will come to their rescue. From December 1947 to May 1948, a cruel civil war between Arabs and Jews rages. After the British leave, the State of Israel is founded on May 14, 1948. The next day, the armies of Egypt, Jordan, Iraq, Syria, and Lebanon invade and a full-scale war erupts.

In December, a seven-car convoy en route to Ben Shemen is viciously attacked. Thirteen of its Jewish passengers are brutally murdered. In February 1948, some four hundred students of the youth village are evacuated from the Lydda Valley in a sad convoy of buses, escorted by British armored vehicles. Dr. Lehmann is heartbroken. By April, the youth village is a besieged military post. In May, the mayor of Lydda recommends that Ben Shemen surrender, but it refuses. Still, the mayor begs the commander of the Arab Legion not to attack the isolated compound, as it does not threaten Lydda in any way. When Arab fields adjacent to Ben Shemen are set ablaze, some of the youth village graduates who have remained rush to put out the fire. Even as war rages in most parts of Palestine, both Arabs and Jews regard the Lydda Valley as a zone of restricted warfare.

But on July 4, 1948, Operation Larlar, designed to conquer Lydda, is presented to Israel's first prime minister, David Ben Gurion. On July 10–11, the 8th Brigade of the IDF takes the northern parts of the Lydda Valley: the villages of Deir Tarif and Haditha, and the international airport. Simultaneously the elite Yiftach Brigade takes the southern parts of the valley: the villages of Inaba, Gimzu, Daniyal, and Dahariya. Within twenty-four hours of the Israeli Army's first division-scale offensive, all the villages Dr. Lehmann so loved and taught his students to love are conquered. And as Zionism closes in on the valley of Lydda from the south, east, and north, it now prepares to conquer the city of Lydda itself.

On July 11, two 3rd Regiment platoons advance from the conquered village of Daniyal toward the olive orchards separating Ben Shemen from Lydda. Strong machine gun fire from the outskirts of Lydda halts them. In the meantime, Moshe Dayan's Regiment 89 arrives in Ben Shemen. By the water fountain Dr. Lehmann built for his Arab neighbors, Dayan forms the regiment into an armored column. One behind the other, they stand at the ready: a giant armored vehicle mounted with a cannon, menacing half-tracks, and machine-gun-equipped jeeps. In the late afternoon the column leaves Ben Shemen and speeds into the city of Lydda, firing at all in its way. In forty-seven minutes of blitz, more than a hundred Arab civilians are shot dead—women, children, old people. Regiment 89 loses nine of its men. In the early evening, the two 3rd Regiment platoons are able to penetrate Lydda. Within hours, their soldiers hold key positions in the city center and confine thousands of civilians in the Great Mosque, the small mosque, and the St. George's cathedral. By evening, Zionism has taken the city of Lydda.

The next day, two Jordanian armored vehicles enter the conquered city in error, setting off a new wave of violence. The Jordanian army is miles to the east, and the two vehicles have no military significance, but some of the citizens of Lydda mistakenly believe they are the harbingers of liberation. Some of the soldiers of the 3rd Regiment mistakenly believe them to mean that they face the imminent danger of Jordanian assault. By the small mosque, Israeli soldiers are fired upon. Among the young combatants taking cover in a ditch nearby are some of the Ben Shemen graduates, now in uniform. The brigade commander is a Ben Shemen graduate, too. He gives the order to open fire. The soldiers shoot in every direction. Some throw hand grenades into homes. One fires an antitank PIAT shell into the small mosque. In thirty minutes, at high noon, more than two hundred civilians are killed. Zionism carries out a massacre in the city of Lydda.

When news of the bloodshed reaches the headquarters of Operation Larlar in the conquered Palestinian village of Yazzur, Yigal Allon asks Ben Gurion what to do with the Arabs. Ben Gurion waves his hand: Deport them. Hours after the fall of Lydda, operations officer Yitzhak Rabin issues a written order to the Yiftach Brigade: "The inhabitants of Lydda must be expelled quickly, without regard to age."

Over the next day, negotiations are held in the rectory of St. George's Cathedral. Present are Shmaryahu Gutman, who is now the military governor of Lydda, and the dignitaries of the now occupied city. The bewildered dignitaries are anxious to save the lives of their flock, whereas the cunning Gutman is eager to expel the lot without giving an explicit expulsion order. When negotiations end in the late morning of July 13, 1948, it is agreed that the people of Lydda and the refugees re-siding there will exit Lydda immediately. By noon, a mass evacuation is under way. By evening, tens of thousands of Palestinian Arabs leave Lydda in a long column, marching south past the Ben Shemen youth village and disappearing into the East. Zionism obliterates the city of Lydda.

Lydda is our black box. In it lies the dark secret of Zionism. The truth is that Zionism could not bear Lydda. From the very beginning there was a substantial contradiction between Zionism and Lydda. If Zionism was to be, Lydda could not be. If Lydda was to be, Zionism could not be. In retrospect it's all too clear. When Herbert Bentwich saw Lydda from the white tower of Ramleh in April 1897, he should have seen that if a Jewish state was to exist in Palestine, an Arab Lydda could not exist at its center. He should have known that Lydda was an obstacle blocking the road to the Jewish state and that one day Zionism would have to remove it. But Herbert Bentwich did not see, and Zionism chose not to know. For half a century it succeeded in hiding from itself the substantial contradiction between the Jewish national movement and Lydda. For forty-five years, Zionism pretended to be the Atid factory and the olive forest and the Ben Shemen youth village living in peace with Lydda. Then, in three days in the cataclysmic summer of 1948, contradiction struck and tragedy revealed its face. Lydda was no more.

When, twenty years ago, I realized that Lydda was our black box, I tried to decipher its secrets. I found the brigade commander and spent long hours with him. I located the military governor and spent long days on his kibbutz with him. I spent time with soldiers from the 3rd Regiment and interviewed students from the youth village. To write this chapter, I dug out the audiocassettes I had recorded at that time and listened to them as they told the story of the death of Lydda.

The brigade commander was born in 1923 in Kovna, where his father worked with Dr. Lehmann. He was raised in a socialist household in Tel Aviv, but at the age of fifteen he was sent to the Ben Shemen youth village, where he immediately became the favorite of his father's old friend. On Shabbat mornings he was invited to the Lehmanns' cottage to listen with them to rare recordings on the gramophone: Haydn, Mozart, Bach. On holidays he escorted Dr. Lehmann as he made courtesy calls in the neighboring villages. Occasionally he went with Dr. Lehmann to visit friends and schools in Lydda. He took to Lydda, its market, its olive presses, its old town. At Ben Shemen he worked in the cowshed, the vineyard, the orange grove; he played handball and developed a taste for the arts. But most of all, he loved music: classical music, popular music, folk music. One of his favorite memories of Ben Shemen is of hundreds of students sitting in silence in the great courtyard listening to an orchestra and choir perform Bach's Peasant Cantata.

But in addition to the humanistic, music-loving world of Ben Shemen, the seventeen-year-old lived in an alternate reality. At night, he and his friends would go to the forest beyond the youth village, where they learned to assemble and dismantle an English rifle, to shoot a machine gun, to throw a grenade. And when the music lover graduated from Ben Shemen, he joined the first platoon of the Palmach Strike Force. In the winter of 1942 he climbed Masada. In the summer of 1942 he went south to stop Rommel's Nazis with Molotov cocktails. At the age of twenty-one he became a company commander. At twenty-three he became a commander in a nationwide training course. At twenty-four he was a regiment commander. When war breaks out at the end of 1947, the Ben Shemen graduate commands one of the elite units of Zionism.

Is the brigade commander aware of the contradiction between his two worlds? Can he combine the Lehmann disciple with the warrior? He has no clear answers to these questions. When he speaks of the fighting up north he is surprisingly open. The voice coming out of the tape recorder says plainly that the mission was the cleansing of the Galilee before the invasion of Arab armies. The Jewish state about to be born would not survive the external battle with the armed forces of the Arab nations if it did not first rid itself of the Palestinian population that endangered it from within. So first they sweep away all the Arabs from the Tiberias-Safed region. Then, in April 1948, they conquer Tiberias, whose Arab population departs under military pressure from the superior Israeli Army. Then they conquer and demolish the Arab villages around Safed. In May they conquer Safed, whose Arab population flees under fire. Then they drive away the villagers of the Hula Valley. By the end of May 1948, the Hula Valley is cleansed of Arabs. The entire Safed-Tiberias region is cleansed of Arabs. All of the eastern Galilee is cleansed of Arabs. Under the command of Ben Shemen's graduate, the eastern Galilee becomes an Arab-free zone, and an integral part of the new Jewish state.

But when the brigade commander speaks of Lydda, his voice changes. Now he sounds quiet, almost agonized. He sounds cautious, perhaps not quite candid, as if when talking about Lydda he is suddenly aware of the contradiction and the tragedy. He speaks slowly as he tells me how he conquered the villages to which he used to accompany Dr. Lehmann on his Shabbat visits: Gimzu, Dahariya, Haditha. He speaks quietly as he tells me how he conquered the valley and the city of Lydda. He describes the morning he was informed that Jordanian armored vehicles had broken into the city and learned, shortly afterward, that some of the 3rd Regiment's Ben Shemen graduates had been attacked. He tells me he was the one who gave orders to shoot anyone walking along the streets of the city, the one who gave orders to evacuate the city. He and the military governor were the ones who sent the people of Lydda out of Lydda in a long column heading east.

The brigade commander is clearly torn. The voice coming out of the tape recorder is unconvincing. It's not that he is purposely hiding anything from me. He himself does not know what he feels. His talk of Lydda is vague; it lacks colors, smells, details. While he remembers his Ben Shemen years vividly, he only vaguely remembers the conquest of Lydda. He does not mention the schools he visited, the families he knew, the community he was so fond of. He does not speak at all about the city he loved and destroyed. Only his muted tone surrenders what he holds back. His first apology: We were surrounded. His second apology: We were under imminent threat from within and without. His third apology: There was no time, I had to make an immediate decision. His fourth apology: Horrible things happen in war. But not one of his apologies seems to convince him, or to begin to explain the suppressed three days of Lydda's death.

Bulldozer is very different from the brigade commander. Although he, too, is traumatized by the war of '48, his mental injury is not the same. Rough and coarse, he tends to raise his voice too much. He's tense and quick-tempered, restless. He admits that in the damned war he lost his peace of mind. In the many years since, he has not been able to find inner calm.

Bulldozer was also born in Eastern Europe but was raised in Tel Aviv. At seven, he was returning from school one day when an Arab threw a bomb from a passing train onto busy Herzl Street, wounding dozens and killing an eight-year-old boy standing nearby. That day it became clear to him that there would be an all-out war with the Arabs. Although as a teen he walked to Arab Jaffa and made Arab friends, he always knew that between us and them there was a sword. He always knew that eventually the land would be decided by war.

He was exceptionally strong. He boxed, rode horses, excelled at sports. The size and strength of his body gave him his nickname and made him the boys' leader and the girls' favorite. At the age of fourteen he became a member of the secret Haganah. At the age of fifteen he began grenade training. At sixteen he trained at a firing range with live bullets. At seventeen he climbed Masada. When Bulldozer joined the Palmach at the age of eighteen, he did so not because he believed in some sort of kibbutz utopia, but because he wanted to be with the best of the best when war arrived.

The first months of 1948 are easy: village raids, roadside ambushes. But after he is trained to be an antitank missile operator, warfare becomes intensive. The 3rd Regiment needs his bazookalike antitank weapon in most operations. April, May, and June are impossible, inhuman. A close friend is killed, then another, and another. Pain becomes rage, and rage becomes apathy. There is no time to comprehend, no time to mourn, no time to weep. They have to drive the Arabs from the Galilee and thwart the Syrians and Lebanese forces invading the Galilee. Conquer the Galilee, cleanse the Galilee, defend the Galilee. Ensure that the Galilee is Jewish.

The raid on Ein Zeitun is the first time they go down into an Arab village not to take revenge but to conquer. Bulldozer vividly remembers the midnight anticipation. He remembers the assault, the firestorm, and the surprise: how easy it is to conquer a village. When the 3rd Regiment boys break into the stone houses they find only burning lanterns, warm blankets, milk boiling over from pots. They walk into homes abandoned by their inhabitants who had taken fright and run away into the night. He recalls the eerie feeling of witnessing a living village become a ghost village in one night.

The first brutal deed Bulldozer remembers carrying out is the prisoner-of-war interrogations. For a moment his self-assured voice is hesitant: May one tell? But after a pause comes the flood, and the need to talk overpowers the imperative not to talk. Because he is big and strong, Bulldozer is assigned to assist the intelligence officer as he interrogates seven of the young men captured in Ein Zeitun. One by one he ties the terrified prisoners to a low bench, so that their foreheads touch the ground at one end and their feet at the other. Once he hits the head of a prisoner with a short stick, and then he hits the prisoner's legs with a long stick. And once he starts beating the prisoners of war he begins to enjoy beating them. He feels he is avenging the dead, that he is doing what his fallen comrades would have wanted him to do. He makes the seven prisoners tell the intelligence officer all that they know. He makes them bleed so much that they cannot stand up.

Next is the conquest of Safed, the first time the 3rd Regiment conquers a city. The beginning is difficult. Bulldozer finds himself nearly alone as an armed Arab mob storms the building he is in. The mob shouts "Slaughter the Jews." Ammunition is running out. He feels the cold shudder of approaching death. But by morning there is a dramatic turn of events. Jewish reinforcements arrive and the Arabs retreat. With his Canadian rifle and fresh rounds of ammunition, Bulldozer hunts down the Arabs seeking refuge between the old stone houses of the ancient city. He feels delight in hunting. Delight in killing. The almost sexual pleasure of laying men down.

After the battle subsides, Bulldozer goes to the local hospital, where he finds three of his buddies lying on the floor in a cold corridor—their faces alien in death, frozen in horror. As tough as he is, he is frightened. A week later, because he is the last to return from a late-night operation in some Arab village, he boards the last truck at the collection point. Half an hour later, he realizes that the boys he is with are lifeless. Once again, he feels fear. He has a sudden, rare moment of understanding of what these few months of war have done to him, what a nightmare he is living.

In late May, he is in the Jordan Valley. He experiences one of his worst hours when he is sent with his PIAT rocket launcher to stop the invading Syrian tanks that are approaching Kibbutz Degania. He stands alone watching the first tank head toward him, watching it target him. At the very last moment he fires his PIAT first, halting the tank while wounding himself.

He experiences another bad hour when he sees the survivors from two Jordan Valley kibbutzim who have escaped their incinerated homes. The shock of seeing kibbutz members turned refugees makes him think for the first time that defeat is possible. He realizes that the war he is participating in might end with the death of Zionism. And if Zionism dies, what will happen in the Land of Israel will be what has happened time after time in Europe. Jews will be Jews again: they will be helpless.

By the time Bulldozer arrives in the Lydda Valley, he is exhausted. He has seen too much, done too much, killed far too much. This time he is not trigger-happy. But when the orders come, he obeys. He marches with the 3rd Regiment platoons from the silvery olive orchards into Lydda. And when the sun rises, he wanders the streets of Lydda looking for a camera shop he can loot—he so loves cameras. Suddenly, there is shooting. There are rumors of invading armored vehicles, of friends trapped in the ditch by the small mosque. When Bulldozer approaches the small mosque, he sees that there is indeed shooting. From somewhere, somehow, grenades are thrown. He instructs one of his subordinates to fire an antitank PIAT into the small mosque. When the shell-shocked soldier refuses and departs, Bulldozer takes the PIAT into his own hands. Although he knows that shooting a PIAT in the narrow alley means that the PIAT operator himself will be hurt, he decides to shoot anyway. He dismantles the door of a public lavatory situated in the narrow alley and tries to hide his huge body in the lavatory as best he can. He does not aim at the minaret from which the grenades were apparently thrown but at the mosque wall behind which he can hear human voices. He shoots his PIAT at the mosque wall from a distance of six meters, killing seventy.

The training group was made up of 120 youth movement graduates from Tel Aviv, Jerusalem, and Haifa whose mission was to establish a new kibbutz on the shores of the Red Sea, close to Eilat. In the summer of 1947, the eighteen-year-old boys and girls trained for kibbutz life in an older kibbutz by the Sea of Galilee. They cleared fields, built communal housing, mended fishing nets, worked in the banana plantation and in the cowshed, took sheep out to pasture. Ten days a month, they studied topography and navigation and learned how to handle a submachine gun and assemble explosives. But for the rest of the month they maintained their communal lifestyle: they held a literature class, an arts seminar, a political economy workshop, and a course on Zionist thinking. They analyzed the inherent contradiction of capitalism, that it tramples the dignity of man; they wondered whether man makes history, or whether history makes man. They read Tagore, Zweig, Hesse, and Rosa Luxemburg; Koestler's *Darkness at Noon*, Gandhi's *The Story of My Experiments with Truth*, Buber's *I and Thou*. They played and listened to music: Mendelssohn, Paganini, and Domenico Cimarosa, to whom they took a special liking. In the woods by the Sea of Galilee, sitting in a circle around a gramophone, the boys and girls of the training group listened again and again to Cimarosa's tragic oboe, whose sad sound was echoed by the rustling of the eucalyptus trees and the lapping of the lake's waves.

In December 1947, a few of the training group boys join their first retaliation operation in a small Arab village in the Upper Galilee. Because women and children are accidentally killed, they decide they might as well blow up the two village homes that contain the corpses of the dead. In January 1948, the training group suffers the loss of its first boy. The girls place candles around his body, and all night they sit beside it, as if in vigil. Then another boy is killed in action. And another. Two more are killed. Some of the boys become cynical and morbid. Others leave the girls letters of last will and testament.

In mid-January, eight of the boys carry out their first roadside ambush: they open fire with a machine gun on an Arab taxi, killing all of its innocent passengers. In mid-February some of them participate in their first commando-style raid: they blow up sixteen stone houses in a remote Galilee village, killing sixty. The mind-set changes. Values and norms begin to devolve. There are still gramophone concerts in the evenings, but the talk now is of revenge. Literary discussions and ideological debates still take place, but just before a military operation there is now a war dance. Like painted Indian warriors, like lustful Arab assassins, the Hebrew boys go round and round with daggers held high, knives between their teeth. And on the eve of May Day, they descend the mountain of Kna'an to conquer a village for the very first time. They drive away the eight hundred inhabitants, loot the village, and blow it up. They erase the village from the face of the earth.

From the tape recorder on my desk rises the voice of one of the girls from the training group whom I know very well. She remembers the apprehension she felt as the boys went down to the village late at night. And how they returned at sunrise, riding looted donkeys, wearing looted kaffiyehs, carrying looted strings of beads. Instead of the tension they have been feeling for months, a sort of euphoria erupts. Suddenly war isn't just serious and somber, it's fun. The boys feel a new sense of power and liberation. Instead of khaki, spartanism, and self-discipline, they feel an unburdening, a throwing off of the yoke of morality. The rooms of the hotel they commandeer for their base are now filled with colorful cloth, strings of beads, copperware, and hookahs. On one of the doors is a handwritten sign that reads EAT, DRINK, AND LOOT, FOR

TOMORROW WE DIE. It is as if not only a conquered Arab village was demolished on May Day, but with it the ethos of the socialist-Zionist edict of being humble and doing right and serving a greater good.

Some of the boys participate in the brutal interrogation of the village prisoners. Others take the bleeding prisoners to the wadi after the interrogation is over. As the prisoners are executed, some of the boys turn their eyes away, but others watch in glee. Meanwhile, in the city of Safed, one of the boys emerges as a talented sniper. His voice on my audiocassette is remorseless. Once he shot a woman, another time a priest, then a child. And every time he felled an Arab, he carved another groove on the wooden butt of his Canadian sniper's rifle. Fifty grooves in all, he says.

Then comes the great battle of Safed, the emptying of Safed, and the looting that follows. "Our yard is like the yard of an Arab village," writes one of the girls in a letter.

> There is much commotion. Hens are everywhere, clucking away. The cattle break into the yard now and then . . . but even in all the excitement, I see the wrong in all these looted possessions, and at the end of the day, it disgusts me, sickens me. I cannot recognize the guys anymore. All of them are drunk with victory and driven by the lust for loot. Each one of them took all that he could and in the joy of triumph they broke loose, expressing feelings of hatred and revenge, turning into real animals. They smashed, destroyed, and killed anything in their path. The thirst for revenge found its fountain and the comrades lost all humanity. I can't believe that human beings are capable of such things: to kill dozens of people in cold blood. No, I cannot say in cold blood. With passion. Day by day, the human feelings in us become duller and duller.

On July 11, 1948, the training group boys march on Lydda. The shooting from the eastern outskirts of town confines them to the olive groves bordering Ben Shemen. Mosquitoes buzz around them, the heat is scorching, and their new iron helmets sizzle on their heads. A few are wounded, others are shell-shocked. The group's first daylight battle is not going well. But after Dayan's storm of fire breaks Lydda's spirit of resistance, the training group boys are among the 3rd Regiment soldiers who penetrate Lydda. They lead the long processions of Lydda's inhabitants, their hands in the air, to the Great Mosque and confine them there, thousands of men, young and old. They hear the shrieking, the howling, the weeping. They see the horror in the eyes of women and children.

The next day, after the Jordanian armored vehicles break into Lydda, one of the training group leaders is wounded when a hand grenade, apparently thrown from the small mosque, explodes and takes his hand clear off. This incident provokes Bulldozer to shoot the antitank PIAT into the mosque. And when the PIAT operator is himself wounded, the desire for revenge grows even stronger. Some 3rd Regiment soldiers spray the wounded in the mosque with gunfire. Others toss grenades into neighboring houses. Still others mount machine guns in the streets and shoot at anything that moves. After half an hour of revenge, there are scores of corpses in the streets, seventy corpses in the mosque. The corpses from the mosque are buried at night in a deep hole dug by some nearby Arabs, and a tractor is brought in before morning to cover the hole.

"We were cruel," writes another of the training group girls. "The damned war turned humans into beasts," writes a boy. And a second boy writes, "I am tired, so tired. Tired in many respects, but especially mentally. I feel too young to carry the burden of all this." But of all of the letters on my desk, the one that upsets me most is by another boy, whom I now know as a mentor and a friend:

From day to day I see the devastation caused by this war to our generation, and to the next. From day to day my fear grows that this generation will not be able to carry upon its shoulders the burden of building the state and fulfilling the dream. I am all anxiety and concern. When I think of the thefts, the looting, the robberies and recklessness, I realize that these are not merely separate incidents. Together they add up to a period of corruption. The question is earnest and deep, really of historic dimensions. We will all be held accountable for this era. We shall face judgment. And I fear that justice will not be on our side. There is an impression that the quick transition to a state, and to a state of Hebrew power, drove people mad. Otherwise it is impossible to explain the behavior, the state of mind, the actions of the Hebrew youth, especially the elite youth. The moral code of the nation, forged during thousands of years of weakness, is rapidly degenerating, deteriorating, disintegrating.

The military governor of Lydda after occupation is the Man of Masada. Although personally he is secular and rational, Shmaryahu Gutman's approach to Zionism is almost mystical. He sees the revolutionary movement as the outburst of life of a people on the verge of extinction. He sees it as an inspired undertaking by a beaten nation that does not wait for the Messiah but takes upon itself the Messiah's mission. He believes that for fifty years Zionism has been an outstanding success. Every time one wave of immigration subsided, another wave emerged. Every time one generation grew weak, another generation took the torch into its strong hands. But in the 1940s something changed. The Arab issue, which had always existed, suddenly put a question mark on the future. Throughout the country, Arab villages became more modern and Arab cities more prosperous. A new Arab intelligentsia developed a strong national awareness and began to crystallize a distinctive, highly dangerous Arab-Palestinian identity. So the old Zionist way of doing things was no longer relevant. There was no longer an option to buy land gradually, bring in well-trained immigrants gradually, and build the Jewish nation gradually, from the bottom up. There was a need for a different sort of action. War was inhuman, but it allowed one to do what one could not do in peace; it could solve problems that were unsolvable in peace.

Six and a half years have passed since Gutman took his first forty-six cadets up to Masada. Since then he has taken up thousands more and single-handedly transformed a generation. Yet his work has gone beyond inspiring youth. In the intervening years, he has turned out to be a superb intelligence operator. A year after the first Masada seminar, using his Arabic, his cunning, and his sharp instincts, he began assisting in preparing intelligence files on the Arab villages. In each file he included an aerial photograph, a map, a demographic breakdown of the population and its leadership, its strengths and weaknesses, its roads and byways, its command points. Every village file contains the village's demise.

For years Gutman's thinking has been clandestine. Only with his best friend, the Haganah's chief of staff, Israel Galili, could he be candid. Only between themselves did they say what could not be said—what the mind understands, the heart whispers, and morality forbids. And when the great, inevitable war was being planned, it was clear to the two close friends that the first task in war would be to guarantee an Arab-free zone—a Jewish territorial continuum. Gutman believed the mission was possible. Knowing the Arabs well, he surmised that they did not yet have a coherent, internal structure or the spirit of a sovereign nation. Once they encountered Zionist organization, determination, and firepower, he believed, they would simply leave.

When the 1948 war breaks out, Gutman is in charge of the Palmach's special undercover intelligence unit. He debates fiercely with the old-guard Arabists of the Haganah, who rely on the peace treaties they signed with friendly Arab villages across the country. He claims that when push comes to shove, even the most loyal village leaders will not be able to withstand Pan-Arab pressure. They will break the treaties and turn against the Jews. While the old guard is still committed to its Arab allies who have been supportive of the Jews for years, the energetic educator and Arabist believes the conflict between Jews and Arabs in Palestine is a total one. The great war is a war of us or them.

Gutman lives in Na'an, the kibbutz he helped to found not far from Lydda. Next to Na'an are the Arab village of Na'aneh and the Bedouin village of Sataria, established fifty-eight years earlier, when the tribe of Sataria was expelled from the estate of Duran to make way for the orange grove colony of Rehovot. In the spring of 1948 the leadership of Kibbutz Na'an meets with the leadership of the Sataria tribe, and the Jews and Bedouins pledge mutual allegiance. Yet Gutman cannot stand the hypocritical innocence of both parties. He rises to his feet. "There is a great war coming," he says to the Bedouin chiefs. "When it reaches us, Kibbutz Na'an will not be able to stand by you and guarantee your future." The tribal chief of Sataria immediately gets the message. The next morning, the Bedouins of Sataria leave their homes and escape to Gaza. Several weeks later, the villagers of Na'aneh do the same. Without lifting a hand, without committing any act of war, Gutman succeeds in achieving his goal. The two villages whose people he has known well and has had close neighborly ties with for fifteen years disappear.

Unlike the brigade commander or Bulldozer or the training group, Gutman gets it. He is fully aware of the strategic and moral dilemmas he is faced with. He has always known that his generation's mission would be to rid the country of its Arabs. And he has always known how terrible it would be to rid the country of its Arabs. That's why he has been looking for "sophisticated" ways to get rid of them. He does not want to kill them or expel them; he wants to induce them to leave of their own accord.

Gutman is assigned to Lydda purely by chance. On July 11, 1948, he is looking for Yigal Allon and Yitzhak Rabin on some intelligence matter. He drives from Na'an to the old Herbert Bentwich estate near Tel-Gezer but finally finds the generals in the conquered, deserted village of Daniyal. As they watch from Daniyal the forces storming Lydda, Allon tells Gutman that he is to be the military governor of the city once it is taken. Gutman asks Allon, "What should I do with the Arabs? Do you have anything to say to me?" "I have nothing to say to you," Allon replies. "You will see how things go, and as things go, you'll act. Do what you think you must do."

At dusk Gutman arrives in Lydda and becomes its military governor. In the dimness of nightfall he sees a mass of thousands flowing in silence toward the Great Mosque in order to turn themselves in under threat that whoever is found outside after curfew will be shot. By nightfall thousands of terrified human beings are gathered in the high-ceilinged house of prayer. It is hot, crowded, and stifling, with no food, no water, no air—there is no room to sit or to lie down. Within hours the ill and the young will suffocate.

At midnight the military governor releases the women and children. Then he releases the flour mill and flour shop owners to provide flour, and the bakers to bake pita bread. He releases the water well operators to provide water. Later on he releases two hundred refugees from Na'aneh and provides them with food, water, camels, and mules so they can escape the city before all hell breaks loose. By morning he releases most of the teenagers. Yet the mosque is still crowded. Things get worse again when the 3rd Regiment takes control of the entire city in mid-morning, and more men pour into the Great Mosque, their hands up in the air, their eyes full of dread.

The sudden shooting at noon on July 12 finds the military governor in the rectory of St. George's, where he is negotiating with Lydda's dignitaries. The operations officer of the 3rd Regiment is sent into town to see what the hell is going on. Minutes later, an agitated young soldier arrives, saying that grenades are being thrown at his comrades from the small mosque. The regiment commander turns to the military governor with a sarcastic smile. "What do you say, Governor? What are your orders?" he asks. The governor is neither sarcastic nor amused. He realizes that if he does not act quickly and firmly, things will get out of hand. He suggests shooting at any house from which shots are fired, shooting into every window, shooting at anyone suspected of being part of the mutiny.

Gutman describes the next thirty minutes as the worst half hour in his life. Decades later he is still flustered when he recounts the events into the tape recorder. The horrific noise. The shooting that won't stop. The wrath of God. And when the shooting does stop, the silence is so sweet. But then news comes of what has happened in the small mosque. The military governor orders his men to bury the dead, get rid of the incriminating evidence.

Gutman now knows that the die is cast, the fate of Lydda is sealed. There is no going back. But as he has not received an expulsion order, he will not give one. He returns to the Arab dignitaries assembled in the rectory of St. George's, gets hold of himself, and does what he must do. He tells the dignitaries that there is a great war coming to Lydda because of its international airport. He says that, as they have just seen, anything might happen in a great war. The terrified dignitaries ask what will happen if they ask to leave. "That is an ominous question," the military governor responds; "I must give it some thought." Retiring to the next room, he rests his head and thinks how much easier it would be if this mass of Arabs were not here. Yet he also decides that no matter what, he will not order the Arabs to leave. When he returns to the dignitaries, he exercises the utmost psychological pressure, then tells them he must consult with his superiors again.

During their third meeting, the Arab dignitaries are in a state of hysteria. They ask to leave Lydda with their one condition being the release of all prisoners detained in the Great Mosque. For the third time, the military governor leaves for consultations. This time he returns escorted by two young officers whom he has asked to witness the fateful conversation.

> DIGNITARIES: What will become of the prisoners detained in the mosque?
> GUTMAN: We shall do to the prisoners what you would do had you imprisoned us.
> DIGNITARIES: No, no, please don't do that.
> GUTMAN: Why, what did I say? All I said is that we will do to you what you would do to us.
> DIGNITARIES: Please no, master. We beg you not to do such a thing.
> GUTMAN: No, we shall not do that. Ten minutes from now the prisoners will be free to leave the mosque and leave their homes and leave Lydda along with all of you and the entire population of Lydda.
> DIGNITARIES: Thank you, master. God bless you.

Gutman feels he has achieved his goal. Occupation, massacre, and mental pressure have had the desired effect. At the end of the day, after forty-eight hours of hell, he does not quite order the people of Lydda to go. Under the indirect threat of slaughter, Lydda's leaders ask to go.

Now Gutman walks across the street from the rectory to the Great Mosque. He faces the mass of prisoners and tells them they are free to go. According to the decision made by the dignitaries of Lydda, he tells them, within an hour and a half all the inhabitants of Lydda will leave Lydda. It is forbidden to carry weapons. It is forbidden to take cars and vehicles. But any other possessions may be taken as long as they leave Lydda immediately.

The military governor can hardly believe his eyes. Thousands of men are leaving the Great Mosque, their heads bowed. No one complains, no one curses, no one spits in his face. With complete submission, the masses march out and disperse. He climbs the tall minaret of the Great Mosque. From the top he watches chaos engulf the town. The people of Lydda grab anything they can: bread, vegetables, dates and figs; sacks of flour, sugar, wheat, and barley; silverware, copperware, jewelry; blankets, mattresses. They carry suitcases bursting at the seams, improvised packs made from sheets and pillowcases. Everything is loaded on horse wagons, donkeys, mules. All is done in a rush, in panic: within an hour and a half, an hour, half an hour.

Gutman descends the minaret and walks to the eastern edge of town overlooking Ben Shemen. The groups of civilians leaving town gather into a procession. The procession gathers into a long, biblical-looking column of thousands. And as the military governor watches the faces of the people marching into exile, he wonders if there is a Jeremiah among them to lament their calamity and disgrace. Suddenly he feels an urge to join the marching people and to be their Jeremiah. For one long moment, he who is their Nebuchadnezzar wishes to be their Jeremiah.

The brigade commander withdraws into himself when he finally describes the marching column. Standing by his command car, he watches the people of Lydda walking, carrying on their backs heavy sacks made of blankets and sheets. Gradually, they cast aside the sacks they cannot carry any farther. In the heavy heat, suffering from terrible thirst, old men and women collapse. Like the ancient Jews, the people of Lydda go into exile.

Watching the column, does the brigade commander feel guilt? Not guilt, but compassion, he says on tape. Then he immediately turns from the human experience to the overall strategic context. "Yitzhak Tabenkin supported the expulsion of the Arabs," he tells me. "Tabenkin was perfectly clear. He was not in a position to give specific orders, but his general instruction to Palmach headquarters was that war presented a one-time opportunity to solve the Arab problem. Yigal Allon, too, said that this was the moment. He said they must not be. Allon was a humanist, but he said that the Arabs must not remain or else there would not be a state." When Allon appointed the brigade commander, he told him explicitly: wherever you fight, Arabs should not remain. So it was in Tiberias and Safed, so it was in the villages of the Galilee, so it was in the villages of the Valley of Lydda—Iraba, Daniyal, Gimzu, Dahariya, and Haditha. "Only in the city of Lydda was there a mess, because the city was large and the troops closed in on it from the east, so the Arabs could not flee during the battle itself."

Was the column the outcome of an early expulsion plan or an explicit expulsion order? "No, no," replies the alarmed brigade commander. "Operation Larlar was conducted by the State of Israel. In July 1948, David Ben Gurion was already the prime minister of a sovereign nation. The troops attacking Lydda were the troops of the just-born Israel Defense Forces. The Holocaust was in the background. Prime Minister Ben Gurion could not instruct the IDF to get rid of the Arabs. Yigal Allon, too, was a farsighted Jew. He understood that Ben Gurion could not give an expulsion order. As a state we do not expel. On the other hand, both Ben Gurion and Allon knew it was impossible to allow an Arab Lydda to remain by the international airport, not far from Tel Aviv. If we did so there would be no victory and there would be no state. Some things were said between Ben Gurion and Allon, but there were no written orders."

There are also no explicit orders between Allon and the brigade commander. But the training the brigade commander received in the Palmach makes any order redundant. He knows what he must do even when he's not told. And when the Jordanian armored vehicles break into Lydda, there is even an excuse. The Jordanian Arab Legion, heading toward central Israel, does attack from the east. The 3rd Regiment is indeed under pressure from within and without. There is a large Palestinian population in Lydda, and there are considerable Jordanian forces massing east of Lydda. So when the Arabs of Lydda ask the military governor if they may leave, it makes strategic sense for them to be told to walk toward the Legion. "It was a favorable outcome," says the brigade commander. "It worked one hundred percent. The column leaving Lydda pushed the Arab Legion eastward, clearing a vast territory without any combat."

And yet when I ask the brigade commander to go back to the place, the moment, the personal experience, he is taken aback. Allon and Rabin have left for another front, so the responsibility for the exodus of Lydda falls to him, and to his deputy, the regiment commander, and the military governor. These four officers have to contend with the dangers of renewed fighting in the east and the chaos caused by the soldiers' wild looting in town. They have to see to the burial of ours and theirs. And the march. The terrible column of tens of thousands leaving Lydda.

"Officers are human beings, too," says the brigade commander. "And as a human being you suddenly face a chasm. On the one hand is the noble legacy of the youth movement, the youth village, Dr. Leh-mann. On the other hand is the brutal reality of Lydda. You are sur-prised by your own surprise. For years you've trained for this day. You've prepared the village files. You've been told there is an inevitable war coming. You've been told that the Arabs will have to go. And yet you are in shock. In Lydda, the war is as cruel as it can be. The killing, the loot-ing, the feelings of rage and revenge. Then the column marching. And although you are strong and well-trained and resilient, you experience some sort of mental collapse. You feel the humanist education you re-ceived collapsing. And you see the Jewish soldiers, and you see the marching Arabs, and you feel heavy, and deeply sad. You feel like you're facing something so immense you cannot deal with, you cannot even grasp."

Bulldozer doesn't remember the column because he was injured when shooting the antitank PIAT shell at the small mosque; he lost consciousness and was taken to the hospital. But when he awoke several days later, his comrades came to visit and told him that he'd done good, he'd killed seventy Arabs. They told him that because of the rage they felt at seeing him bleed, they had walked into the small mosque and sprayed the surviving wounded with automatic fire. Then they walked into the nearby houses and gunned down anyone they found. At night, when they were ordered to clean the small mosque and carry out the seventy corpses and bury them, they took eight other Arabs to do the digging of the burial site and afterward shot them, too, and buried the eight with the seventy. Because after the shooting by the small mosque, they were not hesitant anymore but tough as nails. "The guys stopped being noble-minded," says Bulldozer. "They knew what had to be done and did it. And what they did was in accord with the decision made high up to take the people of Lydda and walk them beyond the border of the Jewish state."

One of the boys from the training group remembers the column well. He remembers that in the morning after the small mosque mas-sacre, his company's assignment was to cleanse the quarter east of the small mosque. He remembers an explicit order to expel, to throw them out. All of them. The idealistic soldiers of the 3rd Regiment went from house to house along the ruler-straight streets of Lydda's modern quar-ter, shouting in Arabic, *"Yallah, yallah."* (Go on, go on.) And they shot in the air to frighten and to hurry the Muslim and Christian families of Lydda's new middle class. The affluent Arabs collected their children in a panic, along with their donkeys, horses, and belongings, and they walked in the scorching heat to the edge of town and then onto the road to Ben Shemen.

Other boys remember less. Their memory is not quite sharp when it comes to Lydda. They cannot recall what they were doing during those decisive hours. All they carry with them from those three days of July are scattered pictures: an occupied city, shuttered windows, white flags. The thousands crammed into the Great Mosque. The shooting by the small mosque. Half an hour of inferno, followed by a deathly silence. And in the silence, the quiet procession of defeated Arabs, their hands in the air. So now the young soldiers can ride looted bicycles all over town and break into Lydda's luxury stores to take cameras, gramophones, radios, carpets, hookahs, and fine copperware. They confiscate trucks, tractors, combines, and orange grove pumps for their future kibbutz. They fill the buses of the future kibbutz with all the goods of Lydda. Then, after an unexplained pause, the men I am interviewing mention the column. They sound shocked even all these years later as they describe the procession of elderly, women, and children who leave behind a long trail of household goods they cannot carry anymore. Sacks of flour, of sugar, of wheat. Bicycles. Mattresses. Children's toys, clothes, shoes.

The training group leader remembers the column exceptionally well. Before he is wounded he breaks into a barber shop to use the clean towels and alcohol to bandage Lydda's children who were wounded during combat. But after being wounded in the ditch near the small mosque and losing the palm of his right hand, he is treated in an improvised military clinic in the town center. While the medics bandage him up and ease his pain with morphine, he hears the stern commands given to put down the Lydda revolt. And the boom of the PIAT, and the infernal rat-a-tat-tat of the machine gun. The next day, when a military ambulance evacuates him to the field hospital in Ben Shemen, it runs into the column leaving Lydda. Through the ambulance windows, the training group leader sees the surreal scene of old men and women and children walking among the donkeys and mules and horse wagons and baby carriages, expressions of calamity on their faces. The training group leader doesn't know whom he pities more: his dead friends, himself, his generation, or the tens of thousands marching through the Lydda Valley.

Gutman remembers, too. After he descends the minaret and marches among the marchers, the military governor is overtaken by emotion. He asks himself if he was right to encourage the regiment commander to shoot into Lydda's houses, if there was a way to avoid all that has happened. Then he silences himself by answering that if it weren't for what happened in Lydda, Zionism would be done for. As he watches the men and women marching, he is shocked to see the imperviousness on their faces, the loss of sovereignty, the loss of dignity. He finds it incomprehensible that a city, a civilization, can break down just like that. Outside town, the military governor sees hundreds, perhaps thousands of people gathered around a well to draw water to quench their July thirst. One person falls into the well; another is trampled to death in the panic. He sees a young woman kneeling to give birth amid the commotion. He sees a boy lost, and a mother shouting for a lost boy. He sees soldiers forcing those marching to hand over cash and wristwatches and jewelry. And he stops the soldiers. He sees how between two lines of armed Jewish boys the great throngs of Palestinians leave the city and become a column. And the column grows longer and longer. The column exits the city of Lydda and crosses the Lydda Valley, passing by the endearing Zionist youth village of Ben Shemen.

Ottman Abu Hammed of Lydda remembers the column best. His grandfather used to work with the Jews in the Atid factory and had helped the Jews with the planting of the olive forest. His father, who used to supply the youth village with vegetables, had befriended Dr. Lehmann and would escort him when he gave anticholera vaccinations in Lydda. He himself had visited the Ben Shemen youth village quite often as a child. He loved the modern cowshed and the swimming pool, and the girls in khaki shorts, with their tanned legs.

Ottman is almost as old as the boys from the training group, but when war breaks out in 1948 he is far more innocent. Lacking a good education and any political awareness, he does not really comprehend what is going on. All he remembers is his father trying to prevent an attack on Ben Shemen; his father meeting the men of Ben Shemen in the fields; his father being charged with treason and escaping the firing squad at the very last minute. For Ottman, Lydda in the summer of 1948 is a booming city. The many thousands of refugees who have fled Jaffa and Sarafand and Na'aneh and settled there have brought money to the town. As food and vegetable prices soar, the locals' profits double and triple. Cafés are open late into the night and belly dancers are everywhere. There is music and fun in town, and girls who are easy to get.

Ottman remembers violence, too. A convoy of Jews on its way to Ben Shemen is attacked and its passengers murdered. The driver of a Jewish jeep is murdered on the main road. One day the corpses of two Jewish young men and one Jewish young woman are brought to town after they have been captured, raped, and murdered in one of the nearby villages. When the violated bodies are paraded in Lydda's high street, Ottman is aghast. But neither the eighteen-year-old nor his family can imagine what is to come. They are totally shocked when Lydda is bombed by a Jewish air force on the night of July 10 and bombarded by Jewish artillery on July 11. They are flabbergasted when a Jewish armored column sweeps the streets of Lydda with fire on the afternoon of the eleventh, leaving behind dozens of corpses. The shock, the horror, the dismay.

Ottman remembers that on the night of July 11, Jewish soldiers suddenly appear in the neighborhood. Loudspeakers mounted on jeeps call for all men to go to the Great Mosque. Ottman walks there with his father, joining thousands of others in the streets. Inside the mosque it is hot and crowded, with no room to sit or lie down. Ottman is terrified. He cries. He wets himself. When news comes of some sort of massacre in the small mosque, fear intensifies. No one knows what to expect. No one knows what else the Jews are capable of. His father shuts his eyes in prayer. Ottman fears the worst. But the next day, after thirty-six nightmarish hours, the Jews come to some sort of understanding with the dignitaries. At last the men are allowed out of the mosque. Although Ottman's father notices the loose soil where the small mosque's victims are buried, he believes life will now go back to normal.

When they arrive home, his mother greets them as if they have returned from the dead. Minutes later, there is a knock on the door. Two soldiers stand there, shouting loudly, "*Yallah, yallah*. Pack your belongings and leave. Go to King Abdullah, to Jordan." One of the soldiers is sensitive and shy. It's clear he doesn't like what he is doing. But the other one, with a thin mustache, enjoys every moment. Father takes a letter written in Hebrew out of his pocket saying that Dr. Lehmann vouches for this decent Arab and asks that no harm will come to this friend of Ben Shemen. But the mustachioed soldier couldn't care less. He discards the letter, presses the barrel of his gun into the father's chest, and says, "If you don't go right now, I will shoot. *Yallah* to Abdullah."

Mother screams. She believes that Father is about to be shot. But Father remains speechless. He is in shock. Bowing his head, he asks Mother to pack quickly all that can be packed. Then he calls for Grandmother, the three aunts, his two sons. Under the barrels of the two Jewish soldiers' guns, the Abu Hamda family hastily collects its belongings: flour, rice, sugar, jewelry, mattresses. They load their belongings onto a horse-drawn wagon and help Grandmother, who is half blind, to mount the donkey.

What hurts Ottman most is the humiliating way the soldiers search the women's bodies at the checkpoint on the outskirts of Lydda. One soldier takes Ottman's cash, another takes his wristwatch. The jute sacks of the Jewish soldiers are now filling up quickly with necklaces and earrings, silver and gold. But it is the humiliation of the women—young and old—that proves how disgraced they all are now.

Ottman holds the horse's reins while Father pushes the wagon from behind. The road is narrow, the congestion unbearable. Children shout, women scream, men weep. A rumor circulates of a mother who has lost her baby boy. A rumor circulates of a mother who has thrown away her baby girl. A Jewish jeep appears out of nowhere, its soldiers blowing its horn. Onward, onward. The Jewish soldiers shoot over their heads. There is no stopping, no going back, no looking back.

In the great rush people took flour and rice with them rather than water. So there is no water now, and the heat is unbearable. When someone falls into the well outside town, people suck on his wet clothes when he is pulled out. People suck watermelons found in the fields, eggplants, anything with moisture, anything that will give momentary relief to their animalistic thirst. Most women are dressed in traditional black gowns and carry sacks on their heads. Some of the men wear traditional djellabas, some fine European suits. Every so often a family withdraws from the column and stops by the side of the road—to bury a baby that

could not bear the heat; to say farewell to an old grandmother who collapsed in fatigue. After a while it gets worse. Now a mother abandons
her howling baby under a tree. Ottman's cousin deserts her boy under
another tree. She cannot stand to hear the week-old baby wailing with
hunger. But Ottman's father instructs the cousin to go back to the tree
and get her son. Yet Father is desperate, too. He appears to be losing his
mind. Pushing the loaded wagon he curses the Jews and curses the
Arabs and curses God.

Not far from Ben Shemen there is a surprise. A group of Jews in
uniform stand by two command cars watching the march. One of them
calls Father's name aloud. Father raises his eyes and walks toward the
commander. The Ben Shemen graduate and the Ben Shemen vegetable
supplier stand face-to-face in the summer fields, both silent. Finally, the
commander tells Father he can stay. Father says that if he stays he will
be considered a traitor and will be executed. The commander walks
back to the command car and brings a jerry can of water, which he puts
on Father's wagon. The commander watches as Father gives water to his
mother, his wife, his sisters-in-law, his sons. And he watches as Father
takes the family wagon and rejoins the column heading east.

I drive to Lydda. It's July, and the heat is as stifling as it was back in July
1948. A thick yellow haze chokes the Lydda Valley. The small mosque
was recently renovated and is locked up, but the Great Mosque is open.
I walk through the same stone gate the inhabitants of Lydda entered,
through the same square courtyard they crowded into, beneath the
same arches of the same high-ceilinged dome they stood under for
thirty-six hours. A few yards away is the regal cathedral of St. George.
Across the alley is the rectory in which the military governor, Gutman,
held talks with the dignitaries of Lydda.

The area in which stood the old stone houses and olive presses and
alleyways of the old city was demolished in the 1950s. But in the square
kilometer of what was once Old Lydda, one still feels that something is
very wrong. There is a curious ruin here, an unexplained ruin there.
Amid the ugly slums, shabby market, and cheap stores, it is clear that
there is still an unhealed wound in Lydda. Unlike other cities where

Israel overcame Palestine, here Palestine is still felt. Unlike other places where modernity overcame the past, here the past is present.

Do I wash my hands of Zionism? Do I turn my back on the Jewish national movement that carried out the deed of Lydda? Like the brigade commander, I am faced with something too immense to deal with. Like the military governor, Gutman, I see a reality I cannot contain. Like the training group leader, I am not only sad, I am horrified. For when one opens the black box, one understands that whereas the small mosque massacre could have been a misunderstanding brought about by a tragic chain of accidental events, the conquest of Lydda and the expulsion of Lydda were no accident. They were an inevitable phase of the Zionist revolution that laid the foundation for the Zionist state. Lydda is an integral and essential part of our story. And when I try to be honest about it, I see that the choice is stark: either reject Zionism because of Lydda, or accept Zionism along with Lydda.

One thing is clear to me: the brigade commander and the military governor were right to get angry at the bleeding-heart Israeli liberals of later years who condemn what they did in Lydda but enjoy the fruits of their deed. I condemn Bulldozer. I reject the sniper. But I will not damn the brigade commander and the military governor and the training group boys. On the contrary. If need be, I'll stand by the damned. Because I know that if it wasn't for them, the State of Israel would not have been born. If it wasn't for them, I would not have been born. They did the dirty, filthy work that enables my people, myself, my daughter, and my sons to live.

To the east, the silvery olive orchards are gone. The remains of the Atid factory are also gone. The fields of the long-gone Arabs of Lydda are now the withering sunflower fields of the Israeli moshav Ginton and the Israeli moshav Ben Shemen. Dr. Lehmann's youth village is still here, but after the 1948 war and after the death of Dr. Lehmann in 1958, its spirit was lost. On the gentle slopes now stand the nondescript buildings of a nondescript educational institution. Only one group of long, red-roofed houses built for the orphans of Europe still stands in testimony to what Ben Shemen once was and what it wished to be. And the courtyard of Ben Shemen is still here. A major project is under way to preserve it.

From the highest point of the Ben Shemen youth village, I look out at the Lydda Valley. I see the city of Lydda and the tall minaret of the Great Mosque. I see the vanished olive orchards, the vanished Herzl forest, the vanished Atid factory, the vanished Lehmann youth village. And I think about the tragedy that took place here. Forty-five years after it came into the Lydda Valley in the name of the Kishinev pogrom, Zionism instigated a human catastrophe in the Lydda Valley. Forty-five years after Zionism came into the valley in the name of the homeless, it sent out of the Lydda Valley a column of homeless. In the heavy heat, through the haze, through the dry brown fields, I see the column marching east. So many years have passed, and yet the column is still marching east. For columns like the column of Lydda never stop marching.

SIX

Housing Estate, 1957

I MEET WITH PROFESSOR ZE'EV STERNHELL IN HIS MODEST JERUSALEM apartment. Sternhell is a distinguished scholar of European fascism and a lauded political activist against Israeli fascism. He is tall and elegant, a true gentleman. For three consecutive days I listen to his life story, trying to understand my own. Listening to Sternhell, I try to understand the Jewish-Israeli tale of the twentieth century.

"I was the beloved, pampered son-of-old-age of an affluent secular Jewish family in Galicia," Sternhell tells me. "My grandfather was a successful textile merchant and my father was his business partner. My mother stayed home and raised me with the help of a maid and a nanny. My older sister, Ada, who was thirteen years my senior, was like a second mother to me. I was showered with love. To this day my most poignant memory is of my father holding me in his arms and pressing his cheek to mine.

"Suddenly war broke out. I was awakened in the middle of the night. All the lights were on as my father said goodbye to us, dressed in the uniform of the Polish army. When he returned from defeat a few weeks later, everything collapsed. My father died, my grandfather died. The Russians occupied eastern Poland and took over half of our large house. We no longer had a nanny or maid. My mother had to work. My mother and my sister did the best they could to shield me. In a world that had lost all sense of stability, they were my only remaining anchor.

"When I was six, in the summer of 1941, the Barbarossa operation began right under our house, which was built on the banks of the Wisla River. I remember the windows shattering, firebombs, the amazing might of Nazi Germany. And within hours, we saw long convoys of terrified Russian prisoners of war. A few months later we were transported to the ghetto. The transition was abrupt: from our grand house to a nook in the ghetto, with its terrible overcrowding, its stench, the hunger.

"Then came the Actions. The ghetto was liquidated in stages, and each time it was a different sort of hunt. I remember when we ourselves were hunted. My mother, Ada, and I hid for three days in an underground hole, some sort of cave. There were a few other people hiding with us, while outside, the ghetto was being decimated. There was a slit through which I watched the hunt. I saw men being shot, children being shot. I was a child of six hiding underground watching through a slit other children who were hiding in treetops as they were shot and killed and fell to the ground.

"I cannot even say what my emotions were. I grew up in the very orderly world of a prosperous middle-class European family. And then, after five years of bliss, this world collapsed overnight. What we thought to be inviolable was violated. What we thought to be the natural order of things was overturned. And it all happened from one day to the next. In the ghetto, one lost one's human foundation, one's human identity. One stopped being human. I was no longer a human being. And in this postcollapse world, it was survival at all cost.

"After the first Action came another. It was a hot summer day, and the Germans were once again hunting Jews. It was a real hunt, like a fox hunt or a hare hunt. Then came the order that everyone who did not have a work permit must assemble in a specified ghetto location. My mother and sister went. I remember it as if it happened yesterday. I remember my sister saying to my mother: we are young, we will work, we will survive. They knew they were leaving me. They knew that only God knew what would happen. But they did not want to frighten me. And they wanted to hope. They wanted to believe they would return. And I did, too. It didn't even occur to me that they wouldn't return, that

I would never see them again. They hugged me and kissed me and left me with my aunt. I watched them walk away, becoming smaller and smaller in the distance.

"My aunt tried as best she could to make up for my mother's absence. My uncle was extremely resourceful; he rescued us from the ghetto. But although my uncle and aunt tried hard to soften the blow, from the moment my mother and sister left, I was alone. From the age of seven, I had no one to talk to. I knew I had to survive on my own. Although I was a child, I knew that I could count on no one and turn to no one. It was a life of utter solitude.

"In the next few months something happened that bordered on the miraculous. My uncle found a home owner in Lvov who had been an officer in the Polish army and was willing to assist Jews. In the terrible anti-Semitic climate of Poland at that time, this was one in a thousand. There was also a working-class family that helped us. These two families saved us. Our forged papers said we were Aryan and that our identity was Polish Catholic. So we wouldn't get caught, my aunt taught me Catholic stories and prayers. It was crucial that the neighbors saw us living as Catholics. Gradually it stopped being a game. I liked it: Easter, Christmas, Christmas presents. The story of Jesus, the image of Mary. Catholicism is genius. You don't stand alone the way Jews and Protestants do. Jesus sacrificed himself for you, and Mary constantly watches over you. You ask her to save you. And when you are a child in the midst of a horrific war and there is carnage all around you, and your father is dead and your mother is gone, you are easily tempted to believe in all this. You hope it will bring you salvation. And you kneel by the altar and you say what every Catholic child says.

"Postwar Poland was dreadfully anti-Semitic. Even though the Nazis were gone, you could smell the hatred for Jews on every street corner. I remember a woman shouting at Jews: 'Scum, you've come out of your holes, too bad Hitler didn't finish you off.' I remember Jews who returned from the camps hiding their identity, and when they were exposed, they were cursed and beaten. There were constant rumors of postwar pogroms. It was crystal clear that Jews had no future in Poland. After all we had been through and all we had seen, we knew that we could no longer be Jewish. We had to replace our old cursed identity with a new one.

"I was officially baptized. My Polish name became Zvigniew Or-lowski. I was an altar boy in the Krakow cathedral. I prayed with the priest and helped him with the holy bread. Every day I genuflected. Being the servant of God's servant gave me proximity to God. But what was even more important than that was not to be Jewish. To be a Jew was to have to run away all the time. To conceal, to lie, to manipulate. And I cut myself off from all that. I ceased to be Jewish. I turned myself into a Catholic in order to live.

"But in 1946, it became clear that even as a Catholic I had no future in Krakow. A Red Cross children's transport train took me from Poland to France, from one aunt to another. I was eleven, and once again I was totally alone. When I reached France, I buried in my heart everything that had happened in Poland. I didn't want to remember anything. I erased the Polish language, my mother tongue, from my memory. I also erased my Catholicism. I adopted a new identity, French. Within a year French became my first language. I studied in a prestigious high school in Avignon, and by the time I was fifteen I was immersed in French culture. Even my accent no longer sounded foreign. I was on the fast track to the Sorbonne.

"France taught me liberty, equality, and human rights. I learned to embrace universalism and secularism, and the principle of separation between state and church. But I always knew that France was not home. Although I wanted to erase the past, I didn't erase the memory of my father, mother, and sister, who were taken from me and died because they were Jewish. I felt I was different; I was from another place. As a Jew, I felt I could never be whole in France. And I was not authentically French. Between France and me there was always a barrier.

"The declaration of the establishment of the State of Israel in May 1948 aroused enormous excitement. You and people of your generation cannot grasp this," Sternhell tells me. "Even before the war, in Poland, our family was Zionist. My aunt in Avignon was active in the Jewish National Fund. There were Zionist posters in every room. I used to read three newspapers every day to follow the drama unfolding in Pal-estine. As a thirteen-year-old boy I feared that the Arabs would slaugh-ter the Jews. But the army of the Jews fought and won and the state of the Jews came to be. It was beyond imagination. Only four years had passed since the Red Army had liberated us. Only six years since the

Nazis had wiped out the ghetto. And now these very same Jews who had been locked up in the ghetto and were hunted down, rose and established a state. Even to someone as secular as myself this was a historic event with a metaphysical dimension. Suddenly there were Jews who were government ministers and Jews who were military officers. A flag, a passport, a uniform. Now the Jews were no longer dependent on gentiles. Now Jews were like gentiles. They stood up for themselves. Even in retrospect, the most thrilling event of my life was the establishment of the State of Israel. I felt an almost religious exaltation.

"In the world of the Holocaust, Jews had no dignity. Jews were human powder, human dust. They were shot as dogs and cats were never shot. They were treated worse than animals. Animals you could pity. Jews you could not pity. The Jew was subhuman. Nothing. Zero. And now, only three years after Auschwitz, the Jew is a human entity. Now, in the Land of Israel, the Jews were fighting back. And they were fighting properly. They fought to win. I saw them in magazine photographs and in cinema newsreels: young and strong and holding guns. Suddenly they were human like all humans. They were capable of fighting for their freedom as the Italians of Edmondo De Amicis's *Heart* fought for their freedom. They were not creatures one could enslave and hunt down and kill. For me, in the south of France, it was a wonder. It was a miracle taking place in real, concrete history.

"At the age of sixteen, I decided to make *aliyah*. I immigrated to Israel on my own, on a boat with a large transport of children coming from Marseille. It was very crowded but it was fun. I remember us standing on the upper deck, watching Mount Carmel come into view, the Land of Israel approaching. And as we disembarked, a few children knelt and kissed the ground. I didn't kneel or kiss the ground, but I felt I had arrived. This was the last station—no more wandering, no more transformations, no more false identities. No more fraud and forgery. No more not being myself. For subterfuge and deceit were not needed here. Something artificial and scary fell away from me. Something that had to do with the perpetual need I felt to justify myself. But in the State of Israel I no longer had to justify or explain. It was a great relief. I didn't speak Hebrew yet, I didn't know what the future held. I was alone, without possessions or protection. But I was filled with the amazing feeling that the long, excruciating journey had come to an end."

• • •

Aharon Appelfeld is a world-renowned author whose Holocaust-related novels—*Badenheim 1939, The Age of Wonders, Iron Tracks*—have been translated into many languages. I sit with him in the basement studio of his Mevaseret-Zion home near Jerusalem. He is short, round-faced, and soft-spoken. Every now and then a devilish spark lights up his eyes. As I had listened to Sternhell, I listen to Appelfeld for a few days. Listening to Appelfeld I once again try to comprehend the Jewish-Israeli story of the twentieth century.

"I was born near Czernowitz in 1932," Appelfeld tells me. "My father was a well-educated industrialist, a former chess champion of Vienna. My mother stayed at home, and she was absolutely beautiful. I was an only child, and my parents spoiled me with ice cream, cakes, toys, books, and folk tales. They wanted me to be a lawyer in Berlin or Vienna. In general, their eyes were always set on Vienna, with its opera, theater, and grand cafés. Judaism was some anachronistic matter of little importance to them. The future was the future of European enlightenment. Our home was spacious and prosperous. We employed a nanny and a cook. We had a piano and many books and fine paintings, multi-colored vases, and a masonry stove that warmed the interiors in winter. And when our small happy family left home, we went to Vienna or Prague or the Carpathian Mountains. Wearing Austrian shorts, socks, and high boots, I loved to step on the soft carpet of autumn leaves in the Vienna parks. When we would return home, my mother would play the piano and put me to sleep with snowy tales that seeped into my dreams. On Sundays, when Father and I would play in my room with the electric train he bought me, Mother would call from the other end of the house: 'Ervin, where are you?' 'I am here, Mother, I am here,' I would call back to her.

"In the summer of 1941, when I was nine, we were vacationing at my grandmother's country estate in the Carpathian Mountains. I was sick and was asleep in my bed at noon. Suddenly there was shooting. I called out for my parents. There was more shooting. I jumped out of the window and hid in the cornfield behind the house. While in the field, I heard the Germans torturing my beautiful mother. I heard my mother screaming. I heard the Germans murder my grandmother and my mother.

"At night Father came home. He had managed to hide and come back for me. He found me in the high corn. Together we returned to Czernowitz, where we found our house looted. The books, the fine paintings, the multicolored vases, the piano, the masonry stove. We were taken to the ghetto, where they put ten of us in a room. It was crowded, it smelled, it was degrading. The moans of the dying elderly filled the air. A few days later we were ordered to march to the train station. There was commotion, shouting, dogs barking. Every now and then there was a gunshot. Inside the cattle cars there was no air to breathe. My father lifted me onto his shoulders so I would not suffocate. When the train stopped, there was a commotion again, and more shouting and dogs barking. Thousands of Jews were pushed off the cattle cars and kicked into the Dniester River. The fittest swam, the weak drowned. Most of the elderly and the children drowned. Because I was his one and only son, my father was able to save me.

"When we reached the other side of the river, we were ordered to march. It was the end of summer and it was getting cold. It rained. For two weeks we walked in mud in the daytime and slept outdoors at night. Some disappeared in the marshes. Some collapsed of fatigue. Some succumbed to diseases. But my father was strong and resilient. Although at nine and a half years of age I was no longer a baby, he carried me on his shoulders much of the way. At last we arrived at an abandoned kolkhoz which had become an improvised concentration camp. Children were separated from adults. Father disappeared. Before I was ten I was alone in the world.

"I realized that if I stayed in the camp I would die. I ran away. The Ukrainian farmers whose doors I knocked on turned me away. I was hungry. I felt it was time to leave this world. At home I'd heard that when the end was near, you leaned on a tree, closed your eyes, and waited for death. So I leaned on a tree, closed my eyes, and waited. But hunger and cold and the dampness kept me awake. A few hours later a ray of sun appeared in the woods, and I walked on. I found shelter in the wooden hut of a Ukrainian prostitute. I became her servant. For six months I milked the cow, cleaned the floor, watched the rough farmers fuck the prostitute in every which way. But when I sensed danger I fled and found refuge with a gang of horse thieves. I was useful to the horse thieves; since I was small, they could smuggle me into barns at night and have me open the gates so the horses could be taken away. But when I sensed danger, I fled again. And so I passed from one underworld to the next. From village to village, from forest to forest. I survived like a field animal. The spoiled bourgeois child I was survived by living for three years like a mouse.

"When the Red Army arrived, I became the kitchen boy of a Russian brigade. The Russians were hungry for food, drink, and women. I watched them conquer, loot, and rape. I watched them drink and cry. When the war ended in 1945 I bade them farewell. I was thirteen and all alone again. I had no orientation whatsoever. I hadn't gone to school, I had no historical perspective. I didn't know where I was or who I was. And Europe was all refugees. Everywhere you went there were refugees, throngs of uprooted children looking for a home. But I had no home. My mother was murdered, my father was gone. The soldiers of the British army's Jewish Brigade found me as they found others. They collected us and smuggled us first into Italy and then to Yugoslavia. But I was still at odds with myself. Who was I, what was I, where did I belong?

"The *Haganah* sailed from Zagreb to Haifa. The boat was filled with people who didn't know each other. Everybody got sick, everybody vomited. When we approached shore I was not at all excited. It was another station on the journey, another ghetto. I knew they would go on hounding me the way they had been hounding me for the past five years. I would have to survive as I had been surviving for the past five years. And in order to survive, I would have to win hearts. Here, too, I would have to prove that there was something valuable in me, something that would make it worthwhile for them to keep me alive."

Aharon Barak, who from 1995 until 2006 served as Israel's chief justice, sits in his cozy office at the Herzliya Interdisciplinary Center. He is a brilliant liberal jurist who reshaped Israeli jurisprudence and is admired worldwide. But I come to him in the same way I approached Sternhell and Appelfeld. I listen to his life story because I want to understand my own. Listening to Barak, I try yet again to comprehend the Jewish-Israeli story of the twentieth century.

"When I was born in Lithuania in 1936, my name was Erik Brik," Barak tells me. "My father was born into a rabbinical family, but he turned his back on all that. He went to the university, studied law, and became the head of the Zionist office in Kovno. My mother was a woman of outstanding intellect. She went to the university and then taught history, German, and Russian. Our home was modest but happy. With my parents I spoke Yiddish; with the Lithuanian nanny I spoke Lithuanian. I was an only child.

"I do not remember life before the Holocaust. Perhaps I have repressed it. So my first memory is of the Holocaust. The German Luftwaffe bombarded the city and soon after that we left home. We put a few of our belongings on a horse-drawn cart and we moved to the ghetto. My next memory is of the Germans arriving in the ghetto, rounding up the Jews and assembling them. A German officer divided everyone: right—left. Those to the right were sent home. Those to the left were sent to death. I was five or six years old. My memory is not clear and the context is not clear. I do not know what the historical truth is. But I remember machine guns mowing down Jews. I remember the Jews of my hometown being murdered en masse by the Nazis.

"Then came the Children's Action. By the beginning of 1944 the Germans realized they would not win the war. But before defeat they wanted to kill as many Jews as they could. They decided to eliminate all Jewish children in the Kovno ghetto. I remember soldiers going from house to house, taking with them any boy or girl under twelve. I was eight. My mother ran home and held me tightly. She took me away and hid me. I was saved just in time.

"Now I had a problem. I was a Jewish boy living in the ghetto, but there should not be a living Jewish boy in the ghetto. So my parents dressed me up as a twelve-year-old: tall shoes, a hat, grown-up clothes. But we lived in fear that someone would see through the disguise and realize I was not an adolescent. One time a German officer realized I was not an adolescent. He looked at me, smiled, and turned away. Once again I was saved.

"My parents recognized that the ghetto was a death trap. Although it was highly dangerous, they decided to smuggle me out. My father was deputy manager of a sweatshop that sewed uniforms for the Wehrmacht. The uniforms from the sweatshop were placed in large canvas sacks and piled on horse-drawn carts. They put me into a sack, closed it, and threw it onto the cart. They put my sack on the top of the heap so that I wouldn't suffocate. That was a big mistake: the cart driver sat on my sack. I was nearly crushed and had a hard time breathing. But the eight-year-old that I was did not utter a sound. After the longest half hour of my life I was thrown into a cowshed. Since I was raised in the ghetto I had never seen a cow. When at last the sack was opened, I felt the tongue of a fat, friendly animal licking my face.

"A few days later my father managed to smuggle my mother out of the ghetto and we were reunited. In early 1944 the Nazis were everywhere, and everywhere there were Nazi collaborators. But one Lithuanian family gave refuge to my mother and me. They built a double wall in one of the rooms of their cottage. My mother and I lived in the one and a half meters between the walls for six months. Only at night was I allowed to get out. To walk in the fields, to breathe fresh air. I even rode a horse. But during the long days I sat with my mother in the dark behind the wall as she taught me everything she knew: math, Latin, history.

"My father stayed in the Kovno ghetto until the end. The ghetto was burned to the ground and its inhabitants were exterminated, but my father survived, though his parents were murdered. Most of my mother's family were also murdered. So when the war ended we were just three: my father, my mother, and me. After the Russians liberated Kovno, they arrested my father but they let him go. So it was clear that we had to flee. We escaped Kovno for Vilna, and Vilna for Grodno, and Grodno for Bucharest. From Bucharest we traveled in a train's coal car to Budapest. From Budapest we went to Russian-held Austria, and then we fled to British-held Austria via a mountain pass. Throughout the journey we experienced anti-Semitism, humiliation, robbery. I remember drunken Russian soldiers taking my father's wristwatch. They humiliated my father. They despised us. They treated us like dirt. For them we were the scum of the earth. I watched how both my parents fought tooth and nail so I could stay alive and we could keep our human dignity. When we reached the British zone, we encountered soldiers of the Jewish Brigade. Here were soldiers with blue-and-white flags sewn onto the lapels of their uniforms, soldiers who spoke Hebrew, soldiers who actually cared for us and wanted to help us. You cannot imagine our excitement. Even now, when I tell you about it, I am all emotions. After all that had happened, Jewish soldiers were a dream. They were a messianic revelation.

"The Jewish Brigade took us to Milan, and from Milan we went to Rome. In Rome they put us up in a mansion previously owned by a fascist count. And suddenly, for the first time in my living memory, we were comfortable. We were taken care of and fed. We were treated as humans. And I went to school. I studied. My mother took me to town to see the opera. But what I loved most was the mansion's cellar, which I discovered one day. There I found the count's fancy clothes and swords and daggers. For the first time in my life I had a world of my own, a world of my own imagination. Left to myself I put on the count's clothes and held his sword and imagined that I was a count, too. Not a Jew, but a count.

"Of the journey to Palestine I remember only the last night. Standing on deck, when we saw the lights of Haifa, my parents held me tight and we all cried. But when we disembarked in the morning it was all quick and efficient. From the port of Haifa we were taken to a rented apartment in Tel Aviv. Days later I was sent on my own to relatives in a Sharon Plain village to learn Hebrew. What struck me immediately was the scent of the soil, the orange groves, the Jewish farmers. A few days later, my aunt took me to an Atta workmen's clothing store in the village of Hod Hasharon. She bought me a bell-shaped Israeli hat, khaki shirts, khaki trousers, and sandals. I had been in the country only a week. I didn't speak the language, I didn't know the land. But when I took off my old clothes I shed the past, the Diaspora, the ghetto. And when I stood in the Atta store in a khaki shirt, khaki trousers, and sandals, I was a new person. An Israeli."

Louise Aynachi is different. She is a woman, she is from Iraq, she is not well known. But like Sternhell, Appelfeld, and Barak, she, too, experienced the great transformation that many Jews experienced in the 1940s and 1950s. Listening to her in the living room of her daughter's fancy apartment in North Tel Aviv, I hear another chapter of the Jewish-Israeli story of the twentieth century.

"For twenty-six hundred years, Jews lived between the Tigris and the Euphrates," Aynachi tells me. "When the British established modern Iraq, they gave Jews equality and full rights. And when Iraq gained its independence in 1932, the Jews' civic and economic rights were maintained. Of the hundred and thirty thousand Iraqi Jews, a hundred thousand lived in the capital, Baghdad, and played a major role in its commercial and intellectual life. Many of the big businesses were owned by Jews, and many of the leading intellectuals were Jews. Jews were also politically influential, and some of them served in parliament. My father was a senior executive at the national train company. My uncle was in parliament. In the Iraq in which I grew up in the 1930s, Jews were not servants but masters. In the modern quarter of Salhiya, on the banks of the Tigris, we lived a life of dignity, prosperity, and happiness.

"In the late 1930s there was a growing German influence in Iraq. *Mein Kampf* was translated into Arabic, and Nazi propaganda was distributed. The pro-Nazi Al-Futuwa youth movement was gaining ground and support. For the rising fascist forces, Jews were the collaborators of the British and the agents of imperialism. And yet, like the Jews of Germany, my family and my circle of friends in Baghdad refused to see what was coming. The Babylonian Diaspora was a perfect Diaspora, they said. It gave Jews what Jews had never had: equality and security, prosperity and prestige. No one could imagine that one day lightning would strike.

"On April 1, 1941, an anti-British military coup occurred. In May, the British put down the mutiny. A day after the British-supported king returned to the capital, nationalist soldiers and civilians, frustrated by the failure of the coup, took out their anger on a delegation of Jewish dignitaries who were on the Al Khurr Bridge on their way to greet the homecoming king. Immediately afterward, Jews were attacked in the Al Rusafa quarter and at Abu Sifyan. For thirty-six hours, pro-Nazi soldiers and youngsters wrought havoc on the Jews. They were joined by poor Baghdad Bedouins and policemen. On the holiday of Shavuot, hundreds of Jewish apartments were ruined and hundreds of Jewish businesses looted. Torah books were violated, synagogues burned. Altogether, seven hundred Jews were wounded and one hundred and eighty murdered. Among the murdered were old men, mothers, and infants.

"When the news of the *farhud*, the pogrom, reached us, my father assembled the family and we all moved to my aunt's home in central Baghdad. We locked ourselves in, terrified. We heard the mob closing in. We saw them waving knives and axes. We saw their eyes inflamed with hatred. The mob broke into neighboring Jewish homes. Women were raped, infants killed. There was literally blood in the streets. There were body parts in the streets. There was chaos. Peaceful Baghdad had suddenly gone mad. The world had shifted from its natural course. The impossible had happened.

"Our family was miraculously saved. For some unknown reason, the mob spared the house we were hiding in. So after the *farhud* ended, we tried to forget. We tried to act as if it had never happened. I married an affluent textile merchant, Naim Aynachi, and we brought three children into the world. Like my parents, we lived in an elegant villa on the banks of the Tigris. Life was as sweet as sweet could be.

"In May 1948, Israel was established. In July, the Iraqi government passed an anti-Zionist law. In September, a highly prominent Jewish businessman was hanged in Basra. Jewish government workers were fired in October. The law curtailing Jewish rights was passed in March 1950. There were threats and sporadic attacks. Now most young Jews in Baghdad no longer believed in the Jewish future of Baghdad. After the *farhud*, many of them became Zionists or Communists, and after the establishment of Israel they witnessed the rising tide of national Arab anti-Semitism wash over Iraq. They understood that twenty-six hundred years of Jewish life in Baghdad would not give them clemency. They knew that the Arab-Jewish honeymoon of the 1920s and 1930s was over. But my father's family and my husband's family still believed in the promise of Baghdad. With all their soul they clung to their happy memories of life by the Tigris.

"In 1950 things got worse. First Jews fled via Iran at the rate of a thousand a month. Then they fled in direct flights arranged by Israel at the rate of two or three thousand a month. In the spring of 1951, ten to fifteen thousand Jews fled Iraq each month. As the community collapsed, even my father and my husband realized there was no other way.

Against everything they believed in, my parents boarded a plane in March 1951. Against everything we believed in, my husband and I and our three children boarded a plane in June 1951. Exactly ten years after it took place, the *farhud* triumphed. On the wooden bench of a Mossad Skymaster I sat crying, watching the Baghdad I loved fade away. Two hours later the Skymaster landed in Lydda."

Sternhell, Appelfeld, Barak, and Aynachi are just four of the 750,000 Jewish refugees who arrived in Israel between 1945 and 1951. Of that number, more than 90 percent arrived in the first three and a half years of the newly founded state. In forty-two months, the number of immigrants absorbed (685,000) surpassed the number of those absorbing them (655,000), a percentage comparable to what would happen if twenty-first-century America took in 350 million immigrants in three and a half years. The numbers were daunting and so was the challenge. In its first decade of existence, the Jewish state experienced a wave of immigration never experienced by any other state in modern times.

The challenge was not only demographic. Many of the immigrants were the survivors of ghettos, forests, and concentration camps. Many of them were unskilled, illiterate, old, and sick. By and large, their ethnic and cultural profile was dramatically different from the profile of the now veteran Israeli population. The traumas they carried with them were unprecedented. And yet the immigrants were taken in and absorbed. By 1957, the vast majority of Israelis were postwar immigrants. Within a decade, Israel's population tripled. Society was totally transformed and so was the country. Before even establishing itself as a free, stable entity, Israel was a new Israel. It was an immigrant state forged in the extremely high temperatures of the post-Holocaust and post-Independence 1950s.

The beginning was dismal. Approximately a hundred thousand of the first immigrants to arrive in the free Jewish state were sent to the vacant houses of Arabs who had just fled Jaffa, Haifa, Acre, Ramleh, and Lydda. Tens of thousands were settled in dozens of Palestinian ghost villages whose stone houses were deemed fit for residence. But by early 1950, the deserted properties could no longer solve the acute problem created by the astonishing human flood. More than a hundred thousand immigrants found themselves in depressing camps established in what had been British military installations, most of them surrounded by barbed wire fences. There they lived in tents, sharing toilets and showers. The camps were muddy, chaotic, and prone to disease. This was not what the immigrants had expected the Promised Land to be like. To deal with the human catastrophe, 121 *ma'abarot*, or refugee camps, were hastily erected throughout the country. At the end of 1949, 93,000 immigrants lived in the tin shacks of these camps. In mid-1951, their number soared to 220,000, and at the end of 1951, to 257,000. Almost every second person recently immigrated to Israel lived in one sort of makeshift installation or another; 11,500 families lived in tents, 15,000 in tiny temporary huts, 30,000 in tin shacks. At the very same time, the country slid into a deep economic crisis. Despite the harsh rationing introduced in 1949, the economy was about to collapse. Unemployment was nearly 14 percent, inflation at over 30 percent, and the government could not pay its debt. The burden of mass immigration was about to crush the young state.

The government finally took action in 1952. It halted immigration, cut the defense budget, raised taxes, and devalued the Israeli lira. Immediately afterward, Israel signed a vital reparations agreement with Germany and began to sell bonds to the Jewish community in the United States. Two years later, the emergency economic measures, German money, and American bonds produced results: inflation and unemployment declined, while growth and productivity rose. When immigration was renewed in 1954, Israel was a tiger leaping ahead with an annual growth rate of more than 10 percent. Between 1950 and 1959, Israel's GDP climbed a staggering 165 percent.

The first national project to lead the Israeli economic miracle of the 1950s was housing. Committed to eliminating the *ma'abarot* and to providing every immigrant with a roof over his head, the government initiated the building of two hundred thousand apartments. At first it built cramped 24-square-meter and 32-square-meter units. Then it built more reasonable 48-square-meter and 52-square-meter apartments. Within a few years, housing estates resembling long white trains dotted the landscape. They were a cheap and functional mass solution to a mass problem. The number of inhabitants in the *ma'abarot* declined from 160,000 in 1952 to 88,000 in 1954 to 30,000 in 1956. Public loans en-

abled most newcomers to buy the new units that the government had
built for them practically overnight. By 1957 the rate of Israelis who
owned their homes was one of the highest in the world. The housing
estate, the *shikun*, became the defining feature of the Israeli welfare
state.

The second national project of the 1950s was agricultural settlement. From 1950 to 1951, Israel built 190 new kibbutz and moshav villages. The average rate of building was one new settlement every four
days. In the years 1951–52, 110 new kibbutzim and moshavim were established. The average rate now was a new settlement per week. In its
first decade as a state, the number of villages in Israel rose by 140 percent, from 290 to 680. Agricultural land use rose from 1.6 million dunams to 3.5 million dunams, irrigated field use from 300,000 dunams to
1,250,000 dunams. The rural population tripled. Agricultural production grew dramatically. While four hundred evacuated Palestinian villages were demolished, four hundred new Israeli villages shaped the new
economy and the new map of Israel.

In the mid-1950s a third national project began: industrialization.
After supplying basic housing to most of the population and after secur-
ing the land and the food supply, the young state turned to modern industry. Almost half of the reparations that Israel received from Germany
were turned into government loans that enabled entrepreneurs to establish factories in remote areas. Some of the new enterprises failed, but
many succeeded. In 1954 the first Uzi submachine gun was manufactured. In 1955 the aeronautics industry was in full swing. In 1957 Israel
began planning its first scientific nuclear reactor. The bromide industry
in the Dead Sea and the phosphate industry in the Negev followed,
along with a metal factory in Yokneam, a tire manufacturing facility in
Hadera, and a steel plant in Acre. Between 1953 and 1958 industrial
production rose 180 percent. By the end of its first decade, Israel underwent a rapid and intensive industrial revolution.

The energy was unceasing. Wherever one went there was demoli-
tion and construction. In accordance with a national master plan devised by the government's leading architects and civil engineers in 1950,
Palestine vanished and the modern State of Israel replaced it. In addition to the new villages, thirty new towns were founded. Roads were
paved, power stations erected, a new port planned. A centralized gov-

ernment used centralized planning to build the new Israel as if the state were a grand engineering project. At the very same time, the state built its own institutions: a parliament, an administration, a judiciary. A popular conscription army that performed many nonmilitary duties—such as teaching its new soldiers Hebrew—became a powerful melting pot of the new society. A state-run education system tripled in size within a decade. A national bank, a national social security system, a national employment service were all established. Public hospitals and public health clinics provided advanced medical care to most Israelis.

Israel of the 1950s was a state on steroids: more and more people, more and more cities, more and more villages, more and more of everything. But although development was rampant, social gaps were narrow. The government was committed to full employment. There was a genuine effort to provide every person with housing, work, education, and health care. The newborn state was one of the most egalitarian democracies in the world. The Israel of the 1950s was a just social democracy. But it was also a nation of practicality that combined modernity, nationalism, and development in an aggressive manner. There was no time, and there was no peace of mind, and therefore there was no human sensitivity. As the state became everything, the individual was marginalized. As it marched toward the future, Israel erased the past. There was no place for the previous landscape, no place for previous identities. Everything was done en masse. Everything was imposed from above. There was an artificial quality to everything. Zionism was not an organic process anymore but a futuristic coup. For its outstanding economic, social, and engineering achievements, the new Israel paid a dear moral price. There was no notion of human rights, civil rights, due process, or laissez-faire. There was no equality for the Palestinian minority and no compassion for the Palestinian refugees. There was little respect for the Jewish Diaspora and little empathy for the survivors of the Holocaust. Ben Gurion's statism and monolithic rule compelled the nation forward.

From the port of Haifa, Svern Sternhell was sent to a Jewish Agency immigration camp in Haifa, but just days later he was sent on to the boarding school of Youth Aliyah in the small town of Magdiel. On his first night there, the sixteen-year-old threw away the European suit his Avignon aunt had sewn especially for his *aliyah*. On his first morning at work he was already wearing the blue workingman's uniform and the black workingman's boots. When he arrived at the orange grove for the very first time, he was as happy as a bird. Sun, blue skies, oranges. For the first time since his family was taken to the ghetto, the world was good.

Within weeks, Sternhell was fluent in Hebrew. Within months he was a skilled farmer. Working in the orange grove, he consumed dozens of oranges a day. Like many others, he exchanged his European given name for a Hebrew one, Ze'ev, but he refused to let go of his European last name because it was the name of his parents and sister. Yet the now seventeen-year-old survivor was determined not to wallow in pain but to suppress it. He was afraid that the weakness of over there would haunt him over here. He was afraid that the burden of the past would jeopardize the future. He knew he must build himself anew on totally new foundations.

Sternhell's new comrades made similar decisions. Although they studied together, worked together, and slept in the same huts, they did not talk about their pasts. Most were Holocaust survivors, a few were refugees from the Arab world. All had experienced trauma. Some had lost their parents, all had lost their homes. Yet these youngsters displayed remarkable optimism. In the sweltering heat of summer and the bone-chilling cold of winter, they did not lament or complain. They were not bitter. They did not allow themselves to think like orphans or feel like orphans. On the contrary, they were determined to turn themselves into Israelis as fast as possible. To milk cows, to work the fields, to join a kibbutz. To forget. To begin the future as if the past had never happened.

Because Sternhell was already a thinker, he conceptualized what his comrades could only intuit. He knew that the Jews needed a shelter and that Israel was that shelter. He understood that the Jews needed a roof and that Israel was their only roof. For secular Jews who had no God and no religion, Israel was also essential for their souls and identities. Without a Jewish state, secular Jews like himself would stand naked in the world. They would have no home, no collective self, and no future. Therefore, Sternhell embraced his new Israeli identity completely. Only in Israel did he not have to justify himself or hide himself. Only as an Israeli could he turn from being an object of history to being a subject of history. Only as an Israeli could he be the master of his own fate.

In the summer of 1952, Sternhell and his comrades moved to a kibbutz up north. Ze'ev worked in the kibbutz in the mornings, studied in Haifa in the afternoons, and returned for guard duty in the kibbutz at night. A small inheritance allowed him to move to Haifa, finish high school, and pass the university entrance exams. In August 1954 he joined the Israeli Army. He went through basic training, a squad leader course, an officer training course. Ten years after he was an altar boy in Krakow, Sternhell was an outstanding combat officer in the Golani infantry brigade. In October 1956, during the Sinai campaign, the charismatic platoon commander discovered that his men were trapped in a minefield. Walking ahead, he led them out of it. Mental agility, physical strength, and fearlessness marked Svern-Ze'ev Sternhell as a son of the land. He had found his place in the world. The haunted boy from the ghetto had become a total Israeli.

From the boat, Ervin Appelfeld was taken to an immigrant camp in Atlit, and from Atlit he was sent to a Zionist youth village south of Jerusalem. On the farm, thirty-four young Holocaust survivors tried to learn the rules of life in this strange new land. They competed to see who would be the first to drive a tractor, who would be more fit and suntanned, who would be blonder, who would look the least like a Jew. They tried to pretend that the ghettos and the forests and the concentration camps had never happened. Czernowitz had never existed; there never was Vienna. Or Father, or Mother.

Appelfeld feared he was about to lose his sense of self. When the teacher would say, "Children, now we will study Hebrew and study the Bible and plant trees and water flowerbeds and everything will be fine and everything will turn out great," the other children seemed convinced. They rapidly shed the past. On the first day they returned from the fields sunburned, and on the second day they returned sunburned, but on the third day they were tanned Israelis. But fourteen-year-old Appelfeld was different. He didn't want to attach himself to a language and a world that were not his own. He didn't want to lose the German language and the theater and the music of his childhood. He was terrified of losing his parents and becoming an eternal orphan. Until one day, after everybody was gone, he sat alone in the dining hall, took out a school notebook, and wrote down in large childish letters: "My father's name—Michael; my mother's name—Bulia; my grandfather's name—Meir Joseph. My home is on Masarik Strasse, Czernowitz." The next day, when Ervin read the list and added a few poignant words evoking his childhood, he felt warmth spreading inside him. "I have a home," he thought. "I have a street. I have a father and mother and grandfather and a city and a park and a soft carpet of autumn leaves. In spite of everything, I have something to hold me in this world. I am not an orphan."

In the 1948 war Appelfeld was a sixteen-year-old paramilitary warrior. Four years after hiding from the Nazis in Ukrainian forests he used a machine gun to defend the Zionist farm he was living on from the neighboring Arabs who were about to slaughter its youth. When the war ended he was sent to the elite Mikveh Yisrael Agricultural School to learn how to grow apples, pears, and plums. A year later he was sent to the new agricultural school of Ein Karem to teach Moroccan and Iraqi immigrant boys how to grow apples, pears, and plums. Six months later he was sent to serve as a caretaker of the girls' agricultural school in Nahalal. In all of these schools Ervin felt totally alone, without family or community. He found no common ground with the arrogant Sabras, the Oriental newcomers, or the ill-mannered Israeli girls. In 1950 he was drafted and trained as a mortar operator. Now his loneliness became unbearable. On Shabbat, when all his fellow soldiers returned home, Ervin had no home to go to. He stayed on base by himself. On Saturday nights he would spend a few hours in the nearby town of Netanya. He would sit at a seaside café watching the people pass by. Some were Holocaust survivors, others were Arab-world survivors, but what Appelfeld saw were human wrecks. He saw the uprooted Jews of the twentieth century, whose lives had been shattered by disaster.

Appelfeld reflected on the gap between Ben Gurion's proclaimed egalitarian and united Israel and the real Israel of the fate-stricken who were now huddled in immigrant camps and housing estates. He reflected on the gap between the pious pioneering rhetoric of Zionism and the new Israeli reality of restless drunks and gamblers and whores who could not find peace of mind. He reflected on the gap between the mobilized monolithic upstairs-Israel and the cacophony of downstairs-Israel. What he saw was an inebriated and licentious immigrants' Israel trying to forget all that had happened.

In the last days of his army service, Appelfeld studied on his own, passed the matriculation exams, and was accepted to the Hebrew University. He rented a cheerless room in Jerusalem's Rehavia neighborhood. The boy who never attended first grade was now the student of some of the world's most renowned scholars: he studied Yiddish with Dov Sadan, Kabbalah with Gershom Scholem, and scriptures with Martin Buber. But Ervin was not impressed by his progress. He had no bearings. He lacked a well-grounded identity and was struggling to contain the numerous transformations he had gone through in a decade. Alone in his room in Rehavia, Appelfeld tried to decipher himself: what had happened to him and who he was; from what sea he had come and on what shore he had washed up.

The one place Appelfeld felt at ease was in Café Peter in Jerusalem's verdant German colony. Here people spoke the Austro-Hungarian German of his childhood and served the Austro-Hungarian dishes of home. At the elegant tables sat elegant ladies who resembled his mother. Here there was no melting-pot edict. Here he could remember his mother and long for her. He imagined that though murdered, she would somehow return. In Café Peter, in 1956, Appelfeld could bring up from the cellar of his memories what the Israel of 1956 kept locked away. In his notebook he jotted down a few lines, then some sentences, then broken paragraphs. Slivers, scraps, fragments. One story, two stories, three. The story of a people gone up in smoke. The story of a world gone up in smoke. The story of a boy who witnessed pre-Holocaust, Holocaust, and post-Holocaust life. And now, a decade after the Holocaust, sitting in a Jerusalem café, he tried to collect himself. To rehabilitate himself, to define himself and to find his own voice.

When his family arrived in Jerusalem, Erik Brik had already gone through five metamorphoses: sheltered childhood in prewar Kovno; persecuted childhood in the wartime ghetto; a childhood of hiding in the wall as the war drew to a close; a refugee's wandering childhood when the war was over; a respite in the Jewish Agency's mansion in the years following the war. But when the Briks settled down in a small apartment on the edge of Rehavia, the eleven-year-old told himself that what was before would not be again. This is our homeland. This is the final beginning. Here he would take root.

The beginning was difficult. Erik was gentle and chubby and well-read. He loved the opera. The Israeli-born sixth-grade Sabras ridiculed him. They saw him as a weak and pale Diaspora Jew. But within months, Erik proved what he was made of. He acquired Hebrew and got rid of his Lithuanian accent. He viewed himself as someone who was born in Israel and acted accordingly. He didn't tell anyone about Democracy Square or the Children's Action or the ghetto or living in the wall. Within a year, it became apparent that Erik was gifted. He was brilliant in math and history, but he also became president of the student council. He was an enthusiastic boy scout, first a cub scout, then den chief, then troop leader. As president of his student council he was chosen to meet Ben Gurion at his famous retreat in the desert. Because of his role in the boy scouts he led work camps in the kibbutz and intended to settle in a kibbutz. Brik internalized the collective values of old pioneering Israel. He identified completely with the Jewish state that gave him refuge. He saw Israel as a dynamic, enlightened, and constructive entity headed for the future. The boy who changed his name to Aharon Barak was now determined to erase his Kovno past and join the Israeli future.

Not so his parents. Leah Brik had been a respected high school teacher in Lithuania, but in Israel she taught third grade in a working-class school. Zvi Brik had been the head of the Jewish Agency in Kovno, but in Israel he was just a clerk. Both felt they didn't receive the recognition they deserved. Both were not fulfilled professionally and realized they never would be. And the Holocaust refused to let go. Zvi had lost his parents. Leah had lost her father, mother, a brother, and a sister. The family was small and sad and had few true friends. There was anguish at home, and much crying. All Leah and Zvi had was their son, on whom they were totally focused. Aharon was promise. Aharon was hope. Aharon was an arrow shot from a hopeless past to a hopeful future.

In 1954 Barak graduated from high school with honors. Because he wanted to continue studying, he didn't join a kibbutz but studied law at the Hebrew University. By 1956 there was a consensus among the Jerusalem faculty: Aharon Barak was a judiciary genius. When he married and set up house in 1957, many of his friends had no doubt that one day the young groom would be Israel's chief justice.

At Lydda airport Louise Aynachi discovered that half of the suitcases she sent from Baghdad were gone and the others had been broken into. The family had no clothes, no food, and the children were crying. From the airport she was taken to a cold room at the end of the terminal. A brusque nurse went through her hair, looking for lice. Although she didn't find any, without giving notice, she sprayed Louise's hair and body with DDT. Then she sprayed Louise's husband, Naim, and then their children, Huda, Nabil, and Morris. Naim was shocked: "From whence have we come," he asked, "and how far have we fallen?"

After the Aynachi family filled out all sorts of bureaucratic forms, the Jewish Agency staff put the family on a truck. For three hours the truck rocked along in the dark, heading for an unknown destination. It arrived at what seemed to be a military camp: army tents surrounded by barbed wire. Louise tried to quell her fears so that her children would not be frightened. She took whatever belongings were left and piled them up in the corner of their assigned army tent. She did her best to put the children to bed on the straw pillow and under the straw blanket. The next morning, when Naim woke up, he was bursting with rage. "In Iraq we were distinguished guests at the king's palace, and here we are nothing. We are not respected, we are not honored, we have no property. We are nothing but homeless refugees in a tent."

One blow followed another. Before the Aynachis had left Baghdad, the Iraqi government had confiscated their assets because they had chosen to immigrate to Israel. When they arrived in Israel it turned out that the small amount of money that Naim had managed to smuggle out via Iran had been stolen by the moneychanger he had put his faith in. On top of that was the DDT, the humiliation of life in a tent, the condescending attitude of veteran Israelis, the scornful attitude of the Ashkenazi immigrants. And the fact that in Israel, Jewish Baghdad was not perceived as the cradle of a great civilization but as the unknown territory of barbarians. Within one week, the Aynachi family experienced a sudden fall from paradise to humiliation and depravation.

Louise held on. Even when it became clear that the money would
not arrive, she didn't crack. Even as she struggled in the chaos of the
refugee camp, she stood firm as she confronted the insults and the deg-
radation. She pretended that all was well for the children's sake, that this
was some sort of sandy summer camp and not the end of the world. Just
a short detour on the way to a new adventure and to a new life in a new
land that would eventually reveal to them its milk and honey.

From the Atlit immigrant camp the Aynachi family was transported
to a *ma'abara* near Netanya—from a tent to a tin hut, from dampness to
heavy heat, from shock to depression. Yet after a few months Naim
found an apartment in Holon, a southern suburb of Tel Aviv. He found
work in Tel Aviv's Atara coffeehouse. The apartment was nothing like
the villa on the Tigris, and work in a coffeehouse was nothing like the
work of a textile executive. But there was a home for the eight family
members that Naim was taking care of (grandparents, aunt, wife, and
children), and his job was not shameful. So after a year Louise felt that
they were rising from the deep pit into which they had fallen. Unlike
many other men who had emigrated from Iraq, Naim was not broken,
he was only very sad. For his remaining days, Naim would remain sad.

More bitter was the fate of Louise's father. Less fortunate than
his son-in-law, Eliyahu Yitzhak Baruch did not find a suitable job in Israel. His property, assets, and money were lost when he left Iraq. And
when he and his wife left the immigrant camp, they had to settle for a
shabby one-room apartment in Struma Square in Holon. Each morning
Eliyahu Yitzhak Baruch left the one-room apartment for the Lodzia
women's undergarment factory; throughout the day, the former train
company executive would stand by the gate of the factory with a ped-
dler's cart trying to sell gum, candy, and chocolate to the impoverished
workers. And each evening when he returned to his small apartment in
Struma Square, Eliyahu Yitzhak Baruch remembered the Tigris. His
heart would cry as he remembered the Tigris, until it could no longer
endure the pain and stopped beating.

By the time I am born, in November 1957, the State of Israel is a triumph. The borders are quiet, the economy is booming, the population
is approaching two million. The decisive victory in the 1948 war gave

birth to the nation, and the decisive victory in the 1956 Sinai campaign has stabilized it. The superhuman endeavor to absorb nearly a million immigrants was a success. Twenty new cities, four hundred new villages, two hundred thousand new apartments, and a quarter million new jobs attest to an unprecedented historical achievement. By now Svern Sternhell has become Lieutenant Sternhell, who has left the IDF for the Hebrew University to study history and political science. Ervin Appelfeld has become Aharon Appelfeld, who is assembling his first collection of short stories. Erik Brik has become Aharon Barak, who is about to receive his law degree summa cum laude. Louise Aynachi is still struggling in a Holon immigrant quarter, but her three children have gradually adjusted to their new homeland. After a decade of war and frenzied state building, bordering in pace on the maniacal, the first signs of stability appear. The young state ceases to be a makeshift camp. It is no longer perceived as a crazy adventure but as a solid political fact. True, there is no peace. The Arab world still looks upon the Jewish state as an artifice, temporary and despicable. But there is no war, either. The victories of 1948 and 1956 are deterring the enemy. A new alliance with France equips the Israeli Air Force with the most modern fighter jets: Ouragans, Mystères, Super-Mystères. West Germany and Great Britain also assist the resolute state, which had proved just a year earlier that it was capable of reaching the Suez Canal. Relations with the United States are good, relations with the Soviet Union are reasonably good. The world watches the Jewish phoenix rise from the sand. Israeli orange groves, Israeli archaeology, and Israeli science raise international interest and admiration.

The autumn I am born, Rehovot, the city I am born in, is getting ready to inaugurate a nuclear physics department. Niels Bohr and Robert Oppenheimer are about to come to the Weizmann Institute to pay tribute to the promising young physicists of the promising young state. At the very same time, Tel Aviv's new performing arts center, the Frederic R. Mann Auditorium, is opened. Arthur Rubinstein, Isaac Stern, and Leonard Bernstein come to nine-year-old Israel to celebrate with the fine musicians and the enthusiastic audience of the Israel Philharmonic Orchestra. The national project of draining the swamps of Lake Hula in the Galilee is completed. The first supermarket is set to open in Tel Aviv.

As the Russians launch their first Sputnik into space, Israeli newspapers stick closer to home, reporting a staggering rise in refrigerator
and washing machine sales. The economic boom and German reparations awaken old appetites: dozens of delicatessens open in central Tel
Aviv. As Israel gears up for its tenth birthday, there is a strong sense of
achievement and even wonder. A First Decade Exhibition is planned, to
be held in the summer of 1958 in Jerusalem, to highlight Israel's success.
The message will be that Israel is now the most stable and most advanced nation in the Middle East. It is the most remarkable melting pot
of the twentieth century. The Jewish state is a man-made miracle.

But the miracle is based on denial. The nation I am born into has
erased Palestine from the face of the earth. Bulldozers razed Palestinian
villages, warrants confiscated Palestinian land, laws revoked Palestinians' citizenship and annulled their homeland. By the socialist kibbutz
Ein Harod lie the ruins of Qumya. By the orange groves of Rehovot lie
the remains of Zarnuga and Qubeibeh. In the middle of Israeli Lydda,
the debris of Palestinian Lydda is all too apparent. And yet there seems
to be no connection in people's minds between these sites and the people who occupied them only a decade earlier. Ten-year-old Israel has
expunged Palestine from its memory and soul. When I am born, my
grandparents, my parents, and their friends go about their lives as if the
other people have never existed, as if they were never driven out. As if
the other people aren't languishing now in the refugee camps of Jericho,
Balata, Deheisha, and Jabalia.

Denial has its reasons. In the first decade, the unique endeavor of
nation building consumes all of the young state's physical and mental
resources. There is no time and no place for guilt or compassion. The
number of Jewish refugees that Israel absorbs surpasses the number of
Palestinian refugees it expelled. And all the while, the vast Arab nation
doesn't lift a finger to help its Palestinian brothers and sisters. In 1957,
most Palestinians don't yet define themselves as a distinct people. They
do not have a mature and recognized national movement. The world
feels sorry for them, but the world denies them political rights and does
not recognize them as a legitimate national entity. It is therefore not
without reason that Israel chooses to see the Arab-Israeli conflict as a
conflict between states, a conflict between the Israeli David and the

Arab Goliath. It is a conflict that marginalizes the Palestinian tragedy, viewing it as some sort of unpleasant peripheral issue.

And yet this denial is astonishing. The fact that seven hundred thousand human beings have lost their homes and their homeland is simply dismissed. Asdud becomes Ashdod, Aqir becomes Ekron, Bashit becomes Aseret, Danial becomes Daniel, Gimzu becomes Gamzu, Hadita becomes Hadid. The Arab city of Lydda is now the new immigrants' city of Lydda. A dozen towns and hundreds of villages and thousands of sites receive new identities. An enormous refugee rehabilitation project is carried out in the homes and fields of others who are now refugees themselves.

Yet the denial of the Palestinian disaster is not the only denial the Israeli miracle of the 1950s is based upon. Young Israel also denies the great Jewish catastrophe of the twentieth century. True, the Holocaust memorial Yad Vashem is being built in Jerusalem. Every April, Israel marks the Holocaust and Heroism Remembrance Day. And in wheeling and dealing with the international community, the tragedy of European Jewry is mentioned and used. But within Israel itself, the Holocaust is not given space. The survivors are expected *not* to tell their stories. A dozen years after the catastrophe, the catastrophe has no place in local media and art. The Holocaust is only the low point from which the Zionist revival rose. The Israeli continuum rejects trauma and defeat and pain and harrowing memories. Furthermore, the Israeli continuum does not have room for the individual. That's also why the Holocaust remains abstract and separate. It's not really about the people living among us. The message is clear: Quiet now, we are building a nation. Don't ask unnecessary questions. Don't indulge in self-pity. Don't doubt, don't lament, don't be soft or sentimental, don't dredge up dangerous ghosts. It's not a time to remember, it is a time to forget. We must gather all our strength now and concentrate on the future.

This denial, too, is not without reason. Although vibrant and confident, Israel is not strong enough to deal with the horror of the past. It is still a scrappy society fighting for its life and its future. The Jewish state is a frontier oasis surrounded by a desert of threat. It is not mature enough for self-analysis. It is not tranquil enough to see its own drama in perspective. There are far too many challenges. There is far too much pain. Without self-discipline and self-repression and a degree of cruelty, everything might disintegrate.

But the price of denial is dear. Yes, Ze'ev Sternhell and Aharon Barak are too ambitious to notice the price. They enthusiastically embrace their new identities, wanting to run as far away as possible from the past. But the introspective Appelfeld looks on with dread at what is taking place around him. People replace a name with a name, a tongue with a tongue, an identity with an identity. To survive, they cleanse themselves of the past. To function, they flatten themselves. They turn into people of action whose personalities are rigid and deformed, whose souls are shallow. They lose the riches of Jewish culture as they are shaped by a new synthetic culture that lacks tradition and nuance and irony. They create a loud, externalized way of life that is eager to display a forced gaiety. They have lost the place they came from without knowing where they are heading.

The two denials are actually four: the denial of the Palestinian past, the denial of the Palestinian disaster, the denial of the Jewish past, and the denial of the Jewish catastrophe. Four forces of amnesia are at work. Erased from memory are the land that was and the Diaspora that was, the injustice done to them and the genocide done to us. As they struggle to survive and cast a new identity, the Israelis of the 1950s bury both the fruit orchards of Palestine and the yeshivas of the shtetl, the absence of seven hundred thousand Palestinian refugees and the nihility of six million murdered Jews. What vanishes under Ben Gurion's hasty development is the beauty of the land, the depth of the Diaspora, and the great historic cataclysms of the 1940s.

It is highly likely that this multilevel denial was essential. Without it, it would have been impossible to function, to build, to live. An obstinate disregard was crucial for the success of Zionism in the first decades of the twentieth century, and a lack of awareness was crucial for the success of Israel in its first decade of existence. If Israel had acknowledged what had happened it would not have survived. If Israel had been kindly and compassionate, it would have collapsed. Denial was a life-or-death imperative for the nine-year-old nation into which I was born.

• • •

To confirm this point I turn to the Spiegels, whom I have known for years and whose familial biography I find striking. The head of the family, Erno Spiegel, is no longer alive, but I manage to speak with his ninety-two-year-old wife, Anna, on her last days of lucidity. Their daughter Yehudit adds her own memories to the family's life story. And as I leaf through the family's records, photo albums, and documents, I find the Spiegel story to be yet another powerful example of the Jewish-Israeli story of the twentieth century.

Anna was born in the Carpathian Russian town of Svalava in 1918. When the Germans invaded in the spring of 1944 she was a twenty-six-year-old beauty. A knock on the door, a yellow Jewish star, the herding of Jews into the local brick factory. Ten days later the Jews were marched through the streets to the train station. They spent three days in a sealed cattle car, then arrived at Auschwitz. Anna's sister-in-law and four-month-old nephew were sent to the left. Lucky Anna was with the hundreds of women sent to the right: first to a crowded shower hall, then to have a total body shave, which led to a total loss of identity. She spent three days in the camp barracks as the flames of the crematorium danced in the windows. But because Anna was young and strong she was sent to a succession of work camps: an airplane factory, an airport, hard labor in the woods. She made the retreating march, with thousands of others, to the Elba River, where those who survived the trek were liberated. On the train to Prague many female survivors were raped by Russian soldiers. In Prague, she was reunited with her brothers and a sister. All returned from hell, though their parents and sister Sheyna would never return. In Prague, Anna met Erno Spiegel.

Spiegel was born in Budapest in 1915 but raised in the Carpathian Russian town of Munkacz. Prior to the war, he served as an officer in the Czech army. In 1941, he was sent by pro-Nazi Hungarians to forced labor camps for two years, and in 1944 he was sent by the Germans to Auschwitz. A twin, Spiegel was taken from the Auschwitz platform to Dr. Mengele's twin compound and appointed by Mengele to be the twins' master. His job was to monitor and organize the twins subjected to Mengele's experiments, including his sister. On several occasions, he saved lives, including his sister's. At night he tried to ease the young twins' loneliness and allay their fears. He promised them that their parents had not died and that when the war ended, he would reunite them with their families. At the end of January 1945, Spiegel left the just-liberated death camp with thirty-two children. Soon after, his surreal convoy of survivors wended its way through the ruins of Europe. After he brought the twins to their hometowns, Spiegel went back to Munkacz and then moved to Carlsbad. He returned to his old vocation of book-keeper. On a visit to the capital, Erno met Anna, and three months later they married in Prague's ancient synagogue.

In May 1948, the State of Israel was founded. In March 1949, Erno and Anna Spiegel and their two-year-old daughter entered the port of Haifa. Israeli soldiers boarded their ship and handed out oranges. Anna was beside herself. The Land of Israel, the State of Israel, Jewish sol-diers, oranges. She felt it was a triumph over Hitler. Anna and Erno together were a triumph over Hitler. Two-year-old Yehudit was a tri-umph over Hitler. The State of Israel was an absolute triumph over Hitler.

From Haifa the Spiegels were sent to the Be'er Ya'akov immigrant camp. The army tents were surrounded by barbed wire, and the March rain penetrated the tarps and turned the floor into a muddy puddle. All around the camp people shouted and complained. The jumble of im-migrants from a jumble of countries spoke a jumble of languages. Baby Yehudit contracted acute dysentery, which endangered her life. In some tents, babies quickly succumbed to the disease and died. And yet Anna Spiegel was happy: our land, our state, a place of our own.

While Anna struggled in the camp, Erno went to Tel Aviv to look for a job. He found work as a bookkeeper in a small accounting firm. The Spiegels saved every penny. Finally, nine months after arriving in Israel, they had enough to move to a one-and-a-half-room apartment in a housing estate on the eastern outskirts of Tel Aviv.

The Spiegels arrived in Bizaron in December 1949. Between Bi-zaron Street and Victory Road were the long white housing estates that had been hastily erected on the sand. Pedestrian paths bordered small muddy yards. At the end of one of the paths, three concrete stairs led from the mud to a small covered entrance. On the right was the apart-ment of the engineer Dr. Fischer, on the left the apartment purchased by the senior bookkeeper, Mr. Spiegel. Thirty-four square meters—one room, one half room, a toilet, a kitchen—that made Anna Spiegel cry: at last they had a home.

Apart from the Jewish Agency's three metal beds, the tiny apartment was empty. But within days, the crates the Spiegels had sent from Carlsbad arrived: blankets, towels, bed linens, crocheted tablecloths, pots, pans, silverware, two tea services. An electric stove, a mechanical meat grinder, a coffee grinder, a poppy seed grinder. The heavy Czech furniture that could not fit through the door of the miniature apartment was exchanged for light, modern Israeli-made tables and chairs. When Erno Spiegel became the bookkeeper of the just-founded Cameri Theater, more furniture was added: armchairs, a sofa, an icebox, a radio. Within one year the empty public housing unit became a warm home enveloped in the aroma of goulash and paprikash and poppy-seed yeast cakes that Anna prepared in her tiny kitchen.

For Erno Spiegel, work was everything: a source of income, a safety net, therapy. Work kept away bad thoughts and memories, he told his wife. Every morning at eight he would put on a suit and tie, don a hat, and take the bus to the theater's office. Every afternoon at four, the bus would take him home. After a light meal he would rest and listen to the news on the radio and read the centrist *Maariv* newspaper. Then, at his desk in the hall, he would audit the accounts of private theater productions for which he was well paid. This was how there was enough money to add another room and to buy Yehudit a piano.

Anna Spiegel was a housewife. In the mornings she cooked spicy Hungarian dishes. In the afternoons she took Yehudit to private piano lessons. She was particular about her looks and her daughter's looks: she sewed, ironed, and embroidered their clothes. Once a week was laundry day. Once a month was seamstress day. Every once in a while, she would take a Hebrew lesson at the Ulpan or attend a gathering of mothers at the women's club. Unlike Erno, Anna never stopped talking about over there. And about the great miracle that happened to her family and to all other Jewish survivors when they came here from over there.

Yehudit attended the housing estate's kindergarten and elementary school, first in the adjacent neighborhood and then in the housing estate itself. Almost all the children in her class were the sons and daughters of Ashkenazi immigrants, almost all of them Holocaust survivors. From time to time someone would say, "Daddy screams at night." From time to time someone would say, "Mommy is sick again." They would discuss the number tattooed on a mother's arm, the number tattooed on a father's arm. Partisans, ghettos, concentration camps. But all these shadows could not obscure the miraculous events taking place around them. In 1953 Israel began to drain the swamps of Lake Hula in the Galilee. In 1954 it was digging the first parts of the National Water Carrier that would eventually bring water from the Sea of Galilee to the Negev desert. In 1955 oil was discovered in Heletz, not far from the Gaza Strip. In 1956 Israel won the Sinai campaign. So in the housing estate's school there were no doubts anymore. It was absolutely clear that the children wearing blue and white for Israel's ninth Independence Day were the children of hope. And Yehudit Spiegel was the most striking among them. There was nothing Yehudit couldn't do. Sports, scouting, English, French, piano. She was the head of her class, the leader of the youth movement, a medal-winning athlete. In her pleated blue skirt and embroidered white shirt, eleven-year-old Yehudit Spiegel was the daughter of triumph. Triumph over Mengele and Auschwitz and Birkenau. Triumph over the damned Germans. Triumph over the horrific past of the Jews. In the name of Erno Spiegel from Auschwitz-Birkenau and in the name of Anna Spiegel from the labor camps she would go forth and conquer the world.

So when I choose the place that evokes the Israel of 1957 more than any other, I don't choose my hometown of Rehovot or a kibbutz or a moshav or a new town. Nor do I choose Jerusalem, Haifa, or central Tel Aviv. I choose the Bizaron housing estate.

In 1957, there are nineteen blocks in the Bizaron *shikun*. In every block there are sixteen families. Most are European: Poles, Russians, Hungarians, Czechs. Almost all of the parents are survivors of death camps, forests, ghettos. Like Yehudit, many of the children were born immediately after the war, in the ruins of Europe. The families are small—no grandfathers, no grandmothers, no uncles or aunts. Every family has only one child, at most two. Behind every living family lurks the shadow of the larger family that has ceased to exist. Over there, Mr. Teicher had another wife. Over there, Mrs. Cohen had two other daughters. Shoshana's mother is in bed all day long because her little brother and her baby sister never came back from the camps. In the tidy, clean apartments of night watchman Weinstock and Labor Party functionary Katz, whose wife suffers endless bouts of migraines and fatigue, no one is allowed to raise a voice, to horse around, to disturb the wives. The demons must not be woken. Although they are only in their thirties and forties, almost every parent in the housing estate is bereft of a father or mother, of a family that is no more. Almost every child in the housing estate knows that his or her parents have a past that one should not ask about. The Bizaron housing estate lives its life under a silent mountain of death.

Yet the housing estate is not gloomy. The pedestrian paths between the long trainlike housing blocks are busy with enterprise and action. Most fathers work as junior clerks in government or trade union offices, or in small private firms. Most mothers augment the family income with part-time jobs. But in every corner there is enterprise. One opens a notions store, another becomes a stationer. One works as a plumber and one as a photographer. Mrs. Shapiro uses a special blender sent from America to make carrot juice that she sells on the estate. Mrs. Levy imports a Singer sewing machine to make fancy dresses for the ladies. One Holocaust survivor is a milkman, another is a policeman. There is a shoemaker in the housing estate, an egg seller, and a bookbinder. One neighbor is a cosmetician, another repairs pantyhose. At No. 20, an attractive young woman sells her body to men. At No. 26 and No. 30, they sell black market butter. In winter, when the kerosene seller rings his bell, everyone gathers with metal jerry cans in hand around his horse-drawn cylindrical red tanker. In summer everyone gathers around the square blue cart of the iceman who wins the children's hearts with merry squirts of ice water. Those lucky enough to have a bathtub at home fill it on Thursdays and throw a carp in to make gefilte fish for Shabbat. And every summer evening the immigrants sit on their balconies to read *Maariv* or the Labor Party's *Davar* or the Hungarian-language *Uj Kelet*. At night the Russians drink vodka, the Poles play cards, the Czechs listen to classical music. From one year to the next, a neighborhood coalesces. Within less than a decade, a hodgepodge of devastated Jewish refugees who reached Bizaron in the hectic summer of 1949 becomes a stable community.

Political allegiance is mostly to Labor. When Minister of Labor Golda Meir comes for a visit, the housing estate greets her warmly. When Prime Minster David Ben Gurion gives a rousing election speech from the back of a truck parked on Victory Road, the housing estate is ecstatic. No wonder: for the Bizaron housing estate, Labor is not just a political party, it is a great omnipotent mother. Labor built the estate and assembled the refugees and gave them shelter and protection. The housing estate's medical clinic, social club, and sports facilities are all Labor-related. Most of the housing estate's men work in Labor-related offices and institutions. On the other side of Victory Road there is a housing estate whose middle-class Middle European residents vote for the Progressive Party. A half a mile away live Oriental Jews who worship Menachem Begin and vote for his Herut Party. A mile away is a Socialist Mapam housing estate. In bloc number 20, several Russian Communists live a life of debauchery. But at the heart of the Bizaron housing estate, Labor has a solid loyal majority. Even the state of mind is that of Labor: restrained nationalism, moderate socialism, pragmatism. Nobody gets too excited, nobody is too righteous, nobody insists on being absolutely just. They have seen it all. They believe in the hard work of laying down brick upon brick. But they also know that to get to the right place, one sometimes has to take a circuitous route.

There are a number of institutions in Bizaron: a cooperative minimarket, a medical clinic, a synagogue, a library, a sports field, a social club. But the most important of all is Habonim, the builders' school. The two-story school is very much the center of life and the melting pot of the estate. Here the sons and daughters of Europe's survivors study math, English, Hebrew, the Bible. But far more important, they become Israelis. They learn about the heroic pioneers who drained the marshes of the Harod Valley, about the wonders of orange growing, and about the remarkable victory in the War of Independence. They learn about the Jewish National Fund's forestry efforts, about the breakthroughs of Israeli science and the achievements of young Israeli industry. The Yiddish-speaking, Polish-speaking, Hungarian-speaking, and Czech-speaking adults of Bizaron see the Habonim school turn their offspring into Israelis.

In every immigrant society, as in every postwar society, the children are the crux. But in the Bizaron housing estate the children are everything. Like Leah and Zvi Brik, the thirty- and forty-year-old parents know they are the desert generation. Though they were saved from annihilation, they know that they will never reach a true haven. For them everything is temporary, fragile, and in doubt. For them life is waiting for the next catastrophe. But their children are something else. Like the Briks' son, their children, too, are arrows shot to the future. For even though the bow was scorched and deformed in the great fire, it can still shoot a future-bound arrow. This is why the fathers will take any job to support the young and the mothers will buy them butter on the black market. This is why the children are sent to whatever private lessons they choose. Because the children's education is the first priority: only what a person knows cannot be taken away from him. Everything in Bizaron is done in the name of the children, so that the children will be able to knock on the gates of a future closed to their parents.

The children get it and don't get it. Only Yaakov's father, Shmuel Gogol, comes to school once a year to say what the other parents don't say. On Holocaust and Heroism Remembrance Day, he tells the young students that from the age of seven he played the harmonica. In Auschwitz, too, he played the harmonica. The harmonica saved him. He was the harmonica player in the death orchestra that played music for those marching to work and those marching to death. All those years he played the harmonica with his eyes shut. Even now when he plays for the pupils of Habonim, he plays with his eyes shut. But the children would rather leave behind Gogol's heartbreaking stories and harmonica music. They want to leave their fathers' nightmares and their mothers' migraines behind. They want to play volleyball, basketball, soccer, go to the scouts and have parties. They want to believe in everything that 1957 Israel tells them to believe in. That we are strong now. That we are the very best. That we will not be taken like lambs to the slaughter. That we will be tall and strong; we will be pilots and paratroopers, engineers and scientists. We will overcome the Germans and the Arabs and the barren desert. We will overcome our weakness and deformed genes and shameful history. Here, in the Bizaron housing estate, we will overcome ourselves. We shall be the new race of Israeli triumph.

So in the housing estate there is a growing gap between one generation and the next. Inside the tiny flats, one cannot escape the anguish. Although catastrophe is repressed, it is present. Black-and-white photo-

graphs of the dead are illuminated by memorial candles. But outside
in the daylight there is great jubilation. When one walks between number 14 and number 16, one can hear the Fischer girl playing the piano
and the Spiegel girl playing the piano and the Belldegrun boy playing
the violin.

After they finish their lessons and chores, the children run to the
kiosk to buy popsicles and soda pop. And as dusk descends they gather
by the big tree on Victory Road to play tag and capture the flag. When
the holiday of Lag BaOmer approaches, the children's excitement
mounts. They collect kindling and branches and plywood for their bonfire. And when the day arrives, the entire housing estate assembles
around the enormous woodpile. The fire is lit. The flames grow taller
and taller. For the parents, the smell of something burning is almost
unbearable. But the children's happiness is as high as the flames. And
this year—after the 1956 victory—is the first year that the effigy of
Hitler is replaced by an effigy of Egypt's president, Gamal Abdel Nasser.
By now we have burned Hitler so many times that he's totally burned
out. So this year it is the nasty nose of the Arab tyrant that is ablaze,
his vicious smile consumed by flames. As we triumphed over the damn
Nazis, we shall triumph over the Arabs. For we are now part of a great
beginning. We are the living proof that Israel's new beginning is a great
success.

In the basement archives of Tel Aviv's City Hall I lean over the old thick
file of house number 14 of the Bizaron housing estate. It's a two-story
structure built in 1949 by the Histadrut's Shikun Ltd., the housing construction company for workers. The land was owned by the Jewish National Fund, and the plans were inspired by those of the working-class
housing projects of 1920s Vienna and 1930s Tel Aviv. Although No. 14
is a long row house, it is variegated in order to give each unit several
exposures and some privacy. In the plans, the 430 square meters of each
floor are divided into eight units, so that each one will have 53.2 square
meters. But in practice, because of the economic turmoil of 1949, the
Shikun Company built only two-thirds of the designated building area.
The drawings make a distinction between the 34 square meters of "the

existing area" of each unit and the remaining 19.2 square meters of "area for the future."

In December 1951, the engineer Dr. Eliezer Fischer submits a request to add to his apartment a bedroom and a bathroom as per the original plans. In May 1953, the bookkeeper Spiegel submits a similar request. In August 1953, Wolf Dovrovsky does the same, as do Zalman Weinstock in September 1955 and Arieh Mendkler in May 1956. One by one the immigrants make good. No. 14 is well built. The walls are made of hollow blocks, the ceilings of reinforced concrete, and the plaster is waterproofed. The northern exposure has nice tall windows; the southern exposure has square windows and rectangular balconies. The architecture is modern but not forbidding, functional but not cheap. It is apparent that a real effort has been made here to give the best accommodations possible to as many people as possible in hard times. Even after they are enlarged, all the apartments resemble one another. At the entrance is a small hall with a kitchenette to the left and a bathroom to the right. Beyond the hall are two square connecting rooms, one of which opens onto the balcony. Access to the front yard is through the kitchenette. During the 1950s, most dusty yards gradually turn into gardens, with plum trees, guavas, chrysanthemums, and rosebushes. By 1957, the sands on which the *shikun*'s long housing blocks were built in 1949 are covered with green vegetation.

The land surrounding the housing estate is dotted with orange groves. Some are Jewish orange groves that bear fruit; others are deserted Palestinian orange groves that are dying. Closer by, new housing estates pop up one after the other. New factories pop up, too. Sypholux manufactures domestic soda fountains, Amcor makes Israel's first refrigerators, Argaz assembles buses. A fenced-off plant of Israel's military industry manufactures who knows what. In 1957 Bizaron is still encircled by breathtaking fields of wildflowers: autumn crocuses, asphodels, bellflowers, and anemones. But they are about to disappear. A wave of development is replacing them with more and more housing estates populated by more and more new immigrants who are rapidly becoming new Israelis.

I leave the municipal archives and drive to Bizaron. A great deal has happened here over sixty years. The neighborhood has gone downhill and uphill and now it is being gentrified. Yet the structures of the housing estate are pretty much as they were. Nineteen long rows, eighteen pedestrian paths, a school still named Habonim.

I walk along the path that separates what was No. 14 from what was No. 16. Here the children of 1957 used to play dodgeball and hopscotch and Simon Says. Here they rolled hoops with sticks and sprayed water on one another, until from the balconies their mothers called them home for supper. The news bulletin would come on the radio, then popular Israeli music, classical music, cantorial singing. As I look across the path, I can almost imagine the Spiegels' neat living room, where Yehudit is playing the piano, and the living room of the Belldegruns, where Arie is struggling with the violin while his close friend Pinchas (Zukerman) masters it. Somewhere an accordion is playing, somewhere a heartbreaking harmonica. And while the Kovno ghetto survivor Abrasha Axelrod writes unforgiving poems in Yiddish, the Mengele twin Erno Spiegel is closing his account books. Dr. Fischer is drafting engineering plans for an overpass to be built in the desert, and plumber Zahlikovsky is playing cards with friends. The photographer Leon Teicher is developing photographs of his two beloved sons, one of whom will fall in one of Israel's future wars. As night descends, the bedroom lights and the balcony lights are dimmed one by one. The children's squeals are quieted. The forced Israeli gaiety and purposefulness of daylight hours disappears into the night. Carpets are being rolled up, armchairs moved aside, beds pulled out from living room sofas. As they finally lie down to sleep, the tenants of the Bizaron housing estate close their eyes. In their dreams—in their nightmares—they see their new neighborhood sinking into the sea.

And yet, walking along the path between what was No. 14 and what was No. 16, I realize that Bizaron is not a tragedy but a miracle. Israel's 1950s are not defined by misfortune but by a fit of human greatness. Against all odds, most of the Holocaust survivors of the housing estate make it. Against all odds, Ben Gurion's Israel pulls through. Ze'ev Sternhell will become a professor of political science. Aharon Appelfeld will become a great novelist. Aharon Barak will become one of the most respected jurists in the world. The children of Louise Aynachi will also do well. Arie Belldegrun will become an extremely successful doctor and investor in Los Angeles. Yehudit Fischer will become a professor of

Hebrew literature in Boston. The surviving Teicher boy, Shlomo, will become one of Israel's best dental surgeons. Yehudit Spiegel will become a psychologist and entrepreneur who, together with her husband, will launch a billion-dollar medical company. In the most astonishing way, Bizaron will have become a hub for Israel's future meritocratic elite. Many of its sons and daughters will conquer their professional worlds. The Israel into which I am born in late 1957 does not only overcome its horrific past, it launches a radiant future.

SEVEN

The Project, 1967

AT THE AGE OF SEVEN, I ALREADY SUSPECTED THERE WAS A SECRET. No one told me what it was or uttered the actual words. But because I was a curious child, I liked to listen to the grown-ups' conversations. And in the scientific community of Rehovot in the 1960s, those conversations revolved around mysterious if not downright sinister-sounding places like the Hill, Machon 4, and Hemed Gimmel. My father was a promising young chemist at the Weizmann Institute, and many of his colleagues, who assembled often in our living room, were among Israel's prominent scientists. They would often discuss what Israel (Dostrovsky) was working on, what Ernst (Bergmann) was up to, what Shalhevet (Freier) was absorbed in, and what Amos (de Shalit) was trying to do. And they would always circle back to the big and nameless thing happening in the Negev, the big, baffling thing that required my fathers' friends and the fathers of my friends to travel down there. In Rehovot itself there was an urgent sense of purpose. On the quiet, manicured lawns of the Weizmann Institute of Science there was a hushed air of anticipation. Although nothing was said, it was somehow evident that the physicists and chemists upon whose knees I was being raised were expected to save our lives.

My uncle, too, went down to the desert in the early 1960s. The neighborhood of square, concrete, flat-roofed villas on the outskirts of Beersheba where he lived with his family was built by the government on the edge of the desert. The engineers left their neat, dim, quiet homes every morning and boarded a gray bus that took them to the secret. In the afternoon the bus brought them home. Children like me knew not to ask what they were actually doing down there. But at the age of eight I understood that Gideon and Roberto and Mishka and Uncle Zeki and Yoskeh did more than just gather together on hot summer nights to sing folk songs and tell funny stories as they ruffled my hair and treated me to thick watermelon slices. I knew that beyond the villas and their well-tended gardens something huge was taking place. Something was happening in the desert that would change everything forever.

At the age of nine, I already knew the secret. One of the first books I pulled down from my father's shelves was *Brighter Than a Thousand Suns: A Personal History of the Atomic Scientists*, the story of the Manhattan Project. Another book I took an interest in was a collection of articles by Israeli academics and intellectuals who opposed the building of an Israeli atomic bomb. I knew to connect the two books, and I knew to connect them to the anticipation at the Weizmann Institute and the solemn mystery surrounding the villa neighborhood in the desert. I realized that I was probably growing up in an Israeli Manhattan Project, surrounded by people who were probably the Robert Oppenheimers, Edward Tellers, and Leslie Groveses of Israel. At the age of ten I already knew that the bespectacled engineers and diffident physicists around me were in their own way part of a mythic undertaking.

Half a century later, the secret is still a secret, but in reality, almost everything has been written about in the international media: Why Israel built Dimona, how Israel built Dimona, and what Israel does there. Officially, however, the nuclear reactor of Dimona is still shrouded in ambiguity. Israeli state policy does not allow Israelis to discuss Dimona publicly. I respect this policy and I obey it, and I cleared this chapter with the Israeli censor. And yet, even when wrestling with this haze of mystery, it is clear that Dimona is still very much at the center of Israel's story.

· · ·

According to nuclear experts such as Frank Barnaby, the Dimona complex is basically rectangular. Close to the entrance are the administrative offices, the classrooms, the canteen, and the library. To the south are Machon 4 (a treatment plant for the radioactive effluent from plutonium extraction), Machon 8 (where uranium is enriched by gas centrifuges), and Machon 9 (which houses a laser isotope enrichment facility). The central area lies beyond Machon 5 (where uranium fuel rods are coated with aluminum before insertion into the reactor). This central area is bisected by lawns and rows of palm trees that pass by Machon 3 (where uranium is produced from yellowcake) and Machon 2 (the main production facility where plutonium, lithium compounds, and beryllium are machined into components for nuclear weapons) and lead to Machon 1, the reactor itself, with its grand dome, 18 meters in diameter and 25 meters in height. The silver dome is the central commanding structure of Dimona. The hub. The core. The center of gravity of the Middle East.

In basic terms, it may be put as follows: In order to create and uphold a Jewish state in the Middle East, a protective umbrella had to be unfurled above the fledgling endeavor, a structure that would protect the Jews from the animosity they provoked when they entered the land. A bell jar had to be placed over them to shield them from the predators that lay in wait.

The first such bell jar was provided by the British. Only within the strong walls of the British Mandate could the plant be built without scrutiny. But even after the British left, Western hegemony in the Middle East provided the Jews with protection from the hostility and malevolence of the Arab-Muslim expanse in which they had elected to build their national home. But in the mid-1950s, Israel's leaders discovered that the protective umbrella of the West was slowly furling. The colonial era was coming to an end, Europe was in retreat, and Israel was left on its own in a hostile desert. At the same time, Arab nationalism was coalescing, being transformed by rapid modernization and swift military buildup.

Israel's leaders panicked. The basic conditions upon which the Zionist endeavor was founded, and within which the Zionist miracle occurred, no longer existed. Although the young state was flourishing, rapidly absorbing immigrants and tripling its population, it was now completely exposed.

By 1955, Prime Minister David Ben Gurion had made up his mind: the old protective umbrella of Western colonialism had to be replaced with a new one. Instead of relying upon the West's hegemony over the Middle East, an Israeli hegemony had to be established. In the summer of 1956, during many hours spent with his advisers, Ben Gurion honed the view that had begun to crystallize for him in 1949. Now he stated explicitly: Israel must go nuclear.

In 1956, only three nations possessed nuclear weapons: the United States, the USSR, and the United Kingdom. Even France would produce and assemble a nuclear bomb only four years later. In contrast to those wealthy countries, the Israel of 1956 was a fragile immigrant state of 1.8 million people not yet capable of manufacturing even transistor radios. The mere thought that this tiny, weak nation would succeed in obtaining nuclear capabilities seemed audacious, megalomaniacal, even unhinged. And yet the founder of the Jewish state was adamant: Israel must acquire a nuclear option. Ben Gurion believed that the Arab-Israeli conflict was deep and irresolvable. He worried that in the long run Israel's military supremacy would not hold. He felt the stress of bearing personal responsibility for his small nation. In closed-door meetings, he analyzed the strategic threats Israel faced and arrived at the conclusion that its ultimate security might very well rest on the existential insurance policy of nuclear deterrence.

Many senior cabinet members and politicians opposed him: Minister of Trade and Industry Pinchas Sapir, Foreign Minister Golda Meir, Minister of Education and Culture Zalman Aran, Leading Member of Parliament David Hacohen, and from time to time Finance Minister Levi Eshkol. So did many physicists (especially Amos de Shalit), senior army officers (chief among them Yitzhak Rabin), and many intellectuals (most prominently, Yeshayahu Leibowitz, Ephraim Auerbach, and Eliezer Livneh). But the debate was neither moral nor ethical. In the Israeli siege-republic of the 1950s and early 1960s, the memory of the Holocaust felt very close, as did the existential threat. Both of these factors underpinned the generally agreed-upon moral justification regarding the right to acquire a nuclear option. Those who opposed articulated realpolitik arguments: some feared economic bankruptcy, others feared diplomatic bankruptcy, and still others feared military bankruptcy; some warned that the nascent alliance with France would dissolve, while others warned against American anger and Soviet wrath. Still others pronounced the whole idea a pipe dream. There was no way a small nation, poor and only partially industrialized, could take upon itself a scientific-technological feat that most great nations had yet to attempt.

The comprehensive, methodical argument against the nuclear option was put forward by two renowned military strategists, Yigal Allon and Israel Galili. Both men were prominent territorial hawks who had now become nuclear doves. Their position was that the prime minister was consumed with historical pessimism regarding Israel's chance to survive in the Middle East and technological optimism regarding Israel's scientific ingenuity, while they were consumed with the exact opposite: historical optimism and technological pessimism. The Allon-Galili argument against the bomb was threefold: In the Middle East there was no possibility of fashioning a stable regime of mutual deterrence. And if no such regime existed, then Israel would be the party most exposed to the horror of a nuclear attack. Therefore, to guarantee its own security, Israel should not acquire a nuclear capability that would initiate a nuclear arms race in the Middle East. Because if such a race was launched in such a volatile region, it would endanger the very existence of the Jewish state.

Ben Gurion remained undeterred. In the summer of 1956, he sent his sorcerer's apprentice, Shimon Peres, to Paris to wield his wand. Improbably, the director general of the Defense Ministry got what he came for. He deftly manipulated the anti-Arab sentiment of the Suez era and the pro-Jewish sentiment of a decade after Vichy, and he appealed to the bruised patriotic ego over Algeria, the demise of colonialism, and the decline of Europe. In a very short time, the thirty-three-year-old graduate of the Ben Shemen Youth Village School—a student of the pacifist Siegfried Lehmann—pulled off one of the greatest strategic feats of the postwar years, persuading a major European power to give a minor Middle Eastern nation its own nuclear option. The option Peres received was all-inclusive, providing engineers, technicians, know-how, and training. According to international publications, it comprised a nuclear reactor, a facility for separating plutonium, and missile capabilities. Ben Gurion's vision, Peres's cunning, and the diligent work of a few other Israelis who joined Peres in Paris convinced France to place in Israel's hands the modern age's Prometheus' fire. For the first time in history, the Jews could have the ability to annihilate other peoples.

In his book *Israel and the Bomb*, Dr. Avner Cohen provides the following details: In September 1956, an initial understanding was agreed upon for the construction of a small model EL-3 reactor. On October 3, 1957, the dramatic agreement for the construction of a large G1 reactor and a secret plutonium separation plant was signed. In the beginning of 1958 a huge hole was dug in the Rotem Plateau, 14 kilometers southeast of Dimona, and work on the reactor began. In February 1959, twenty tons of heavy water were purchased from Norway. In the early 1960s, uranium was extracted from local phosphate rock as well as purchased clandestinely from America and South Africa. In April 1963, an agreement was signed with the French armament manufacturer Dassault for the purchase of MD-620 missiles. On December 26, 1963, the Dimona reactor went critical. In 1964, the underground plutonium separation plant was completed. At the end of 1965, plutonium was produced. In March 1965, the Jericho missile system was tested. By 1967, Israel had reached the capability to assemble its first nuclear device.

On an early summer evening, I park my car on a quiet side street of Tel Aviv's affluent suburb Ramat Aviv. I locate the apartment building, ring the intercom, and take the elevator to the eighth floor, where a tall, broad-shouldered man in his early eighties awaits me. His handshake is firm, his tone gruff. "Come in," he commands. "I've been waiting for your visit for a long time."

The furnishings in the living room are simple and homey: blond wood Scandinavian sofas and armchairs, a worn Persian rug, walls hung with watercolors and oil paintings—lively landscapes of Israeli orange groves painted by my host himself. A bottle of Chivas Regal and a bowl of salted almonds have been placed on the table. The television murmurs in the corner, talking heads discussing yet another snippet of news about the Iranian nuclear threat. "Bullshit, it's all bullshit," my host says. "The Iranians already have a bomb. A bomb is no big deal. If a country has the desire and the means, and minimal engineering capabilities, it will have a bomb. If you're determined to build a bomb, you'll build a bomb."

He should know. Avner Cohen claims that Israel indeed built its first atomic bomb in late 1966 and early 1967. My host was the director general of Dimona at that time. He was the man in charge. I look him over as he regards me. I know, he knows that I know, and I know that he knows that I know, but we do not say a word about it. My host pours whisky into two tumblers and raises his glass toward mine to wish us a productive evening. After decades of silence, he would like to say his piece while somehow still abiding by the official vow he has sworn to the State. He is willing to circle the secret, come very close, but not reveal it or his part in it. He asks me to omit his name as long as he is alive. But even the euphemisms he uses cannot obscure the great drama to which he bore witness, and in which he played a critical role.

He was born in Jerusalem in 1926. His first memories are bloody: during the Arab uprising of 1929, his father rescued wounded residents of the Old City, and when he returned home, the car seats were covered with blood, as were his suit and hands. In the 1930s his family moved to Rishon LeZion, where his father became a prosperous orange grower. Life in the agricultural colony was comfortable and happy. The orange grower's spoiled son had little time for school. He preferred playing sports and developed an impressive physique that complemented his technological curiosity and extraordinary daring. At the age of eleven, he was already driving his family's old Austin-Morris on the sands surrounding Rishon LeZion, and at the age of sixteen he won girls' hearts in his father's fancy new Buick. His adolescence did not have a memorable ideological dimension; it proceeded from game to game, from party to party, from girl to girl. Until, on a beautiful spring morning in 1943, his father was gunned down by an Arab while driving out to the family orange grove.

The murder of his father was a defining experience. It did not loosen its grip on him as he completed a chemical engineering degree at Haifa's Technion, or when he excelled in a Haganah company commanders course. During the War of Independence, the memory of his father's murder gave him the motivation and the cruel strength of an avenger. In December 1947, he received the command of a northern infantry corps platoon, and in January 1948 he defended isolated kibbutzim in the eastern Galilee. In April and May 1948, he led the conquest of Palestinian villages in the eastern Galilee, and in June and July he fought the Egyptian army in the south. In October 1948 he drove Palestinian villagers from their homes in the north. During ten months of fierce fighting, the twenty-two-year-old platoon commander saw hundreds of Arabs killed by his men and buried dozens of his fellow soldiers, many of them friends. The war toughened him and hardened his heart. It taught him that he was resourceful, capable, and bold. At the end of the war, the platoon commander felt that there was no such thing as mission impossible. There was nothing in the world that could not be conquered.

After the war he worked as an engineer, and in 1951, he was called upon by Israel Dostrovsky. Dostrovsky led a double life: a brilliant scientist at the Weizmann Institute of Science in Rehovot, he was also the commander of a secret Israeli Army unit, Hemed Gimmel. Dostrovsky appointed his new recruit as the operations officer of Hemed Gimmel. The engineer's first assignment was to conduct a mineral survey of the Negev to search for bitumen, phosphorus, and uranium. He remembers well the journey to the desert, especially the moment he broke open a desert rock with a geologist's hammer to find a fish-scale-like substance glowing green in the night. But the decisive moment occurred on his return from the desert. Back in Rehovot, he met with Dostrovsky, who took from the safe in his office a big metal lump covered in wax paper. The professor placed it in the hands of the excited young major and asked him if he knew what it was. "Like lead, but much heavier than lead," the young man answered. "Uranium, it must be uranium." Both men were silent, but they both understood, without saying it explicitly, what the purpose of Hemed Gimmel was and what its mission was: to create a new bell jar for the Jewish state.

On the table in the Ramat Aviv living room is a stack of international scientific journals alongside a copy of Avner Cohen's book. My host praises Cohen's book, and in this manner he signals that we both know what we are talking about. We will conduct our conversation under the shroud of opacity.

"There was no general plan," my host begins. "Professor Ernst

David Bergmann did his thing, and Israel Dostrovsky did his thing, and they both began to talk to the Norwegians and the French. I worked on uranium recovery from phosphate rock, Dostrovsky worked on heavy water, and the physicists studied nuclear science. But all of these activities were not coordinated, and they were not part of a consolidated work plan. They stemmed from the understanding of about a dozen people that this age was the nuclear age, and that Israel must be at its forefront; that if Israel fell behind the Arabs in the nuclear arms race, it would cease to exist. The Arabs were too many to defeat, and eventually they would be too strong to defeat. What happened in the Galilee villages in the spring of 1948 and in the fall of 1948 will not happen again. The clock was ticking. We were in a race against time. The citizens of this country didn't understand, but we understood. The army generals didn't get it, but we did. That's why we rose every morning at five and worked until well after sundown. That's why we read, studied, experimented, improvised, invented. Wherever a new capability appeared, we quickly harnessed it. We progressed step by step. And because it was the mid-1950s, and the spirit was that of the mid-1950s, no one asked where we were running to; everyone just kept running, running all the time. From the mid-1950s until the end of the 1960s, no one ever stopped running."

The marathon began in Rehovot, where Dostrovsky's team built the cumbersome Kleinschmidt apparatus that distilled heavy water in a unique process. The operation officer's team brought phosphate rock from the Negev and developed various methods to extract uranium from it in vats of solvent. The distillation of water enriched with heavy oxygen (O18) was an immediate success. It turned 1950s Israel into one of the leaders in the field. But the uranium extraction was slow and arduous. Years of hard work yielded only a few grams. But both processes forged an initial capability in the field of nuclear research. Both aroused international interest and allowed Israel to enter international partnerships. In the laboratories of the Weizmann Institute, amid the orange groves, Israel acquired its nuclear foothold.

The first nuclear ties between Israel and France were brokered by Ernst David Bergmann in the late 1940s. In late 1956, Bergmann signed a preliminary agreement with the French to build a nuclear reactor in Dimona. Shimon Peres forged the diplomatic alliance on nuclear matters and the French signed the binding agreements in 1957. But the two young men who nurtured and deepened the ties with the French, the undercover scientific attaché Shalhevet Freier and the operations officer of Hemed Gimmel, received few accolades. Working directly with the French Atomic Energy Commission (CEA), these two energetic men gained the trust of the French and fostered a scientific, technological, and strategic intimacy between Paris and Rehovot. In 1956 and 1957 the operations officer made frequent visits to Paris, hammering out an agreement with the French that required each side to keep the other fully apprised of its advancements. In 1957, my host moved to France in order to study the most critical stages of the nuclear process, and in 1958 he received access to France's holy of holies, its most advanced atomic facility. From that moment on, everything was open to him, everything revealed. After completing his military service, the young operations officer of Hemed Gimmel became the engineer in charge of the most sensitive and most secret part of the French-Israeli nuclear program.

In the winter when I was born, the action returned to Israel. Seven years after he went down to the Negev in a command car in search of uranium, the engineer again went down to the desert in a command car in search of the best location to build the French-Israeli reactor. The survey team included eight Frenchmen and two Israelis. The Israelis detested each other. The pedantic Colonel Manes Pratt, former Ordnance Corps commander and an engineer by profession, was in charge of building Israel's Los Alamos, while the brash and sometimes impetuous engineer was to be responsible for the most critical part of the future installation. But at this point in the plot, both Israeli men were minor characters. The decision makers were the French. And when the command car convoy reached triangulation point 472 on the Rotem Plateau, the French concurred that this was the spot. The Israeli nuclear reactor would be built fourteen kilometers southeast of the town of Dimona.

According to the official agreements, the reactor was to have been a modest affair of the type EL-102, with an output of only 24 megawatts. But according to Avner Cohen, on the ground, the reactor that the

French company Saint-Gobain built for Israel resembled the G1 reactor it had built in Marcoule for the French Republic. According to international publications, the output of the upgraded reactor in the desert was at least 24 megawatts. And according to those same publications, it included a secret plutonium separation plant that was not mentioned in the official agreements. I have reason to believe that during the three years he spent in France, the engineer probably took part in the planning of the most essential unit of the Israeli reactor. And during his frequent visits to Israel, he surely observed its construction. He may well have been the one who solved the severe problems that arose from the proximity of the separation plant to the reactor itself. Still, the engineer has no doubts about the matter: however significant his or Manes Pratt's contributions might be, Dimona was France's grand gesture toward Israel. It was the parting gift of a declining colonial power to the young frontier nation that the West erected in the East and was now leaving on its own.

Because of his intense rivalry with Manes Pratt, the engineer was not present in Dimona when the construction of the reactor was completed in 1961. And he was not present at the Negev Nuclear Research Center, as Dimona was officially known, when the French departed in 1962. Nor was he present when the reactor was activated and went critical at the end of 1963. In fact, during the first years of Dimona, the engineer watched from afar. But when he was appointed to the helm of Dimona in 1965, he discovered to his surprise that his most important work would be political.

By 1960, the United States knew that France was building a nuclear reactor for Israel on the Rotem Plateau. President John F. Kennedy was committed to the nonproliferation of nuclear weapons and was staunchly opposed to the production of nuclear weapons in Dimona. According to an agreement signed between Israel and the United States, American inspection teams were allowed to visit the desert reactor once a year, beginning in 1962. On their first four visits, the Americans discovered nothing. But with every visit, Israel's posturing became less and less convincing to the Americans. By 1965, according to Avner Cohen and others, Israel faced its most dramatic juncture.

The engineer does not tell me so explicitly, but it is clear: before he turned forty, the role of the son of an orange grower from Rishon LeZion was to deal with the Americans. His mission was to win them over—pleasantly, calculatingly, elegantly—so that Dimona could continue to function. And in order to achieve this goal, according to non-Israeli sources, simulated control rooms were built, the entrances to underground levels were bricked up, and pigeon droppings were scattered around some buildings in which the forbidden installations were housed to give the impression that they were not in use.

The Saturdays on which the Americans visited Dimona were tense and exhausting. The national leadership followed from afar every moment of conversation between the engineer and the inquisitive inspectors. Every moment was critical, any mistake could be fatal. But the engineer's self-confidence and charm worked wonders. The March 1966 inspection passed without incident, as did the following inspection in April 1967.

But there was one last hurdle for the Israelis to overcome. Immediately after he was appointed president in 1958, Charles de Gaulle made it clear that he adamantly opposed the nuclear cooperation between Israel and France. In 1960, he ordered its cessation. But pro-Israeli French ministers allowed the completion of the construction work in Dimona in 1961 and 1962. Even in 1965, when de Gaulle became hostile toward Israel, the French-Israeli nuclear cooperation continued. As I now learn, without French raw materials and French technology, Dimona could not have functioned throughout the 1960s. Senior members of the French Atomic Energy Commission understood this. They felt obligated toward Israel because of the young state's scientific contributions, because of the Holocaust, and because of the intelligence it provided on Algeria. Even those among them who were not Jewish believed that Israel represented a historical act of justice and regarded it as a Western bulwark in the East. The engineer's dramatic task was to maintain the alliance with the professional leaders of the French nuclear project who defied their president in order to make Dimona possible.

I want to question the engineer about the final stage of the process, but I know he will not answer my questions about production directly. After so many years of adamant silence, he will not yield easily now. So

I ask for another whisky. Outside the living room windows, evening descends.

In order to ease his way forward, I place in front of my host an almost inscrutable entry from the journal of Munia Mardor, the CEO of RAFAEL Advanced Defense Systems. It was published in his memoir, but its significance was only noticed some years after publication by Aluf Benn of *Haaretz* and was later quoted by Avner Cohen in his book. It is dated May 28, 1967:

> I went to the assembly hall. . . . The teams were assembling the weapon system, the development and production of which was completed prior to the war. The time was after midnight. Engineers and technicians, mostly young, were concentrating on their work. Their facial expressions were solemn, pensive, as if they fully recognized the enormous, perhaps fateful value of the system they brought to operational alert. It was evident that the people of the project were under tension, the utmost tension, physical and spiritual alike.

The engineer laughs. He knows what Mardor wrote, but he dismisses it out of hand. He won't speak about Dimona's decisive moment, but he will say something about Dimona's spirit. "We never trembled with excitement, we never opened bottles of champagne. We were physicists and chemists and engineers who did what we were supposed to do, without dramatic flourishes or lofty words."

Yet the race was not finished. On May 17, 1967, shortly before the Six Day War, two Egyptian MiG 21 jets made a brief high-altitude reconnaissance flight over Dimona, causing alarm in Jerusalem. The engineer had to take extraordinary steps to protect his unique project. But in the year following the war, the engineer faced his greatest technological challenge—and opportunity. Post-1967 Israel felt a sense of urgency because of the extinction fears that the nation experienced in the weeks prior to the war. But because of the decisive victory, post-1967 Israel also had a new sense of omnipotence. The outcome of this mixture of fear and omnipotence was technological chutzpah. According to Avner

Cohen, during the engineer's third year as director general of Dimona, the facility tripled its production capability.

After this success, and another, and a third, the engineer's audacity knew no limits. Under his command, Israeli scientists, engineers, and technicians developed remarkable know-how. They turned Israel into a self-sufficient nuclear nation. No longer a French protégé or an American dependent, the Jewish state was now perceived worldwide as an advanced nuclear power.

And then there was the final stage of the process. The American inspectors' visits of 1968 and 1969 passed without a hitch. Together with the physicist Amos de Shalit, the engineer would exhaust the inspectors and lead them astray and yet again manage to obscure the secrets of Dimona. But after the eighteen-hour inspection of July 12, 1969, Golda Meir changed tack and undertook a forthright dialogue with the Americans. Under the influence of Henry Kissinger, the United States also changed tack. In late September 1969, in a meeting between the newly elected U.S. president, Richard Nixon, and Prime Minister Meir, the United States and Israel reached an unwritten understanding concerning Dimona. The reactor on the Rotem Plateau had become a fait accompli, and the international community accepted and adopted Israel's policy of opacity regarding its existence.

What interests me most is the event the engineer says occurred in December 1966. This was the moment in which, according to international publications, Israel assembled the first metallic sphere that could take out a city. Were there really no goose bumps? Did the hands not tremble? Was there really no sense that we had eaten the forbidden fruit? Did the engineer feel no fear or trepidation at all?

My host does not confirm or deny the relevant international publications. "But let's say they are accurate," he says, smiling. "What's all the fuss? Isn't it clear that Israel must defend itself? Isn't it clear that Israel must deter its enemies? Someone had to do that job. Someone had to be at the Weizmann Institute in 1955 and in France in 1960 and in Dimona in 1966."

It had to be done, so he did it. And he did what he did as best he could, helming one of Israel's first high-tech enterprises. And this enterprise demonstrated Israel's acumen and cunning and wherewithal, surpassing all expectations and guaranteeing Israel a half century of life.

As I glance up from my notes to the beaming face of the engineer, my first thought is of his murdered father. Though the murder occurred four years after the end of the Arab Revolt, the shooting in the orange grove in the spring of 1943 affected the engineer in the same way that the wave of violence of 1936–39 affected his generation. The murder turned him into a tough, formidable fighter bent on revenge. The spoiled and intellectually indifferent adolescent became a fearless soldier, free of inhibitions. He fought as commander of a Golani infantry platoon, as the operations officer of Hemed Gimmel, as an engineer in France, and as the director of Dimona. He invested his inner strength and his steely determination in the Jews' national struggle for their land and against the Arabs. The obligation to guarantee the existence of Israel swept aside all other concerns. At every juncture the engineer had only one mission: To make sure the Jews would not die. To make sure that no enemy would rise up from the bush and fell them one fine spring morning.

My second thought is about the Arab villages the engineer destroyed in 1948. Even if he does not say so, it is clear that a straight line leads from those villages to Dimona. The expulsion of 1948 necessitated Dimona. Because of those dead villages it was clear that the Palestinians would always pursue us, that they would always want to flatten our own villages. And so it was necessary to create a shield between us and them, and the engineer took it upon himself to build that shield. We would not allow the Palestinian tragedy to jeopardize the monumental enterprise designed to end our own tragedy.

My third thought is about the engineer himself. The more I listen to him, the more I understand that he cannot delve any deeper. He does not possess Ben Gurion's historical acuity, Amos de Shalit's tragic insight, or Dostrovsky's dialectical shrewdness. He truly does not comprehend the complexity of his actions, the problematic aspects of his deeds. He has no perception of the enormity and the horror of his accomplishments. He is possessed by a strong national imperative, an iron will, an impressive propensity for action. But he does not have the ability to see his life's work in perspective. His ability to *do* is derived from his ability not to see the implications of his deeds.

My host looks at me quizzically, as if trying to read my thoughts. I answer his silent questions candidly. I tell him that his accomplishments are almost incomprehensible in scope. In the mid-1960s, Israel was a nation of 2.5 million people that nevertheless succeeded in acquiring for itself a capability that Germany, Italy, and Japan still do not have. Despite its small size and the difficult circumstances in which it existed, it was perceived as one of the six leading powers of the world. And it did not stop there. Immediately after crossing the threshold, according to international publications, it built an arsenal of dozens and dozens of nuclear warheads: A-bombs and H-bombs, low yield and high yield, nuclear artillery shells and nuclear mines. If even a fraction of what has been written over the years is true, I tell him, then we're talking about a stupefying success. According to non-Israeli nuclear experts, even during the early years, when the engineer was in charge of Dimona, the facility in the desert succeeded in producing its wares not only with French separation technology but with an Israeli method. Those experts claim that with proven imported technology and with home-grown, novel technology, the scientific installation produced what no one imagined it could produce: an astonishing capability of mass destruction.

The engineer smiles. He neither confirms nor denies.

But the technological achievement is only part of the story, I say. No less astounding than Israel's ability to build a bomb was Israel's decision to act as if it did not have a bomb. In the beginning there were two schools of thought: those who believed in the bomb absolutely (like Moshe Dayan and Shimon Peres), who thought that national security could be based on the bomb, and those who opposed it absolutely (like Allon and Galili), who believed the bomb would ultimately endanger national security. But after the security seminar Ben Gurion conducted at a retreat on the shore of the Sea of Galilee in 1962, a synthesis of these two approaches emerged: a doctrine according to which Israel would be a nuclear power but would act is if it were not. This way it would not goad the Arabs or accelerate the nuclearization of the Middle East; it would not adopt a reckless and immoral security strategy. Concerning anything and everything nuclear, Israel would be much, much more cautious than the United States and NATO. Concerning anything and everything nuclear, Israel would be the responsible adult of the international community. It would well understand the formidable nature of the nuclear demon and would keep it locked in the basement.

The engineer smiles with what seems to be appreciation of this analysis.

I go on. There is a third achievement that is just as important, I tell him. The Dimona decade (1957–67) is also the first decade of Israeli normalcy. It is not only physicists and nuclear engineers who travel to Paris in those years. Painters and sculptors study at the École des Beaux-Arts, writers and poets frequent Latin Quarter cafés. Returning to Israel, they bring with them Sartre, Camus, Brassens, Prévert, and a new individualistic spirit. So do their colleagues who travel to New York and London. Some are influenced by W. H. Auden, some by Philip Larkin, others by Andy Warhol. Tel Aviv becomes a city of cultural and artistic fervor in which young Israeli-born artists and writers rebel against old-guard Zionist edicts. In Kibbutz Hulda, young Amos Oz writes his first groundbreaking short stories. In Jerusalem, A. B. Yehoshua writes modernist novels expressing the voice of a new generation. While a French nuclear reactor is built in the Negev, Israel becomes a modern Western nation, in which "I" replaces "We." There is a remarkable link between these two processes: Dimona is not only an expression of modernity and individuality but a facilitator of modernity and individuality. Under its new bell jar, the new Israelis can be more relaxed and less mobilized. They can be far more liberal and loose than they were before, and they can actually pursue personal happiness. Dimona enables the inhabitants of the Jewish national home to live relatively sane and full lives that are not fundamentally different from those of Western Europeans.

For almost half a century, I say to my host, the three achievements were valid. The bell jar solution worked. Dimona was astounding in its existence and in its opacity, and in the quasi-normalcy it fostered. Dimona symbolized the best of Israel of the 1960s: the vision, imagination, soberness, daring, tenacity, power, restraint, and resolve. A stern rule of rationality. A security-mindedness that was not imperialistic. A patriotism that was not chauvinistic. A unique combination of diplomatic ingenuity and intelligence sophistication. And a modicum of modesty. A matter-of-factness. A concise understanding of reality and a valiant effort to manage this reality. An attempt to find a rational solution to an insane situation. Dimona gave Israel half a century of relative security and gave the Middle East forty-six years of relative stability. Because of the regional conflagrations that erupted periodically during this period, Israelis did not consider the much greater fires that could have broken out. Dimona prevented total wars. It brought about peace agreements. But after forty-six years, the question remained: Was it right? And what would happen when the Arabs possessed a demon of their own? Didn't the engineer and his colleagues open the gates of a future hell?

The engineer likes my analysis but dislikes my questions. He rises from his armchair and says he would like to show me something. He walks slowly to the next room and returns with an oblong album in his hands. The front cover is made of a thin sheet of copper, hammered with the likeness of a dome amid palm trees in the desert.

The photographs in the album are almost all of the dome. The construction of the dome, 1960. The completion of the dome, 1961. Prime Minister Ben Gurion in front of the dome, 1963. Prime Minister Eshkol in front of the dome, 1965. Prime Minister Meir in front of the dome, 1970. Defense Minister Dayan in front of the dome, 1972. And the small group of nuclear engineers who led Ben Gurion, Eshkol, Meir, and Dayan on their tours of the dome. I see the exultant expression on Dayan's face, the solemn expression on Meir's face.

I recognize the faces of many of the engineers, who are in their late thirties and early forties. I remember them dancing at Independence Day parties and playing with us children in the sand on summer holidays at the beach. I remember them telling jokes and performing magic tricks for the ten-year-olds we were. And here they are showing Golda Meir and Moshe Dayan the secret. Here they are displaying the quiet resolve of the 1948 generation. They are neither triumphant nor anxious, neither prideful nor fearful. But the expressions on their faces and the way they hold themselves seem to say: It had to be done, and so we did it. It was not for us to ask why.

In many of the photos, the engineer is in the lead. Brisk and determined, he walks ahead, his bald pate shining above thick horn-rimmed glasses and thick lips. He exudes confidence and conviction. He appears proud of the Citroën D3 in which he meets the dignitaries at the helipad and in which he takes them on a tour of his desert kingdom. But the photographs betray nothing of the secret itself; even in this secret album, the secret is kept. Instead I see the heavy trucks of the Solel Boneh building company in the dust of the desert construction site, the emerging streamlined structures of sixties modernism, the palm trees and casuarinas. I see new lawns, bougainvillea plantings. And a large silver dome like a cathedral for a tragic modern age.

And yet, one of the photographs sends a shiver up my spine. It is a photograph of an empty room. Under the dome everything works without human intervention. Everything takes place in silence. If the international publications are correct, in this silence are produced a few dozen grams of enriched uranium every day, and a few kilograms of plutonium every year. If these publications are right, the quiet and matter-of-fact Israelis of my childhood processed the plutonium and fashioned it into black metal buttons. Are these black metal buttons what Golda Meir sees as she faces the camera, terror in her eyes?

There is only one secret the engineer is willing to divulge as he closes the oblong album. In the beginning, he tells me, Golda didn't much like him, and she didn't much like the facility he was in charge of. But gradually she grew to like him and began to take a greater interest in the facility. She called it *varenye*. *Varenye*, the jar of fruit preserves that Eastern European Jews kept in the cupboard for times of trouble, so if a pogrom broke out they would have something to feed their families until the fury passed. When the engineer would enter her office to report the goings-on in Dimona, the prime minister would ask, "Nu, what's new with *varenye*?"

In October 1973, it looked as if Golda Meir's Israel might be in need of its *varenye*. Israel was forced to consider its Dimona capabilities, and it decided to make threatening use of them. But even then, Meir was very careful. She acted responsibly and sensibly. According to non-Israeli sources, Israel revealed its nuclear missiles for a brief moment, for Russian and American satellites to photograph, but never seriously considered using them. Immediately after the danger passed, Dimona disappeared again. But the trauma remained. The Yom Kippur War proved unequivocally that Dimona was Israel's unseen anchor, an inseparable part of its existence. Without Dimona, Israel was like a lone tamarisk in the desert.

But the historical respite that Dimona gave Israel is nearing an end. Israel's nuclear hegemony in the Middle East is probably coming to a close. Sooner or later, the Israeli monopoly will be broken. First one hostile state will go nuclear, then a second hostile state, then a third. In the first half of the twenty-first century, the Middle East is bound to be nuclearized. The world's first multirival nuclear arena might emerge in the world's most unstable region.

I describe my concerns to my host. At this very moment, Iranian engineers are doing exactly what you did in the 1950s, 1960s, and 1970s, I say to him. At this very moment all kinds of mini-Dimonas are being built in Natanz and Parchin. Nuclear scientists are being sent abroad to learn everything they can from the West. Intelligence agents are stealing what they can from both East and West. The Iranians are now running the marathon you ran from 1951 to 1967. And they are not alone. Egypt, Saudi Arabia, Turkey, and Algeria have all expressed nuclear interest, especially if Iran succeeds. They all believe that if we have a right to our Dimona, they have a right to theirs. And when other Middle Eastern nations exercise their rights, our Dimona will turn from a blessing into a curse. We will revisit Allon's and Galili's warnings and discover that they were right. Half a century later we will revisit the essays of the intellectuals I read in my father's library and discover how prescient they were. The thing that allowed Israel to flourish from 1967 into the second decade of the new millennium will become the biggest threat facing Israel. It might turn the lives of Israelis into a nightmare.

The engineer does not have an argument to refute mine. Quite the opposite. He can definitely foresee a Middle East glowing in radioactive green. He doesn't mince words. Disparaging the Arabs in the most politically incorrect terms possible, he concludes that they won't behave the way we behaved. They won't act responsibly. If they acquire the capability, they'll use it. Right here, in the skies over Tel Aviv. As far as the engineer is concerned, there is only one answer: a preemptive strike. He who comes to kill you, rise up and kill him first. Even though he believes they already have a bomb, strike them nonetheless. Strike them with everything we've got. Be proactive now, as he and his colleagues were proactive then. "We cannot sit idly," he bellows. "We cannot wait until one fine spring day a white mushroom cloud rises over what is left of our homes."

I show the engineer parts of an article I wrote in the fall of 1999, when *Haaretz* newspaper hired a Defender jeep to take me to the desert to circle the secret installation in the Negev.

> From the beginning Israel well understood the dangers inherent in Dimona. It built Dimona but decided not to make irresponsible use of it. It did not use the unconventional advantage of Dimona in order to gain the upper hand in conventional diplomatic gamesmanship, conventional political gamesmanship, or conventional military gamesmanship. It did not incorporate Dimona into its day-to-day security strategy, did not base its military assumptions on it, and did not make political capital of it. It did not calm the Israeli public with it and did not weaken the army's readiness with it. It really kept it only as an option, as an alternative only to be thought of for the worst possible calamity. As an ultramodern answer to the fundamental, primeval anxiety of Israeli existence.
>
> Seemingly, opacity is a joke. An agreed-upon convention. Something that everyone knows but of which no one speaks publicly. But in truth opacity is genius. There is something profoundly wise about Israel's desire not to know about Dimona, to see it only in the grainy photographs taken from a very great distance with a telephoto lens. To hear news of Dimona only from foreign sources and international publications. Alongside the decision that Dimona was essential, there developed in Israel an understanding that Dimona is impossible. And in order to reduce to a minimum the possibility that any use might one day be made of it, Israel understood that it could in no way rely on Dimona. Life should be lived as if Dimona does not exist.
>
> But Dimona is here. And when the dusty Defender climbs the hill

recommended for viewing the secret and the morning fog lifts, you can suddenly see what you see in satellite photos: how the concrete and asphalt and palm trees of Dimona were laid and planted in all of this desert. How the Negev Nuclear Research Center was laid in this vast desert like a tiny square of well-organized Western outpost. Like an isolated settlement of Israeli modernism encircled by electric fences.

I step out of the jeep and look around me at all that surrounds Dimona—the open maw of the Little Crater, the steep descent to Sodom—and think about the people who built it. Mostly, they were not comfortable with words, feelings, or insights. They were the physicists and chemists and engineers of the Jewish generation of the mid-twentieth century. They labored under the intense impression of what had happened to the Jews in the first half of the twentieth century. And so when the State of Israel reached an impasse and told them to break that impasse, they broke it. They built the reactor that in more ways than one is the core of the Zionist revolution.

They did this without thinking too much. Without slogans or clichés or stray thoughts. They did it with the certitude of good engineers pulled by the great magnet of national commitment. And a duty to serve, for better or for worse. No questions, no qualms. Just action.

And now when the sun rises high above the mountains of Jordan, when the desert air begins to warm and the silver dome shines in the distance, I think about its place in our lives. Because in the most basic sense, it is our real taboo. Our common secret-not-secret. It is the real thing, scientific and concrete, that embodies the root of our existence here. And the unique predicament of our existence here. That's why we prefer to avert our gaze from Dimona. That's why we prefer not to know much about it. That's why we prefer to know that it is there, but not what it is. That's why we chose to ignore the tragedy enmeshed in Israel's great secret.

The engineer places the article on the table in front of him, removes his glasses, and tells me affectionately that I think too much. I think of the things that he would rather not think about. This is how he and his generation were raised. Make the best of every moment so that tomorrow will be better than today and the day after tomorrow will be better than tomorrow. "If everyone spent as much time thinking as you do," he tells me, "they would never act. If everyone had spent as much time thinking, these thoughts would have paralyzed them and kept them from building Dimona."

"But you invited me," I tell the engineer. "You wanted to talk. You thought it was important to present things in the right context. You thought it important that what you did would not be forgotten."

The engineer fixes me with his piercing gaze. "I know my days are numbered," he says. "Another month, another six months, another year. In a certain sense I am the last of my generation. Of those who were there in the beginning, the doers, I am truly the last. And that's why I wanted to place in your hands a certain understanding. Not knowledge, but understanding. Through you, I wanted to ensure that your generation will know what my generation did. We never talked. We bit our lips. But it is unacceptable to me that because we didn't talk, our part will be forgotten. That's why, after a long deliberation, I invited you over this evening. That's why I spoke to you as I did. I have never spoken like this before. This is my legacy."

The engineer is tired. We drink another whisky, the last one for the evening. In the background Daniel Barenboim plays the Kreutzer Sonata. "What a genius," the engineer says. "A self-hating Israeli, but still a genius. Unbelievable how many geniuses this country has spawned. Unbelievable what music and literature and poetry this country has created. Here, on the edge of the desert, in the line of death, we have built a nation of talent and joy and endless creativity."

The engineer asks me about the book I am writing. Because he opened his heart to me, I open my heart to him. I tell him about the valley, the orange grove, Masada, Lydda, the housing estate. I tell him Dimona was the inevitable outcome of the valley, the orange grove, Masada, Lydda, and the housing estate. And I dare say to him that there is a tragedy here. We brought not only water to the Negev but heavy water. We brought not only agricultural modernity to the land but nuclear modernity. Because between the Holocaust and revival, between horror and hope, between life and death—we did the colossal deed of Dimona. And to this day it is still impossible to know if this deed is a blessing for generations to come or a malignant curse.

Perhaps it is no coincidence that we are speaking now, I say to my host. You are a doer, a man of action, whereas I am an interpreter of actions. You are a builder, and I try to fathom the meaning of your buildings. You are experience and I am consciousness. And you need consciousness. Even your neighbors don't know what they owe you. All around you is a hedonistic, pleasure-seeking Tel Aviv that has forgotten what it owes you. And you see how the wheels of history are starting to spin in reverse. There are the Bushehr reactor and the Natanz centrifuges in Iran. For the first time in your life, you're not thinking only as an engineer, in terms of problems and solutions. You, too, are now consciousness. You see context. And the context fills you with pride, but it also fills you with dread. You realize what you've done, and it is too big for you. Too big for any human being."

The engineer has had enough. It's late, and he is tired. He promises to think about what I've said. He rises from the armchair and leads me past the watercolors and the oil paintings of the orange groves of his childhood. When he takes me to the door, he suddenly pats me tenderly on the shoulder and tells me that this evening he has said things that he hadn't imagined he would say, revisited places he never thought he would revisit. And he makes me promise that I'll treat his radioactive material with care. That I'll do him justice, and I'll do Dimona justice, and I'll do the State of Israel the justice it deserves.

A month later, the engineer died.

EIGHT

Settlement, 1975

ONE CANNOT UNDERSTAND THE SETTLEMENTS WITHOUT UNDERSTAND-ing the Six Day War. In May 1967 the Egyptian army entered the Sinai desert and blockaded the Straits of Tiran, directly threatening the State of Israel. The international community failed to respond, and many in the Jewish state panicked. They feared a Pan-Arab invasion that would crush Israel. But when Israel launched a preemptive strike on June 5, 1967, it had the upper hand. Within three hours the Israel Defense Forces destroyed the air forces of four Arab states. Within six days it conquered the Sinai desert, the West Bank, and the Golan Heights. The Arab armies were overwhelmed and Arab states were humiliated as tiny Israel tripled its size and became a dominant regional power. Nineteen years after it was founded, the Israeli republic had become an empire. Nineteen hundred years after the destruction of the Second Temple, Jews were again the masters of Jerusalem's Temple Mount on which the ancient temples once stood.

One also cannot understand the settlements without understanding the Yom Kippur War. On October 6, 1973, when the nation was fasting to observe the high holiday of Yom Kippur, the Egyptian army caught Israel by surprise. It crossed the Suez Canal and captured the Bar Lev fortification line, which was built to defend Israel's southern flank. Simultaneously the Syrian army crossed the northern border, crushed Israeli defenses, and occupied most of the Golan Heights. Within days thousands of Israeli soldiers were killed, wounded, or captured. The air force lost a third of its jets. At times, it seemed Israel was about to break; Defense Minister Moshe Dayan, shaken to his core, spoke in apocalyptic terms about the imminent destruction of the Third Temple. Only after ten days of bloody fighting did Israel seize the initiative. It struck the invading armored divisions, crossed the Suez Canal, and threatened the Egyptian capital, Cairo, while simultaneously closing in on the Syrian capital, Damascus. But the belated military accomplishments did not dispel the trauma of near defeat. The war was perceived as a grand failure. Faith in Israel's leadership and army was fractured. So was Israeli self-confidence. For the first time in its history, Zionism was not a process of expansion but of retreat.

The settlements were a direct response to these two wars. The swift turn of events in 1967—from fear of annihilation to resounding triumph—sideswiped the rigorous self-discipline that had held Zionism together for seventy years. The Israeli nation was drunk with victory, filled with euphoria, hubris, and messianic delusions of grandeur. Six years later, the almost instantaneous shift from an imperial state of mind to cowering despondency was followed by a deep crisis of leadership, values, and identity. The nation was filled with despair, self-doubt, and existential fear. Let down by Israel, many sought comfort in Judaism. The two diametrically opposed war experiences, which occurred within six years of each other, threw the Israeli psyche out of balance. The incredible contrast between them gave birth to the settlement.

In 1980, when I was a twenty-three-year-old student, I first came to realize that the settlements were a calamity in the making. When I was twenty-five, I wrote a pamphlet for the Peace Now movement that described the settlement project as folly. It was the first text I ever published, and it assumed that if the number of Jewish Israelis to settle in the West Bank were to quintuple from about 20,000 to 100,000, Israel would be lost. Today there are nearly 400,000 Jewish-Israeli settlers in the West Bank. My dire warnings—as a student, as a peace activist, and as a journalist—were in vain. The grand and noble campaigns of the Israeli peace movement and the international community to stop the expansion of the settlements failed. The nightmare we envisioned turned into reality.

That is why some thirty years later, I am driving to Ofra—the mother of all settlements—not to fight it, but to understand it. To understand how the settlements turned from rightist fantasy to historical fact. To understand what the forces were that impelled late-twentieth-century Israel to erect a futile, anachronistic colonialist project. To understand how Ofra came to be.

On a cool winter day I drive east from Tel Aviv to Ariel on the highway, crossing the green line and cutting across Samaria, the northern West Bank. Along this road, twenty small settlements and one settlers' town were planted. Then I drive south, from Ariel to Eli, and from Eli to Ofra. Along this road, which follows the water divide line of the Shomron Mountain range, are another twenty or so settlements, situated amid Palestinian villages. The jagged precipices of the mountainous landscape are as stunning as the demographic reality is appalling. Under December's crystal clear skies, it seems that the entanglement created by the West Bank settlements cannot be undone. Occupation seems irreversible. The most beautiful region of the biblical land of Israel is now the most distressing region occupied by modern Israel. It is sublime and depressing here, majestic and sad. Perhaps even hopeless.

A day earlier, I had met with Yoel Bin Nun, one of the founders of the Gush Emunim settlers' movement, and of Ofra, in his home at the southern West Bank settlement of Alon Shvut. On a cold, wet night, as the wind howled outside, I asked him how he had come to found the settlers' movement. What were the forces that brought Israel to build settlements in the territories it occupied in June 1967?

Bin Nun's answer was his life story, which begins with the arrival of his mother in Palestine on one of the last ships to leave Europe in the summer of 1939, on the eve of World War II. Growing up in the late 1950s in Haifa, he received an enlightened religious education and was a member of a moderate national religious youth movement. In the mid-1960s he studied in the restrained and reserved atmosphere of the elitist Mercaz HaRav yeshiva in Jerusalem. And then, in the spring of 1967, he experienced a defining moment. Three weeks before the Six Day War, Rabbi Ziyehuda HaCohen Kook assembled his students to share with them a yearning he had secreted in his heart for two decades. "Where is our Nablus?" the elderly founder of the yeshiva cried out, as if experiencing a divine revelation right there and then. "Where is our Hebron? Where is our Jericho? Where is our Kingdom of Israel? Where is the House of God?" A storm was brewing outside the tall windows as an incensed Bin Nun paced the room.

When war broke out in early June, Bin Nun fought in the alleys of east Jerusalem. Twenty-two days after hearing Rabbi Kook's prophetic fulminations he found himself on the Temple Mount, the rabbi's cries echoing in his ears. He told me that he felt as if the skies had opened and touched the earth. "All of a sudden," he said, "the land was calling to us, beckoning us. The land filled our soul." It was as if the Bible were suddenly alive. A historic event of biblical magnitude had occurred: the State of Israel had returned the people of Israel to the Land of Israel.

As Bin Nun spoke to me his eyes were ablaze. He stood up, he sat down, he walked back and forth in his living room tugging at his beard. He told me about the first gathering of hundreds of rabbis and yeshiva students in Jerusalem two months after the war: "Everyone there was convinced that this land was our land and we would never leave. The germ of the Gush Emunim settlers' movement was formed on that day. True, it did not yet have a name, or a platform. But in the summer of 1967 it was already clear that the national religious community, who up until the Six Day War did not dare covet Greater Israel and did not swear by Greater Israel, was now completely devoted to Greater Israel." Religious Zionism was determined to settle Judea and Samaria and make them an integral part of the sovereign State of Israel.

Yet not much happened between the Six Day War and the Yom Kippur War. Yes, Gush Etzion, to the south of Jerusalem, was rebuilt after being abandoned and destroyed in 1948; in Hebron a new Jewish community was established, forty years after the massacre of 1929. But the overall number of settlers in the West Bank was less than three thousand, and not one of them lived in Samaria. The Labor government did not allow the expansionist yearning of the national religious movement to be fulfilled. Yet the Yom Kippur War weakened the Labor government. The postwar trauma and bewilderment allowed the messianic impulse that already existed to become a determined and aggressive political force. The dam that had kept at bay those eager to settle Judea and Samaria could no longer stand against the rising tide.

Bin Nun reconstructed for me the sequence of events. As the 1973 war drew to a close, a group of young religious women met with Prime Minister Golda Meir and suggested that she establish a Jewish settlement in Samaria to boost morale and to prove that the Yom Kippur trauma could not break the spirit of the people of Israel. Meir thought the young women had lost their minds. But when Hanan Porat, Benny Katzover, Menachem Felix, and Yoel Bin Nun returned from war in the early winter of 1974, they picked up the struggle from the point at which the women had left off, organizing a sit-down strike near Golda Meir's residence and offices. To their surprise, hundreds and then thousands joined them. A mass movement was born that pressured the government to allow the building of a first Jewish settlement north of Jerusalem.

The standoff between the energetic zealots and the enfeebled Labor government lasted a year and a half. Time and again the determined young believers tried to seize land for settlement in Samaria, and time and again they were evacuated. Time and again illegal outposts were erected in the West Bank, and time and again they were demolished. But the ongoing confrontation with the establishment forged, consolidated, and empowered what was now the confident settlers' movement of Gush Emunim. More and more religious young people identified with the new protest movement and joined it. Even among the nonreligious there was growing sympathy for those who were perceived as the new pioneers of a new era. There was something attractive and tempting in the enthusiasm and devotion of those determined to go to Samaria. Even Israelis who realized that settling occupied territory was illegal and immoral and irrational found it difficult to resist settlement. Gush Emunim was seen as the new torch of Zionism, at a time when other torches were being extinguished.

It was not the rabbis who led Gush Emunim, Yoel Bin Nun told me. The real leaders were a dozen or so dynamic and charismatic young men in their late twenties and early thirties. They had in them a rare combination of fervor and pragmatism, idealism and slyness. They had both religious faith and political skill. They admired the historical Labor Movement, and they despised what Labor had become. Combining messianic Judaism with Israeli chutzpah they were determined to replace—even to inherit—the idealistic pioneering movement that the Labor Movement had once been. In flannel shirts, army coats, and knitted yarmulkes, these men became Israel's new avant-garde. They mobilized thousands, inspired tens of thousands, and had the tacit support of hundreds of thousands. They evoked fear in the hearts of Israel's elected government. While the moribund Labor Party was seen as yesterday's leader, Gush Emunim perceived itself as the leader of tomorrow. It challenged secular Zionism and democratic Israel and demanded to establish in Samaria its own Ein Harod.

Ofra is no Ein Harod. It did not issue from a desperate Diaspora but from a sovereign state. It did not intend to give the Jews shelter but to build the Jews a kingdom. It did not stand up to a foreign power but against the Jewish democratic state. And yet, for its founders, Ofra is the direct descendant of Ein Harod. Like Ein Harod, it pitched a tent where no Jews had lived for thousands of years. Like Ein Harod, it was founded against all odds. Like Ein Harod, it evinced the triumph of willpower. In its own way, Ofra tried to impose its own Zionist utopia on reality, just as Ein Harod did fifty-four years earlier.

Pinchas Wallerstein welcomes me to his red-roofed Ofra home with a warm handshake. Another founder of Ofra, Wallerstein is very different from Bin Nun. Short, clean-shaven, vigorous, and practical, he is not a man of deep thought but of swift action. Yet, like Bin Nun, he answers my questions with his life story: his impoverished childhood in the Haifa working-class suburb of Kiryat Atta; a father who left home at 5:00 A.M. every morning to distribute fresh bread from a horse-drawn cart; a mother whose ready smile hid a heavy Holocaust anguish. Both his father and mother were alone in the world; their families had been annihilated. Yet their young son, an Israeli Sabra, was determined not to be miserable, not to feel poor or bitter. Although he was small and dyslexic, he became a social dynamo. Although he was expelled from his high school yeshiva, he was a leader in the national religious youth movement, which became his real home. Although he lived on the fringes of Israel, he admired the kibbutz and dreamed of being a kibbutznik. In the 1967 war he was badly injured and was hospitalized for two years. But he overcame his disability and his dyslexia, married and had children, and finished school. He was always restless, always looking for something else, somewhere else. After the 1973 war, Wallerstein realized that he wanted to find a way to resuscitate Zionism. At the age of twenty-five, he became the leader of a group of young men and women seeking to settle in Samaria. But only in early 1975 did he come up with a practical idea that would actually make settlement in Samaria possible: rather than clash with the government, he would lull it into accepting and later endorsing a cunning settlement fait accompli. The pragmatic Pinchas Wallerstein then made all the preparations needed to spearhead the first settlement on Shomron Mountain.

Another founder of Ofra, Yehuda Etzion, greets me with suspicion. What exactly do I want? What am I looking for in Ofra? The tall, bearded settler finds it inconceivable that a left-wing journalist like me can be balanced and fair. Yet after an hour of idle chat, he softens. He makes me strong Turkish coffee, offers me raisins and roasted almonds, and begins to talk. Etzion is a person of depth. Unlike Bin Nun and Wallerstein, he felt the yearning for the land of biblical Israel from early childhood. He remembers the fury his parents felt after the War of Independence because Ben Gurion did not insist on keeping the Old City "in our hands." He remembers the admiration for the brutal Stern Gang of pre-Independence Israel who vowed to forcibly evict the British from the land. And yet even for Etzion, the Six Day War was the tipping point, the big bang. When East Jerusalem was liberated he felt a delirious joy, he tells me. He felt a yearning for the Temple Mount, where the First and Second Temples once stood. He experienced the realization that the Temple Mount was what mattered, and the determination to climb up the mount. To bring the Bible to life.

Six years after the skies opened in 1967, the skies came crashing down with the Yom Kippur War. The questions hit him as he was carrying corpses down from the Golan Heights: What has happened to us? Why have we fallen? How did we become so terribly weak?

Yehuda Etzion tells me that worse than the war was the political avalanche in its aftermath. Suddenly the government of Israel was willing to give up everything. Outside pressure was building, but from within there was no real resistance. On the contrary, there was cynicism, nihilism, defeatism. In the winter months that followed the war he realized that something had gone terribly wrong, that something profound had been lost. Over the years Israel had experienced a spiritual decline. Secular pioneering Zionism had been replaced by complacent Zionism and seized by a secular weakness of will. There was cultural assimilation. There was mental surrender to the West. And war made all these underlying processes apparent. True, the Third Temple had not fallen this time around, but it might fall when encountering the next challenge. So the mission of salvation was now on the shoulders of believers. The torch had been passed to religious Zionism. And it was the mission of religious Zionism to light the fire on the mountaintops. One settlement on Shomron Mountain would not solve the problem. But one settlement was certainly feasible. And it could make a statement. It would lead Zionism in a totally new direction.

Etzion tells me that Gush Emunim had a strategic rationale for building Ofra: the understanding that eventually Israel's permanent border would pass along the last Jewish furrow. They believed that no territory without Jewish settlement would remain Jewish. But Etzion admits that this hawkish strategy was only a small part of the ambitious endeavor. "Nablus, the capital of Samaria, is the most significant city in the land of Israel," he tells me. "It's the city where Joshua renewed the covenant with God after the conquest of Jericho. Nearby Elon Moreh is the site where Abraham built his first altar after he entered Israel. At Elon Moreh, God said to Abraham: 'To your offspring I shall give this land.' So divine revelation takes place in Elon Moreh and in Nablus. The first *aliyah* of the people of Israel to the land of Israel was *aliyah* to Shomron Mountain. Secular Zionism never climbed Shomron Mountain. It remained in the plains. The renewal and revival of Zionism after the Yom Kippur War was not just about taking strategic control of the highlands of the West Bank. It was about bringing the people of Israel to the mountain of Israel. We would revive Zionism and save Israel by climbing up the mountain, by realizing that without a spiritual depth the State of Israel cannot hold. We would revive it through the understanding that the Zionism of the plains is doomed. Our way is the way of our fathers; we must go back to the land of our fathers, go back to the mountains we lost. We must bring Zionism back to the mountains and bring the mountains back to Zionism."

Whereas Wallerstein is matter-of-fact, Etzion is imposing. In the simple living room of his modest Ofra home, his words touch me. Although I reject his worldview and despise his actions, I am not indifferent to what he says. Surprisingly, I recognize the great forces that pulled him to Ofra. I can understand what he says about the plains and the mountains and the history of Zionism. With horror I realize that the DNA of his Zionism and the DNA of my Zionism share a few genes.

Through the rectangular window of Etzion's living room I can see Ba'al Hazor Mountain. Its summit is the tallest in Samaria: 1,010 meters. That's why in the mid-1970s the Israeli Air Force chose it for the site of a highly advanced early warning station. As Etzion and I talk, I can see through his window the enormous, science-fiction-like metal spheres that scan and protect the skies of Israel. Beyond its strategic importance, the radar station has historical significance, too. It gave Etzion the excuse to gain a foothold in Samaria. In the winter of 1974, at the age of twenty-three, the slim, fair-skinned Etzion managed to become a subcontractor to the Jerusalem contractor who was building the secret station. Etzion's mission was to put up the security fence surrounding the Ba'al Hazor installation. This is how the inventive zealot was able to assemble a small work squad of nationalistic young men who came daily to the mountain to erect the fence. This is why Etzion had reason to demand that a place be found for the fence workers to sleep. This is the way he managed to find a way into forbidden territory.

When Etzion talks, he is calm, concise, unsentimental. He is always careful not to claim too much credit for himself, not to brag. But when he tells me about his first days on the mountain, his eyes light up. And when I say that he must have felt God's presence when he went up the mountain for the very first time, he does not contradict me. "You know I don't like to talk," he says. "I never liked talkers. I always said, 'Go and do.' But you are right. That winter we understood our role. Suddenly it was clear that the land of Israel was calling upon us and that God was calling upon us. A religious duty was thrust upon us. And that duty fueled our bodies and souls. It fueled my entire existence. Most of the time I dealt with the small details: I put gas in the Land Rover and loaded it with metal poles and rolls of barbed fence. But when the Land Rover was climbing Ba'al Hazor and the mountaintop came into view, I would talk to the heavens. And I would say, 'We are here, we are doing all we can do, so please now do your part.' Yes, I had a dialogue with God. I was saying to God what the sons of Israel said when they brought their baskets of first fruits to the temple: 'Here, we have done our share. Please do your share and bless your people, your Israel.' "

In the beginning of 1975, everything begins to come together. Yoel Bin Nun is tired of the raucous demonstrations that Gush Emunim held throughout the West Bank. Pinchas Wallerstein is looking for a pragmatic way to penetrate Samaria. Yehuda Etzion knows that the cover story of the work squad won't hold for long. The three realize that it is time for a different kind of action, discreet and clever.

First Etzion wants to settle on the western saddle of Ba'al Hazor Mountain. He wants Ofra to be founded on the site where God showed Abraham the Land. But his more practical comrades convince him that his desire is futile. The only way to break into Samaria is to take over the deserted Jordanian military base of Ein Yabrud, to raid land that is not private property and that already has buildings to settle in. And the only way forward is to take action at once, before momentum is lost and the youth lose hope and the settlers' movement disintegrates.

The operation is planned like a military offensive. Etzion's work squad is to come down the mountain at the end of the workday and arrive at the deserted base below. Wallerstein's group is to arrive from Jerusalem at the very same time. Simultaneously, Gush Emunim's leader, Hanan Porat, is to contact the sympathetic defense minister, Shimon Peres, so that when the army discovers that the base has been invaded, he will put pressure on the army to look the other way, to accept this invasion. Between the cracks, Ofra will be founded and become a fact on the ground.

On Sunday, April 20, 1975, Wallerstein leads a small convoy of cars from the Gush Emunim office in Jerusalem to Samaria. In the late afternoon the work squad comes down Ba'al Hazor Mountain. By evening the two groups meet at the Ein Yabrud base and take it over. A few hours pass until the regional military commander arrives and instructs the trespassers to leave. Etzion and Wallerstein refuse. They claim that they are acting on behalf of the Ministry of Defense. While the two are taken to the army's headquarters in Ramallah, Porat puts enormous pressure on Peres and three of his hawkish aides. Late that night, Peres instructs the army not to assist the settlers but not to evacuate them, either. Etzion and Wallerstein immediately grasp the historic significance of these vague instructions. A bottle of wine is found and glasses are raised in the army's headquarters. At midnight the two young leaders are driven back to Ein Yabrud in an army jeep, victorious. Determined, resourceful, and crafty, they have overpowered the government of Israel. In Ofra they have laid the foundation of the last colonial project of the twentieth century.

In early March 1975, Palestinian terrorists attack Tel Aviv's Savoy Hotel, murdering eight guests. The UN does not condemn the attack, and the PLO leader, Yasser Arafat, sees his international standing grow stronger. In late March, Henry Kissinger's attempt to reach an Egyptian-Israeli interim agreement fails. President Gerald Ford instructs his administration to reassess the United States' relationship with Israel. The vital American-Israeli alliance is in crisis. At the very same time, America's East Asian policy is in a state of collapse. On April 18, 1975, Phnom Penh is conquered by the Khmer Rouge. On April 20, 1975, the last Communist offensive on Laos is launched, and on April 30, 1975, South Vietnam falls. American helicopters rescue the last Americans from the rooftop of the American embassy in Saigon. In Israel there is a widespread feeling that the West might abandon it, too. Western weakness, internal weakness, and international isolation are almost palpable. Many Israelis fear that what happened in Saigon will happen in Tel Aviv, and that Israel's fate will be similar to that of South Vietnam. No wonder there is an instinct to cling to Ofra. Not only raving right-wingers but many realistic centrists view Ofra as a symbolic response to the national and international slide toward the abyss. That is why many Israeli officials—senior and junior—secretly assist Ofra, and why leading public figures encourage Ofra and contribute to it. Within less than two years, a groundswell of support turns Ofra from a temporary encampment into a viable settlement.

Pinchas Wallerstein speaks like an entrepreneur when he describes Ofra's early days. First they had to cover the broken windows of the Jordanian base's buildings with sheets of plastic, he tells me, and improvise a kitchen, organize a mess hall, bring water tanks, and deploy chemical toilets. Then they had to pave a path in the rocky terrain and pitch tents, and divide the long military barracks into small family housing units. Then they illegally drew water from the regional (Palestinian) water system and siphoned electricity from the regional (Palestinian) electric network. They dug a cesspit. They founded a field school, a metal workshop, a computer programming firm, and a small aircraft ladder factory. They brought in the first prefabricated houses. Then they got into night-long discussions about their vision for Ofra. Ofra wouldn't be a kibbutz or moshav or a bedroom community, they decided. It would encourage private initiative and allow private property. Ofra would be Israel's first community settlement.

Yehuda Etzion speaks about Ofra's early days like a romantic ideologue. "The first principle of Ofra was that its residents would all work here," he tells me. "The second principle was that no Arab would be permanently employed here. The third principle was that Ofra would have a strong agricultural foundation." For Etzion, agriculture was the crux. He believed then, as he believes now, that there is no way to hold on to the land without working the land, that there is no way to return to the land without direct physical contact with it. That's why he cleared the first plot of land with his bare hands and planted daffodils the very first summer and cherry trees the first autumn. As the settlement grew stronger, he dedicated himself to the cherry orchard, convinced he was doing what God wanted him to do.

Neither Wallerstein nor Etzion gives me a convincing answer regarding the Arabs. Did they not see the Arabs they had settled among? Yes, they did see them. Did they not know that all around Ofra were the Palestinian villages of Silwan, Mazraat, A-Sharkiya, Ein Yabrud, Beitin, and Taybeh? Yes, they did know that those villages existed. Did they not understand the inherent contradiction wedged between Jewish Ofra and the dense Palestinian population surrounding it? Yes, they did understand.

Wallerstein tells me that the Arabs of 1975 were not the Arabs of today. The villages were small, poor, and primitive. Their presence was much less evident. The villagers were not hostile or violent. They showed no signs of Palestinian nationalism. In the first years, the settlers of Ofra visited the villages and traded with the villagers frequently and did not feel that the local Arabs threatened them in any way. On the contrary, at that time the villages had a primal beauty that amplified the biblical magic of the mountainous, historically charged region in which Ofra had planted itself. The Arab villagers did not seem to be a genuine obstacle.

Etzion, on the other hand, knew better than that. He spoke Arabic, had spent long hours with Arabs, and had bought Arab land. He even had some sympathy for traditional Arab ways. He appreciated the fact that unlike secular urban Jews, rural Arabs were one with the land. I sense that Etzion knew from the outset that there would be a war to the death between Ofra and the villages, and that he believed that at the end of the war, the villages would vanish. The historically minded national religious leader never forgot Ein Harod. He was convinced that what would save Ofra was some sort of future cataclysm that was bound to come and to achieve in the West Bank what the cataclysm of 1948 had achieved in the Valley of Harod.

And yet, when I listen to Wallerstein and Etzion, I realize that they did not have a well-defined doctrine regarding the Arabs. When they came to settle in Samaria, they were more ignorant than evil. They saw Israel's 1970s weakness and realized that the Israeli crisis was not only political but spiritual. They felt obliged to deal with the crisis, but the solution they came up with was absurd and completely ignored the demographic reality on the ground. Wallerstein and Etzion did not realize this because they did not think through the consequences of their actions. They were young and rebellious and they were part of a juvenile movement that enjoyed breaking a taboo, crossing a line, and challenging the establishment. But they never knew where they were really headed. They never realized what sort of mess they were about to create. They established Ofra without comprehending its repercussions.

Pinchas Wallerstein is Ofra's secretary general for four years. He leads the way in expanding it from the abandoned Jordanian base into the privately owned Palestinian fields surrounding it. He doubles its population. He builds a kindergarten, a school, a minimarket, a post office, and a synagogue. He sees to it that Ofra gets a bus line and a telephone line. He initiates and plans Ofra's first fifty-house neighborhood. In 1977, after the right-wing Likud Party comes to power, he coaxes Menachem Begin's cabinet into recognizing Ofra as a legitimate and legal settlement. As a result of that recognition, the once piratelike outpost receives generous support from all branches of government: housing, health, welfare, education, and defense. Within less than five years, the unlawful stronghold becomes a solid and viable settlement. Ofra is home to settler movement gatherings, to the settlers' weekly magazine, and to the settlers' political organs. The mother of all settlements is now the capital of all settlements. It is the icon of the settler movement and the settlement phenomenon.

But Pinchas Wallerstein wants more. Ofra is not enough. Like others in the Gush Emunim leadership, he watches in pain in 1979 as Israel's right-wing government hands over the Sinai desert to Egypt in exchange for peace. He sees that the process of contraction is gaining momentum and might soon reach the West Bank. Although Ofra is a success, it does not stop the landslide its founders had planned to stop. That's why Wallerstein thinks it is essential to take over vast territories of the West Bank. He seeks to prevent an Israeli-Palestinian peace agreement by establishing dozens of Ofras. And he does. In 1979 Wallerstein is nominated head of the regional council of the Binyamin District. He paves roads, builds industrial parks, establishes Jewish communities. Energetic, creative, and shrewd, he gets successive Israeli governments to endorse and advance the Gush Emunim dream. In his twenty-eight years in office he establishes forty settlements, enlarging the settler population under his jurisdiction from one thousand to forty-three thousand. Simultaneously, he plays a leading role in the settlers' Yesha Council, which compels Israeli governments to build and support 140 settlements and dozens of illegal outposts throughout the West Bank. He helps bring hundreds of thousands of settlers to the occupied territories. After succeeding in Ofra, Wallerstein realizes that there are no limits. There is no power in post-1973 Israel that can stop him. That's how Wallerstein is able to build one Ofra after another. One Ofra, ten Ofras, a hundred Ofras. Along with his friends and comrades he institutionalizes the Gush Emunim revolution. He creates a new demographic-political reality that redefines Israel and changes the course of Zionism.

Yehuda Etzion also wants more. For four years, he works in his cherry orchard. To this day he remembers with delight the screech of the chains of the tractor that broke the land of Ofra for the very first time. He brings the cherry plants from the Valley of Jezreel and lays out the orchard with pegs and white ropes. He recalls digging the holes for the trees, watering the holes. The first section of the orchard is sour cherry, the second section is Japanese plum, the third is sweet cherry. Then he plants another orchard, twenty miles away, of peaches, nectarines, and grapes. Four years after the initial planting the first harvest arrives. He recounts to me the exhilaration he feels when the decorated wagon drives into Ofra carrying its first fruits.

But Etzion also realizes that although Ofra has taken root, its success is local and limited. Prime Minister Menachem Begin has betrayed the Land of Israel, he insists, by returning the Sinai. The Israelis of the plains are not standing by the Land of Israel. Retreat is in full motion, and it seems clear that Judea and Samaria might fall. Americanism is the new Hellenism and it is making Israel un-Jewish, weak, hollow, and rotten. Israel can only be saved by a new idea or a deed or an event that will transform history.

The Temple Mount has always fascinated Yehuda Etzion. As a child, he went with his father to West Jerusalem to look over the border toward the site that the Holy Temple once occupied. By the time the Six Day War broke out, Etzion was obsessed with the Temple Mount. And even when he was striving to build Ofra, he always knew that it was only a station on the road to the Temple Mount. "The Temple Mount is the focal point of the land," Etzion tells me. "But it is in the hands of gentiles. As long as the Al-Aqsa mosque and the Omar mosque stand on the Temple Mount, there can be no salvation for Israel."

In 1979, as Wallerstein begins his work at the Binyamin District Regional Council, Etzion begins meeting in Jerusalem with Yehoshua Ben Shoshan, Menachem Livni, and Shabtai Ben Dov. All four agree that no Islamic abomination should stand on the Temple Mount. The Temple Mount embodies the covenant between God and Israel. It is the source and the focus of Jewish life. The Etzion Four see the Temple Mount as the place to launch the revival of a Judaic Israel. Only dramatic action on the Temple Mount will make it possible to restart Zionism, so that this time it will be right and pure and truly Jewish.

• • •

Wallerstein does not know this at the time, but in 1980 his path parts from Etzion's. They still live house by house in Ofra and are still Ofra's moral leaders. Wallerstein admires Etzion's spirit, and Etzion respects Wallerstein's work. But in their daily lives they are working on two very different enterprises. Wallerstein is determined to establish more and more settlements, which he does. But Etzion becomes convinced that Wallerstein's settlements are not enough. They are vital for the cause, but they will not solve the core problem. What is needed is a profound internal change. What is needed is revolution. It is necessary to replace the State of Israel with the Kingdom of Israel. Western democracy will have to make way for the great Jewish court, the Sanhedrin. God Almighty will have to intervene in modern history and save his people, his Israel.

At this point the conversation with Etzion becomes far more fascinating than my conversation with Wallerstein. Yehuda Etzion has never before spoken about the Temple Mount plot as he speaks now, revealing his innermost hopes and fears of that time. "When we founded Ofra, we already knew that our struggle would pit truth against falsehood," he tells me. "The government's attempt to make Samaria a Jewish-free zone was false. Our fight with the government was a fight between the good angel and the evil angel. Jewish legend teaches us that such a fight ends with a surprising outcome: the evil angel says 'Amen' in spite of himself. After being beaten, he is forced to see the truth. This is what happened in our case, too. Even though the forces we encountered were far superior, in the end our truth won. Even Labor's leaders said 'Amen' in spite of themselves.

"Ofra's success gave us a tremendous boost. It strengthened our faith and emboldened us. A lot of what happened later happened because of Ofra's success. From all over the country and from all walks of life people came to see us and be with us. They were surprised by what we had accomplished. Suddenly, they saw a light on the mountaintop. So after we lit the light of Ofra, we lit the light of Elon Moreh, and we lit the light of Shilo, and we lit the light of Beit El. While secular Zionism remained below in the lowland, we climbed up and lit more and more bonfires on the mountaintops.

"But I lived in fear. What was accomplished was far from secure.

What was built was not yet stable. Everything still seemed vulnerable and reversible. And then there was the shameful peace agreement with Egypt, and the duplicity of the government, with Labor drifting further and further away from what it once was. So much so that I felt I could no longer trust the national leadership. I felt betrayed by it. And so I had to fight the State of Israel, which had ceased to be the emissary of the nation of Israel. I was obliged to act on my own for the good of the nation of Israel. As there was no real leadership to speak of, and no real state to speak of, the duty rested on me.

"In the late 1970s I was introduced to the writings of Shabtai Ben Dov. Ben Dov prepared an operative plan for the establishment of the Kingdom of Israel. I learned from him that settlements were not enough, that there was an urgent need to replace the set of foreign values that Israel had adopted. American and European concepts had to be done away with. We needed to embrace concepts that followed directly from the Torah of Israel. We had to leave democracy behind and go back to the source. We had to foment a Kingdom Come revolution.

"I knew that the Temple Mount was the focal point. The mountain is where our Father in heaven connects with us. The fact that the Temple Mount is not in our hands is the most damning testimony of how low we have sunk. The mosques on the Temple Mount are a humiliation to the people of Israel and the history of Israel and God. Blowing up the mosques would allow us to break through to the heavens. It would pave the way to sanctity, divine presence, the Sanhedrin, and the Temple. It would be a purge that would end the old corrupt era and usher in a new pure one, that would replace the secular State of Israel with a Torah-inspired kingdom.

"A third world war? An Islamic march on Jerusalem? Tens of thousands of casualties? I thought about these scenarios but came to the conclusion that they were pessimistic and alarmist. I realized that when the Dome will collapse all hell would break loose. But I didn't think that thousands of tanks would move on Israel and that hundreds of missiles would be launched. But I also thought that even if I was wrong, the risk was worthwhile. Ben Gurion thought that the foundation of Israel justified the war it begot. Now things are no different. It was absolutely clear to me that making Israel a holy state justified suffering a war against all of Israel's enemies."

• • •

In the early 1980s, as Pinchas Wallerstein mobilizes more and more of the resources of democratic Israel to build settlements in Judea and Samaria, Yehuda Etzion mobilizes more and more settlers in Judea and Samaria to bring about a revolution that will topple democratic Israel. Wallerstein tries to impose a colonial stalemate in the West Bank, while Etzion tries to ignite Armageddon on the Temple Mount. Their success with Ofra makes the two men outrageously ambitious. While the pragmatic Wallerstein succeeds in making the Israeli republic a subcontractor of the Greater Israel edifice, the messianic Etzion wishes to replace the Israeli republic with a kingdom.

Even today, when he reconstructs the events of thirty to forty years ago, Wallerstein is energetic, forceful, and detailed. He remembers every road he opened, every industrial park he initiated, every budget he extracted from the government. He circumvented here and he maneuvered there, and he pushed and he shoved and he made mainstream Israeli politics flow to the riverbed of Gush Emunim.

But Etzion is pensive and introspective. He quietly tells me how he came to the conclusion that the time had come. Not one Ofra and not a thousand Ofras would suffice. So he carries on with the cherry orchard and with buying land from Arabs and with planning the Ofra synagogue and with weekly meetings of the Gush Emunim leadership. But his mind is elsewhere. His heart is with the Temple. He collects ancient cedar logs that were purportedly once part of the Second Temple. He imagines the Temple, thinks of the Temple, reconstructs the Temple in his mind. And he knows for certain that without redeeming the Temple there will be no redemption. Because he has never been put off by unconventional thinking, he is not put off now by the unconventional idea that is capturing his mind. And because he has always been disgusted by people who talk but don't act, he knows he must act. He goes up the Mount of Olives at night to observe the Temple Mount, and he studies its defenses. He draws maps and acquires aerial photos and collects every piece of relevant intelligence. And he makes a detailed plan. He mobilizes men and instructs them to get explosives. He reaches a point where he has four major explosive devices (20 kilograms each) that will bring down the four pillars of the Dome; then he reaches a point where he has twelve medium-sized explosive devices (7 kilograms each) that will bring down the twelve columns surrounding the Dome. He is ready. "In my mind," Etzion tells me, "I already saw the Dome collapsing on itself with a huge cloud of rising dust. And then the confusion stops and Israel's stuttering stops and there is clarity at last as one chapter ends and another begins. One era closes and another era opens. And all is different now, for we have done our share and God is bound to do His."

When, in the spring of 1984, Israel's Secret Service arrives in Ofra to arrest Yehuda Etzion, the community is up in arms. The official leadership denounces his deeds, but many others are supportive. It is soon revealed that Etzion is not the only Ofra resident who is a member of the now notorious Jewish underground. Several Jewish terrorists live in Ofra. A number of the terrorist operations the clandestine ring has managed to pull off earlier were planned in Ofra. From Ofra came the instructions to booby-trap the cars of three Palestinian mayors, which left two of them without legs. Only five years after Ofra settled among the Palestinians, it became a terrorist hotbed that bred ideological Jewish murderers. Ofra was home to militant messianic ideas and to a radical school of thought that believed in transforming the land by using unrestrained force.

The exposure of the Etzion-led underground is a shock. And the shock is healing. Now even the Ofra settlers realize that messianism is radioactive, that combining metaphysics with politics breeds insanity. After the initial storm subsides, the zealots' way is rejected. The Ofra majority chooses pragmatism over fundamentalism, moderation over extremism, Wallerstein over Etzion. The settlers enlarge Ofra and strengthen it. They acquire more land and found new neighborhoods. As a community they survive two intifadas. They suffer their losses and bury their dead. They withstand the outbreaks of violence and the constant uncertainties of living in a disputed territory. True, once in a while violent Ofra gangs take the law into their own hands and carry out brutal attacks on the neighboring Palestinian villages. Even Wallerstein himself gets into a shooting incident in which he kills a Palestinian boy after his car is stoned. But as a rule, Ofra does not openly revolt against the state. It advances its agenda not by fighting state and law, but by using them. Adopting Old Labor's step-by-step approach, Ofra goes from strength to strength. In 1983 it has five hundred residents. In 1995 it has twelve hundred residents. Today it has approximately thirty-five hundred.

And yet, when I sit with Yehuda Etzion and hear him talk, I know that he has remained a part of Ofra's DNA. For Etzion is right: Ofra as such is futile. Settlements as such are hopeless. In spite of Wallerstein's longitudinal and lateral roads, the settlements have remained isolated Jewish islands in the Arab West Bank. In spite of Wallerstein's communities and industrial parks and highways and bridges, the settlers are a minority in Judea and Samaria. As the international community will never recognize them as legitimate, the settlements are built on precarious ground. As Israel of the plains never really embraced the settlements, they remain distant and detached, living beyond mountains of darkness. Like Algeria and Rhodesia, they will not survive. They are at a dead end.

Pragmatic Wallerstein does not have a solution. He won the war of the hills, but his victory is Pyrrhic. The homes he built don't have long-lasting foundations; the trees he planted have no deep roots. The only way to save his monumental project is Yehuda Etzion's way. The only way to believe in the future of Ofra is to believe in cataclysm or divine intervention, or both. Etzion is honest enough to say it, but every intelligent person in Ofra must know it: they harbor in their heart a great belief in a great war, which will be their only salvation.

There will be war, no doubt about it. Because of 1948 and 1967, and because of Ofra, there will be war. But war will not save Ofra or Israel. The reality created by Wallerstein and Etzion and their friends has entangled Israel in a predicament that cannot be untangled. The settlements have placed Israel's neck in a noose. They created an untenable demographic, political, moral, and judicial reality. But now Ofra's illegitimacy taints Israel itself. Like a cancer, it spreads from one organ to another, endangering the entire body. Ofra's colonialism makes the world perceive Israel as a colonialist entity. But because in the twenty-first century there is no room for a colonialist entity, the West is gradually turning its back on Israel. That's why enlightened Jews in America and Europe are ashamed of Israel. That's why Israel is at odds with itself. Although the founders of Ofra wished to strengthen Israel, in practice they weakened it. So when the great war does break out, it will meet an isolated, ostracized, and divided Israel—an Israel that will hardly be able to defend itself.

On this clear winter day, everything is still quiet. The radar station on Ba'al Hazor Mountain scans the blue skies. The white homes of Ofra and the stone houses of the Palestinian village of Silwan watch one another. In the distance lie the vineyards and the cherry orchard and the gray rocks and the mountain soil. A thousand years of memory and a thousand years of silence and an uncertain future.

Yehuda Etzion carries on. He tells me about the project he has taken up since his release from prison, a plan for a New Jerusalem: a Jerusalem without mosques and without Arabs, a Jerusalem of the Third Temple. Pinchas Wallerstein carries on, too. "We were not mistaken," he says. "We built a splendid project. We did what our forefathers did in Hanita and Ein Harod. We followed Labor's ethos and used Labor's methods. In the last quarter of the twentieth century we did in Samaria what Labor did in the Valley of Harod in the first quarter of the twentieth century."

"But this is exactly what the argument is about," I interrupt. "The question is whether Ofra is a benign continuation of Zionism or a malignant mutation of Zionism." The answer, of course, is that it is both. On the one hand, the spirit and the modus operandi are remarkably similar. No fair-minded observer will deny the assertion that in a sense Ofra is Ein Harod's grandchild. But on the other hand, the historic and conceptual context is completely different. In this sense, Ofra is not a continuation but an aberration, a grotesque reincarnation of Ein Harod.

Wallerstein doesn't get it, so I try to explain. I tell him that from the beginning, Zionism skated on thin ice. On the one hand it was a national liberation movement, but on the other it was a colonialist enterprise. It intended to save the lives of one people by the dispossession of another. In its first fifty years, Zionism was aware of this complexity and acted accordingly. It was very careful not to be associated with colonialism and tried not to cause unnecessary hardship. It made sure it was a democratic, progressive, and enlightened movement, collaborating with the world's forces of progress. With great sophistication Zionism handled the contradiction at its core. It managed to arrive at the great war of 1948 just and strong and came out of the war with a Jewish democratic nation-state that had clear borders and a massive Jewish majority. It had turned the conflict between an emigrant community and a native population into a conflict between sovereign states. Gone was the danger that our fate would be the fate of Algeria or Rhodesia, that Zionism would be perceived as just another ill-conceived colonial project.

"But after 1967, and after 1973, all that changed," I tell Wallerstein. "The self-discipline and historical insight that characterized the nation's first years began to fade. You settlers took advantage of the feebleness and of the political vacuum created by the wars. You abused Labor's weakness and Likud's recklessness. But although you think you outsmarted everybody, you were wrong. You were wrong to think you could have done with Ofra in 1975 what was done in Ein Harod in 1921. You were wrong to think that a sovereign state could do in occupied territories what a revolutionary movement can do in an undefined land. You didn't grasp the deep wisdom of the 1950s housing-estate-Israel and the 1960s Dimona-Israel. Ironically, you brought back the Palestinians Ben Gurion managed to keep away. You have turned a conflict between nation states into a conflict between a settlers' community and an indigenous community. By doing that, you endangered everything. Your energy was remarkable, but on everything that matters you were utterly wrong. Out of an understandable yearning for the Zionist past and for Zionist glory, you contradicted Zionist logic and undermined Zionist interests. You brought disaster upon us, Wallerstein. On our behalf, you committed an act of historic suicide."

Angry and dejected, I walk from Pinchas Wallerstein's home to the home of Israel Harel. Harel is my colleague at *Haaretz* newspaper, a columnist and longtime partner in conversation about the nation's future. He is pleasant, wise, and low-key. Unlike Wallerstein and Etzion, he is neither defiant nor obstinate, but thoughtful and sad. In 1967 he was among the first paratroopers to reach the Temple Mount, and in 1973 he was among the first paratroopers to cross the Suez Canal. As a young student he was one of the founders of the Greater Israel movement, and as a young journalist he settled in Ofra a year after it was founded. He initiated and edited the Ofra-based settlers' weekly magazine, *Nekuda*, and he founded the settlers' representative council, Yesha. Although I like Harel and respect him, I am now cruel to him. "The more I look into Ofra and the more I think about it," I say, "I come to the conclusion that you simply went mad. A zealot's fever blinded you; a collective national-religious fervor made you not see the Arabs all around you. Your tribal psychology and bizarre ideology led you to lead Israel to a dead end."

My excitement doesn't affect Harel. Through his thick glasses he looks me right in the eye and replies with surprising candor. "Any person coming to live in Ofra is required to give answers," he says. "From our first moment here we were required to give answers." He lists four of them:

1. A wave of immigration will come—from the USSR or from the U.S.—and will sweep away the demographic problem.
2. Of their own accord, the Arabs will leave and go to live with their brothers in Jordan.
3. The State of Israel will not transfer its population by force but will encourage the immigration of individual Arabs to Arab states.
4. There will be a war resembling the war of 1948.

"Then I was right," I cry. "Ofra's assumption is that the Arabs will not stick around. Its secret hope is that there will be a great war and the Arabs will vanish."

Harel politely ignores me and continues. "We always knew a day might come when we would be forced to leave," he says. "It was not talked about. It was concealed in the darkest corners. But from the day Ofra was founded, every person here knew this. But we all knew something else, too. There is a belief here that a grand event will happen, like the 1967 war or the 1948 war. And that grand event will prove that we were right. It will redeem our struggle and will convince the people of Israel to join us. The people of Tel Aviv will understand how hollow their existence is, that without us they have no roots, no depth, and no life. The masses will come. And then, when a million Jews live on the mountaintops, there will really be a new map. And there will be a new consciousness. What began in Ofra will make Israel Jewish and Zionist once again."

Only when I listen to Harel do I comprehend: Gush Emunim was so strong because it was the liberation movement of religious Zionism. By going to Judea and Samaria it tried to turn a petit-bourgeois Shabbat-keeping community into a revolutionary movement. By establishing settlements, it tried to move religious Zionism from the fringes of the Zionist narrative to its center. That's why the yearning for Ofra was not only political or religious, but visceral. Only in the disputed territory outside of the borders of sovereign Israel was the national-religious tribe able to assert itself. Only in this undefined territory could it define itself. Only in Ofra could national-religious youngsters raise their heads and find a place in the world. That's why they refused to see the folly of Ofra, why they shut their eyes to a reality that was closing in on Ofra from the very start. That's why they did not understand that in the twenty-first century, Ofra simply could not be.

But for the time being, Ofra is here: thirty-five hundred strong and counting. And when I leave Israel Harel and stroll to the commercial center and visit the day-care nursery and the kindergarten and the school, I am impressed by how lively it all is. Life is good here. Not a cloud in the sky. That is, as long as you don't raise your eyes and see the neighboring Palestinian villages. As long as you don't know exactly how the land under your feet was acquired. As long as you are not aware of how the calm is maintained here.

This is what is so deceptive about Ofra. To begin with, it was a pregnancy outside the womb. It was conceived outside state law, state borders, and state sovereignty. But even today Ofra lives beyond international law, devoid of international context, bereft of international goodwill. So at the very same time Ofra exists and doesn't exist. Although vibrant and dynamic, it is clear that sooner or later Ofra's internal logic will be crushed by the exterior logic it revolted against and ignored.

I think of the Rhodesian farmers who felt safe on their vast farms in the 1960s. They had it so good. They looked down upon critics and skeptics. In their eyes, their reality was so solid they could not see how fragile it was. They were wrong to believe that their virtual reality of affluence was a sustainable reality of survival. And I remember the Nezer Hazani settlement in the Gaza Strip, which I visited just before it was evacuated and demolished during the 2005 disengagement. I remember the very deep fear that the destruction of Nezer Hazani aroused in me. It was just like Ofra, prosperous and self-assured. But then the bulldozers razed it to the ground. Within a day it was gone. First it was and then it wasn't. Vanished.

I feel for Ofra. I feel strongly for the Ofra that I am furious with.

The Ofra archive is as neat and tidy as a pharmacy. In one of the white boxes I find an old statement by Yehuda Etzion: "Our real goal: to establish a proud kingdom that is spiritually robust and politically powerful." In another white box I find a tattered map that shows the sixteen concrete buildings of the Jordanian Ein Yabrud base scattered on the rocky mountain slope. And black-and-white photographs: a lonely Arab stone house overlooking the first settlers as they take hold of the Ein Yabrud base. Some 8 mm footage: energetic young women sweeping the deserted military barracks. A baby carriage, a water tank, hanging laundry. Young men in shorts and undershirts building vigorously. Young women in T-shirts painting walls white. Twenty-three-year-old Yehuda Etzion in a red bell-shaped hat. Twenty-six-year-old Pinchas Wallerstein speaking excitedly to his fellow settlers. The innocence and the blindness of April 1975. The determination to climb the mountain and to light the fire. To force God to intervene in history and save his people, his Israel.

NINE

Gaza Beach, 1991

Twenty years after occupation began and twelve years after Ofra was founded, the first intifada broke out. In December 1987 the Palestinians residing in the West Bank and the Gaza Strip revolted against Israel's ongoing military rule. Tens of thousands took to the streets. Cities and villages and refugee camps were engulfed by protest. An unprecedented Palestinian rebellion challenged Israel and nearly brought down its reign over the occupied territories. But after the initial shock the Jewish state fought back. It mobilized its army and trained it to become an effective police force. It unleashed the Shin Bet, its efficient secret service, on the unarmed masses that rebelled against it.

Within a few months the Israeli military built several detention camps in which thousands of Palestinians were imprisoned after having been convicted by military tribunals. Within a few years, the intifada rebellion was in decline. The systematic and determined use of oppressive force worked. The Palestinian campaign lost momentum. Gone were the mass demonstrations. Gone was the notion that the popular uprising would force Israel to end occupation. Thousands of Palestinian civilians languished in the detention camps. In many ways their mass imprisonment tainted Israel's democratic identity.

In March 1991 I was a young journalist about to become a father.

When I reported to a military base not far from Lydda for my annual reserve duty, I had no idea what that duty would be. Once told I was to serve as a jailer in a Gaza detention camp, I was horrified. An antioccupation peacenik, I was not willing to compromise everything I believed in, and for the first time in my life I seriously considered breaking the law, refusing to serve, and going to jail.

But as the IDF bus was taking me and my fellow reservists south, I had a better idea: I would write about the experience. I would put on paper the experience of an Israeli citizen who was suddenly transformed into a military jailor. Documenting occupation, I believed, would be a far more effective act of protest than refusing to take part in it. In the twelve days I spent in the Gaza beach detention camp I took notes, and in the three days that followed I wove the notes into a three-thousand-word piece. "On Gaza Beach" was first published in *Haaretz* and then in *The New York Review of Books*. By the time it came out in English, my eldest daughter, Tamara, had been born.

The setting is idyllic, a few hundred yards from the white sands of the Mediterranean shore. At six in the morning, when the fishing boats go out, I feel as if I am in the Crete of the 1950s. All that is west of me captures the heart: blue sky, blue-green waves, hopeful fishermen. But the fresh breeze that blows into my watchtower blows east, into the barbed wire fences, and onto the dark military tents. It lifts the spirit of the jailed Palestinians, and lifts the spirit of the jailing Jews.

The watchtower guards turn their eyes to the changing colors of the morning sea. So do the early-rising prisoners. In the tin shanty where the toilets are located, two of the prisoners stand on tiptoe, clinging to the only narrow window from which the Mediterranean can be seen. One day, when Free Palestine is established, its government will surely lease this piece of land to some international entrepreneur who will build the Gaza Beach Club Med. One day, when there is peace, Israelis will come out here for a short holiday break abroad. By these blue-green waters, they will drink white wine and dance the samba. On their way home they will buy embroidered black Palestinian dresses in the air-conditioned duty-free shop of the international terminal separating prosperous Israel from peaceful Palestine.

But for the time being there is no free Palestine, and no peace. That's why we must get the morning delivery ready. A long line of blue-uniformed prisoners are being led under the curling wire fences. And those who prod them with barrels of M-16 rifles are my buddies. In the faint light of an early April morning, the Jewish soldiers grip their rifles tightly. They tell the prisoners to stop, to advance, to stop. And while the fresh breeze blows in from the sea, they tell the prisoners to hold out their hands in front of them. A young soldier goes from one to another, clamping on handcuffs.

This is Gaza Beach Detention Camp. It is one of several such camps built in a rush in recent years after the eruption of the Palestinian uprising in December 1987. More than a thousand Palestinians are imprisoned here. Most of them are not terrorists but demonstrators and rock throwers. Many are in their teens. Among them, here and there, some are physically small and seem to be boys.

The detention camp has two interrogation wards and four compounds. In each compound there are twelve old brown army tents. In each tent there are twenty to thirty prisoners. In the past, fifty or sixty men were crowded into each tent. Now conditions have improved and they are considered reasonable.

Each of the four compounds is surrounded by a conventional wire fence topped with barbed wire. Outside this fence is a narrow path for the jailers. Then comes an additional, outer fence—a sort of improvised wall made of metal barrels filled with cement. As the jailers pace back and forth between these fences, it occurs to me that it isn't clear who are the confined and who are the confiners. The entire camp strikes me as a grand metaphor for everybody's imprisonment. Both Israelis and Palestinians are fenced in here.

The internment facility has a dozen watchtowers. Some Jewish soldiers are struck by the similarity between these and certain other towers that they have learned about in school. But the shock is merely emotional. The watchtowers constructed in Europe in the 1940s were all made of heavy German and Polish wood, whereas the towers in the Gaza Beach facility are of flimsy Israeli metal produced up in the Galilee. The towers are equipped with searchlights, but they are rarely used. This is because the camp is suffused all night with an extra-strong yellowish light from hundreds of powerful lampposts. When the electric

system is not turned off, as required, at early dawn, the bulbs and bea-
cons go on glowing into the light of day.

The detention facility has a mess hall, a canteen, showers, toilets.
Palestinian prisoners are assigned to scrub the Israeli soldiers' toilets
three or four times a day. Alas, some soldiers find that the hygiene stan-
dards achieved by the Palestinian scrubbers are not satisfactory. The
prison facility also has a set of tents for reservists, a commander's office,
and an operations room. There are two kitchens: one for the jailers, one
for the jailed. The two are separated only by a net. At times when the
guards run out of coffee, their cook asks the prisoners' cook to pass him
two or three bags of the tasteless stuff through the net. The same sort
of coexistence is found in the one medical clinic. A doctor may attend to
a reservist's eye infection immediately after he has patched up the leg of
a prisoner injured by an overzealous interrogator. Thus everything is in
order. The Gaza Beach Detention Camp runs by the rules.

Given the circumstances they are trapped in, the officers in charge try
to do their best. They are decent men. On their orders, the prisoners
receive plenty of food and cigarettes, and according to policy, they are
given considerable autonomy. For the most part, the imprisoned are allowed to run their own kitchen and quartermastership and are given the
supplies to do so. The prison commanders and the prisoners' leadership
negotiate daily. They allow life here to proceed calmly. It is two years
now since an officer shot to death a prisoner who tried to attack him—
and kept shooting while the young man rolled over on the ground in his
blood. Nowadays, unlike in the past, families and lawyers are given the
right to visit every Friday. The Red Cross drops in regularly.

Yet an evil stench is in the air that even the Mediterranean breeze
cannot carry away. Although unjust and unfounded, the haunting analogy is pervasive. Here it is not suggested by anti-Israel propaganda but
rather in the language the soldiers use as a matter of course. When A.
gets up to do guard duty in one of the interrogation wards, he says, "I'm
off to the Inquisition." When R. sees a line of prisoners approaching
under the barrels of his friends' M-16s, he says with quiet intensity:
"Look. The *Aktion* has begun." And even N., who harbors strong right-
wing views, grumbles to anyone who will listen that the place resembles

a concentration camp. M. explains with a thin smile that he has accumulated so many days of reserve duty during the intifada that soon they will promote him to a senior Gestapo official.

And I, too, who have always abhorred the analogy, who have always argued bitterly with anyone who so much as hinted at it, can no longer stop myself. The associations are too strong. They well up when I see a man from Pen Number 1 call through the fence to a man from Pen Number 2 to show him a picture of his daughter. They well up when a youngster who has just been arrested awaits my orders with a mixture of submission and panic and quiet pride. They well up when I glance at myself in the mirror, shocked to see myself here, a jailer in this ghastly prison. And when I see the thousand or so humans around me, locked up in pens, in cages.

Like a believer whose faith is wavering I go over the long list of counterarguments, all the well-known differences. Most obvious, there are no crematoria here. And in the Europe of the 1930s there was no existential conflict between two peoples. Germany, with its racist doctrine, was organized evil. The Germans were in no real danger whatsoever. But then I realize that the problem is not in the similarity—no one can seriously think there is any real similarity. The problem is that there isn't enough lack of similarity. The lack of similarity is not strong enough to silence once and for all the evil echoes.

Maybe the Shin Bet is to blame for this. Every night, after it has managed to break some youngsters in the interrogation ward, the Israeli Secret Service hands over to the Israeli paratroopers who control the city of Gaza a list of the close friends of the broken youngsters. And anyone standing at the gate, like myself, can see the paratroopers' jeep leave the detention camp after midnight and drive into the occupied, darkened city, which is under curfew, to arrest those who are said to endanger the security of the state. I will still stand at the gate when the paratroopers return in their military vehicles with boys of fifteen or sixteen, who grit their teeth, their eyes bulging from their sockets. In some cases they have already been beaten. The soldiers gather around to watch them undress, to watch them shiver in their underwear. As they tremble with fear, even S., who owns a plastics factory in the occupied territories, cannot believe his eyes. "How have we come to this?" he asks. "How have we come to chasing such kids?"

Or maybe the camp doctor is to blame for the analogy haunting me. He is no Mengele, of course, but when I wake him in the dead of night to treat one of the nocturnal detainees who has just been brought in— barefoot, bruised, looking as if he is having an epileptic fit—the doctor shouts at him. And although the detainee is barely seventeen and complains that he was just beaten on his back and on his stomach and over his heart, and although there are indeed ugly red marks all over his body, the doctor shouts loudly at him, "I wish you were dead." And then, turning to me, he laughs and says, "I wish they were all dead."

Or maybe the screams are to blame for my inability to rid my mind of the comparison. At the end of my watch, as I walk from the reservists' tent to the showers, I suddenly hear horrific screams. Strolling in my shorts and clogs, a towel slung over my shoulder, toilet kit in hand, I am stunned by the literally hair-raising screams coming from the other side of the galvanized tin fence of the interrogation ward. From the various human rights reports I have read, I know what might be going on beyond the fence. Are they using the "banana-tie" method of torture or the other, more brutal methods? Or are they simply applying a crude, old-fashioned beating?

Whatever the method, I do know that from this moment on I will have no quiet. Because fifty yards from the showers where I try to rinse off the day's dust and sweat, people scream. Eighty yards from the mess where I try to eat, people scream. A hundred yards from the bed where I try to sleep, people scream. And they scream because other people, wearing a uniform like my own, make them scream. They scream because my Jewish state makes them scream. In a methodical, orderly, and absolutely legal fashion, my beloved democratic Israel makes them scream.

Don't be emotional, I tell myself. Don't jump to conclusions. Doesn't every nation have its dark cellars? Doesn't every nation have its secret services and its special units and its hidden-away interrogation facilities? It just happened to be my bad luck that sent me to the place where I can hear how it all sounds. But as the screams get louder I know there is not a grain of truth in what I have just told myself. Because in this specific interrogation facility they don't interrogate dangerous spies or traitors or terrorists. There are no ticking bombs here. And in the various prison compounds Israel erected in recent years, thousands upon thousands are being held. Many of them are being tortured. In our case the issue is not a dozen deadly enemy agents, and the issue is not a limited and precise operation of counterespionage. The thing here is cracking down on a popular uprising, a forceful occupation of another nation. And therefore what I see and hear here is an entire population of ours—bank clerks, insurance brokers, electronics engineers, retailers, students—imprisoning an entire population of theirs—tile layers, plasterers, lab workers, journalists, clergy, students. This is a phenomenon without parallel in the West. This is systematic brutality no democracy can endure. And I am a part of it all. I comply.

Now the screams grow weaker. They change to sobbing, wailing. Yet I know that from this moment on nothing will be as it was. A person who has heard the screams of another is a transformed person. Whether he does something about it or not, he is transformed. And I have heard the screams of another. I still do. Even as the screaming men stop screaming, I still hear them screaming. I cannot stop hearing.

So although there is no basis for comparison, I begin to understand how it was with other guards who stood in other places over other people locked behind other fences. How these guards heard others' screams— and heard nothing. For in most cases, the evil do not know they are evil. Those who carry out atrocities don't know they are doing so; they are simply obeying orders. Or waiting for a promotion. Or doing what they have to do to get on, when all they really want is to be home, safe and sound. And they worry about their taxes, and about their kids' problems in school. But as they are thinking about home and wife and bills to be paid, their hands unthinkingly hold the weapon; their eyes are on the fence behind which other people are sobbing.

Most reservists are shocked when they first arrive here. They find the sight of other people caged in pens inconceivable. When they hear the screaming for the first time, they are shaken. Yet only two out of sixty reservists refuse to do guard duty in the interrogation ward. Only four or five are really tormented. The others adjust. After a day or two in the detention camp, most reservists find it almost natural to see people enclosed behind barbed wire. The interrogation ward becomes part of routine service, as if this is the way of the world. As if this is what the

IDF was originally assigned to do. And those moral doubts that surface in the first days of service give way to the banality of a soldier's life. When is the next furlough? When can we call home? When will the new uniforms arrive? For after all, this is just another army base, although this specific army base does not protect the border or train soldiers for combat but rather locks boys up. This army base puts boys out in the yard with hoods over their faces.

When we line up for guard duty at one-thirty in the morning, I look at my fellow reservists—at their faces, their slouching bodies, their oversized trousers and disheveled appearances. Are we the soldiers of evil? Are we agents of cruelty? Are we the heartless gatekeepers of oppression? When it comes right down to it, we don't want to be here, either. We don't like this work. It's not for us, this whole fucking business. Like most Israelis, we'd prefer our Israel to be a sort of California, but the trouble is that this California of ours is surrounded by ayatollahs. The trouble is that although we are solid citizens of a consumer-oriented, technological democracy, we find ourselves in deep shit. And when we stand in this weary semicircle—tired, desperate, and miserable, with our tattered belts and with lousy coats that don't keep us warm enough— we, too, feel like victims.

But it's not that simple. When the formation breaks up and I climb the ladder to tower number 6, I realize that what makes this camp tick is the division of labor. The division makes it possible for evil to take place apparently without evil people. This is how it works: The people who vote for Israel's right-wing parties are not evil; they do not round up youngsters in the middle of the night. And the ministers who represent the right-wing voters in government are not evil; they don't hit boys in the stomach with their own fists. And the army's chief of staff is not evil; he carries out what a legitimate, elected government obliges him to carry out. And the commander of the internment facility is not evil—he is doing the best he can under impossible circumstances. And the interrogators—well, after all, they are doing their job. And it is, they are told, impossible to govern the occupied territories unless they do all this. As for the jailers, most of them are not evil, either. They only want to leave all this behind and get back home.

Yet in some mysterious way, all these nonevil people manage together to produce a result that is evil indeed. And evil is always greater than the sum of its parts, greater than all who contribute to it and carry it out. Despite our unkempt exteriors, our clumsiness, our pathetic petit-bourgeois ways, we are evil in Gaza. But this evil of ours is a cunning evil. For it is an evil that happens, as it were, of its own accord, an evil for which the responsibility is no one's. Evil without evildoers.

From watchtower number 6 I can see the sea, the camp, the city of Gaza. Gaza is a city with no hope, no cure. It is the city of the people whose houses and villages we took in 1948 and whose place of refuge we conquered in 1967. It is the city of those whom we exploited during the long decades of occupation, denying them human rights and civil rights and national rights. So in Gaza there are no excuses. Gaza is not even needed for our defense like some strategic heights in the West Bank; it is not even a historically charged terrain like some parts of Judea and Samaria. Gaza is clear and simple. It is the epitome of the absurdity of occupation. It is futile occupation. It is brutal occupation. It corrodes our very existence and it erodes the legitimacy of our existence.

I look down at the tents and fences and barbed wire. For the last time I try to comprehend the inner logic of the place, the necessity that, so to speak, created it. And I summon up all our just claims, all our mitigating circumstances: Aren't we refugees, too? Aren't we, too, victims of violence? And if we are to survive in the Middle East, we must be strong. When attacked, we must respond. The IDF and the Shin Bet are all that protect us from total chaos. Only the willingness to use force is what keeps us alive here.

But it doesn't work here. In the Gaza Beach Detention Camp it cannot work. Because there are places and there are situations that are clear-cut. And this is such a place. This is such a situation. There are no complexities here, no mitigating circumstances. This is what the Palestinians have brought upon us by means of uprising: they deprived us of the illusion of bearable occupation. They have told us that if we are to occupy Gaza, we must have a Gaza Beach prison. And if we are to have such a prison, we must betray ourselves. We must betray everything we were to be and everything we are to be. So the question now is not land for peace. The question is land for our decency. Land for our humanity. Land for our very soul.

• • •

Twenty-two years have passed since I observed my Palestinian enemies and my Israeli commanders from watchtower number 6. The watchtower no longer exists. Two and a half years after I returned home from Gaza Beach, the 1993 Oslo Peace Accords were signed. In a rare moment of bliss, Israel's decency overcame Israel's brutality, and Palestinian realism overcame Palestinian extremism. Within months, the occupation of the city of Gaza was no more. By the spring of 1994, the Israeli detention facility was dismantled. But the Palestinian government never leased the coastal terrain to a Club Med entrepreneur. It handed it over to its own security forces—far more brutal than Israel's. Later on, that secular Palestinian government was overthrown by the radical Islamists, Hamas. After a short lull, the conflict resumed. Once again Israelis and Palestinians were caught in their well-known vicious circle: violence, counterviolence, countercounterviolence. So the grand metaphor of Gaza Beach still applies: the intimacy of the jailers and the jailed; the complexity of the besieged laying siege to the siegers; the jailers imprisoned by their jailed. The fact that the actual reality we live in is surreal.

Perhaps this is the reason that even today, the sights I saw and the sounds I heard in the Gaza Beach facility still haunt me. I am haunted by the notion that we hold them by the balls and they hold us by the throat. We squeeze and they squeeze back. We are trapped by them and they are trapped by us. And every few years the conflict takes on a new form, ever more gruesome. Every few years, the mode of violence changes. The tragedy ends one chapter and begins another, but the tragedy never ends.

TEN

Peace, 1993

LIKE THE SETTLEMENTS, PEACE, TOO, WAS AN OUTCOME OF THE 1967 AND 1973 wars.

In the abstract, the desire for peace had always been a part of Zionism. It was there in the late 1920s when Herbert Bentwich's son Norman realized that the Jews were not alone in Palestine and joined the Jerusalem intellectuals who formed Brit Shalom, the Jewish Peace Alliance. It was there in the early 1930s, when Yitzhak Tabenkin settled the Valley of Harod and Jewish radicals rose against Zionist colonization that led to the dispossession of Arab tenants. It was there in the late 1930s, when the Rehovot writer and orange grower Moshe Smilansky warned that we have partners in the land and that we must learn to live with them. It was there in the early 1940s, when Shmaryahu Gutman led his cadets to Masada and Jewish humanists denounced the militaristic chauvinism that was capturing the hearts of the young. It was there in the late 1940s, when Palmach battalions emptied the Arab villages and conquered Arab Lydda, and Smilansky's nephew Yizhar wrote *Khirbet Khizeh*, a seminal novella about the savagery of expulsion. It was there when the young State of Israel was building and arming itself in the 1950s, and left-wing parties demanded a peace initiative that would deal justly with Palestinian refugees. And it was there in the early 1960s, when Ben Gurion built the Dimona reactor and men of morals denounced the nuclearization of Israel and the Middle East.

For seventy years the yearning for peace existed on the fringes of Zionism, trying to restrain the baser instincts of the Jewish national movement. But after the Arab uprising of 1936, mainstream Zionism wanted more and more land, more and more power. It paid lip service to peace, but it was not willing to pay a real price for it. It saw immigration, settlement, and nation building as its main goals, and it did not consider peace to be an absolute value or a supreme cause.

The real, mainstream Zionist peace movement was born only after the wars of 1967 and 1973. Only the new horizon opened by the Six Day War and the trauma of the Yom Kippur War turned the battle for peace into a central struggle of Israel's public arena. In those same years the Greater Israel idea and the demand to annex the occupied West Bank sprouted, too. The decade of the first settlements was also the decade of the first peace demonstrations. From the tectonic shifts of the late sixties and early seventies rose both the New Right and the New Left. Both rebelled against Labor's intractable ways. Both rebelled against a stagnant reality. Both offered a radical solution and a recipe for instant utopia. As they wrestled against each other and defined each other and empowered each other, the peace movement and the land movement became the shaping forces of the new Israel.

This time I don't have to travel far; Yossi Sarid lives just five miles from my home. From the corner window of his roomy apartment in north Tel Aviv, the Mediterranean Sea beckons, blue and placid. The man who was an icon of the Israeli Left welcomes me with a weak handshake. We've known each other for years. In one election campaign, I even volunteered to be his unofficial adviser. But over the years we've had our differences. This time Yossi knows I've come not to argue but to understand. Where did the peace movement come from, I ask. What was it all about? What did it get right and where did it go wrong? Why has it lost its way?

Sarid was born in Rehovot in 1940. Both his parents were raised in the bleak Polish town of Rafalowka and made *aliyah* in 1935. Several years later, the Nazis arrived in Rafalowka, led the Jews to the forest, instructed them to dig holes in the ground, and shot them into the holes they had just dug. Yossi's mother, Duba, lost her mother and father, sister and brother. She became clinically depressed. His father, Yaakov, lost his entire family but kept an optimistic, upbeat attitude toward life. In 1945, Yaakov seated his son Yossi on a kitchen stool and told him why he had decided to change their surname from Schneider to Sarid (remnant): because they were the last remnants. For Yossi, that moment in the kitchen was formative. Listening to his father, he was certain that they were all alone on this earth.

Yaakov Sarid did well. Within a few years the schoolteacher became school principal, then director general of all socialist schools, and then director general of Israel's Ministry of Education. Yossi Sarid did well, too. He was a gifted child who excelled in every field, often surpassing his peers. But Duba Sarid remained sad all her life. On the nineteenth anniversary of the Rafalowka massacre she took her own life.

From an early age, Yossi was bound for great things. His mother wanted him to be a poet and professor, while his classmates were convinced he would become a great national leader. Wherever he went, Sarid stood out for his quick thinking, sharp tongue, and arrogance. As a boy and as a teenager he was brilliant, rebellious, and conceited. He never accepted authority. He was a sore loser. A stark combination of ambition, talent, and a provocative disposition pushed him from one achievement to the next. At sixteen he published poems in Israel's most prestigious literary journal. At twenty-three he was a leading news editor at Israel's state-run radio. At twenty-four he was the youngest spokesperson ever of the long-ruling Labor Party.

Sarid defines himself as one who was born of Labor's womb. His parents were both active members of the Labor Movement. The neighborhood was Labor, school was Labor, and the youth movement was Labor. Labor was his only frame of reference. No wonder the young party spokesman quickly won the trust and affection of the party elders. Prime Minister Levi Eshkol, Finance Minister Pinchas Sapir, and Secretary General Golda Meir all treated him as a beloved son. The inarticulate, aging rulers groomed their eloquent spokesman and, in a sense, adopted him. They gave him the backing of an all-powerful establishment, while he gave them access to a young Israel and a news media they did not understand. By now it was clear that in due course Sarid could inherit Labor and become prime minister.

Immediately after the Six Day War, Sarid went to study in the United States. Liberal New York, where he spent his graduate school years, was absorbed in the struggle against the Vietnam War. The dynamic Israeli joined the struggle. He identified with Students for a Democratic Society (SDS), took part in protest marches, and became part of the antiwar movement. When he returned to Israel in 1969, he was a different person. Now Israeli policy seemed to him combative, thoughtless, and outdated. Although he ran Labor's election campaign, he was at odds with the government's hawkish line. When he realized that Golda Meir was reluctant to give back the occupied territories for peace, he was outraged. The Meir-Sarid lovefest became an ugly mutual hate relationship.

In the early 1970s, Sarid had already made up his mind: occupation was a disaster, the settlements were a fatal mistake, peace was essential. Israel must retreat to the 1967 border and negotiate with the Palestinian Liberation Organization. Among the radical Left and liberal intelligentsia, some agreed with him. But in Labor he was an outcast, and his new political position—absolute heresy. Under Golda Meir and Moshe Dayan, Israel was bewitched by the empire it had just won and would not listen to the sober warnings of an arrogant prince who had been indoctrinated by the American antiwar movement.

The Yom Kippur War shattered the imperial delusions of Meir and Dayan. It also gave birth to a new political culture based on protest. Sarid became its champion. He mastered the media and fought passionately against the establishment, the settlers, and corruption. The 1977 electoral upheaval that brought Menachem Begin and the right-wing Likud to power made Sarid even stronger. Labor was now in the opposition, and so were the elite associated with it. Many in academia, the media, the business sector, the judiciary, and the civil service felt alienated.

Opposition and alienation suited Sarid just fine. They were compatible with his defiant, haughty nature. Now he was the star. He stood up against Likud and against the settlers and against the rise of a nationalistic-religious Israel. More than any other Israeli he expressed the critical, bitter mindset of post 1973 and post 1977.

Sarid's finest hour came in 1982. As Menachem Begin and Ariel Sharon led Israel to a deceitful and outrageous war in Lebanon, Sarid was the first Zionist member of the Knesset to oppose it. For a while he was public enemy number one: reviled, attacked, ostracized. But when it turned out that the war was indeed folly, Sarid was vindicated. For the hundreds of thousands of Israelis who took part in antiwar demonstrations, Sarid was the undisputed hero of the Israeli peace movement. As the peace protest movement gathered steam, so did Sarid.

Two years later, Sarid quit Labor and joined the left-wing Meretz Party. Although he eventually became leader of the small party and even served for a while as education minister, he never regained the stature he had enjoyed in the 1970s and 1980s. Breaking away from Labor led the promising maverick to a life of frustration and resentment on the fringes of Israeli politics. Although much respected, Sarid embodies a resounding missed opportunity. His is the road not taken.

Sarid's face is heavily lined, etched by disappointment. He is slim, almost bald, and is dressed in a strikingly unfashionable manner. The coffee he drinks is milky and weak. The furnishings in his living room are functional. Although he is still a consummate storyteller, quick-witted and wry, he cannot mask his discontent. The hours I spend with him leave me bewildered and disheartened.

"I'm here not only because you are the icon of the Israeli peace movement," I tell Sarid. "I am here because your biography is the biography of the Left. You were the pillar of the new peace movement that replaced the fading Labor Movement. But the transition from Labor to peace was not only political. It was a deep mental shift from building to protesting, from doing to talking, from leading to opposing. And you are the embodiment of that transition. You are the incarnation of the shift from the Labor culture of socialist-Zionist action to the peace culture of liberal-Israeli protest."

Sarid doesn't deny this. He sees the correlation between what happened to the Left and what happened to him. "What shaped me," he says, "were the disappearance of my parents' home in Rafalowka, the happiness I experienced in Rehovot, and the sanity of Israel in its first nineteen years. But the Six Day War undermined the order of things. And then America opened my eyes. The Yom Kippur War enraged me because it could have been prevented. So when I came of age, politically speaking, I could not be the prince of continuity I was expected to be. I was the wayward son. Rather than walk in the footsteps of the elders, I wanted radical change. I wanted to topple and destroy the national leadership that had betrayed us."

"Therein lies the problem," I say. "Both you and the peace movement were always *against*. Against Meir, against Begin, against occupation. But though you were right to be angry, your failing was that you were always about negation. Protests. Demonstrations. Unlike the old Laborites, you never built anything. You never put up a home or planted a tree. And you never accepted the heavy responsibility of dealing with the complexity of Israeli reality. Emotionally, you remained stuck in the adolescent protest stage of the 1960s and 1970s. The naysaying character of the peace culture made it sterile and eventually unattractive. Politically and emotionally it was unproductive and barren, even corrosive. There was not enough love, not enough compassion. And there was too much judgment. That's why you couldn't fill the vacuum left by the fading Labor culture. After you performed the grand acts of patricide and matricide, you didn't succeed in becoming fathers and mothers yourselves. You did not nurture, you did not inspire, you did not lead. You didn't offer the nation a mature political choice. At the end of the day, your generation achieved only a fraction of what the founders had. It was on your watch, not theirs, that Israel became a rudderless nation, lost at sea with no captain and no compass and no sense of direction."

Sarid has a reply at the ready. As he fiddles with his frameless glasses with his small, nail-bitten fingers, he begins shooting long salvos of sharp words.

"Focusing on occupation was the right thing to do," he says. "Occupation is the father of all sins. Occupation is the mother of atrocity. When we occupied the West Bank and Gaza, we opened a door, and evil winds swept through it. All the depravity you see in today's Israel is because of the occupation. The brutality. The deceit. The decay. Even the army is now rotting because it was forced to be an occupying army. Because of occupation we have been held captive by an insane gang of messianic zealots who may yet destroy us like their forefathers destroyed the Second Temple. Don't you see it? I am afraid we are doomed. And I saw it all coming. I saw it in advance. When I saw the first seeds of occupation, I knew they were the seeds of destruction.

"There is something else," he continues. "You asked me what the real impetus of the peace movement was. Well, let me put it this way: The Israeli peace movement was actually a struggle for normalcy. What we wanted was normalization. The previous generation told us that war was our lot. This is the way things are. In this region and this country, war is normal. But we raised our heads and looked around and saw that in other parts of the world, perpetual conflict is not normal. This is not how others live. This is not how nations sort out their differences. Germany and France, for instance. Vietnam, China. Later the Soviet Union. So we rejected Moshe Dayan's notorious statement, 'The sword shall devour forever.' We looked for a way that would guarantee that the sword shall *not* devour forever. It is not fair to say that we were all about protest and negation. We are the ones who brought a new hope of peace. We said that war upon war is not a decree. We said that peace is within reach. We said we want the normal life other people have, and we want to enjoy the peace other people enjoy."

"That's just it," I challenge Sarid. "You discovered the world, but you ignored our own history. You forgot 1948 and the refugee problem that it created. You were blind to the chilling consequences of Zionism and the partial dispossession of another people that is at the core of the Zionist enterprise. You also failed to realize the gravity of the religious conflict and identity clash between the Western Jewish democratic Israel and the Arab world. You didn't take into consideration the fact that given our history and our geography, peace is hardly likely."

Sarid understands me, but he answers as if he doesn't understand a thing.

"History is not a train station," he says. "Because even if you're stuck at the most remote train station, you can be certain that if you missed the train, another will come. It might take an hour, a day, a week—but the next train will come. Not so history. In history, if you missed the train you were supposed to get on, there is no certainty that there will be another. That's why I am so angry now. And exasperated. And disillusioned. I have no doubt that had I been prime minister in the late 1980s, I would have reached a peace agreement with the Palestinians.

Perhaps I would even have managed to save a few settlements. Perhaps an inch of east Jerusalem. But because the Israeli leadership of the day was cavalier and callous, time slipped by and opportunity slipped by and the train left the station. Now I don't see another train coming. No train at all. And that only makes me more pessimistic and gloomy. I don't love the land as I once did. I don't feel I belong to the nation as I once belonged. In my nightmares I see millions of Palestinians marching to Jerusalem. I see millions of Arabs marching on Israel. I am well over seventy now. I have nothing to lose but the grave I will be buried in. But sometimes, when I look at my grandchildren, my eyes tear up. I am no longer certain that their fate will not be the fate of the children of Rafalowka." Sarid died at home, of cardiac arrest, in December 2015. At his funeral, the novelist Amos Oz eulogized him as a "courageous, stubborn, and perceptive man, first and foremost an educator."

I meet with Yossi Beilin in his posh office in a Herzliya high-tech tower. His suit is light, his tie white, his hair silver-gray. Even though he is in his midsixties, the face of the peace statesman turned business adviser is the face of a boy, marked by only a few lines. Although eight years younger than Sarid, Beilin is far more mature. Throughout the years, he has been the responsible adult of peace: not a man of protests, but a man of deeds; not a man of overwhelming emotions, but a man of calculated action.

Beilin was born in Tel Aviv in the same summer as the State of Israel. His home was imbued with Jewish history and a commitment to Zionism. Years earlier, his grandfather had been a delegate to two of the first Zionist Congresses. His father was the well-read bookkeeper of Tel Aviv's Journalist Union, his mother a teacher of Arabic, Bible, and archaeology, who contributed to the Labor daily *Davar*. Their home was the humble apartment of a family that had lost much of its fortune but not its pride or its passion for learning. On the walls hung photographs of the founders of Zionism and victims of pogroms and the Wailing Wall. Both of Beilin's parents felt that they were privileged to live in the time of redemption, and they instilled this feeling in their young son Yosef.

Beilin was an ambitious boy. He had the resolute drive of the son of poor Ashkenazi Jews. In elementary school he was industrious, diligent,

and eager, and he was accepted on scholarship to the prestigious Herzliya Gymnasium. He never wasted time, never rebelled, never cut loose.
In the afternoons he worked as a juvenile radio reporter. At eight he
became observant; he put on tefillin and ate kosher. But his real God
was flesh and blood: David Ben Gurion. On Fridays, the young Yossi
would walk to Jewish National Fund Boulevard to watch the old man
with the unruly white mane get out of his limousine and enter the simple two-story residence from which he led the Jewish people with infi-
nite wisdom. When Ben Gurion retired, Beilin cried bitterly.

The Israel Beilin remembers from his youth was a future-bound
country. The Weizmann Institute in Rehovot, the reactor in Dimona,
the performing arts center in Tel Aviv, the National Water Carrier.
Economic growth was faster than that of Singapore and South Korea,
Beilin is amazed to recall. The borders were quiet, the Arabs were distant, the Palestinians were not an issue. There was a deep feeling of security and calm. The Jewish tragedy was at last behind us. Zionism had
succeeded in turning the miracle of redemption into the modern and
enlightened State of Israel.

In May 1967 there was a moment of fright. In the days leading up to
war, people in Tel Aviv talked of digging mass graves in the city's parks.
Some feared a second Holocaust. But the resourceful and resolute IDF
that Beilin served in was raring to fight. Beilin, too, was impatiently waiting for the war of his generation. When war did break out, the Israeli
military machine worked like a Swiss clock. It crushed the Arab armies
within days. The nineteen-year-old soldier was struck by the sight of the
burned corpses of Egyptian soldiers lying in the sand, their eyes agape.
When the transistor radio he was holding in his hand announced that
Jerusalem had been liberated and that the Temple Mount was in our
hands, Beilin cried like a child. He felt that justice had been done; what
was not achieved in 1948 was achieved in 1967. The state that was as old
as he was proved strong enough to defend itself and fulfill its rights.

In the late 1960s and early 1970s, Beilin studied at university (political science and literature), wrote for *Davar*, and was active in politics
(Labor). He worked hard, studied hard, and married young. Although
he was not a hawk, occupation never really troubled him. He even supported the establishment of some early settlements. He had absolute
trust in Golda Meir, Moshe Dayan, and their Labor government. Once

again the borders were quiet, the Arabs were distant, and the Palestinians were not really an issue. Everything was just as it should be.

The sirens of October 6, 1973, caught Beilin at home, having just returned from Yom Kippur prayers to his young wife and their two-year-old son. He thought it must be a mistake. Could the Arabs really be foolish enough to attack after the humiliating defeat they had suffered in 1967? But hours later, the twenty-five-year-old reservist was in uniform, serving as a radio operator in the supreme command headquarters. With his own ears he heard the Israeli army collapse. The soldiers at the Suez Canal were crying for help. The generals were shouting at each other. There was no order, no discipline, no dignity. The communication networks were screaming in panic. The venerated Moshe Dayan walked the corridors like a defeated marshal. The face of the chief of staff was gray with horror. In the halls of Israel's supreme command there was talk of the end of the Third Temple.

While war was still raging, Beilin turned his back on religion, stopped putting on tefillin and eating kosher. He drove and wrote on the Sabbath, and he never again walked into a synagogue to pray. Not only was his faith shattered, the world he trusted had crumbled. The gods he worshipped seemed now like nothing but deceitful idols. "It was like a religious revelation, but in reverse," Beilin tells me. "There was terrible pain and a terrible void because of the sudden disappearance of the *shekhinah*, of divine presence. Nothing was valid anymore. Nothing was secure or trustworthy. There was no one up there who was wiser than myself and saw what I didn't see. There was no God and there were no leaders, and there was no one to whom I could raise my eyes. I was all alone. I bore all the responsibility. I was personally obliged to make sure there was not another war or calamity, and that the Third Temple was not destroyed."

In the decade after the Yom Kippur War, Beilin became the promising young thinker of Labor. In 1977 he was Shimon Peres's aide and Labor Party spokesperson. By 1984 he was cabinet secretary of a Likud-Labor coalition government. Then he became a peace entrepreneur. In 1987, he stood by Shimon Peres's side as the foreign minister tried to negotiate peace with Jordan's King Hussein. In 1989, he held indirect talks with a PLO representative in The Hague. In 1990, he signed a joint Israeli-Palestinian declaration in Jerusalem. After Yossi Sarid left

Labor and became marginalized, Beilin took his place as the great white hope of peace. He was the man seen most likely to fashion the historic conciliation between Israel and the Palestinians.

In June 1992, Yitzhak Rabin led Labor to victory in the national elections and formed a center-left government. Rabin despised Beilin and Beilin disdained Rabin, but the opportunity was irresistible. After the failure of the Lebanon War and after the Palestinian uprising of 1987–92, the Right was crushed. For the first time ever, there was a peace majority in the Knesset. The prime minister was committed to reaching an interim agreement with the local Palestinian leadership within six to nine months. A man like Beilin wouldn't miss such an opportunity. A man like Beilin would not wait for the prime minister to lead the way to peace.

As deputy foreign minister, Beilin acts on his own accord. On December 4, 1992, he sends his envoy, Dr. Yair Hirschfeld, to a clandestine, unauthorized meeting in London with the PLO's finance minister, Abu Ala. On January 20, 1993, he sends Hirschfeld and another envoy, Dr. Ron Pundak, to negotiate with Abu Ala in Sarpsborg, south of Oslo. On February 11, 1993, he sends Hirschfeld and Pundak to a second round of talks in Sarpsborg. Prime Minister Rabin and Foreign Minister Peres don't have a clue, but in Sarpsborg a serious document is being drafted. It is agreed that Israel will withdraw its forces from the Gaza Strip, consent to an autonomous Palestinian administration in the West Bank, and open direct negotiations regarding a final status accord.

Only in mid-February 1993 does Beilin show Peres the draft of the Norway paper. He downplays the matter and in a sense deceives his superior. Though he informs Peres, Peres does not fully comprehend the significance of the Sarpsborg talks. Therefore, when the foreign minister reports to the prime minister, neither of them really gets it. Rabin is not keen on the plan, but he does not instruct Peres to stop the negotiations. The befuddlement of Israel's top two statesmen plays into Beilin's hand. Just as Yehuda Etzion, Pinchas Wallerstein, and Hanan Porat extracted from the 1975 Rabin-Peres government a vague approval to settle in Samaria, Beilin extracts from the 1993 Rabin-Peres government a vague approval to negotiate with the PLO. There is a crack in the dam. A speedy process is under way.

In the spring of 1993, three additional rounds of talks are held. In

May, the director general of the foreign ministry, Uri Savir, joins the
Israeli team in Norway. In early June, Yoel Zinger, legal adviser and
Rabin confidant, comes aboard. On June 6, 1993, Rabin instructs Peres
to halt negotiations. It seems he has suddenly realized how significant
they are and panicked. A few days later he acquiesces. Now the negotiations center on mutual recognition between Israel and the PLO. They
are navigated by a team of four who meet secretly every weekend in Tel
Aviv, Jerusalem, or Herzliya: Rabin, Peres, Beilin, and Zinger. But the
lead navigator is Deputy Foreign Minister Beilin. He is the only Israeli
who knows where he is heading and the only one who understands the
meaning of every move. He is the one leading the prime minister and
the foreign minister—and the national agenda.

"Did you ever discuss the historic significance of what you were
doing?" I ask. "Never," answers Beilin with coolheaded candor. "Did
you discuss the risks involved?" "Never." "Did you consider alternatives?" "No." "Did you realize you were on the road to establishing a
Palestinian state?" "I did, though Rabin and Peres—not quite. We assumed that the Oslo talks were a secret channel that would remain secret. The political outcome was supposed to be a limited autonomy
agreement between the Israeli government and the local Palestinian
leadership in the West Bank and Gaza Strip. No one foresaw the historic handshake between Rabin and Arafat. No one knew that Israel's
partner would be the Palestine Liberation Organization. What the Israeli team dealt with were details. Much thought was given to minor
matters that in retrospect had no real importance."

At the end of July, as their self-confidence rises, the Palestinians say
they will not sign the interim agreement if there is no mutual recognition. Rabin is outraged, but by now he is trapped. He has locked himself
into a commitment to political breakthrough, and as there is no breakthrough with Syria, the Palestinians are his only chance. Therefore he
yields once again to Palestinian demands and walks the path on which
Beilin is leading him. On August 18, Rabin authorizes Shimon Peres to
secretly sign the agreement in Oslo. On September 10, Yitzhak Rabin
recognizes the PLO. Then, on September 13, Rabin surrenders to a
highly significant last-minute maneuver by Arafat, changing the phrase
"Palestinian team" in the agreement's preamble to "PLO." An hour
later, the prime minister of Israel goes out to the White House lawn

with the president of the United States and the leader of the Palestinian people and makes history. Yossi Beilin sits in one of the back rows on the lawn, not quite believing what he is seeing. He brought Rabin and Peres here. He brought Israel here. He touches peace.

"I'll tell you how I see it," I say to Beilin. "To begin with, you were not a great believer in peace with the Palestinians. Following the Yom Kippur trauma, you wanted peace, and you realized that occupation was dangerous, and you thought an agreement that would return the West Bank to Jordan would solve the problem. But by the end of 1988, Jordan's King Hussein no longer wanted anything to do with the West Bank. And by 1992 your next go-to option, negotiating with the local Palestinian leadership, was no longer on the table. All you were left with was Arafat. But Arafat was no easy matter. Arafat represented the entire Palestinian people—not just the residents of the occupied territories, but also the Palestinian refugees and the Israeli Palestinians. Arafat was the embodiment of the armed struggle against Zionism. So if there was to be a peace agreement with Arafat, it was to be completely different from the one discussed with the local Palestinians. An Arafat peace agreement should have been based on a Palestinian about-face: recognizing the Jewish people, recognizing the Jewish national movement and its national rights, relinquishing the Palestinians' right of return.

"In hindsight, it seems clear that you did not think about the religious, cultural, and existential dimensions of the conflict. You did not remember the Arab rejection of the Balfour Declaration of 1917, the Arab outrage at the UN partition plan of 1947, and the calamity wrought by the war of 1948. All you saw was the relatively easy problem of 1967, namely, occupation, which you thought you could solve in a relatively easy manner. That a person of your intelligence was tempted to make peace in such a hasty way is unconscionable. Rather than use the unique circumstances of the early 1990s to begin a long process that would eventually lead to a true peace, you opted for the appearance of peace. You thought you were manipulating Peres and Rabin, but in reality it was the Palestinians who manipulated you. Although they were at a strategic disadvantage, they still managed to knock you to the ground."

Beilin listens quietly and patiently. One of his virtues is his ability to remain detached, ice-cold. "If it were up to me," he says, "I would have gone for a final-status agreement right there and then. I would have solved all the core issues you mentioned in a short time. But in 1993 Rabin did not want a final comprehensive peace. I had to sew a suit he would be willing to wear. I knew the suit was far from perfect. I knew that any delay would serve the enemies of peace. But since I was not calling the shots, I had no other way. I had to work within a set of given circumstances. Immediately after the White House ceremony I flew to Tunisia and started to negotiate a real peace agreement with Arafat's most senior deputy, Mahmoud Abbas. It took time, and meanwhile things happened. Baruch Goldstein committed the Hebron massacre in February 1994. Then Yigal Amir murdered Yitzhak Rabin in November 1995. Events happened that I could not foresee. To this day I am convinced that if Rabin had not been assassinated, peace would not have been assassinated. We would not be having this conversation because Israel would have peace with Palestine, Syria, and the Arab world."

The peace story is also my story. For upper-middle-class secular Ashkenazi Israelis like me, peace was not only a political idea; in the last quarter of the twentieth century, it defined our identity. Peace was the social integrator and the pillar of fire of our tribe. Peace was our religion. In 1965, when I was in third grade, our most sacred song was the peace song "Tomorrow." But the peace promised by the song was abstract. It had soldiers shedding their uniforms, but it had no Arabs. It was a peace one yearns for but doesn't really believe in. When I was in tenth grade, our most sacred song was the "Song for Peace." The peace of this song was one of protest: it was the chilling outcry of dead soldiers. It had defiance, but it, too, had no Arabs. The peace of the "Song for Peace" was angry and confrontational and political, but it was amorphous just like its predecessor. Still, its demand for peace was exhilarating.

The transition from the peace of "Tomorrow" to the peace of the "Song for Peace" characterized my generation. After the Six Day War and the occupation of the West Bank and Gaza, we believed peace was possible. After the Yom Kippur War we—rightly—thought Israel had missed the opportunity to prevent war by making peace. After the political upheaval of 1977, the establishment of the settlements, and the

Lebanon War, peace became our plaint against the Right and the settlers. Peace was not based on a sober historical diagnosis, and it did not
offer a realistic strategic prognosis. Peace was an emotional, moral, and
intellectual stance vis-à-vis an ongoing, intolerable conflict, and an Israel changing its face.

When I was in high school I would often go to peace movement
gatherings. I listened with admiration as luminaries like the novelist
Amos Oz, the journalist Uri Avnery, and the former colonel Meir Pa'il
promised peace. When I was a soldier on leave I used to participate in
the thrilling Jerusalem torch-bearing peace marches, and I listened
with devotion as Yossi Sarid and Yossi Beilin promised peace. When I
was a university student I was an enthusiastic activist in the peace movement. I wrote and distributed peace pamphlets, and I believed with all
my heart in the promise of peace. But only when I turned thirty and
began listening seriously to what Palestinians were actually saying did I
realize that the promise of peace was unfounded. It played a vital moral
role in our lives, but it had no empirical basis. The promise of peace was
benign, but it was bogged down by a systematic denial of the brutal reality we live in.

I worked out a theory. The theory assumed we lived in a tragedy: an
almost eternal struggle between two peoples sharing a homeland and
fighting over it. For seventy years we Jews had the stamina needed to
withstand this tragedy. We were vital enough to be jolly and optimistic
while enduring an ongoing conflict. But as fatigue wore us down, we
began to deny the tragedy. We wanted to believe there was no tragic
decree at the heart of our existence. So we had to pretend that it was not
by tragic circumstances that our fate was decided, but by our own deeds.
The territories we conquered in 1967 gave us an excellent pretext for
this much-needed pretense, as it allowed us to concentrate on an internal conflict of our own making. The Right said, "If we only annex the
West Bank, we'll be safe and sound." The Left said, "If we only hand
over the West Bank, we'll have peace." The Right said, "Our dead died
because of the Left's illusions," while the Left said, "Our dead died because of the Right's fantasies." Rather than face a tragic reality imposed
on us from without, we chose to create a simplistic narrative of Right
against Left. It's not the Arabs' fault, it's the Jews'. It's not the Middle
East, it's the Israeli government. It's not the fundamental Israeli condi-

tion but some specific mistake made by some specific Israeli politician. In an ingenious way, we turned the tragedy in which we live into a morality play. We created a virtual reality that enables us to blame ourselves rather than face the cruel reality we are trapped in.

From this general theory I worked out a theory of the Israeli Left: its fundamental flaw was that it had never distinguished between the issue of occupation and the issue of peace. Regarding the occupation, the Left was absolutely right. It realized that occupation was a moral, demographic, and political disaster. But regarding peace, the Left was somewhat naïve. It counted on a peace partner that was not really there. It assumed that because peace was needed, peace was feasible. But the history of the conflict and the geostrategy of the region implied that peace was not feasible. The correct moral position of the Left was compromised by an incorrect empirical assumption.

Why did the Left cling to this empirically incorrect assumption? Because this assumption enabled it to deny the tragedy of 1948 and to ignore the schism between its new liberal values and the Zionist predicament. It is well known that the euphoria of 1967 led the Right to believe that Greater Israel was possible. What is less generally acknowledged is that the same euphoria led the Left to believe that Greater Peace was possible. The struggle between these two fantasies empowered both sides and enabled Israelis to escape reality. Instead of sticking to the sound, rational position of ending occupation simply because it is immoral and destructive, the Left endorsed the unsound and irrational belief that ending occupation would bring peace. There was a tendency to see the settlers and settlements as the source of evil and to overlook Palestinian positions that were not occupation-based. There was a magic belief that Israel was the supreme power that could end the conflict by ending occupation. The Left adopted the peace illusion because it had a messianic dimension: it promised Israel a new existential condition. It was to replace the badlands under our feet with the open blue skies of an imaginary future.

So it transpired that peace stopped being peace. It was no longer bound by a realistic analysis of power, interests, opportunity, threat, and alliance—by sound judgment. It ignored Arab aspirations and political culture. It overlooked the existence of millions of Palestinian refugees whose main concern was not the occupation but a wish to return to their lost Palestine. It was not based on a factual state of affairs, but on a sentimental state of mind. It was a wish, a belief, a faith. In the Israel I grew up in, peace was an existential need that gave birth to a messianic concept. It enabled Israel's WASPs (White Ashkenazi Supporters of Peace) to believe they could be Israelis without being brutal. It made it possible for progressive Zionists to delude themselves into thinking that they could appease Zionism's disinherited other. Thus it became the totem of the secular tribe. Peace promised us that we could be pure and righteous and beautiful. Peace meant we would not have to fight for centuries, for we could write a happy ending to our tragedy.

I drive up to Jerusalem to meet with Ze'ev Sternhell, Menachem Brinker, and Avishai Margalit, three of the leading intellectuals of the Israeli peace movement. Two of them were my university professors and the third a political mentor. I ask them what went wrong, what thwarted the peace process.

Sternhell says that Oslo was too little too late. But the real problem was that the Left never managed to advance beyond the well-established Ashkenazi elites. It never managed to build a party that resembled the European social-democratic parties. "This is why we didn't save Israel in time," Sternhell tells me. "This is why I am now racked by anxiety," he says. "Israel is my life, but I see Israel fading away. I see a terminal illness consuming the nation I so love."

Brinker surprises me by echoing my own theory. He says that like the Right, the Left succumbed to messianic delusions following the Six Day War. It was convinced that Israel was omnipotent. It was certain that everything was in our hands. "We were naïve, but we were also arrogant," says Brinker. "In principle our position was right, but we refused to see that it was inapplicable. First the Arab states said no. Then King Hussein said no. And the Palestinians were always fickle. But we never seriously dealt with these difficulties. We insisted that if Israel did A, B, and C, there would be peace. That's why we were vulnerable to attacks from the Right. Time and again the Right exposed our internal contradictions. It proved that the Arab partners we were counting on were not really there."

Margalit surprises me, too. Not for a second did he believe in Oslo, he says. One does not hop over a chasm in two jumps. He anticipated violence, killings, and a loss of momentum. He saw in advance that euphoria would evaporate and the counterforces would have the upper hand. He never trusted Rabin, Peres, or Barak. He did not believe peace would be achieved at Camp David. But he never publicly criticized the peace process because he didn't want to sabotage it. As a movement, the peace movement did have great achievements, he tells me. "Over the years we dominated the debate regarding occupation. We even scored a verbal victory over the Right, which eventually adopted our wording regarding the two-state solution. But on the ground, we lost badly. We didn't stop colonization. We never managed to forge a coalition wide enough and strong enough to stop the settlers. Now it's too late. It's almost irreversible. I don't see a power within Israel fierce enough to stop the state founded by my parents from becoming an apartheid state."

I take a seat in a café in the German colony in Jerusalem. Nearby, on Lloyd George Street, stood the headquarters of Peace Now, where I spent many long nights as a student. Here we tried to stop the Lebanon War—and failed. Here we tried to stop the settlements—and failed. Here we tried to bring about peace—and failed. Here we failed to stop the secular Right and the religious Right from taking over the sane Israel we loved. It was a powerful experience. The struggle emboldened us. The protests bolstered our virtuous view of ourselves. The hope for peace gave us meaning. But after listening to Sarid, Beilin, Sternhell, Brinker, and Margalit, I ask myself what was our flaw. Why did we fail in such an astounding way?

My answer is simple. We were right to try peace. We were right to send Beilin's team to meet with the Palestinians and offer them a grand deal: a demilitarized Palestine living side by side with a Jewish democratic Israel along the 1967 border. But we should never have promised ourselves peace or assumed that peace was around the corner. We should have been sober enough to say that occupation must end even if the end of occupation did not end the conflict. Our goal was to draw a border, to win international recognition for that border, and to gradually and cautiously withdraw to that new border. Our task was to convince the Israeli public that an occupying Israel is doomed and a postoccupation

Israel will be viable and strong. Our mission was to design the greatest Zionist project of all: dividing the land.

But we did not. We failed to say to the world and to our people that occupation must cease even if peace cannot be reached. We failed to tell ourselves the truth about the Palestinian wish to return to their pre-1948 villages and homes. Rather than deal courageously with reality as it is, we fell for the romantic belief in "peace now." So when the great moment of opportunity arrived in 1993, we missed it. In Oslo we tried to impose a flawed concept of peace on a Middle East reality that soon rejected it. But even after rejection was apparent, we clung to the flawed concept. As buses exploded on the streets of our cities, we kept singing the hymns of our imaginary peace. This is how we lost the trust and respect of our countrymen, who turned away from us because we failed to acknowledge that our wished-for peace was turning into a macabre farce. Our failure was not caused by the forces we encountered, but by our own weakness: by our lack of intellectual integrity and courage, and by our immaturity. We never deigned to inherit the legacy of the founders of Israel that we were supposed to inherit, and we didn't continue in the footsteps of those we were supposed to follow. The peace clan balked at the historical continuum. It refused to take the reins of true responsibility and remained a 1970s-style protest movement.

Sarid, Beilin, Sternhell, Brinker, and Margalit were the teachers and leaders of my generation, and I feel close to them. I feel empathy and affinity. Even when I argue with them, we are of one stock. Sarid, Margalit, and Brinker understood the folly of occupation in the summer of 1967. Beilin and Sternhell saw the light after the 1973 war and the 1977 upheaval. It is to their credit that they grasped this facet of the story very early and clearly. They were courageous enough to fight a consensus that regarded them as loonies or traitors. But my mentors fostered an oedipal political culture whose main theme was patricide. In a sense, they never grew up. They never became leaders. And they made the mistake of detaching the occupation issue from the wider context of Israeli life and Middle East reality. They were blinded three times over: They saw the inner circle of the conflict in which an Israeli Goliath stands over a Palestinian David, but they didn't see the outer circle in which an Arab-Islamic Goliath stands over an Israeli David. They saw that for the Palestinians the 1967 occupation was disastrous, but they did not see that for many Palestinians there are other matters that are far more severe and visceral than occupation, like the homes they lost in 1948. They knew that Israel had to deal with the challenge of occupation, but they overlooked and dismissed the other critical challenges facing the state. Because of these three cognitive flaws, their vision was impaired and their scope of reality grew more and more narrow, until finally they were disconnected from reality. The well-meaning leaders of the Israeli Left and the Israeli peace movement became irrelevant.

I drive back to Tel Aviv to meet with Amos Oz. We've known each other a long time. Over a period of twenty years, we have been meeting to discuss life and literature, to debate peace and politics. Although I truly love him, in recent years I have often disagreed with him. Oz is *the* peace prophet. He is the guru of the peace movement and the chief rabbi of Israel's peace congregation.

I find Amos in a surprisingly good mood. In Italy they have just produced an opera based on his poetic novel *The Same Sea*. His books have been translated into dozens of languages and are read in dozens of countries. The Jerusalem orphan who found a home in Kibbutz Hulda is Israel's most distinguished author. But his head remains level, and he is as humble as he has always been. In a plaid shirt and old beige trousers he sits in a remote corner of a tidy, plain café in Ramat Aviv. He rises to his feet, shakes my hand, and greets me warmly.

"I am not an Orientalist," Oz says. "But what I do every morning, from five A.M. on, is to try to get into other people's heads, to imagine how they see the world. In June 1967, when I returned from war in the Sinai desert to Jerusalem, dressed in uniform and carrying an Uzi submachine gun, what I saw was not David's capital. I saw the Arab shoeshine boy looking at me fearfully. And I remembered my childhood in British Mandate Jerusalem and the intimidating, surly British soldiers. I understood that although Jerusalem is my city, it is a foreign city. I knew I should not rule over it, that Israel must not rule over it. Old Jerusalem is our past, but it is not our present, and it endangers our future. We must not be tempted by what many are fond of describing as its holy silence.

"When I came back to Hulda, I realized that what I saw in Jerusalem, others did not see. Both the Right and mainstream Labor thought of 1967 as the completion of 1948. What we were not strong enough to do then, we were strong enough to do now. What we didn't conquer then, we conquered now. I thought that state of mind was dangerous. I realized that the West Bank and Gaza Strip are the Palestinians' poor man's lamb. I knew we must not take it. Not one inch, not one settlement. We must keep the territories only as a surety until peace is reached.

"Labor's lions thought as I did: Levi Eshkol, Pinchas Sapir, Abba Eban, Yitzhak Ben Aharon. But the foxes wanted to annex. And when the lions did not roar, the foxes raised their heads, and I was alone. The journalists Uri Avnery and Amos Kenan preceded me, but within the world of Labor I was the first. I wrote against Moshe Dayan's desire for 'living space' and against the rhetoric of land liberation. I called for the establishment of a Palestinian state. I thought both morals and realism dictated only one solution, the two-state solution.

"I was savagely attacked. Even in my own Labor paper, *Davar.* Even in my Kibbutz Hulda. A fellow columnist demanded that *Davar* stop running my articles. Others treated me as a traitor or madman. At the very same time, Israel's most respected novelists and poets were endorsing the idea of a Greater Israel: Nobel laureate Shmuel Yosef Agnon and poet laureates Uri Zvi Grinberg, Nathan Alterman, and Chaim Gouri. I saw the nation drifting away, changing its face. It was no longer the Israel I thought I knew.

"By the early 1990s it was all very different. Reality had struck and changed both Israelis and Arabs. The 1973 war made the Arabs realize they could not take us by force. The 1987–92 Palestinian uprising made the Israelis realize there is a Palestinian people, and they will not go away. They were here, and they were here to stay. After a hundred years of mutual blindness we suddenly saw one another. The illusion that the other would disappear was gone. That's why the views held by only a handful of Israelis after the Six Day War were eventually adopted by the majority. The ideology of the 1967 Left became the platform of Rabin, Peres, the 1993 government. Peace had moved from the fringes to the very center.

"I saw up close the process Rabin and Peres went through. I knew them well. They both used to come visit me on Friday nights at Hulda. What changed Rabin were the young people of Israel. He realized that the boys of the twenty-first century would not fight as he did in 1948. What changed Peres was the world. He was visiting many countries and listening, and he realized that he did not want Israel to be the new South Africa. For different reasons and in different ways, both Rabin and Peres realized that the conflict had to end. The predictable hawks they were became hesitant doves.

"When Peres secretly sent me a draft of the Oslo Accords, I saw the problem. I understood that in reality, what we had here was a tricky tripartite agreement between the government of Israel, the PLO, and the settlers. But still I thought it was a good beginning. I believed Oslo would bring down the cognitive wall separating Israelis and Palestinians. And once the wall came down, there would be progress. We would advance step by step toward a true historic conciliation.

"I made one big mistake. I underestimated the importance of fear. The Right's strongest argument is fear. They don't say it out loud because they are ashamed to, but their most compelling argument is that we are afraid. It's a legitimate argument. I, too, am afraid of the Arabs. So if I were to start the peace movement all over again, that's the one change I would make. I would address our fear of the Arabs. I would have a genuine dialogue about the Israeli fear of extinction.

"Desperate? I am not yet desperate. Oslo was not genuinely implemented because it was a baby unloved by both parents. But it's not too late. The settlement problem can be resolved. Both sides know compromise is essential. They don't love each other. They cheat on each other. They shout at each other. But whether they like it or not, they see each other. In this sense the emotional breakthrough of 1993 was real. The taboo was broken. The cognitive block fell away. In spite of everything, we now face the Palestinians, nation to nation, to discuss the division of the land. That is no small feat. Peace is an experiment that has not yet failed."

So I end my peace journey in Hulda, where Amos Oz lived for half his life. Hulda is Ben Shemen's twin sister: it began as an agricultural farm that was to teach Jewish immigrants how to work the land of Israel.

Located in the center of the country, it was founded by the Zionist movement in 1908 on land bought from Arabs, near the Jaffa–Jerusalem railway and the Arab village of Hulda. An olive grove in memory of Theodor Herzl was planted here, too, and a baronial house called Herzl House was built. But in the summer of 1929 the Hulda farm was attacked and burned down by its Arab neighbors. So when the moderate, harmony-seeking socialist Gordonia commune settled here a year later, in the Herzl house in the Herzl pine forest beside the olive grove, it was to make a statement: although we were shot at, and our houses were burned down and our trees uprooted, we shall not give up our dream.

For eighteen years the Zionist commune of Hulda and the Palestinian village of Hulda lived side by side. The utopia-building pioneers and the tradition-bound villagers were good neighbors. But when hostilities erupted after the 1947 UN partition plan, things changed. On March 31, 1948, Arabs attacked a Hulda convoy wending its way to a besieged Jerusalem, killing twenty-two passengers. Ben Gurion decided enough was enough. Six weeks before declaring the establishment of the State of Israel, its would-be founder decided that the Jews must go on the offensive and conquer the Arab villages along the road to Jerusalem. On April 6, 1948, just after 2:00 A.M., the soldiers of the first-ever Zionist battalion left Kibbutz Hulda, crossed the Herzl forest, and attacked the Arab village of Hulda. By 4:00 A.M. the village was conquered. Its inhabitants fled, and within weeks its houses were demolished and its fields were pillaged. Much of the land of the Palestinian village of Hulda was transferred to the kibbutz.

Forty-five years later, I traveled with Palestinian refugees through Israel. In April 1993, as the secretive peace process was under way in Norway, I brought Jamal Munheir back to Hulda. I had been looking for the Hulda refugee throughout the West Bank and finally found him. The seventy-year-old Palestinian remembered his village as if he had just left it. He never suspected anything, he told me. How could he have suspected? Throughout the years he watched his Jewish neighbors, first with suspicion, then with wonder, and then with admiration. He saw them arrive as pale and poor Jews from Russia and saw them grow stronger and take root and turn their olive grove into a piece of paradise. They learned to grow wheat, tend sheep, and press olives for oil. And from his broad field, which bordered on theirs, he sensed that his new neighbors were decent and hardworking. Although their ways were peculiar and their women were half-naked and they had a communal arrangement that did not allow a man to own his own property, they had devotion. Although they were not God-fearing, they were respectful. The kibbutzniks stood by courteously and patiently as the Palestinian girls drew water from the deep old well that the village shared with the commune. And they would visit the village guesthouse, the *madaffa*, and they invited the villagers to visit their own communal dining hall. They bought vegetables from the villagers and supplied them with medicine and medical assistance. Jamal did business with his neighbors, too. And at night he would sit with the Arabic-speaking field guard, Aharon. Aharon would tell Jamal the fairy tales of Hans Christian Andersen and Jamal would tell Aharon ancient stories of demons. They would sit silently by the fire, sipping strong black coffee from small cups and listening to the distant sounds from surrounding villages, where jackals were howling into the great night.

But then, in April 1948, a Jewish army positioned a mortar by the deep old well and began to bombard the village. And the Jewish soldiers came up the path the girls used to walk with earthenware jugs of water balanced on their heads. And there was machine gun fire all over the village. Jamal Munheir took his old mother and put her on a camel and escaped with his family to Dayr Muhaysin. And when Dayr Muhaysin was attacked, on the very next day, he escaped with his mother and family to Abu Shusha. And two weeks later he watched from Abu Shusha as bulldozers razed his family's homes in Hulda. He watched as a vast cloud of white dust rose over the village he was born in and his father was born in and his grandfather was born in.

A month later, the Jews reached Abu Shusha, and Jamal Munheir escaped to Al Qubab. From Al Qubab he escaped to Ein Ariq, and from Ein Ariq to Yatta, from Yatta to Amman, and then back to Yatta. To this day he is a penniless refugee in the West Bank village of Yatta, on the outskirts of Hebron.

But during all those wanderings and during all those years, Jamal told me, he never forgot Hulda. So when I drove him in my car over the dirt road to Hulda in the spring of 1993, he smiled a wide child's smile and murmured: Hulda, Hulda. Nothing in the world like the soil of Hulda. He took me to the site where the threshing floor for the grain harvest had been, to the pile of rubble that was once his aunt's house, to the pile of rubble that was once his uncle's house, and to the pile of rubble that was once his own house. He told me he didn't know how to say what's in his heart. Only God knows. Only Allah himself. For there is no place in the world but this place. There isn't and there won't be any other place. This is Jamal Munheir's one and only place in the world.

From the ruins of the village we drove to the Herzl forest, and I parked by the Herzl House. As we sat under the old pine trees, a gentle wind rose and caressed our faces. All around us was the forest's silence. Jamal raised his hand and pointed to the sea of land in front of us and said, "This is my plot. This is my land. These are the hundreds of dunams of the Munheir family."

"You were a rich man," I said. Immediately, I realized I have made a terrible mistake. Jamal erupted, "My heart burns when I come here. I go crazy when I come here. We were respected people. Englishmen and Jews and Arabs listened to us. Our words carried weight. But today, who are we, what are we? Beggars. No one listens to us. No one respects us. We, who owned all this land, don't even have one grain of wheat. Only a UNRWA refugee certificate."

He went silent. Under the old pine trees the only sound was that of my small tape recorder recording the silence. Until Jamal turned to me again, crying, saying that from the beginning of time his forefathers lived here and died here and were buried here. They plowed this plot of land for hundreds of years. From this old well they drew water for generations. Until the Jews came to Hulda and wiped out the Munheir family. Until the Jews conquered and pillaged Hulda. "Where is Rasheed?" Jamal cried. "And where is Mahmoud, and where are all the village people? Where is our Hulda?"

Of all the houses in the village of Hulda, only the *madaffa* guesthouse remains. Small and charming, it still stands at the top of the southern hill, commanding breathtaking scenery. Its black basalt stones are solid, its roof flat, its windows arched. Today, it is used as a sculptor's workshop and is surrounded by a sculpture garden. As I approach the building, nearly twenty years after I was here with Jamal Munheir, the sound of sirens breaks the quiet. It is spring again—and it is Israel's Memorial

Day. The sirens engulfing me are the sirens of memory. So I stand at attention facing the *madaffa*. In the howling sirens, I see the vanished village of Hulda.

In the two decades that have passed since Jamal Munheir led me through his Hulda, the remains of the village were obliterated. Nothing is left now but the *madaffa*, carob trees, a few hedgerows of prickly pear cactus, the remaining wall of a house, another wall, a pile of rubble. The Palestinian village of Hulda was succeeded by the Israeli kibbutz of Mishmar David. In recent years Mishmar David fell on hard times and ceased to be a kibbutz. So now the kibbutz that succeeded the village is gone, too. It is being replaced by an upper-middle-class community of Israel's new bourgeoisie. A giant bulldozer razes one of the kibbutz's old egalitarian homes. Arab workmen build villas for Jews on what used to be an Arab village, on what used to be Jamal Munheir's home and land.

This time I am on my own, but I make the exact same journey I made with Jamal years ago. I drive to the Herzl forest and park by the Herzl House and walk among the old pine trees. There is the same silence here, the same gentle wind.

First I walk up the external stairs of the colonial Herzl House to the second-story porch. I look out at the forest and think of the solace that the forest was to have been for the Jews. Then I go on to the statue commemorating a well-known guard who fell here while defending the forest and the house in 1929. Then I go out of the forest and walk down the path that separated the Hulda commune's olive tree grove from Jamal Munheir's wheat fields. It is one of the most beautiful paths in the Plain of Judea. On each side of it is a sad row of tall palm trees marching into the horizon. The wind is soft, the skies are a constable blue. The silhouettes of the Hulda kibbutz are to my left, the silhouette of the vanished Arab Hulda to my right.

Hulda is part of my own biography. As a child I came to this forest on winter weekends to forage for mushrooms. As an adolescent I rode my bike here with my friends, looking for adventure. As a soldier on leave I brought girlfriends here in my father's car. Later, as a peace activist, I came to Hulda in my red VW Beetle in order to drive Amos Oz to Peace Now demonstrations. But since my visit here with Jamal Munheir in the spring of 1993, Hulda has changed for me. My homeland has changed for me. Peace has changed, too. I realize now why Israel's peaceniks live against occupation. I understand now what brilliant use we WASPs make of the conflict's present in order to protect ourselves from the unbearable implications of the conflict's past. For we must protect ourselves from our past and our deeds and from Jamal Munheir. We concentrate on the occupation so that we can justify to ourselves the magnificent vineyard that stands in the midst of Hulda like some proof of wrongdoing.

Planted in 1999, the Hulda vineyard is now one of the largest in the country. Six different varieties of grapes grow here, including Merlot, Cabernet Sauvignon, and Sauvignon Blanc. The vineyard is well tended and thriving, and at the end of every row blooms a bush of pink roses.

Rows 1 through 190 of the vineyard are Hulda West. Here, between the kibbutz and the path, stood the Zionist olive grove. Rows 191 through 285 are Hulda East. Here, between the path and the well, lay Jamal Munheir's wheat field. Good earth, bad earth. Earth shifting under our feet.

I go down to the wadi. The deep water well is now blocked up. I find the square pool into which the well water was drawn. I walk up the path the Palestinian girls used to walk with earthenware jugs on their heads. I walk up the path that the Israeli soldiers climbed, under the cover of the three-inch shells that the mortar positioned by the well shot at the village. I stand once again atop the village hill, scanning the Hulda Valley. Two miles away is the yellow summit of Tel Gezer by which Herbert Bentwich settled nearly a century ago. A mile and a half away are the gray ruins of Abu Shusha, where in 1940, Yosef Weitz came to the conclusion that in order to survive, Zionism would have to cleanse the land of its native Arab inhabitants. And here is the kibbutz of Hulda rising forth from the fields. The Herzl forest, the Herzl House, the well. The Hulda vineyard. The two rows of sad palm trees marching into the horizon.

It's Hulda, stupid. Not Ofra, but Hulda, I tell myself. Ofra was a mistake, an aberration, insanity. But in principle, Ofra may have a solution. Hulda is the crux of the matter. Hulda is what the conflict is really about. And Hulda has no solution. Hulda is our fate.

Our side is clear. Kibbutz Hulda's intentions were not malevolent. It did not wish to dominate. It did not seek to exploit or dispossess or supplant. All the Hulda pioneers wanted was to form an intimate community. Their dream was to gather a family of forty or fifty free individuals who would work the land in partnership and equality and commune with nature and thereby prove that it was possible to cure the disease inflicted on the Jewish people by Diaspora life. They sought to offer a way out of modern man's crisis of alienation and subjugation to the machine and plant in the soil of Hulda a new beginning of harmony and justice and peace.

Could we *not* have come to Hulda? And then, when war came, could we *not* have fought for our lives in Hulda? Could we *not* have sent our soldiers to conquer the neighboring Arab village of Hulda? Could we *not* have taken the village's houses and fields? Could we *not* have hardened our hearts and treated our neighbors brutally and brought calamity upon them?

Their side, too, is clear. Could they *not* have protested our penetration into their valley? Could they *not* have attacked and burned and destroyed our colonial agricultural farm? And then, a generation later, could they have prevented the brutal attack on the Hulda convoy that was part of an inevitable war? And after their catastrophe could they *not* have hated us for conquering their village and taking their fields and sending them into exile? And can this hatred ever be overcome? Can the Palestinians be expected to give up the demand to see justice done for the village of Hulda? Can anyone expect the children and grandchildren of Jamal Munheir ever to accept the fact that we build houses on their ruined homes and grow six varieties of grapes in their pillaged fields?

What is needed to make peace between the two peoples of this land is probably more than humans can summon. They will not give up their demand for what they see as justice. We shall not give up our life. Arab Hulda and Jewish Hulda cannot really see each other and recognize each other and make peace. Yossi Sarid, Yossi Beilin, Ze'ev Sternhell, Menachem Brinker, Avishai Margalit, and Amos Oz put up a courageous fight against the folly of the occupation and did all they could do to bring about peace. But at the end of the day, they could not look Jamal Munheir in the eye. They could not see Hulda as it is. For the most benign reasons, their promise of peace was false.

The one Israeli leader who saw with cruel clarity what I now see in Hulda was Moshe Dayan. In 1956, at the funeral of the young security officer Roy Rotenberg, who fell patrolling the Israeli-Gaza border, Israel's then chief of staff said the most sincere words ever spoken about the conflict:

> Yesterday at dawn Roy was murdered. The quiet of the spring morning blinded him, and he did not see those who sought his life hiding behind the furrow. Let us not cast blame today on the murderers. What can we say against their terrible hatred of us? For eight years now, they have sat in the refugee camps of Gaza and have watched how, before their very eyes, we have turned their land and villages, where they and their forefathers previously dwelled, into our home. It is not among the Arabs of Gaza, but in our own midst that we must seek Roy's blood. How did we shut our eyes and refuse to look squarely at our fate and see, in all its brutality, the fate of our generation?
>
> Let us today take stock of ourselves. We are a generation of settlement, and without the steel helmet and the gun's muzzle we will not be able to plant a tree and build a house. Let us not fear to look squarely at the hatred that consumes and fills the lives of hundreds of Arabs who live around us. Let us not drop our gaze, lest our arms weaken. That is the fate of our generation. This is our choice—to be ready and armed, tough and hard—or else the sword shall fall from our hands and our lives will be cut short.

As the years went by, Dayan's insight has been dimmed and forgotten. Israelis could no longer bear its cruel wisdom. The Six Day War enabled us to escape its piercing sagacity. The Right nurtured its self-righteous illusions. The Left was mesmerized by its own moralistic illusion. And for two generations, the sin of Ofra obscured the sin of Hulda. But Hulda is here. Hulda is here to stay. And Hulda has no solution. Hulda says peace shall not be.

I descend the hill to the well, the vineyard. It's so beautiful and calm here. But the soil is hard. The land is cursed. For it is here, in the Valley of Hulda, that history's door creaked open on April 6, 1948. It is precisely here, at the end of the Herzl forest, that the Jews crossed the threshold between the commune's olive grove and Jamal Munheir's fields and entered the forbidden. After eighteen hundred years of power-less existence, Jewish soldiers employed a large, organized force to take another people's land and to conquer dozens of villages—of which Hulda was one of the first. Here, by the old well of Hulda, we moved from one phase of our history to another, from one sphere of morality to another. So all that has haunted us ever since is right here. All that will go on haunting us is right here. Generation after generation. War after war.

ELEVEN

J'Accuse, 1999

ARYEH MACHLUF DERI WAS TO HAVE BEEN A PARISIAN LAWYER. HIS upbringing in the northern Moroccan city of Meknes was prosperous enough to allow him to dream of a life of success and recognition in France. In the 1960s, King Hassan II extended his patronage to the Jews. There was harmony between Arabs and Jews in the young North African kingdom. Life had order and meaning and a quiet Mediterranean rhythm. The Jewish community was strong. But when Eliahu and Esther Deri realized that their five-year-old son was a mathematical genius, they expected him to spread his wings and fly beyond the happy Moroccan-Jewish community they lived in. And because they always looked to France—its modernity, its enlightenment, the equal rights accorded by France to Jews—the Deris hoped their son would find a future there. They imagined he would be a lawyer or a doctor or a math professor in Paris or Lyon or Marseille.

Eliahu Deri was orphaned at the age of ten. One morning he found his beloved mother lying lifeless in the bed next to him. The following ten years were difficult for him. He was bullied by his older brothers, and he worked for sixteen hours a day as a tailor's apprentice, sewing and ironing uniforms for the French army. But as he got older and married and became his own man, Eliahu did well. He opened a shop in the

center of Meknes and became a successful tailor. The rapid modernization of North Africa in the 1950s and 1960s doubled and tripled the
demand for the high-quality European suits that were his forte, and
politicians, businessmen, and officers all called on his shop. Within a
short time, the penniless orphan from the crowded Jewish ghetto, the
mlach, was able to move his young family to the well-to-do Ville Nouvelle, the new city, to a spacious apartment in a smart building with a
concierge. They had two maids, a television, gilded furniture, and summer vacations in the best resorts of Tangier. While Esther's Arab servants cooked and cleaned and tended to the children, she would sneak
off to the cinema across the street to watch Humphrey Bogart films.
Aryeh grew up like a prince, playing soccer and swimming and devouring Jules Verne novels. On the high holidays, Eliahu Deri would take his
two older sons to synagogue dressed in well-cut suits and silk bow ties
so that everyone could see just how far the poor orphan had come. The
Deris lived a comfortable life of promise typical of the postwar Jewish-
Moroccan bourgeoisie.

There was a delicate balance in Meknes. On one hand, the *mlach*
preserved the Jewish community and Jewish identity; on the other hand,
the Ville Nouvelle offered the riches of France. The Deri family, and
many like them, attended synagogue on Sabbath mornings, but their
children played soccer and went to the cinema on Saturday afternoons.
They maintained a close relationship with the Arab majority, all the
while vigilantly safeguarding the uniqueness of their own identity. In
the postwar years, postcolonial Meknes managed to keep alive the semi-
colonial harmony of the enchanting Levant, where Arabism, Judaism,
and French culture were woven together into a modern yet traditional
fabric.

The Six Day War tore this fabric apart. Overnight, in the summer
of 1967, everything changed. Arab customers stopped calling on Eliahu
Deri's shop. Arab employees started whispering behind his back. One
day a passerby spat on Deri's elegant suit and muttered *"Sale Juif,"* dirty
Jew. Deri came home incensed. "We are going to Israel," he announced.
Without letting the neighbors know, they sold all they could sell. They
put their furniture into a shipping container, transferred money with
the help of the Jewish Agency, hid cash in the double linings that Eliahu
sewed into the children's winter coats, and told friends they were going

on vacation to France. They summoned a taxi late one night and drove to Casablanca. From Casablanca they flew to Marseille, where they boarded a ship to Haifa.

Esther Deri remembers that when they left Meknes she cried. And when they boarded the plane in Casablanca she cried again. Life had been good in Morocco. But though she begged and cajoled her husband to return, he didn't listen. The Arabs' sudden change of heart had humiliated him. Only at the transit camp in Marseille did he begin to regret his hasty decision, and only at the port of Haifa did he begin to understand what he had done. When it turned out that their baggage hadn't arrived, he lost his temper. When he didn't receive the housing promised to him in Marseille, his wife and five children watched with horror as an enraged Eliahu Deri overturned a table.

Aryeh Machluf Deri remembers that in the transit camp in Marseille there was already tension between his parents. But they hoped for the best and bought everything needed to make life in Israel easier: a refrigerator, a washing machine, a mixer. The ship was actually fun. The kids went wild on deck, and in the evenings the grown-ups danced the tango and the pasodoble. But when they disembarked in Haifa, his father was a different person: loud, tense, lost. He was incapable of understanding the rules of the new world he had chosen so hastily. He would raise his voice, shouting and crying. He lost his dignity.

The family was sent to the coastal town of Rishon LeZion, south of Tel Aviv. Their apartment was tiny and bare: Jewish Agency metal beds, army blankets, and nothing else. When their money didn't arrive, Eliahu went to the bank every day. When their container didn't arrive, he went to the Jewish Agency every day. He demanded a better apartment in a better location with better conditions. He became enraged. His blood pressure rose. He shut himself in his room and didn't come out. He lay in bed all day crying.

Three months later, the family moved from the fifty-square-meter apartment in Rishon LeZion to a hundred-square-meter apartment in Bat Yam. There was a little more room now, but the neighborhood was bad. Many of the immigrant Libyan families in the Eli Cohen housing estate lived on the edge of society. Some neighbors were decent and hardworking, but others were petty criminals. There were drugs, prostitution, street gangs. Because of Eliahu Deri's debilitating depression, it was up to Esther Deri to protect her four sons and her daughter. She locked them up at home so they would not learn the ways of the street.

One evening two ultra-Orthodox young men in long black coats knocked on the door. They had heard that the Deri boys were talented and suggested that two of them enroll in a religious boarding school in Netanya. Esther Deri was taken aback. She knew nothing about ultra-Orthodoxy, and the idea of sending her boys away scared her. It seemed inhuman. But her fear of drugs, prostitution, and street gangs was even stronger. After a long, heartbreaking deliberation, Esther deposited her eldest, Yehuda, and her gifted Aryeh in the hands of the two young men. The two brilliant Moroccan boys were sent to the Sanz boarding school in Netanya, where they were totally cut off from their sister and brothers and mother and broken father.

The rabbi at the Sanz Yeshiva was an impressive spiritual figure who immediately captured Aryeh Deri's heart. But the place itself was dilapidated, dirty, and miserable. Aryeh did not understand why he was being punished, why at the age of nine and a half he had been taken away from his mother. At night he would cry bitterly. During the day, he tried to escape. He collected bottles from trash cans, sold them back to the local grocery store, and with the money bought a bus ticket back to Bat Yam. At home he cried and persuaded his mother to let him stay—until the rabbi arrived and told Esther that her boy was a promising Torah scholar. Looking around the dismal housing estate, she agreed to place her boy in the care of the rabbi once again.

In the meantime, Esther began working shifts in a trade-union-owned textile factory in Bat Yam. Eliahu got out of bed and began cutting raincoats for a trade-union-owned haberdashery. Honor did not return, and neither did plenitude, and there was not much happiness. But after the abrupt transition from Morocco to Israel that had initially crushed the Deris, the family was making a new life for itself—living the gray, depressing routine of the Oriental-Israeli proletariat.

Aryeh, the child prodigy, took another road. He spent his first summer in the State of Israel in the miserable ultra-Orthodox boarding school in Netanya. He escaped, returned, and escaped again. Months later, he managed to get himself transferred to another ultra-Orthodox boarding school, and then to yet another. In Hadera, living conditions were disgraceful, too, and loneliness was devastating, but the ten-year-old became an observant Jew. The headmaster, Rabbi Shukrun, treated Aryeh like his own son and took a personal interest in his education. When Aryeh went home once a month he watched Arab movies on television on Friday evenings and played soccer on the Sabbath, but in school he wore a yarmulke and studied the Talmud. Three years later, he was transferred to the Sephardic Porat Yosef Yeshiva in Jerusalem, and two years after that, he moved to a mixed Sephardic-Ashkenazi yeshiva. At the age of sixteen he was accepted to the prestigious Hebron Yeshiva. After seven and a half years in inferior and mediocre Sephardic institutions, Aryeh Machluf Deri had reached the Eton of the Ashkenazi ultra-Orthodox world.

Hebron was also the school of David Yosef, the son of Israel's chief Sephardic rabbi, Ovadia Yosef. The chief Sephardic rabbi's son, a mediocre student, needed the help and guidance of the brilliant and charismatic Deri, and in return he suggested that Aryeh become tutor to his younger brother. At the age of eighteen, the son of Eliahu and Esther Deri was taken into the Yosef household. Ten years after the ship *Moledet* docked in Haifa with a spoiled secular-traditional boy from Meknes on deck, Aryeh Deri was an up-and-comer in the royal court of Israel's Sephardic Jewry.

Aryeh's dream was to establish an elite yeshiva for Sephardic students. But life in the chief rabbi's household gave him a taste for politics. After Deri married Yaffa, a beautiful orphan, a friend convinced him to devote his life to public service. His self-proclaimed mission was to persuade the Sephardic rabbi Yosef and the Ashkenazi super-rabbi Elazar Shach to co-sponsor a new Sephardic religious party. Thus Shas was born. In 1984, at the age of twenty-five, Aryeh Deri ruled over an Oriental ultra-Orthodox party that garnered four seats in the Knesset in its debut election campaign. He was about to change the face of Israel.

At the age of twenty-six, Deri was a powerful adviser to the minister of the interior. At twenty-seven, he was director general of the Ministry of the Interior, and at twenty-nine, he became minister of the interior. Though he did not possess any experience in public administration or any previous knowledge of Israeli society, Aryeh Deri became a star overnight. He advanced the cause of both ultra-Orthodox Jews and Oriental Jews. But because he was a dove, the Left took a shine to him. Because he assisted the settlers, the Right appreciated him. And because the agenda he set forth at the Ministry of the Interior benefited many outside his constituencies, he gained the respect of business and media. Deri managed to promote the two minority communities he represented without alienating other communities. At the age of thirty he was the first ultra-Orthodox Oriental Jew to break into Israel's inner circle of power. He was the most electrifying, promising figure of a new Israel.

In June 1990, Israel's most powerful daily newspaper, *Yediot Aharonot*, published a series of investigative articles claiming that Deri was corrupt. The state comptroller and then the police opened inquiries. Deri fought back with a vengeance. He attacked *Yediot Aharonot*, the state comptroller, and the police. The people's hero became the people's enemy. He was perceived not only as a bribe taker but as one who willfully disregarded the rule of law. Gone was the affection of the Left, gone was the support of the Right, gone was the acceptance by the elite. Aryeh Deri retreated to within the bounds of the one domain that stuck by him: the traditional Oriental community.

For three years Deri lived a double life. On the one hand, he remained a successful minister of the interior who contributed greatly to Israel of the early 1990s. He was instrumental in the absorption of mass Russian immigration, in preventing Israeli involvement in the first Gulf War, and in maintaining a crucial and courageous alliance with Prime Minister Rabin. On the other hand, he had lost the legitimacy of a normative political figure. Therefore, he devoted his exceptional energy to the construction of a parallel Israeli universe: a religious Oriental world funded by the government it challenged and undermined. The Shas leader used the political power he still had to build a sectarian education system and a sectarian welfare system that would supplant the dysfunctional universal system of Israel's decaying welfare state. He took advantage of his management and organization-building abilities to establish an alternative kingdom of the oppressed and downtrodden. As enlightened Israel rejected him, he rejected enlightened Israel. Rather than being a unifier and a healer, Aryeh Deri became the Oriental leader who would lead the Oriental-traditionalist revolt against the secular Ashkenazi state that Zionism had founded.

• • •

The revolt's first eruption occured in the 1996 election campaign. These were the years of the Oslo Accords. The government was the government of peace. In the upper echelons of Israeli society, the feeling was that Israeli secularism was back in power. But in the lower echelons, the revolt of Israel's oppressed Jews was simmering. Nationally, the movement's icon was Benjamin Netanyahu; ethnically, its identity was channeled through Shas. Deri understood this. He saw the latent potential embodied in cultural discontent. He also saw the fear gripping Israel when the peace promise was swept away by a wave of terrorism. That's why he offered his voters something else: something mystical. Deri rediscovered Rabbi Yitzhak Kaduri, a hundred-year-old Kabbalistic mystic, and made him the star of the election campaign. Kaduri talismans and blessings were handed out en masse, and the ancient rabbi was flown by helicopter from town to town to address rallies of desperately poor traditional Oriental Jews who clung to his every, often unintelligible, word. By using Kaduri and Kabbalah, Deri got a quarter of a million votes, and ten seats in the Knesset from Israelis who had rejected the secular progress that had established the state. He took many Sephardic Jews back to their traditional mystic roots, a source of both pride and consolation.

The revolt's second eruption came in late April 1997. Israel's secular and dovish elites regarded the Netanyahu-Deri government as illegitimate. Deri was fighting for his life in court. Suddenly, on Passover Eve, the state decided to indict Deri on suspicion of persuading Prime Minister Netanyahu to appoint a pliant attorney general in the hope that he could evade further corruption charges. The police had recommended breach-of-trust charges against Netanyahu and other Ashkenazi suspects in the affair, but unlike the Sephardic Deri, none of them was charged. The outcome was outrage. In the Hebrew University's stadium, across from the Knesset and the Supreme Court, tens of thousands of Shas supporters gathered to cheer Deri and to identify with him. Ethnic civil war was close at hand.

But Deri restrained himself and his people. He told the immense, angry crowd not to resort to violence. But the words he chose to use on that blazing hot day were perceived as his farewell to the state and to Zionism. "The vision of Zionism has failed," he said.

> Now secular Israelis are afraid that Shas will change the secular char-
> acter of the state. They call themselves Zionists, but they are not
> really Zionists. Their movement is a movement of heresy. They see
> our fathers and mothers as primitives. They want to convert them.
> They sent them to remote towns and villages where life was hard.
> They gave their children a good-for-nothing education. Until we
> came and began taking care of all these people who were suffering in
> all these remote places. That's why they are afraid of us. That's why
> they persecute us. And this persecution is both ethnic and religious.
> But the more they humiliate us, the more we will grow. We shall
> change the character of the State of Israel.

The revolt's third eruption comes in the spring and summer of 1999. On March 17, 1999, the Jerusalem District Court finds Aryeh Machluf Deri guilty of taking bribes amounting to $155,000. A week later, he is sentenced to four years in prison. In an irregular move, the reading of the court's decision is transmitted on the radio in a live broadcast lasting for nearly two hours. Not only do the judges convict Deri but they describe him as corrupt and malicious. When he emerges from the courthouse, his supporters are despondent. It seems he is politically dead. But within hours, Aryeh Deri gathers strength. With elections only two months away, he decides to make his own tragedy the main issue of the election campaign. He locks himself in his office with a videographer and gives the speech of his life. "*J'accuse*," he cries. For two hours, two narratives merge as he settles his own score with the rule of law and settles the score of Sephardic Judaism with the State of Israel. Aryeh Machluf Deri is now the symbol of the Oriental narrative: of rejection, humiliation, and persecution; of the unwillingness of the secular Ashkenazi establishment to honor and respect traditional Oriental Jews; of the exclusion of the Jewish-Israeli other.

Deri's *j'accuse* is a hit. To meet demand, tens of thousands of videocassettes are produced in Europe daily and flown to Israel overnight. This time there is no need for Kaduri's talismans. There is not much interest in Rabbi Ovadia Yosef, either. The election campaign is all about Deri. Development towns, impoverished boroughs, and remote villages are on fire. Everybody wants to see Deri, to touch Deri, to identify with Deri. While one Israel convicts him, another finds him innocent and makes him a hero. A surge of protest arises out of the Israeli ethnic divide. The trauma of arrival in the 1950s, the agony of absorption in the 1960s, the sense of discrimination in the 1970s, and the flickers of protest in the 1980s now come together in mass support for the leader of the Oriental revolution who has just been criminally convicted. Deri is no longer just a politician, he is a martyr. He becomes the bearer of the cross of Oriental pain and tragedy. The 430,000 votes he and his party receive sixty days after the court reads aloud its damning decision brings the Oriental revolt to its apex. In June 1999 almost every sixth Israeli gives his vote to a revolutionary leader who challenges the existing order and has been sentenced to four years in jail. Shas gains seventeen seats in the Knesset, up from ten in the previous election.

In July 2000, Israel's Supreme Court rejects Deri's appeal but reduces his sentence to three years, finding that the bribe he received from his yeshiva friends was only sixty thousand dollars. Questions are raised: If so little is left of the original indictment after a decade-long legal battle, is Deri's unprecedented punishment still justifiable? Are there really no other senior Israeli politicians who received illicit funds from friends without being punished at all? But the law is the law, and the sentence is now final.

On September 3, 2000, the first day of the new school year, Aryeh Deri takes his young daughters to the Sephardic elementary school he founded in Jerusalem and named after Margalit Yosef, the late wife of the chief Sephardic rabbi. Facing the TV cameras he bids farewell to his three weeping girls. From school he goes to prison. Shas supporters want their leader to enter prison not as a felon but as a king: tens of thousands are waiting to support him as he exits Jerusalem, and traffic on the Jerusalem–Tel Aviv highway comes to a halt as a convoy of nearly a thousand cars and buses, led by a cavalcade of motorcycles, follows Deri from the capital to Maasiyahu Prison. Outside the prison, tens of thousands more gather. Rabbi Ovadia Yosef assures the crowds that just like the biblical Joseph, Deri will leave prison to become king of Israel. Deri himself asks for forgiveness but swears he has not broken the law and promises he will not crack. Escorted by a phalanx of policemen, with his acolytes chanting their support, Deri walks through the prison gates and bids farewell to his wife, Yaffa, and his parents. And when night comes, as he lies on his narrow iron bunk bed in his private nine-square-meter windowless cell, he buries his face in his hands and listens to his admirers singing outside the prison walls. He pictures the distraught faces of his wife and parents, and he thinks about his long journey. Suddenly he can't take it anymore. He cracks. After ten turbulent years, he cries into the night just as he used to cry at boarding school: "My God, why have you forsaken me?"

"So what is the crux of your story?" I ask Deri ten years later. "And what is the crux of the Oriental Israeli story? Do the two really converge?"

We are sitting in the out-of-the way Jerusalem office to which Aryeh Deri retreats to be on his own, to think. The walls are covered with photographs of Rabbi Ovadia Yosef and other lesser-known Sephardic rabbis. On the shelves are volumes of the Bible, the Mishnah, and the Talmud. On the desk are yesterday's papers. After he makes me strong black coffee, Deri suggests I try some of the exquisite Belgian chocolates he has just received from a friend. Then he sits down, strokes his trim beard, pats his black yarmulke, and looks up at me. His eyes light up; he is ready, relaxed, almost at peace. Years after his incarceration, he no longer feels rage. From his black leather armchair he can recount his own biography with calm and perspective. At times it seems even he is surprised. He cannot believe that so much has happened in his life in such a short period of time, cannot believe that his life has turned into such a dramatic tale. "Unbelievable," he mutters, more to himself than to me. But when I press him to tell me more, his eyes narrow and he chokes up.

"I am not the typical Jewish-Oriental Israeli," Deri tells me. "The vast majority of immigrants from the Arab countries arrived in the 1950s, whereas I arrived only in 1968. The great traumas of most Arab-speaking immigrants were the indiscriminant spraying with DDT that they all received upon arrival and the degrading immigrant camps that I did not experience. But when I arrived in Bat Yam in the late 1960s, I saw all around me the damage wrought by the 1950s. I saw a splintered Oriental society.

"What happened is quite clear," Deri elaborates. "Oriental-Jewish culture was founded on three pillars: the community, the synagogue, and the father. The father was very strong—too strong. He was the family's provider and king. He told his wife what to do. He told his children what to study and how to behave. Even when modernization came, with its French and English influences, the father and the rabbi remained dominant. Religion, tradition, and patriarchy preserved the Oriental-Jewish community for a thousand years. We did not go through European-style secularization. We didn't have Western enlightenment and a revolt against religion. We lived a life that combined religion, tradition, and rudimentary modernity. We looked up to the rabbi and feared the father, and thus we survived as a community.

"On arrival in Israel," Deri says, "the communities were dispersed. There was an intentional policy of dispersion. The rabbi lost his authority, the community disintegrated, and the synagogue was very much weakened. But worst of all is what happened to the father. The father figure was broken. Here he could not provide for his family as he had in Morocco or Iraq. Here he didn't have the authority he had in Tunisia or Libya. He lost his bearings. He was depressed. He ceased to be relevant.

"This was our crisis, too," Deri says. "When we arrived in Israel, there was no community, no synagogue, and no rabbi. My father was mortified. He understood that what had happened to our neighbors was about to happen to us. The family sank into miserable poverty. We children began to misbehave and use foul language. A cousin of ours was killed in a shoot-out between rival street gangs. What saved us was our mother. After the initial shock, she realized she couldn't rely on our father, so she gathered enough strength to act on her own. Because she is a wise, strong woman, she locked us at home so we wouldn't stray. But when she realized this wasn't enough, she consented to the two rabbis who knocked on her door and sent us to boarding school. Personally, emotionally, this was horrific for her. But because she loved us so much she did not let her heart overrule her head. She didn't quite know where she was sending us. She didn't know we would become ultra-Orthodox. But she knew we needed a social framework that would save us from the streets."

"What you are saying," I challenge Deri, "is that it's all accidental. Your parents were more secular than religious, more modern than traditional. They loved Humphrey Bogart, they danced the pasodoble. So had it not been for the young rabbis who knocked on your door, you might not have been religious at all. If a fine secular institution had come knocking, you might have become the leader of a renewed social-democratic Labor."

Deri nods but is careful not to confirm my hypothesis in his own words. He just smiles his mischievous smile and carries on. "Listen," he says, "I have no issue with Labor, or with the Ashkenazis. At home, no one ever said the Ashkenazis screwed us. The feeling was that we endured a catastrophe. I understood what happened back in the 1950s. After all, Israel was a poor, young state surrounded by enemies. It was fragile, recovering from war, with a population of six hundred fifty thousand people in all. And suddenly this tiny Ashkenazi nation is flooded with the entire Sephardic Diaspora of the Middle East—communities arriving one by one from Yemen, Iraq, Morocco, Tunisia, Algeria, Libya, Lebanon, and Egypt.

"So the state builds housing estates for the new immigrants. It sets up factories for them. Within a few years it dismantles the dreadful immigrant camps and gives the newcomers a roof and a workplace. That's quite an accomplishment. But what the Ashkenazi-dominated state does not understand is that it is taking away from the Oriental immigrants their community and honor and tradition. It takes apart the social and normative structures that have kept them together in the Diaspora. They have no tools to deal with the new world, no education relevant to it, no awareness, no sense of where or why. They have no authority, no compass. All they have is the violence and dereliction of the street. And so a generation is lost. And then another. Dozens of slums and remote development towns become what Bat Yam's Eli Cohen has become: neglected, crime-ridden, and bleak. Hundreds of thousands of Oriental-Jewish youngsters in Israel are raised with no father, no discipline, and no meaning to their life.

"Those who were saved," Deri says, "are those who had strong mothers. This is a mother's generation. The mothers are the true heroines of Israel's Oriental story. But as in my case, the mother could not cope alone. She needed a boarding school. Those who went to a religious boarding school, as I did, became Torah scholars. Those who went to secular boarding schools became engineers or insurance agents.

Only the combination of a strong mother and a decent boarding school could save you from the chaos. Only if you were sent away from home could you survive the collapse of your father and the breakdown of your culture.

"I told you I don't hold a grudge against Labor," Deri says. "That's true and not true. There is one thing that does make me angry: the spiritual aspect of absorption. When it built the immigrant camps and the housing estates and the remote factories, Labor had no malice in its heart. But in spiritual matters it certainly did. The veteran Ashkenazim of Labor thought that most of the people who emigrated from the Arab world were primitive and therefore had to be put through a process of secular European indoctrination. The melting pot was a Western melting pot that was supposed to totally transform us. Those Labor Ashkenazim didn't honor our civilization. They didn't see the beauty of our tradition. That's why they severed us from our roots and our heritage. That was a terrible, vicious mistake. What these people did was to destroy, not build. They took the soul we had and did not give us another in its place. And since they didn't really give us a new culture or identity they left us with nothing. Facing extreme economic and physical hardship, we found ourselves standing in the world spiritually naked.

"Into this void stepped the ultra-Orthodox," Deri says. "In the first years, I was not really God-fearing. I learned what I was taught and did as I was told and dressed as I was instructed. When I was by myself, at home, I was not profoundly religious. Only when I reached Jerusalem at the age of thirteen did I discover the richness of the world of Torah. I was deeply drawn to the Porat Yosef rabbis who treated me like a son. I was attracted to the mysticism of the Old Jerusalem Kabbalists. The Western Wall captured my heart. The holiness of Jerusalem enchanted me. I began observing Judaism religiously.

"I didn't encounter the Oriental issues until later," he says. "Because I was transferred from one Sephardic hothouse to another, I didn't encounter non-Sephardic Jews. I didn't encounter non-Orthodox Israel, either. Only in the Hebron Yeshiva did I notice that the Sephardic students bowed down to the Ashkenazim, and their leaders bowed down to the Ashkenazi leaders. There was no anger toward the Ashkenazim, on the contrary. There was gratitude for taking us in and accepting us and teaching us. But there was a self-abasement that I didn't like, that I was not willing to be part of. And gradually I noticed other things I hadn't noticed before: there was no Sephardic spiritual leadership, no Sephardic political representation, no quality Sephardic education. We were totally dependent on the Ashkenazim. We were picking up the crumbs they were kind enough to let us have.

"At first I didn't think politically," Deri continues. "I was not really a part of Israeli society and didn't understand how it functioned. That's why all I wanted was to establish a high-quality yeshiva for Sephardic boys. But in Rabbi Ovadia's house I started to understand politics. I saw the persons and the powers shaping Israel. That's how I got the idea for Shas. I believed an alliance between Rabbi Shach and Rabbi Ovadia would produce a political body that would give representation to Sephardic Judaism and enjoy the religious backing of the Ashkenazim. I didn't want to rebel. The thought of some sort of Israeli Black Panthers was totally foreign to me. All I wanted was to give my people a voice and a place of honor. To return the divine crown to its rightful place."

Deri leans over his wide desk, his eyes glittering. "Only when I became director general of the Ministry of the Interior did I truly understand the Oriental-Jewish problem in Israel. Only then, in office, did I truly leave the closed world of ultra-Orthodox Judaism and come to know Israeli society. And suddenly I realized that of the hundreds of municipalities I was responsible for, the weak ones were almost all Arabic or Oriental. I suddenly realized that most of the suffering in Israel is Oriental suffering. In every remote development town I visited, I found neglect. In every impoverished neighborhood, I found Oriental Jews who had lost their pride and their identity. I found communities destroyed, families torn apart, their honor and tradition taken away, and the spark in their eyes extinguished. While on the surface Israel was thriving, just below the surface there was an Israel that was fatherless and rabbi-less and hopeless. Traditional Oriental Israel was left to fend for itself and quite often it failed miserably.

"In my first years in government," Deri tells me, "I wanted to integrate, not self-segregate. I was very popular at the time. I was a political star and a media darling. I established close relationships with many secular Ashkenazi politicians, journalists, and businessmen. They liked my directness and openness and energy. We found common ground between their Israeliness and mine. So I believed it was possible to bridge the gaps between the Sephardics and Ashkenazim, between religious and secular. I believed that just as the elite accepted me, they would accept the public I represented. I felt my purpose was to heal and unite. To strengthen the Oriental Jews and the ultra-Orthodox Jews, but to integrate them into a multitribal Israel in which they would find a place.

"But then the newspapers came up with their allegations. The state comptroller, the police, and the judiciary came after me. Both the right- and the left-wing elite turned their backs on me. Rabbi Shach, whom I loved and admired more than any other person I knew, deserted me. He never forgave me for trying to form a peace government with Shimon Peres in 1990. I was alone. I was without my new friends from the secular world, and without my old rabbi and the Ashkenazi ultra-Orthodox. Now I was not loved but persecuted, not a hero but a pariah. All I had left was my tribe: Sephardic Jews. Only they believed in me and embraced me. The Oriental Jews identified with me. They saw me as someone whose life story was similar to theirs. They were convinced I was a Moroccan Jew who had opened his heart to Israel and was accepted by Israel until one day Israel slammed the door in his face and did all it could to break him.

"It was hard not to break," Deri whispers. "The loneliness was awful. I had no one to turn to or look up to. Simultaneously I lost the Israel that I had taken for a mother and Rabbi Shach, whom I had taken for a father. So I was attracted to the Kabbalah. I went up to the Galilee on religious retreat. I traveled to the Ukraine to lie upon the tomb of Rabbi Breslau of Uman. Although I am not a man of mysticism, I needed the comfort of mystics. I turned to fundamental faith. The support of Sephardic Judaism, mysticism, and fundamental faith gave me the power to stand tall when everything was collapsing around me. At night, I found myself talking aloud to our Father in heaven.

"So the use of Kaduri's talismans and blessings in the 1996 election campaign was not purely manipulative," Deri continues. "It also expressed my personal distress and my emotional need. So was the rage of the 1999 election campaign. *J'accuse* wasn't only a brilliant political maneuver but an authentic emotional outcry. All during the 1990s, there was an astonishing correlation between what was happening to me, Aryeh Deri, and what the Oriental Jews of Israel were experiencing.

Fifty years after it was founded, Israel was facing an internal revolt that was about to change its identity.

"They perceived me as a threat," Deri tells me. "Here stood a person who was as good as they were. Not afraid, not ashamed. An organizer, a planner, a leader. And that person operated in the most modern and effective way. But he represented Judaism and he spoke for Oriental Jews. And he took the ultra-Orthodox out of the ghetto they lived in, and he rescued the Oriental Jews from under the oppression they lived in. And throughout the country he created change—he built alternative schools and community centers and gave people other options. He threatened Ashkenazi Israel's cultural hegemony and chipped away at its identity as a Western nation. And he was growing stronger by the day, leading the most important revolution in Israel's short history.

"This is why they had to take me out of the game," Deri says. "To remove me from government and cut me off from state resources. To assault my character so that even my constituency would denounce me. That's why they investigated me like they had never investigated anyone else—with a fine-tooth comb. And judged me like they had never judged anyone else—against all evidence. They lynched me and created the impression that I was an evil octopus. And in a sense they succeeded: they expelled me from politics and jailed me and turned me into a demon.

"But in another sense they failed: their attacks on me convinced the masses to follow me. A million Israelis felt that when they tried to take me out, they tried to take them out, too. When they locked me up, they kept them out, too. After they had finally raised their heads, they were pushed back half a century. The DDT, the immigration camps, the condescension. That's why in 1999 we got seventeen seats in the Knesset. If elections had been held a month later, we would have gotten twenty-five or even twenty-eight seats. We would have replaced Likud as the leading right-of-center political force. And the plan was that when I got out of prison we would do just that. We'd pick up where we left off and gain thirty seats in the Knesset. But while I was in jail, I decided not to re-open the wounds, not to reignite the fire. It's not that the wounds are not there. And the fire, too, lingers. You wouldn't believe how much pain is still out there. But I came to the conclusion that enough was enough. What had happened was extremely dangerous. Israel almost went over the cliff. And I don't want that repeated. When I think now about what nearly happened, I shudder. Only Providence prevented the great fire of the 1990s from burning down our house. As I relaunched my political career and reentered the public arena I wanted to do things differently. Now I want to deal with the old pain in a new way."

Deri and I are almost the same age. Our collective generational experiences are similar, and our perception of reality and our political opinions are not far apart. We have common beliefs and a common language. Deri is wired in a very direct Israeli way. He is quick and sensitive and his high IQ is matched by his inflated ego. There are sparks of genius in him. I like him. And yet, Deri lives in a faraway place. He has other commitments and loyalties. He is a citizen of a world I don't know. He is so present yet so elusive, so open yet so inscrutable. He gives me the feeling that even he hasn't quite figured out who he is and who he would like to be. A wanderer between worlds and between identities, he embodies the great Israeli social and cultural chaos.

And yet Deri is not the issue but the metaphor. He will be fine. After a thirteen-year leave of absence, he is back in the public arena and is once again the political leader of Shas. (After the March 2015 election, in which Shas won seven Knesset seats, Deri joined the Netanyahu government as minister of the economy and minister for the development of the Negev and Galilee. In January 2016, he returned to his old post as interior minister.) His charisma is somewhat eroded and he has lost his larger-than-life stature, but he is a powerful player again in Israel's power game. So as I leave his Jerusalem office I think not of him but of his community. The Oriental-Jewish story is simple and cruel, I think. Between the mid-nineteenth century and the mid-twentieth century, Arab world Jewry experienced a relative golden age. As it was close to French and British colonial rulers, it enjoyed their patronage. It won rights it had never enjoyed before. Many Jews in North Africa and the Middle East benefited from all that Baghdad, Damascus, Beirut, Cairo, Alexandria, Tunis, and Casablanca had to offer. But by the 1940s and 1950s the magic of the Orient had evaporated. Colonialism retreated,

Arab nationalism was on the rise, and Zionism was triumphant. Within a few years a civilization collapsed. Thousand-year-old communities disintegrated within months. With one swing of history's sword the soft underbelly of the old Levant was sliced open. The enchanting, pluralist Orient was gone. A million Jewish Arabs were uprooted, their world destroyed, their culture decimated, their homes lost.

The Zionist story is also simple and cruel, I think. Israel was to have been home to the Jewish people of Eastern Europe—that is what the state was designed to be. But between 1939 and 1945, the Jewish people of Eastern Europe almost ceased to be. Having no other choice, Zionism turned eastward. The result was ironic. In 1897, when Zionism was gaining momentum, only 7 percent of the world's Jews were Oriental. In 1945, after the Holocaust, only 10 percent of the world's Jews were Oriental. But in Israel, by 1990, over 50 percent of Jewish Israelis were Oriental. A state designed for one population was populated by another. A state based on one culture was overtaken by another. But Zionism did not—and could not—acknowledge the sea change that had taken place. It could not admit that the original blueprint did not fit the new circumstances. So Zionism pressed on, willfully ignoring the harm it was doing. The Israeli melting pot worked with brutal efficiency: it forged a nation, but it also scorched the identities and scalded the souls it was to have saved.

So when Deri was born in Meknes in 1959, the first secular Oriental-Israeli uprising erupted in the poor Haifa neighborhood of Wadi Salib. When Deri was in the wretched Hadera boarding school in 1970, the second secular Oriental-Israeli uprising erupted in the poor Jerusalem neighborhood of Musrara, with the appearance of the local Black Panthers. When Deri was a yeshiva student in Jerusalem in the mid-1970s, a secular, cultural Oriental uprising erupted with new Oriental music, ignored by mainstream radio and TV but played in every nightclub along the Bat Yam promenade. Deri was not aware of all these developments because he joined Israel late and because even then he lived in an ultra-Orthodox enclave. Even when Begin was elected in 1977 with the enthusiastic support of Oriental Israelis, Deri was not enthusiastic at all. As a disciple of Rabbi Shach, who never believed in the Zionist state, he did not approve of Begin's Jewish nationalism. Yet after Begin faded away and left behind the orphaned masses of Oriental Israelis, Deri saw the vacuum and was quick to fill it. First he presented Rabbi Ovadia Yosef as an alternative father figure to Begin. Then he introduced Rabbi Kaduri as a comforting mystical figure. Then he defined himself as the martyr of Oriental Judaism. In this way he managed to detach himself from the political and the mundane and acquire for a while the otherworldliness of a semimythological figure.

As I drive out of Jerusalem I listen to a compilation of songs by Zohar Argov. Argov was born in the same Rishon LeZion neighborhood that Deri's family was sent to in 1968. For months the Argovs and the Deris lived not far apart. In the early 1970s, the tender, aching songs of the shy, lanky singer conquered downstairs Israel and became the anthems of its struggle. They were sold on cassettes in Tel Aviv's chaotic central bus station, they were sung at weddings, they were a hit in the Oriental nightclubs that popped up in Bat Yam, Jaffa, Netanya, Lydda, and Ramleh. For years Argov was not recognized by upstairs Israel. And when he was finally embraced, he took an overdose of drugs and died. Although his heartbreaking songs deal mostly with love and loss, they seem to fill my car with the great pain of the downtrodden. As I drive down the highway that the Deri convoy traveled to Maasiyahu Prison, I hear in Argov's ballads the howl of the long-suffering Oriental Israel.

When I was a child, Oriental Jews were not recognized as such. Although they already constituted almost half of Israel's population, they were oppressed and ignored. In an odd sort of way they were present and not present, belonging and not belonging. They were followed by a constant cloud of doubt and suspicion. They were not our lot, not really us.

In the army I was already a minority. In the paratrooper platoon I served in, elitist Ashkenazim like me were mocked. But only after the 1977 political upheaval that brought Menachem Begin to power—and the violent, inflammatory election campaign of 1981—was political power transferred to the other people. One could no longer ignore the fact that Oriental Jews were the majority. They came out of the immigrant camps and housing estates and development towns to which they had been confined for over a generation to capture the city square. Politically speaking, they were Likud. Socioeconomically, they were contractors and small business owners. Culturally, they were fans of Zohar Argov, whose music I did not yet appreciate.

But in liberal Ashkenazi circles, the surge of Oriental Jews brought about an ugly response. The racism of the 1980s and 1990s was even more repulsive than that of the previous era, scornful and maligning: They are nouveau riche. They don't behave. Their English is atrocious. They are so sensitive regarding their honor. They are Indians. Levantines. Likudniks. They disgrace the state we founded and eventually will take us down with them. In these comments, I saw the dark side of Israel's enlightenment, a lack of a civility in people who claim to be civilized. The Oriental story fascinated me. As I listened to more and more immigrant stories, and to more and more stories of oppression, I realized we had done wrong. I feared that the pain of Oriental Israelis might one day blow us to pieces.

In a sense, it is just like Aharon Appelfeld's story. The same state that denied the Diaspora and denied the Holocaust and denied Palestine also denied the Orient. Perhaps there was no other way. In order to survive, the establishment tried to forge one strong people and build a unified state. But the human price was heavy. The long-term consequences were severe. We have wounded millions of Oriental Jews.

Yet there is another way to look at all this. There is a politically incorrect truth here that is not easy to express. And this truth is that Israel did a favor to those it extracted from the Orient. The Jews there had no real future in the new Baghdad, the new Beirut, the new Cairo, or the new Meknes. Had they stayed, they would have been annihilated. But forcing them to forgo their identity and culture was foolhardy, callous, and cruel. To this day, many Oriental Israelis are not aware of what Israel saved them from: a life of misery and backwardness in an Arab Middle East that turned ugly. To this day Israel is not aware of the pain it inflicted when it crushed the culture and identity of the Oriental Jews it absorbed. Neither Zionist Israel nor its Oriental population had fully recognized the traumas of the 1950s and 1960s. Neither has yet found a way to honor it and contain it—and make peace with it. This is why the wound lingers on.

In a Tel Aviv café, I meet Gal Gabai. A friend and colleague, Gabai is a journalist and the anchor of a popular political talk show. I ask her what makes her identify with Aryeh Deri. "You are a secular feminist left-winger," I say to her. "You are committed to democracy, liberalism, and the rule of law. Why are you mesmerized by this ultra-Orthodox politician who was convicted of taking bribes and whose world is so distant from yours?"

Gabai, who is a decade younger than Deri, says that ever since she was a young girl in 1970s Beersheba, she remembers being torn between two polar forces. One was *ruge raas:* the edict to hold your head high. The other was *khshumeh:* shame, the need to hide from others, not to let them see you in your disgrace. For dozens of years *khshumeh* was stronger than *ruge raas*, shame stronger than pride. "There was a feeling that there was something wrong with us, with Oriental Jews," Gabai says. "That there was something tainted and inferior. That's why we bowed down to the Ashkenazim and abased ourselves before them. There was a subtle, complicated sort of self-loathing, a deep unease with one's self. Until Deri came and proved that we could stand tall and proud—walk among the Ashkenazim as equals. Deri brought North African Jewish tradition to center stage. He said we were just as good, if not better. He awoke the *ruge raas* in us. He let us lift our heads high. He gave even Oriental yuppies like me the ability to be at peace with ourselves and feel worthy. Deri meant I could be accepted in Tel Aviv without turning my back on Beersheba. He meant we could succeed in the West without betraying the East.

"I remember the overwhelming identification with Deri in my grandmother's housing estate in Beersheba," Gabai recalls. "Deri enabled the housing estate to go back to the traditions that Labor never recognized and the Likud never encouraged. Deri offered a traditional cultural option that was not shameful, backward, or fanatical. He put a stop to our mimicry of the Ashkenazim. He wiped away the shame. He won us over by not wearing a costume, by not disguising himself. Unlike the Oriental Israeli leaders who preceded him, Deri was authentic. He was at peace with himself and at peace with his Oriental identity. While others pretended to be Europeans, Deri said proudly he was a Moroccan. This was liberating. You cannot imagine, Ari, how liberating this was. At last one of us, a Moroccan from Meknes, was not afraid of who he was and was not afraid to say it. He was proud of himself, even full of himself.

"I have a theory," Gabai says. "In Israel, belonging is bought with blood. We Oriental Jews didn't bleed enough into the river of belonging. We were not murdered in the Holocaust. We did not get killed in the War of Independence. We did not participate in the formative saga of Holocaust heroism revival. We were imported here and we were imported late. We were imported only because European Jewry was exterminated and there was no other way to grow the state. That's why there is always a shadow hovering over us: this place was not really meant for us. This communal house doesn't quite suit us. It was, and it remains, alien to us. We have no other home, but for us, Israel is not quite home. We are not at ease here as one should be in one's home.

"Let me put it this way," Gabai continues. "In its terms of reference and in its mission statement, the State of Israel never planned for Aryeh Deri or Gal Gabai. That's not who it had in mind. But at the end of the day, the European fort was housed by Arab-speaking Jews. By Aryeh Deri and Gal Gabai. But the fundamental structure of the fort and the ethos of its builders sentenced Aryeh Deri and Gal Gabai to remain outside in a sense. Western Zionism feared us. It feared the Arabism we brought with us: the Arab music, the smells and tastes of Arab cuisine, Arab mannerisms. Think about it, something amazing happened here. After the Holocaust, Zionism imported a million Jewish Arabs here so they'd save it, demographically, from the Arab world. But after it brought these Jewish Arabs, Zionism panicked because of their Arabic identity. It sensed danger in my grandfather's Moroccan music, and in my grandmother's Moroccan cooking, and in my father's Moroccan tradition. It feared that we Oriental Jews would dissolve Western Zionism from within.

"That's why they steamrolled us," Gabai says. "They had to dominate us. The problem was not one of socioeconomic injustice. It wasn't about housing or welfare or income. The new immigrants from Poland and Romania had it hard, too. But the difference between them and us was that from the very beginning they belonged. They were the ones the State of Israel was meant for and planned for. From the outset we were under suspicion. So we were culturally castrated. We were expected to relinquish what we were previously. We had to prove daily that we were not Arabs. The outcome was an internal struggle that is tearing us apart to this day. We do not accept ourselves and we do not love ourselves. We are split between worlds that don't really intersect. And we are always asked to present proof. We have to prove we are not inferior and not flawed. We have to prove we have totally assimilated. We must prove daily that we are not Arabs anymore.

"You wouldn't get it," Gabai tells me. "You are from here. You belong. In Israel you are always at home. You own the place. But I was raised knowing that there was an inner circle that I was not a part of. There was an alpha group, and I was not in it. Because there was so much love at home, I was empowered. I had my own well of strength. So I insisted on breaking in. I wanted to be with the strong, with those who belonged. That was also the message I got from my family. Their first message was education: study, study, study. But it was clear that knowledge on its own would not suffice. To really get ahead one had to bleach oneself. Progeny bleaching was the best vehicle for social mobility. My beloved grandmother would say it to me in her native tongue: 'For you, Gal, a Moroccan will not do, only a Polish boy.' And this went right into my subconscious. No way would I have a Moroccan spouse—if I'd married a Moroccan he would have been an earnest social worker and I would have been a caring high school teacher, and in the evenings we would listen to nice ethnic music in our three-room apartment in a Beersheba housing estate. But because I was ambitious, I had to mate with white power. I had to dilute the black in me with white sperm.

"Our home was filled with music. Even when times were hard, our rooms were filled with the warm sounds of Moroccan music. But my grandmother took me to a classical music concert and when we came out it was clear that I would play the mandolin—not the Moroccan *oud*, but the Russian mandolin; not Farid al-Atrash but Tchaikovsky. I love Tchaikovsky. I love the mandolin. But within me there is always a yearning for what was lost, a yearning for Arabism. When I visit Arab friends, my eyes tear up. When I watch Arab movies, I am all emotion. I know that there, in Morocco, my father was at ease. In Israel he was never at ease. And he passed his unease to me. Although I live in Tel Aviv and I host a television show, I am not at ease within my own skin. I don't delude myself. For me Arabism is closed off. But in a sense, Israeliness is closed off as well. Although my three kids are half-Ashkenazi, Ashkenazi Israel does not accept me as I am. Israel still suspects me.

"That's why Deri was so important," Gabai says. "Before and after

Deri, most Oriental Jews in Israel channeled their pain to nationalist politics and Likud support. This was artificial and wrong, as most Oriental Jews are not extremists. And when Deri came along it was different. He addressed the Oriental-Jewish inferiority complex and the Oriental-Jewish sense of longing. He made our pain legitimate. But what was really wonderful was his alliance with Rabin. When Yitzhak Rabin and Aryeh Deri formed their alliance in the early 1990s, it was much more than a political compact. Rabin represented the kibbutz, the Palmach, and Tel Aviv; he was the mythological Sabra and warrior of Zionism. Deri was Meknes–Bat Yam–Jerusalem. He was the hero of Oriental Israel. When Rabin and Deri stood together, we could all stand together. When Rabin and Deri looked each other in the eye, we could all look each other in the eye. There was mutual recognition. There was a way to combine political moderation with ethnic pride. Now the Oriental Jews could prove themselves not by hating the Arabs but by being a bridge to the Arabs. For the first time there was hope that Zionism would make peace both with the Arabs without and the Arabs within. But then Rabin was assassinated and Deri was convicted and everything fell apart. The moment of grace of the early 1990s passed. And the more Deri was persecuted, the more rage there was. People were angry at the white establishment that hounded him. But people were angry at Deri, too. Perhaps everybody in politics is corrupt, but he should not have been. He should have been cleaner than clean. Because he had a mission. He was endowed with a crucial historic role. He was our entry ticket. He was supposed to let us in, make us belong. But because he'd fallen, this couldn't happen. Our hope seemed to have been an illusion. And we all knew we didn't stand a chance. We could not be ourselves. All we could do was to adjust, to mimic, to give up and mimic. To go back to *khshumeh*."

Gabai stops. Tears fill her eyes. "When my friends read what I've said to you, they'll be terribly angry," she says. "They think the only way forward is to deny our past and deny our pain. They say we must not look back, not wallow in what happened. That's why they pretend that the ethnic wound has formed a scab. They want to believe that socioeconomic mobility and intermarriages have diluted the problem and put out the fire. They think the Oriental-Ashkenazi divide is the one divide Israel is about to overcome. But I tell you that is not the case. I see my brothers and sisters suffocating. I see their torment. When two thugs at the Shaar Aliyah immigrant camp took my then nine-year-old mother by force and cut her glorious long hair and left her shaven and humiliated and helpless, they wounded her soul. They told her not to be herself. And when my Ashkenazi schoolteacher in Beersheba looked at me in that condescending way and told me with her eyes that my place was at the bottom of the social ladder, she wounded my soul. She told me I was flawed. One way or another, all Oriental Israelis were wounded. That's why the Oriental soul is a wounded soul. It was wrenched out of tranquillity and thrust into turbulence. And from turbulence into shame. And from shame into self-denial. Into forced Westernization. But underneath Westernization lie bitterness and discontent. Our great enemies are bitterness and discontent. Deri was to have freed us from them. He was supposed to head the defiance that would lead to reconciliation. So when Deri fell, so did we. We found ourselves again in the darkness. And in the darkness we ache. We bleed. We cannot find comfort or remedy or home."

TWELVE

Sex, Drugs, and the Israeli Condition, 2000

NINI SAYS, "FINALLY YOU CAN REALLY *LIVE* IN ISRAEL." HE TRULY FEELS it. As the millennium approaches, it is the first time that Nini can be cool here. It used to be that every time he came back from a trip to Amsterdam, he would ask himself why he came back. But this year he suddenly noticed that he is fine here in Tel Aviv. He can breathe. Tel Aviv is free and fun. It feels as if, all of a sudden, everybody has decided that enough is enough. Everyone is fed up with the bullshit, the politics, the terrorist attacks. The religious fanatics. The occupied territories. The military reserve duty. All the pressure that has always fucked up everybody's head here.

Itzik Nini is a dancer at Club Allenby 58. At thirty-one he is good-looking and buff. Clad in a torso-hugging black T-shirt, camouflage army fatigues, and tall black boots, he looks like a European clubber. Actually, he hails from small-town Binyamina, but he came to Tel Aviv at the age of thirteen. He saw everything, tried everything, experienced everything, including all of the clubs: the Coliseum, the Penguin, the Metro. He left and came back and left again. He pursued the life of an actor-model-performer, shuttling between Tel Aviv's trendy Sheinkin quarter and Amsterdam's nightlife. So he knows that there are some things you still can't do here. Like S&M. There isn't enough openness for that just yet. It *is* the Middle East. And anyway, S&M is more of a Western thing. But apart from that and a few other things that are really hard-core, he suddenly feels that everything has opened up here. Almost anything goes. Change is truly awesome. Even he is sometimes blown away.

What caused the change? Nini says it is peace. Because of peace Israelis are more relaxed now, more self-assured. He can see it from his window on Yehuda Halevi Street in downtown Tel Aviv. Everything is calmer. People sit in cafés for hours. They're in the groove. No more old ladies shouting, "Shame on you, what are you doing having a good time and going to clubs and getting laid when soldiers are getting killed?"

There is another thing: MTV. Video clips really got into people's heads here and turned them on. Now when you see kids of fifteen from some remote development town coming to the city with piercings and tattoos, you know it's because even in their traditional hometowns they watch MTV. They see what's happening in the world, and they want to be a part of it. They want to live. They so badly want to live.

But the real cause of change, Nini says, is drugs. They've hit in a really big way over the last five or six years. And every year it gets more intense. Every time he comes back from Amsterdam he notices it. So now the feeling in Tel Aviv is that it's okay. Everybody is doing drugs. The whole world is doing drugs. And they do fantastic things, these drugs. It's time to say it. They make everyone happy. They liberate you. They open things up, especially Ecstasy. It's the drug of the millennium, Ecstasy. It's not a trip, it's not LSD. It doesn't remove you from reality but makes you feel better within reality. It started off as a drug for very angry people. It was a pill that softened them, made them gentler, more loving. And that's what it did for Israelis. It made them less uptight, less tense. Look at the street, you can see it. Sometimes you get the feeling that they poured loads of Ecstasy into the National Water Carrier to make everyone happy and laid-back. Take the gays, Nini says. Only a few years ago being gay was really underground. When he walked down the street with his long hair in a ponytail, people would shout: You maniac, you fag. And the gay scene was hidden, in the dark, not more than one or two hundred people. But now there are thousands, tens of thousands. And they are not ashamed anymore. They're not afraid. They don't give a shit. "Did you see the Purim carnival in Rabin

Square?" he asks. "Did you see the Love Parade? And the night Ehud Barak won the elections over Binyamin Netanyahu and Aryeh Deri—the gays were partying in the streets. And Shirazi's events—hot as can be." Everyone has come out of the closet. Millennial Israelis have pried apart the iron bars that imprisoned them.

Nini says that even the tough Oriental guys don't say a word now. And the straights now envy the gays. It's difficult to tell who is what. "All the straights look like gays now, and the gays look like straights," he says. "Everything is topsy-turvy. There is openness we never had here. It sounds strange, but love is in the air. Tel Aviv is now no less exciting than New York. Maybe it's even more exciting. And there is no less of a happening here than in Amsterdam—maybe even more. All over the world they get it. The word is out that Tel Aviv is hot. Very hot. And the scene here is really classy. It's worthwhile coming here just for the scene. It's getting to be a bit like Ibiza. Gays, straights, after-parties, pills. Open and sexy and totally free. Not at all like Israel once was."

Chupi says that when you think about it, it's pretty amazing. Just five or six years ago, house music was completely marginal in Israel. In 1993 and even in 1994, when he showed up with his box of CDs and started playing these really long tracks, people thought it was spacey, music from another world, from the next millennium. They didn't understand it and they didn't know what to do with it, not even how to dance to it. They still wanted music to have words and meaning. To have a human voice. Even at the Allenby 58 club, they didn't want it at first. It was too weird.

"Who in Israel knew then what Chicago House was?" Chupi exclaims. "What Detroit Techno was, or New York Garage? Who knew the difference between highs and peaks? Who knew then that the most important thing is the DJ? People did not realize then that the DJ isn't some technician who changes CDs, but the musician who creates the one-time music of that particular evening. They didn't know that he is the one creating those combinations in the mixer, and that with perfect timing he hits those peaks that suddenly bring everyone together, that suddenly make a thousand people one. Because of the DJ, a thousand people raise their hands together and take off their shirts together and shout together in bliss. The DJ liberates them for a few hours from the conflict and the wars and the stress and all the shit of this country."

Chupi says he had to be persistent. He had to put youngsters and club owners alike through a rigorous education, to get the dance crowd used to the new thing. He had to create his own crowd by himself, the house music crowd. And then connect the people to the music, and then connect the people to one another with the music. His goal was to make Allenby 58 the mecca of house music. He went to Europe and met the leading DJs and brought back the newest tracks, and along with a few others he created a music scene here that rivals those of London, Amsterdam, or Paris. It worked. So anybody who is anybody in hard-house or club-trance knows that Tel Aviv is now one of the best. Israel is awesome. No one knows exactly why the crowd here is so special. Perhaps it's the wars, the pressure. Perhaps it's the sea, the weather. The atmosphere, the attitude toward life. But what is clear is that the Israeli crowd has an amazing hunger like no other crowd anywhere.

His real name is Sharon Friedlich. He is the son of middle-class German Jews who gave him an education in classical music. He is short and burly, his hair cut short and oxidized. By the mid-1990s he had become a mega-DJ. "When you are a mega-DJ," Chupi tells me, "you have megapower. When you take your place in the elevated booth behind the glass, you know that if you just press one button, it's as if you are pressing some point in the heads of a thousand people simultaneously. This is power. Total, sexy power. Because now they are really in your hands. You control them. And if you want to, you can send them to heaven. You can make them horny. The energy of the dance floor is sexual energy. And what they beg you for is climax. You get to decide whether you'll give them what they are now desperate for. They are totally dependent on you. But if you are good, you wait. You don't hit peak after peak. You play with them. You arouse them, but you don't yet give it to them. It drives them crazy. And they shout louder, 'Give it to us.' And then, finally, when you give it to them, the club is like a ball of fire. Like an atomic blast. God is a DJ; DJ is God. It's as if you've touched a thousand people in every part of their body. And you see all the blood rushing through them, the sweat dripping from them. And they are yours, utterly yours. They thank you and worship you because you gave them something powerful and total. Something that nothing else in life gives them. Something you cannot find in the real life, outdoors."

Shirazi says a real revolution has taken place in Israel. It's not the Israel he grew up in anymore. In these last five years, everything has turned upside down. And his scene, the gay scene, is the perfect example. Until he launched his Friday night extravaganzas at Allenby 58, the gay scene was really on the fringe. It was tucked away, in places that were dim and secret. Only a few hundred people knew about them, and they didn't want to be seen going in or coming out. Israel of the 1970s and the 1980s didn't tolerate homosexuality. Israel was totally straight. It was a conformist society, hailing old-fashioned masculinity and sticking to strict conventional norms. But when Allenby 58 opened in 1994, Shirazi persuaded the owner, Ori Stark, to let him have Friday nights. They called it the Playroom. And they sent out invitations. At first, they were afraid. They didn't know how straight Tel Aviv would react. They didn't know if Tel Aviv's gays would dare come to such a big place in the middle of town. But it turned out that Tel Aviv was not that straight anymore. It turned out that the gays dared. They came in droves, in their colorful coats and their wild outfits and their extravagant attitude. They came without any shame. On the contrary, they came with chutzpah and pride. "Standing there, at the entrance of Allenby 58 and watching that amazing gay crowd congregate, I actually had tears in my eyes," Shirazi says. "I knew something big had happened. Something huge. We were liberated at last. The gays of Tel Aviv were liberated, and Tel Aviv was liberated. Israel was a new Israel.

"The gays are the scene leaders," Shirazi says. "Because what the gays have is totality. Gays are very total people, that's what makes our parties so over the top. If it's costumes, then it's costumes all the way. And if it's drugs, then it's drugs all the way. And if it's sex, then it's sex all the way. Anyone who comes to our Friday night parties sees it immediately. Everything is up-front. Everything is on offer. There is no such thing as busting your ass all evening so that at the end maybe she'll give you her phone number and go with you to the cinema. With us it all goes down in seconds. We look each other in the eye, walk off to the side, find the toilets, and fuck. And all around you the temperature keeps rising. There are go-go dancers, strippers, drag queens. Flickering lights, the beat of house music. It's intense as can be.

"But it's not only the gays," Shirazi continues. "Every night that Allenby 58 opens its doors, you get this feeling that something is happening, here and now. You can't stand calmly at the bar. You can't just sip a drink. The music, the strobe lights, the meeting of flesh. Chupi's guys stripping off their shirts. And the frenzy. The sexual directness. The desire for an outlet. This hyperenergized Israel that suddenly appeared in the mid-1990s insists on partying. Insists on devouring life."

Shirazi was born not far from here, on Sheinkin Street. But it was a different Sheinkin then, Shirazi says. A quaint, quiet neighborhood, with Orthodox neighbors and a small park, a neighborhood that no one ever thought would become Tel Aviv's SoHo. He brought himself up, worked his way up from nothing, until with hard work and perseverance, he acquired his present status as a scene leader. As king of the gays. And every week he has to surprise them. Every Friday night, he must invent some new, ever intensifying thrill. One week it's a sailor party, the next it's a Eurovision song contest party. One Friday it's a Fascist uniform party, another it's cross-dressing. And every two months, he holds his flagship after-party at Hauman 17, which calls for a dawn pilgrimage to Jerusalem.

Time after time he tells me that he is a patriot. He loves Israel absolutely. He feels so proud when any Israeli wins anything abroad. When the blue-and-white flag is raised up high in any sports stadium, it actually gives him chills. But he was especially proud when the transsexual Israeli Dana International won the Eurovision contest in 1998. That was like an official seal of proof that Israel had changed, that Israel had adopted a new identity. "And now they say that Allenby 58 is perhaps the fifth most important club in the world," he tells me. "There is a very strong international spotlight on the Tel Aviv scene. People realize our scene is world-class. DJs and drag queens from all over Europe want to come here. Because the truth is that although life is demanding here, life here is so much fun. Israelis really love fun. We are addicted to fun. We must have a good time all the time. We must party on and on. Perhaps it's everything we've been through, perhaps it's because of all of the troubles we still have, but we have this deep need to release all this pent-up energy. So what comes out at the end, in the Tel Aviv night, is some sort of unique warmth you won't find anywhere else. This is what erupted here in the 1990s, in Allenby 58 and in Tel Aviv and in much of the country. This is what came out of the Israeli closet, when people suddenly opened up and started living. And this is the incredible thing you see here on the dance floor at two A.M., when everybody is sweating and calling out to the DJ, and guys are taking off their shirts and touching each other and feeling each other and becoming one body of flesh."

Michal Nadel says it feels like a tribe. When it really happens and the vibe is good and the rhythm is good and bodies are moving together, then everyone becomes one. She thinks it's all very primitive and wonderful. When she gets into it and closes her eyes and moves her head from side to side, she can actually hear in the music the beating drums of ancient African tribes, the hooves of wild horses. "There is something very sensual about it, rhythmic and deep and sweeping," she says. "And everybody is together in this sexy, insane thing. So you can get close to people. You can touch them. That doesn't mean anything will come of it, though something could come of it. But mainly it's these sort of little caresses. Very gentle. Because the feeling is that people have no barriers. But they are not aggressive. They don't threaten one another. You feel close even to people you don't know. And when you smile at someone, he smiles back. Because we are all together here, brothers and sisters. We are all one in this incredible happening."

Michal's father was a three-star general in the Israeli army. Her brother is a combat pilot. But Michal's Israeliness now manifests itself in new ways. Every Thursday at midnight, she stands at the door of Allenby 58. In an extravagant getup, with her provocative mannerisms, she tells the bouncers who to let in and who to turn away, all the while looking for the guy she'll have fun with at dawn. Selection is power, Michal tells me. It is the power to fish people out of the ocean, to decide who shall be accepted and who shall be rejected. "Because Allenby 58 is for 1990s Tel Aviv what Studio 54 was for 1970s Manhattan," Michal says. "Something glittery, trashy, gaudy. Everybody wants to get in. Sometimes thousands crowd the doors. Guys in leather pants, girls with their breasts half bare. Because everyone knows that I will only let in the gorgeous ones. I will let in those who are not just pretty and hand-some and rich, but those who come with an open mind and an open heart, and are willing to kill for it. Those who are ready to devote them-selves to the alternative reality we create here, the reality that's not Old Israel but New Israel, that's not real life but much better than real life. Full of house music and house sex and house drugs. Full of this roar of an ecstatic tribe."

Ori Stark is Allenby 58's thirty-eight-year-old owner, and the tall, blond, and charming Ravid Zilberman is its twenty-five-year-old bar-woman. He is Tel Aviv's acknowledged Prince of the Night, and she's his girl. They've been going out together for a while now, and they love to talk about the scene they've created.

Ravid says that if you enter Allenby 58 in the daytime you see that there is nothing to it. What was once a cinema house is just an ugly gut-ted hall with cement walls and a bit of a stench. But as soon as it gets dark and the evening begins and people start streaming in and the lights start to flicker and the music erupts, then all at once everything is elec-trified. Your skin starts to tingle, because you know something will hap-pen. You enter something that is not quite real, a dream that makes your head spin. And all your barriers fall away. All your inhibitions. You are transformed. Even a nice middle-class girl like Ravid is transformed. After coming to Allenby 58 for a while she has become a totally differ-ent person.

"Sex and drugs are an important part of it," Ravid says. "There's no question about it. When people are high they get turned on. And they don't give a damn. But it's not only sex and drugs. In the Tel Aviv clubs, Ecstasy isn't only in the blood, it's in the air. Everybody gets into the high. Everybody is vibrating. And it's not some animal thing. There is a sort of code that makes you feel safe, protected. You can cut loose pre-cisely because you feel protected.

"There are all sorts of people," Ravid says. "There are the uptown girls who come to be seen with their rich beaux, but they're not interest-ing. And there are the tough Oriental downtown guys who are much more real and are just grateful to be let in. Then there are the Chupi freaks, who go wild on the dance floor, half naked and sweaty and crowded together. Hugging, flailing, grinding, creating a whirlpool of energy so strong that it sweeps up all the others, too. And on Saturday nights the soldiers come. It's incredible to watch the soldiers. Water and oranges, that's all they have—they don't even drink alcohol. But even so, from midnight to six A.M. they never stop. They give everything they have on the dance floor. And when the night is over they go straight from Allenby 58 to the buses that will take them to Lebanon or to the territories or to some godforsaken skirmish. Really, Israel is such a crazy place. And when these kid soldiers kiss their girls goodbye and put on their uniforms and go, I can't help but get emotional. It really breaks my heart.

"We are five girls at the bar," Ravid says. "Our role is to play the game. We only pour beer for people, but they really admire us. To be a barwoman at Allenby 58 is to be the best of the best. You're a goddess. When you wear a short, tight skirt and a little halter top, with your back bare and two hundred hungry guys crowding around your bar, you have to know how to play it. How to flirt with them in the right way. Gently. And all in all they respect you. Because at Allenby 58 you are allowed to try but not to intimidate. If you get the sign, okay. You take it upstairs to the gallery, to a dark corner, or a dark room. Anything goes here. But if you don't get the sign you move on. You don't make a fuss. Because at Allenby 58 we have this code. Actually, it's a kind of culture, a pretty defined world. But it's a different world. It's the world of today's Israel, the world of the new Israeli generation."

Ori tells me that they are now a movement. They brought out tens of thousands to Barak's victory celebration in Rabin Square, and they brought out two hundred thousand to the Tel Aviv Love Parade. "Who else in the country can bring two hundred thousand people to the streets?" he says. "Perhaps Deri's political party Shas, but no one else. True, it's not a political movement. It has no platform, and it's not saying anything. It's not the sixties now. Che Guevara is dead, Janis Joplin is dead, Woodstock is dead, and there are no more revolutions. There is no innocence, either. No one thinks he can change the world. There is no new idea here, no new message. And yet the government and the parliament and the establishment should pay attention to what is happening here. Because this nation is all about war and death. Even our religion is very sad, with its Yom Kippur and all, always telling you to suffer and sacrifice. But here we have something very powerful that says 'Fuck it.' We don't have to suffer and sacrifice anymore. Because now we are a fifty-year-old nation, and the armies of the surrounding Arab nations won't invade us. No one will conquer and destroy us. So we can breathe. We must breathe. And not only breathe, we even have to smile, laugh, go wild.

"We deserve it," Stark continues. "Of all the people in the world, we deserve it. So let us live. Peace has already happened, and if it hasn't, it will. In a short time, we will have a Palestinian state with Jerusalem as its capital, and it will be all right. So how much longer can we go on carrying this weight, this baggage we've been lugging around for five decades? The government and the parliament and the establishment don't get it yet because they were all brought up on Ben Gurion, who sent everyone to the Negev. But now there is a huge divide here. You can see it at Allenby 58, young people saying, 'Enough, it's time for fun.' There is a new generation in Israel and it's demanding happiness."

Ori Stark is the son of a Labor official and an actress. In the Tel Aviv suburb where he grew up, he was a good Labor boy: boy scouts, high school, active army service. But he always suffered a bit from the stifling atmosphere of Old Israel. So in 1982, after the Lebanon War, he got himself discharged from the military on psychological grounds. He went to London and studied the club scene, and when he came back he was ready. He became known as Ori the Handsome, the young lover of a top fashion designer, the new prince of Tel Aviv's nightlife. By 1983 he had produced his first big party, which featured 8 mm blue movies and attracted thousands. Then, for a decade, he opened and closed a dozen bars and clubs, until one day, at the end of 1993, immediately after Oslo, he walked into the enormous, neglected hall of the Allenby movie theater and knew this was it. The next big thing. Here he would establish his kingdom of happiness. He would make the empty cinema a shrine to happiness. For Ori hates sadness. And in this out-of-this-world venue he would make himself and others happy and celebrate to the very end.

Does he read the papers? Does he follow politics? Does he have an ideology? I ask him. "Sure," he answers. He supports the Left, always has. For a while, he even went to peace demonstrations. But today he believes that the party-now scene is more relevant than the Peace Now movement. "Allenby 58 is where it's at, where politics is really happening," he says. "In the past, Tel Aviv clubs celebrated machismo and senior officers and military heroes. But now no one cares about that hierarchy. If the commander of an elite commando unit comes in—fine, but who the fuck cares who he is. The heroes here are singers and actors and people who make other people feel good. And this is what the next Israeli century and the next global millennium is going to be about. Not that I will be mayor and Shirazi will be my lieutenant, not that it's all going to be one big love parade. But fun will take center stage. It will happen. It's already happening. The young don't read the papers anymore, but they dance like crazy. They will not go down to the desert, or build kibbutzim, or be army heroes, but they will wildly pursue pleasure and fun.

"In the sixties and early seventies, people wanted meaning in life and in music," Ori says. "Then came disco. But disco was ashamed of having no message. Now there is no shame, no pretense, no pressure to say anything. You don't sing about love, you have sex. Sex now, sex right now, sex in the toilets. And this new physical authenticity is what's real, this need for stimuli and pleasure and excitement. This is what Israel is now about. Forget the Zionist crap. Forget the Jewish bullshit. It's party time all the time.

"You can see it here," Ori says. "Look around you. No more poses, no more pretenses. The sound system is so loud you can't even talk. So you can't ask her what kind of wine she likes and who did she vote for in the last elections. There is no foreplay. It's all instant, quick. What's your name? Let's go. These kids live on the Internet. They click and buy. So their love is Internet love, too. They have no patience. Satisfaction is needed on the spot. And when they leave the toilets after a quarter of an hour, I watch them: there is no embrace, no affection, no tenderness. He goes this way, she goes that way. That's it. We came, we came, we went."

They call themselves the Nation. The Dance Nation. At 3:00 A.M. on most Thursday nights, Allenby 58 is at its peak. Nini gets onstage and begins his provocative performance, Chupi orchestrates his most intense climaxes, Shirazi is surrounded by his muscled boys, Michal joins the early morning dancers, Ravid is overwhelmed by the dozens of ex-

posed bodies that storm her bar, and Ori strides regally among his subjects. And when the lights cut the dark hall with pulsating rays of pink
and white, and the floor is full, and the stairways are crowded, and the
top balconies are heaving, it seems that there is something here that is
more than nightlife, something more than one more hot night in one
more hot city at the dawn of the new millennium. There is a great revolt
going on. Though it is confused and undefined and awkward, with no
ideals or slogans or grand pronouncements, it is the most captivating
revolt I have ever witnessed.

They are very good-looking, these youngsters. Here is an Israeli
success story few write about. The combination of sea and sun and
markedly different gene pools has created a unique sensual beauty here.
And the closed, intense space of Allenby 58 makes this sexy beauty all
too apparent. They are also very intelligent youngsters—quick think-
ers, quick responders. But they are no anarchists. They totally accept
the rigid laws of the prevailing economic regime. Even their world apart
is built on the organizing principles of hierarchy and selection and marketing and profit. And when the weekend ends, they'll begin another
week at an accounting firm or a television studio or a start-up company.
Yet at dawn at Allenby 58 these youngsters do make a statement. Without uttering a word, they make a statement through their liberation,
through their sexual openness and their rhythmic ritual. They make it
in trying to create a space of their own that is ritualistic, lustful, and
fun. On the dance floor and on the balcony and in the darkest recesses
of the club, they desperately attempt to reach some sort of personal authenticity, some sort of Israeli totality. In a consumerist era and in a
place of constant stress that doesn't offer its young authenticity or meaning anymore, this is what they are after. This is why they are so devoted
to the ritual that is Allenby 58: the Ecstasy and the ecstasy, this house
music and this house of fun.

At five o'clock in the morning the pilgrimage to Jerusalem begins. The
capital's early risers cannot believe their eyes: one by one, the cars arrive
in the sleeping city, strange futuristic music blaring from their windows. The youngsters in the cars, asking for directions to Hauman

Street, are smiling and red-eyed and dressed like vampires or satanic demons carrying pitchforks, or just sailors, princesses, and pink fairies. Under the gray dawn skies, among the garages and workshops and cheap furniture outlets of this remote industrial zone, a great flow converges on the dark warehouse that is Hauman 17. A sea of revelers is drawn to the club as if it were exerting a magnetic force, beckoning them with an ominous rhythmic beat.

The Shirazi after-parties are only for those who are totally enthralled by the scene. If you are not in full costume, then your face is at least shining with glittery makeup and your clothes are phosphorescent. Nini is right: it's the gays who are leading now. They set the tone, they are in command of the dance floor. But Shirazi is right, too: it's not just the gays, it's the mix. And the mix works. Something extremely poignant happens when all of these different sexual energies collide in one space, under one roof. Wiry boys with shaved heads hug each other by the stage. Gorgeous girls in diaphanous shirts dance by the bar. The strong smell of hashish fills the air. And every minute, some couple goes off to do it in the other room. Boy-girl. Boy-boy. Girl-girl.

It's all upside down: it's Tel Aviv in Jerusalem, night in the daytime, a bacchanal on one of Judaism's holiest days—Rosh Hashanah, the New Year. Thousands are crowded in the cavernous hall of Jerusalem's leading club, proving they can celebrate ten or twelve or fourteen hours of house music without becoming aggressive, impatient, or rough. Proving that anyone who thinks the new Israel is a fundamentalist theocracy doesn't know what the hell he is talking about.

Without the drugs it wouldn't have worked, but the drugs can't explain it all. Many factors are at work here. Israel is an immigrant society that has no deeply rooted, nonreligious conservatism. Israeli society is a survivor society that is hungry for life. Israel is a nation on the edge. Here, at Hauman 17, the outcome is a burst of energy unlike anything seen in London, Paris, or New York. So although this Shirazi after-party is an end-of-the-spectrum phenomenon, it says a lot about the spectrum itself. It says a lot about the cultural and emotional landscape of young Israel at the beginning of the new millennium. For what one hears on the dance floor of Jerusalem's Hauman 17 is the liberating roar of secularism. What one sees is the revolt of twenty-first-century youngsters against the demands and decrees and constraints imposed upon them by the Zionist project. No more, they say. Let us live. Let us seize the day.

Onstage a performance begins that only a few years ago would have been considered outrageous: an ex-boy gets down on his knees to worship the enormous erection of a boy who is still very much a boy. Outside, it's noon, the high noon of a high holiday in Jerusalem. But no one in the roaring hall seems much bothered about the lewd worship ritual taking place onstage. For this is not what matters. What matters are the other things these young people worship: liberation, freedom, the breaking of every taboo. Leaving behind their inhibitions. Crossing every boundary. Living to the extreme. Waving their hands in the air, these sweaty, half-naked boys worship at the altar of personal pleasure. Waving their hands in the air, these slim, provocative girls worship at the altar of deafening delight. And everyone in the hall is trying desperately to fashion a nation from all this. Trying to fashion an alternative nation, an alternative reality, an alternative meaning. Rising up against Israel's past. Rising up against Israel's fate. Rising up against the Israeli condition.

THIRTEEN

Up the Galilee, 2003

MOHAMMED'S LIGHT BROWN EYES LOOK INTO MY EYES AS HE SAYS, "YOU must understand it won't work. Your Jewish mind came up with this Jewish democratic invention, this intellectual conceit. But the invention won't work. The conceit is untenable. So instead of talking throughout this long trip we're going to take together, what we should do is sit down quietly and cobble together a new compact. Because you have no other ally. I am your only ally. Instead of going to the ultra-Orthodox Jews, you should come to me. Instead of trying to scare up half-Jews and quarter-Jews and eighth-Jews from every corner of the world and bringing them here to Israel, you should talk to me. Because I am here, in your backyard. I am here and I am not going anywhere. I am here for good.

"Talk to me," the Palestinian-Israeli attorney Mohammed Dahla says. "Talk to *me*, give *me* your hand, make *me* your partner. Because, like it or not, you are a minority in the Middle East. And though your nation takes part in the Eurovision song contest and plays basketball in the European league, if you open an atlas and look at the map you will see three hundred fifty million Arabs all around you, and a billion and a half Muslims all around you. So do you really think that you can go on hiding in this artificial construct of a Jewish state? Do you really think you can protect yourself with this contradiction of a Jewish democracy? To insist upon the Jewish character of the State of Israel is to live by the sword. And over time, you will no longer be able to do so. The world will change, the balance of power will change, demography will change. In fact, demography is already changing. Your only way to survive in the Arab-Muslim world is to strike an alliance with me. I am your only hope. If you don't do it now, tomorrow may be too late. When you turn into a minority, you will come looking for me, but I won't be here. By that time I will not be interested in whatever you'll want to offer. It will be too late, my friend."

Early in the morning, we set out on our journey from Jerusalem to the north. Driving from Gedera to Hadera, my friend and foe Mohammed Dahla says to me, "Look at this architecture, so foreign, so alien to the land. It's as though some kind of invading force emerged from the sea and landed on the beach. There is no sensitivity to the terrain, no understanding of its features. The immigrants who arrived here from far away didn't have a feel for the country and its history. They built with dizzying speed. They built tall and arrogant. But the buildings seem barely glued to the ground. They don't rise from it, they don't belong to it. That's what makes them so incongruous. They are aggressive urban edifices with an unpleasant concrete face.

"And look at the road signs," Mohammed says. "Most of them are in Hebrew and English, not Arabic. Because what you want is for tourists to travel around the country and believe that there really is a Jewish state here. But I am in your way, along with another 1.6 million Arabs. That's why you find us so difficult. To keep your nice little fiction of a European-Jewish state, you try to hide our existence. You try to eradicate our landscape and our history and our identity."

"Is the idea of a Jewish state totally unfounded?" I ask Dahla. "Don't the Jewish people have the right to self-determination? Aren't Jews allowed to have their own nation-state within the 1967 boundaries?" Dahla tells me that the Jewish people now living in the country have the right to self-determination. But one can understand why the Palestinians rejected the UN partition plan in 1947. And one must understand that there is no parity of rights here. "There is no balance between my right and your right," he says. "At the outset, the Jews had no legal, historical, or religious right to the land. The only right they had was the right born of persecution, but that right cannot justify taking 78 percent of a land that is not theirs. It cannot justify the fact that the guests went on to become the masters. At the end of the day, the ones with the superior right to the land are the natives, not the immigrants—the ones who have lived here for hundreds of years and have become part of the land just as the land has become a part of them. We are not like you. We are not strangers or wanderers or emigrants. For centuries we have lived upon this land and we multiplied. No one can uproot us. No one can separate us from the land. Not even you."

Dahla was born in 1968 in the Galilee village of Turan. He studied hard and worked hard and made his way by himself. After excelling at the Hebrew University's School of Law, he became the first Arab law clerk in Israel's Supreme Court. In 1993 he opened what would become a flourishing law practice in Jerusalem, and in 1995 he was the co-founder of the Legal Center for Arab Minority Rights (Adalah). In 2000, Dahla married Suhad, a lawyer and television presenter. Their first son, Omar, was born in 2002.

For two intense years, in the mid-1990s, Mohammed and I were co-chairs of the board of the Association of Civil Rights in Israel (ACRI). So as we travel north in his blue Mercedes, we conduct a conversation founded in a universe of shared values and concepts: human rights, minority rights, liberal democracy. But unlike previous conversations we have had, this time each of us brings with him his national history and perspective. And also his existential anxiety. This time Mohammed surprises me by unfurling for me his full worldview—and he tells me why he no longer believes in the partition of the land, in a two-state solution.

Growing up in a village, his identity was local, he tells me, the identity of a dutiful village son. Only at the university did he acquire a national Palestinian identity, and already then, the two-state solution seemed to him artificial and insufficient. It did not solve the problem of the Arabs of 1948 (the ones who remained in or returned to Israel after the war). Nor did it address the calamity of the Arabs expelled by the war. But when the Oslo Accords were signed in 1993, he was temporarily persuaded that the only viable solution was the two-state solution.

Then in 2000 he realized it was hopeless. The peace process was actually a process of subjugating the Palestinian people to Israeli will and preserving occupation. Israelis were not ripe for a historic conciliation. They were not willing to give Palestinians their elementary rights. So there was no way but struggle. Israeli society had to be shaken, disrupted. And eventually the solution would be a binational solution, one democratic state between the Jordan River and the Mediterranean Sea: a state that would have a Jewish law of return and a Palestinian right of return. One political entity that would leave the settlers of Hebron where they are, as it would allow the refugees of the Palestinian villages destroyed after 1948 to return to their homes.

This is our second journey to the Galilee. In the first week of October 2000, Palestinian Israelis rioted throughout the north. What began as sympathy protests for the Palestinian cause after the failure of the Camp David talks quickly turned violent. Israeli police came under attack, and in response they shot dead thirteen Palestinian Israelis. On the last day of that brutal week, Mohammed took me in his Mercedes to see the fighting for myself. We visited a Jewish community that objected to Palestinians buying property within its limit. We visited the smoke-filled city of Umm el-Fahem just as the flames were dying down. We dropped in on Sheikh Raed Salah, leader of the extremist Islamic movement. The bright-eyed sheikh talked about the abandoned mosques of ruined villages throughout the country and about the danger looming over the Al-Aqsa mosque, and he declared that the Jews had no historical rights to the Temple Mount and that their Temple Mount story was pure fiction. Then we went to a tent of mourning for a young *shaheed*—a martyr for the cause. In the village of Kana, the bereaved father who had just lost his seventeen-year-old son told us proudly that every day his boy came back from the demonstrations sorry that he had come back alive, until one day he did not come back alive. Then we walked around the empty streets and deserted restaurants of Nazareth. Everywhere we went, what struck us most was the silence, the mute silence of fear. It felt as if both the Israeli Jews and the Israeli Palestinians were terrified of what they had just done. As though both sides had taken refuge within their homes in a kind of voluntary curfew, while they waited anxiously for the future to unfold.

Now, though, two and a half years later, there are crowds everywhere, of Israeli Jews and Israeli Palestinians. The Wadi Ara region is bustling with Jewish visitors. There is not a seat to be found in Nazareth's restaurants. Hebrew speakers and Arabic speakers are scooping up hummus with pita side by side. Grilled meats are being ordered in loud Hebrew and loud Arabic. It's as if peace has been restored and the wounds of October 2000 have healed. As if the riots never happened.

So when Mohammed and I walk once again through the doors of Sheikh Salah's modest office, we are in for a surprise. The sheikh's eyes are not as bright as they were, and his brow is furrowed. In reasonable Hebrew he tells me that Israel will soon attempt to expel the Arabs from this land. Avigdor Lieberman's proposal to make Umm el-Fahem part of the future Palestinian state is an elegant means of population transfer, he says. Now the feeling in the Arab villages is that history is repeating itself, that 1948 is about to happen again.

Sheikh Salah wears a plain dark coat over his white gown and a knitted white skullcap over his gray head of hair. Now as then, he's dignified and gracious. But from across his dusty desk he warns me that international Zionism is making a grave mistake by allying itself with the imperialist interests of the United States, and by thinking that in the twenty-first century it is possible to re-create the oppressive colonial rule imposed by the British and the French on the Middle East in the twentieth century. International Zionism, Salah says, doesn't understand that although the Arabs were silent for a hundred years, they will be silent no more. A billion and a half Muslims will be silent no more. "I am not a prophet," he says. "The future is in God's hands. But if you turn the conflict from an Israeli-Palestinian one to a Jewish-Islamic one, the consequences will be dire. The Zionist Protestants in America want Armageddon. So there is great danger now to the world and to the Middle East, and definitely to this land. There is great danger to the Al-Aqsa mosque. I am deeply worried. I fear a catastrophe is coming, one that will imperil the future of the Jews."

We leave the sheikh and are off to Mohammed's homeland, the Galilee. When we pass Alonim junction ("Kafr Manda junction," Dahla insists), Mohammed says that he doesn't necessarily share all of Sheikh Salah's views, but that he respects his convictions and modesty, and his record of action. He is referring to the March of the Flags, the weekly pilgrimages Sheikh Salah leads, bringing buses full of believers from the Galilee to the Al-Aqsa mosque. It's an impressive operation, meticulously run, that is constantly growing in size. So although Mohammed is not a religious man, and although he was exposed to the West and adopted many of its values, he says that for him Sheikh Salah is a very important identity anchor. "While your story of the temple built by King Solomon three thousand years ago in Jerusalem is pure fiction," Dahla tells me, "Sheikh Salah represents fourteen hundred years of real Islamic existence in this land. It captures my heart. There is something very deep in this continuity. When I listen to the sheikh, I connect, as if through a time tunnel, to early Islam and to Caliph Omar Ibn al-Khattab, for whom I named my son. I connect to the greatness of Islam. It gives me a deep sense of calm, a sense of self-assurance. I know that we are not destined to be defeated. I know we are not a minority. The idea of being a minority is alien to Islam—it suits Judaism, but it is alien to Islam. And when you look around you see that indeed we are not a minority. In this land there is a Jewish majority that is actually a minority, and an (Arab) minority that is actually a majority. So every time the authorities go after Sheikh Salah, I offer my help. As someone whose expertise is Israeli law, I do all that I can do for him."

We turn toward the Jewish moshav of Tzipori. ("Saffuriyya," Mohammed teaches me.) "By 1948 it was a huge village of thousands, so today there are tens of thousands of descendants—some in Syria, some in Lebanon, and some in Galilee villages. Even my sister's husband is from Saffuriyya," he says. "His children also see themselves as sons of Saffuriyya. And on your Independence Day, we all gather here for an enormous memorial rally. We shall not forget," Mohammed promises. "We shall not forget and we shall not forgive."

He wears a light suit, a golden tie. He is of average height and build, energetic, with a dark complexion. He is proud of the fact that his skin color is the color of this soil. For he is mixed with this soil, he says. As we park the car, Dahla points to some skeletal prickly pear bushes in the Tzipori National Park and at some remnants of stone terraces nearby. He tells me that the Palestinian catastrophe of 1948 was not exactly like the Holocaust, but that he is not willing to accept the Jewish monopoly on the term "Holocaust." "It's true that here, there were no concentration camps," Dahla says. "But on the other hand, unlike the Holocaust, the Palestinian catastrophe of 1948 is still going on. And while the Holocaust was the holocaust of man, the Palestinian catastrophe of 1948 was a holocaust of man and land. The destruction of our people," he says, "was also the destruction of our homeland."

Tzipori's houses are nice and neat, white-walled and red-roofed. In one of the front yards, a beautiful young mother opens her arms as her one-year-old takes his first steps toward her. But Mohammed says he doesn't know how people can live here. "In theory, the countryside is pastoral and inviting, but in reality it is a graveyard. In theory, you are walking in your garden, but really you are walking on corpses. It's not human," Mohammed says. It's like the movie he saw once about an American suburb built on a Native American cemetery whose ghosts haunted the families who chose to live on top of their graves. "I am not into mysticism," Mohammed says, "but I feel the spirits here, and I know they will not stop haunting you."

The religious kibbutz of Beit Rimon sits at the summit of the rocky ridge of Turan, overlooking the village where Mohammed was born and his father was born and his grandfather and his grandfather's grandfather. "For hundreds of years we were here," says Mohammed. "From time immemorial. Tens of thousands of dunams on this ridge were designated by the British high commissioner for the benefit of the villagers of Turan, until the government of Israel seized these ten thousand dunams in order to plant Beit Rimon Aleph and Beit Rimon Beth and Beit Rimon Gimmel at the top of the ridge. So here, like everywhere else, the Jews rule over the Palestinians from above. The Jewish masters live up above, while the Palestinian servants live down below."

After we climb the mountain road to the kibbutz and find a way around its locked iron gate, Mohammed's mobile phone rings: the family of a terrorist who tried to blow up butane gas cylinders outside the kitchen of a Jerusalem pub is asking Dahla to represent the freedom warrior. Mohammed agrees on the spot and calls the Russian compound police station in central Jerusalem to inquire about the whereabouts of the detainee. When he is done, I ask him if he considers Beit Rimon a settlement. Does he think what will ultimately happen to the settlements in the occupied territories should happen to Beit Rimon? "The logic is the same logic," answers Mohammed. "The mind-set is the same mind-set. There is even a physical resemblance—the same planning, the same architecture. It's alien. It's an alien force coming from above and imposing itself on the landscape." It is early afternoon, and the air is clear, with good visibility. "Look at that Jewish community there, and that Jewish community there," Mohammed says, pointing first to the right and then to the left. "They are so orderly, so regimented, so European. They are totally different from our villages, which grow from the bottom of the wadi up the hill like a climbing plant. It is so clear that they invaded my Galilee. That's why they were established. To separate village from village. To prevent the Galilee from being an Arab land. So the Arab Galilee cannot demand territorial autonomy and cannot demand to secede from Israel and to join the State of Palestine."

"Do you seriously consider demanding a Galilee autonomy?" I ask. Dahla answers, "For me, the preferred solution is a one-state democracy for both peoples. But if there is no movement toward a binational state, we cannot settle for a shrunken and fragmented Palestinian state that doesn't even have its own airspace. That will not be a state, it will be a joke. So if you continue to insist on a two-state solution, the issue of the autonomy of the Galilee will have to be raised. And this autonomy cannot be only cultural, it must be territorial, with policing authority and effective control of the land and of natural resources. We will need three such autonomies: the Galilee autonomy in the north, the Arab Triangle autonomy in the center, and the Bedouin Negev autonomy in the south. And Palestinians living in Jaffa or Ramleh or Lydda must have personal autonomy linked to one of the three Palestinian cantons within Israel."

We pass by Mohammed's village of Turan, but for Mohammed it is more important to show me the ruins of the neighboring village of Lubia than to stop at home. He does tell me that his village is totally surrounded. Here is Beit Rimon, where he cannot live. Here is the Tzipori industrial park, where he cannot build a factory. Here is the base of an army that is not his army. Here is the monument for the Golani Brigade, which commemorates a memory he is not a part of. "So if I think I was saved," Mohammed says, "if I think my family managed to escape the catastrophe of 1948 because we went into exile in Lebanon for only a few months, here I am constantly reminded that I am not welcome. That I am on perpetual parole. That I have no rights here. For the monument that towers over the Golani junction, our Maskana junction, celebrates the victorious and omits the defeated. With its McDonald's restaurant and its Israeli armored vehicles and its blue-and-white flags, what the Golani junction says to me is loud and clear: We vanquished you. And because we vanquished you, our power allows us to celebrate ourselves within your territory. In the heart of hearts of your Land of Galilee."

Dahla's blue Mercedes descends the road to the South Africa Forest of the Jewish National Fund, then climbs up the gravel path among the pines and conifers. "It's not an innocent forest," says my friend Mohammed. "It's a forest of denial. By planting this forest you misled yourselves into thinking that you can deny your crime." Then he tells me when it first hit him. In the late 1990s, he participated in back-channel talks between senior Palestinians and Israeli peaceniks in Scandinavia. In one of the conversations, the Palestinians demanded reparations for their suffering and asked that these reparations be paid by Israel to the future Palestinian state so it would be able to utilize them just as the reparations paid by Germany to Israel were utilized for national projects. That's all they demanded. But the peaceniks went berserk. Because of this one request, the talks collapsed. Dahla and his colleagues returned home empty-handed, with no recognition of the historic justice they were seeking.

A short time later, he came to this forest with his mother's relative Mahmoud, a son of the village of Lubia. He walked with Mahmoud up this forest path, and when they reached this spot, Mahmoud recognized the ruins of his home. And he wept. "Gone is our homeland," he cried. "Gone is our life." And the successful Israeli attorney Mohammed Dahla stood by his side and wept with him.

"So what are you saying?" I ask Mohammed. "That the injustice done to Palestinians is an injustice not to be forgiven," he answers. "Because at this very moment, as Israelis lay out picnic lunches under the trees of the South Africa Forest, the refugees of the village of Lubia rot in the Yarmuch refugee camp in Syria. And the refugees of Saffuriyya rot in the Ain al-Hilweh refugee camp in Lebanon. So justice demands that we have the right to return. At least those rotting in the refugee camps should be allowed to return.

"I don't know how many there will be," Mohammed says. "Not millions, but perhaps hundreds of thousands. But I see them returning. Just as my family returned from Lebanon, coming down the slopes of the rocky ridge of Turan with their donkeys and belongings after months of exile, so will the others return. In a long convoy they will all return."

Azmi Bishara welcomes us to his private office in Nazareth. The Galilee-born philosopher had established a secular radical-nationalist Arab party in the mid-1990s and was a controversial but effective member of the Knesset ever since. There is no banner on the building that houses the headquarters of the leader of the Balad Party, no nameplate on the door, but his office is airy and comfortable. On the wall hangs a framed embroidered map of Palestine—all of Palestine: Jaffa but not Tel Aviv; Lydda but not Rehovot; Nazareth but not Migdal HaEmek. A photograph of Gamal Abdel Nasser is hanging there, too, of course. The Egyptian president and Pan Arab leader of the 1960s is Bishara's hero, and as we sit on the sofa, he looks down on us from a large black-and-white photograph, in a gray suit and black tie, grinning mirthfully under his narrow mustache.

An outspoken Knesset member since 1996, Bishara is now very cautious. As he awaits a Supreme Court decision that will determine his political future, he looks more like a well-fed cat than a dangerous tiger. Friendly, warm, and obliging, he pours me strong black coffee and asks how I managed to lose so much weight and how my love life is. He tells me about an essay he has just written and a novel he has just completed. He looks wary, as if he is perhaps suffering from political fatigue. But he emphasizes how important it is for him not to be disqualified politically by the Court. If the Court doesn't let him run in the coming elections—because he refuses to recognize Israel as a Jewish state—its decision will be perceived as a historic pronouncement. It will be viewed as an attempt to send Palestinian Israelis back to where they were in the 1960s. Even the appearance of formal democracy will dissolve.

"Will riots break out again as they did in October 2000? Will Israel be torn to pieces by the conflict between Israeli Jews and Israeli Palestinians?" I ask him. Bishara acknowledges that he is in no position to make any threats right now. But Dahla raises his head and says what Bishara is careful not to say: if the Palestinians' rights are not respected and the Palestinians' equality is not guaranteed, that will lead to the beginning of the countdown to the outbreak of Palestinian riots within Israel.

As we leave Nazareth, Mohammed tells me, "Bishara is my other identity anchor. He symbolizes our modern Palestinian pride. He is the icon of the modern generation, a generation that did not experience defeat and expulsion, a generation that does not fear Israel precisely because it knows Israel. This generation has learned from Israeli chutzpah, impudence, cheekiness, and therefore it does not beg but demands. It does not defend but attacks. It doesn't think like a minority and doesn't feel like a minority because it realizes it's not really a minority. The future is ours," Mohammed Dahla concludes. "No matter what tricks you try, you will not be able to maintain a Western state with a Jewish character here. All you will accomplish is to bring about a role reversal. We will be masters, and you will be our servants."

Some weeks later, the Supreme Court will allow Bishara to run for parliament once again. But four years later, in 2007, Bishara will flee Israel after being questioned by police on suspicion of passing information to the Shiite militia Hezbollah on strategic sites for rocket strikes during the 2006 Lebanon War. Dahla's secular hero Bishara will go into exile and become a star on the Pan Arab satellite television network Al-Jazeera, while most Israelis will regard him as a traitor. Dahla's Islamist hero Sheikh Raed Salah will go into jail and out of jail, but he will remain the most influential subversive Palestinian leader within Israel. Right now night begins to fall and Mohammed is very tired.

But all that is in the future. He asks me to take his place at the wheel. As I drive back south in the dark while he sleeps beside me, I think about him and about myself. What are our chances, I wonder. Will we survive this horrific history?

I love Mohammed. He is smart and engaged and full of life. He is direct, warm, and devilishly talented. Had he wished to, by now he would have been a judge or a member of parliament or a mayor or one of the leaders of Israel's Palestinian community. He is as Israeli as any Israeli I know. He is one of the sharpest friends I have. We share a city, a state, a homeland. We hold common values and beliefs. And yet there is a terrible schism between us. What will become of us, Mohammed? I wonder in the dark. What will become of my daughter Tamara, your son Omar? What will happen to my Land, your Land?

FOURTEEN

Reality Shock, 2006

WHAT WENT WRONG?

The obvious answer is occupation, but it's not only occupation. If today's Israel were as clearheaded, determined, and focused as it was in its early years, it would have dealt with occupation by now. Sooner or later, common sense would have prevailed. After making some initial errors of judgment, a reasonable national leadership of a reasonable republic would have taken action. One way or another it would have ended occupation. But though occupation is wrong, futile, and malevolent, it is not the source of all evil. Something else happened to Israel that is much more far-reaching, pervasive, and complex—something most observers of Israeli affairs have surprisingly overlooked.

In less than thirty years, Israel has experienced seven different internal revolts: the settlers' revolt, the peace revolt, the liberal-judicial revolt, the Oriental revolt, the ultra-Orthodox revolt, the hedonist-individualistic revolt, and the Palestinian Israelis' revolt. In a sense, each and every one of these upheavals was justified: they sought justice for an oppressed minority and addressed latent but vital needs. They all brought to center stage forces that were previously willfully ignored or marginalized. But the outcome of these seven revolts was the disintegration of the Israeli republic. What was fought for during the fifty years

prior to statehood and cultivated in the first twenty-five years of statehood was very much eroded in the four decades years following the 1973
war. So while most of the upheavals were just and necessary, their cumulative effect was destructive. They did not advance Israel as a functioning liberal democracy. They did not reconfigure Israel as a strong,
pluralistic federation of its different tribes. Instead, they turned the nation into a stimulating, exciting, diversified, colorful, energetic, pathetic, and amusing political circus. Rather than a mature and solid
state body that could safely navigate the dangerous waters of the Middle
East, it became an extravagant bazaar.

The settlers rose against political discipline and restraint. The
peaceniks rose against historical and geostrategic reality. The liberals
rose against the all-too-powerful state. The Orientals rose against Occidental domination. The ultra-Orthodox rose against secularism. The
hedonists rose against the suffocating conformism of Zionist collectiv-
ism. The Palestinian Israelis rose against Jewish nationalism. Yet all
these rebellions had one thing in common: they bucked against Ben
Gurion's state of the 1950s and 1960s that had built the housing estates
and erected Dimona and stabilized the young modern Jewish state.
After being conscripted and regimented and mobilized for over a generation, Israelis had had enough. The Israeli individual wanted something of his or her very own, and every Israeli tribe wanted something
of its very own. Every scorned and slighted human sentiment wanted to
burst out and be free to express itself. But all these different individuals
and tribes and sentiments never found a way to coexist. They never
worked out a new political framework that would allow Israel to represent them properly while acting as a cohesive whole. The outcome was
a fascinating, vibrant society—and a booming economy—but a dysfunctional system of government, an Israeli republic that was not quite
there.

Up to a point, all the revolts were necessary. They were part of a
crucial process of growing up and opening up. But from a certain point
on, they became petty and dangerous. And they could not be stopped,
even though, by now, Israel's problem was not Ben Gurion's monolithic
statism. By now the problem was the lack of leadership and lack of direction and lack of governability created by the revolts themselves. A na-

tion that was once too forceful was now too feeble. Israel had become a state in chaos and a state of chaos.

Conventional wisdom has it that 1967 was the pivotal year in Israel's history. True and not true. Actually, there were three pivotal years: 1967, 1973, and 1977. Within one decade, Israel experienced an extraordinary victory, a distressing defeat, and a monumental political upheaval—when after nearly thirty years of Labor's leadership, the right-wing Likud Party won the elections. The three dramatic events shook the nation to its core. They brought about occupation and then institutionalized it. But in hindsight, it seems that the most decisive of the three defining years was 1973. The trauma of the Yom Kippur War terminated the reign of Israel's ancien régime. It promulgated a deep distrust of the state, its government, and its leadership. It empowered the individual and weakened the collective. It crushed Ben Gurion's legacy and his concrete state.

As a result, the state was in flux. Old grievances resurfaced, old wounds were reopened. There were no longer any real shepherds or masters. No one had moral authority anymore. No one had the capacity to lead or to educate or instruct. Hierarchy broke down. The sense of purpose was gone. The common set of core values disintegrated. In the heat of revolt, the melting pot itself melted away. After being forced to be one, the different tribes of Israel began going their different ways. And it was the same with Israeli individuals. After being overorganized and overmobilized and overdisciplined for half a century, they were not willing to take orders from anyone. They trusted no one. They became unknowing anarchists.

The mass Russian immigration of 1989–1991 added to the chaos. The one million immigrants who arrived in Israel within three years invigorated its economy and shared its Jewish majority but added to the lack of cohesion. By the time they arrived in Israel, the old Zionist melting pot was no longer functioning. The well-educated newcomers felt they were superior to the ones absorbing them. Hence, they did not shed their old identity and endorse an Israeli identity as previous immigrants had done. They maintained their Russian values and their

Russian way of life and they largely lived in Russian enclaves. While contributing to Israel's science, technology, arts, and military power, they intensified the process of turning Israeli society into a loose confederation of tribes not quite connecting to one another and not sharing one binding national code.

Israel has never had a constitution. Its electoral system and political structure have always been shaky. But now there was no governing ethos and no governing elite. No one was in control and no one was in charge. Israel became impossible to rule. What made things worse was that the old ruling elites now turned their back on the state they felt they had lost, and the new, rebelling forces never bothered to create a dedicated, meritocratic elite of their own. The outcome was a gaping vacuum at the top, with no worthy leadership, no effective civil service, a weak public sector, and a disintegrating national ethos. The new political game was the blame game: Left blamed Right and Right blamed Left. But as this vicious circle went round and round, no political force took overall responsibility for running the nation in a mature and rational manner. Israel was out of its political mind.

What enabled the charade to continue was a regional stroke of luck. The thirty-three years following the Yom Kippur War were Israel's most peaceful. Few have noticed this because there was so much noise—Palestinian terrorism, Palestinian uprisings, a war in Lebanon, two Gulf wars. But in fact, from 1973 on, Israel was not once attacked by the military forces of a neighboring Arab nation. It was not even threatened. The impact of Dimona and Israel's air superiority was overwhelming. But deterrence was not the only factor. Israel enjoyed the benefits of a rare period of corruption-fueled stability in the Arab world. Egypt and Jordan actually signed peace agreements with the Jewish state. Other, less conciliatory Arab nations did not want to pick a fight. The decline of the Soviet Union, the rise of America as the only superpower, and their own internal weakness convinced Arab dictators that war with Israel was not an option. Therefore, Israelis enjoyed an exceptionally long period of strategic stability, which allowed them to ignore the outside world and indulge in their fancies and follies.

Reality first struck in October 2000, after the collapse of the Camp

David talks. The wave of terrorism that rattled their cities for three years reminded Israelis where they lived and what they faced. But under the leadership of the old-time warrior Ariel Sharon, Israel rose to the challenge. After their initial surprise, the IDF and the Shin Bet waged a sophisticated and effective counteroffensive. Israeli society proved to be far more resilient than expected. By 2004, Israel managed to stop suicide terrorism. The result was euphoria, and a regained sense of security and self-assurance that led to an economic boom. The 2005 unilateral pullout from Gaza—the disengagement—was also initially perceived as a success and contributed to the general sense of safety. The generals agreed that our strategic position had never been better, and as Israel grew more and more prosperous, the nation was once again pleased with itself and intent on celebrating its dolce vita.

On July 12, 2006, reality struck once again. The Second Lebanon War was not a major war. It lasted 33 days and took the lives of 165 Israeli soldiers and civilians and some 1,300 Lebanese, but it never really endangered Israel's existence. Though the war was nothing like the Yom Kippur War, for the first time in its history, Israel was not able to defeat an enemy. And the enemy this time was no superpower; it was not even another state. The enemy was the Iranian-backed Hezbollah militia, only eight thousand men strong. Israel's inability to stop Hezbollah from launching rockets at its northern towns was shocking. Its vulnerability and its impotence were shocking. For over a month, more than a million Israelis lived under fire. Approximately half a million Israelis fled their homes. The nation was helpless and humiliated.

Then came a moment of reckoning. The question that echoed throughout the country was what had happened to us. Had we lost it? Returning from a depressing tour in the half-deserted towns of the Galilee, I tried to answer this question in an essay I wrote for *Haaretz:*

What has happened to us?

First and foremost, we were blinded by political correctness. The politically correct discourse that reigned supreme over the last decade was disconnected from reality. It focused on the issue of occupation but did not address the fact that Israel is caught in an existential conflict fraught with religious and cultural land mines. It paid too much attention to Israel's wrongdoing, and too little to the historical and geopolitical context within which Israel has to survive.

Israeli political correctness also assumed that Israeli might is a given. Therefore, it was dismissive of the need to maintain this might. Because the army was perceived to be an occupying force, it was denounced. Anything military or national or Zionist was regarded with contempt. Collective values gave way to individualistic ones. Power was synonymous with fascism. Old-fashioned Israeli masculinity was castrated as we indulged ourselves in the pursuit of absolute justice and absolute pleasure. The old discourse of duty and commitment was replaced by a new discourse of protest and hedonism.

And there was something else: Israelis were besotted with the illusion of normalcy. But on its most basic level, Israel is not a normal nation. It is a Jewish state in an Arab world, and a Western state in an Islamic world, and a democracy in a region of tyranny. It is at odds with its surroundings. There is a constant and inherent tension between Israel and the world it lives in. That means that Israel cannot lead the normal European life of any EU member. But because of its values, economic structure, and culture, Israel cannot *but* attempt to lead a normal life. This contradiction is substantial and perpetual. The only way to resolve it is to produce a unique, positive anomaly that will address the unique negative anomaly of Israeli life. This is what Zionism accomplished in the three decades leading to the founding of the state, by formulating unique social inventions such as the kibbutz and the Laborite social economy of the Histadrut. This is what Israel did in its first three decades, by striking a delicate balance between Israel's unique national requirements and its inhabitants' need for personal space and a degree of sanity. But after 1967, 1973, and 1977, this balance was lost. In the 1980s and 1990s, Israelis went wild. We bought into the illusion that this stormy port was actually a safe harbor. We deluded ourselves into thinking that we could live on this shore as other nations live on theirs. We squandered Israel's unique positive anomaly, all the while chipping away at our defensive shield. Ironically, those who wished Israel to be normal brought about a chaotic state of affairs that could not but lead to the total loss of any normalcy whatsoever.

Both political correctness and the illusion of normalcy were strictly phenomena of the elite. The public at large remained sober and strong. Middle Israel did not forget Israel's existential challenge. In times of trouble, it was tough and resilient. But the Israeli elite detached themselves from historical reality. Business, the media, and academia dimmed Israel's vision and weakened its spirit. They did not read the geostrategic map. They did not remember history or understand history. Their constant attacks on nationalism, the military, and the Zionist narrative consumed Israel's existence from within. Business inculcated *ad absurdum* the illusion of normalcy by initiating sweeping privatization and establishing an aggressive capitalist regime that didn't suit the needs of a nation in conflict. Academia instilled *ad absurdum* a rigid political correctness by turning the constructive means of self-criticism into an obsessive deconstructive end of its own. The media promoted a false consciousness that combined wild consumerism with hypocritical righteousness. Instead of purpose and promise, the Israeli elite embraced self-doubt and cynicism. Each sector undermined Zionism in its own way. They misled Israelis into believing that Tel Aviv was Manhattan, that the market is king, and that mammon is God. By doing so, they didn't give young Israelis the normative tools needed to fight for their country. A nation with no equality, no solidarity, and no belief in its own cause is not a nation worth fighting for. It's not a nation that a young woman or a young man will kill and get killed for. But in the Middle East, a nation whose youngsters are not willing to kill and get killed for it is a nation on borrowed time. It will not last for long.

So what we see now, as rockets pound our cities and villages, is not only a failure of the Israeli Army to defend its citizens, but the grave outcome of the historic failure of the Israeli elite. This Israeli elite turned its back on reality, turned its back on the state, stopped leading Israel, and stopped holding Israel together. With every fiber of its being, Israel wished to be a modern-day Athens. But in this land and in this era there is no future for an Athens that doesn't have in it a grain of Sparta. There is no hope here for a life-loving society that doesn't know how to deal with the imminence of death. Now we must face reality. We must reconstruct our nation-state. We must restore the delicate balance between forcefulness and normalcy. And we must

rebuild from scratch our defensive shield. After years of illusions, delusions, and recklessness, we must recognize our fate. We must live up
to our life's decree.

Sadly, wars are a testament of Israel's national strength. Israel's remarkable victory in 1948 exemplified how determined and well-organized
the society formed by Zionism in Palestine was in the twenty years
prior to the War of Independence. Israel's astonishing victory in 1967
showed how cohesive and modern the nation-state that Ben Gurion
forged was in the twenty years prior to the Six Day War. And Israel's
alarming impotence in 2006 revealed how disoriented and dysfunctional the bizarre political entity that rose from the ashes of Old Israel
in the twenty years prior to the Second Lebanon War was. Yes, occupation is killing us morally and politically, but occupation is not only the
cause of the malaise but its outcome. In the twenty-first century, Israel's
immediate challenge is not an ideological one. It is not a choice between
peace and war. The immediate challenge is the challenge of regaining
national potency. An impotent Israel cannot make peace or wage war—
or end occupation. The 2006 trauma provided Israelis with an accurate
picture of the overall condition of their political body: an enfeebled national leadership, a barely functional government, a public sector in
decay, an army consumed with rot, and a startling disconnect between
metropolis and periphery.

But the 2006 experience also provides a detailed panoramic picture
of the world Israel lives in: Iran on the rise, Hezbollah building up in
the north, Hamas building up in the south. Peace has failed. Occupation has failed. Unilateralism has failed. Any stretch of land from which
Israel withdrew—in the north and in the south—was taken over by an
Iranian-backed terrorist entity able to menace Israel with its rockets. As
the threat of a nuclear Iran hovers above, the peril posed by tens of
thousands of rockets encircling Israel is imminent. Faced with renewed
existential danger, Israel has no relevant national strategy. It is confused
and paralyzed.

The combination of a grim new geostrategic reality with the inherent internal weakness of the state itself is overwhelming. True, the Second Lebanon War bought Israel time. For the next few years Hezbollah

would think twice before launching a new attack. It would not want to see Lebanon devastated again as it was when it last provoked Israel. But when this lull ends, what Israel will face might be ten times worse than what it encountered in the traumatic summer of 2006. Next time Tel Aviv, Ben Gurion airport, and the Dimona nuclear reactor might be under fire. Hundreds or thousands of Israeli civilians might be killed as every site and every home in the Jewish state will be within reach of the rockets of those enraged by Israel's very existence.

In the first Zionist century, Jews proved to be vital and resourceful. They rose to every challenge. Great obstacles that endangered and nearly ended their national endeavor were surmounted. The Arab uprising of 1936–39 was overcome. The war of 1948 was won. By 1967, Dimona secured the existence of the tiny young state. In 1973, the fighting spirit of the Israeli rank and file rescued the nation from the jaws of defeat. So the question posed following the 2006 debacle is whether Israel still has what it takes. Whether in the second Zionist century Jews can rise up to the challenge and defend their national endeavor as they did in its first one hundred years.

The fundamentals are good: we have a strong economy, a vibrant society, extremely talented individuals with impressive common sense and resilience. But the political structures and institutions of the Israeli republic are ailing. Malaise runs deep. The seven Israeli internal revolts have eroded the sovereign nation from below. The elite's disaffection has eroded the sovereign nation from above. The binding Israeli narrative has fallen apart. As a result, there is no one to speak up for the silent and sane Israeli majority. There is no great idea or even a reasonable political platform to address Israel's real challenges. In its seventh decade, Israel is much less of a solid nation-state than it was when it was ten years old.

As war rages on in the north, I decide to revisit Tel Aviv's night scene. By now Allenby 58 is closed, but Jerusalem's Hauman 17 has turned a huge garage in southern Tel Aviv into the new mecca of dance, drugs, and casual encounters. As the Israeli army struggles desperately to push into the Hezbollah-held territory in southern Lebanon, I spend an evening in the sweaty, crowded club, then continue on to a Russian dance

hall in Bat Yam, and then visit a new venue that has just opened next to
the Ayalon highway on the southern outskirts of Tel Aviv. I end the
night at a hip underground club in Tel Aviv located in a cellar, its walls
painted black. Straight stuff, gay stuff, mixed stuff. A lot of dark stuff.
"People really need it hard," a twenty-five-year-old blond psychology
student tells me as she offers me a tiny vial of cocaine, which I politely
refuse. "Ecstasy was love-sex, coke is alienation-sex," she continues.
"After peace fell apart and suicide bombers struck, the naïve scene of the
1990s was replaced by hollow-eyed parties like the one you see all
around us tonight. It's hard-core, in your face, but there's no love, no
affection. No hope whatsoever."

I look around me. The kids are good-looking all right, as sexy as
ever. Lustful and provocative. But there is war up north tonight. Young
soldiers are struggling in the bush at this very moment, stifling the fear
in their hearts, smelling death close by. And the distance between what
the soldiers are enduring in Lebanon and what the clubbers of Tel Aviv
are doing in the black-walled cellar is incomprehensible. They are nearly
the same age, same background, same education. But they are worlds
apart. Planets apart. They are playing out Israel's schizophrenia.

All of Israel's wars had this sort of tension. In 1948, while citizens
were being shot on the road to Jerusalem, others were flirting in Tel
Aviv cafés. In 1969, while soldiers were taking fire in Suez Canal outposts, other Israelis were having a ball in Tel Aviv's discotheques. This
duality was part of Israel's health and strength. It was as if there was a
covenant between us: today I will stand on guard while you party; tomorrow I'll party while you stand on guard. This way we don't turn our
nation into a barracks where life is not really worth living. This way we
continue to live while we defend our right to life.

But now it is different; now there is a complete disconnect. This is
what is so eerie about the war of 2006. Soldiers are fighting, and northern civilians are refugees in their own country, but many others just go
on not really caring. Many of the rich are vacationing on their yachts,
while the upper middle class is finding refuge in Eilat. There are summer cruises and summer parties and summer drugs. It is as if the nation
were not at war, as if it were not being challenged. And that is the real
threat—that is what is so scary. There is no Israeli togetherness. The

state cannot defend its citizens, and its citizens don't go out of their way to stand by their state. There is no glue holding everything together.

This time we survived. It was only a preview of what might happen in coming years. But what will happen when it's not just a small Shiite militia that's attacking us? What will happen to these beautiful dancers and to this sexy Tel Aviv when some of our really powerful rivals decide to strike? Returning from a quick encounter, the twenty-five-year-old blonde rejoins me at the bar. Looking around with glazed eyes and a bewildered smile, she says to no one in particular, "It's a bubble. It's an amazing bubble. It won't last."

THE STRAUSS STORY IS A HOPEFUL ONE. IT IS NOT ONLY A STORY OF A SUCcessful family and how it made its money, but a story of Israel's industrious capitalism. It is not only the story of one family, but the story of what has flourished in Israel—and how it flourished.

Richard and Hilda Strauss married in Ulm, Germany, shortly after Adolf Hitler rose to power. On May 1, 1934, Michael-Peter was born. A year later, as Hilda was holding her firstborn in her arms, she heard Goebbels speak over the wireless. When the Nazi propaganda minister vilified the Jews, she felt a sharp pain in her body: she knew that disaster was imminent. In April 1936, the Strauss family loaded their belongings into their car and left for Switzerland. In her diary Hilda wrote, "We are emigrating. Where to? To the land of our ancestors, to our homeland, to the Land of Israel. Why? Because we are no longer wanted in the land we were born in, the land we loved. We want to stay proud, as we should be, so our children can rejoice that their parents are Jews not only in their religious persuasion but in their soul. That's why we are leaving for a new homeland."

On June 18, 1936, the Strausses arrived at the port of Haifa. Their disembarkation is documented in a crisp black-and-white photograph: Richard in wide, white linen shorts, a white shirt, and a white cap; Hilda in a long, checkered summer dress, holding a rambunctious Michael-Peter, who is wearing shorts and no shirt. At first the family lived in the moshav village of Ramot Hashavim, then they moved to the southern colony of Be'er Tuvia, and then to the northern colony of Nahariya. The climate was hot, conditions were harsh, and the 1936–39 war with the Arabs was brutal. Richard, who held a Ph.D. in economics, felt lost in his chosen land. He found it difficult to relinquish his academic dreams and adjust to his new life as a taxi driver in a remote Mediterranean province. "Disappointment seeps in slowly, like the venom of a snake," Hilda wrote in her diary. "Disappointment is 77 times greater in a new land in which we do not yet have a home. The days are very long and full of suffering. Only the boy's cheerful laughter keeps the soul alive."

In April 1937, the Strauss family finally received the plot of land it had bought months earlier: a nine-dunam rectangle on the eastern edge of Nahariya. Along with the land came a forty-square-meter house, a cowshed, rudimentary agricultural tools, an irrigation system, and a track line on the boundary of the property complete with open carts for the transport of produce. The house was small, the question marks huge. Hilda wrote in her journal, "What does the future hold? What will become of us? Our fate is in the hands of strangers, and we can only fulfill our duty and trust God."

A few weeks later a first ray of optimism penetrated the tiny Nahariya home. Hilda wrote in her diary, "It is eight days now that there are cows in the cowshed. There is milk at home. Fresh white milk. We must work hard to acquire the expertise required to run a dairy farm."

The Strausses were a prime example of the spirit of free enterprise that characterized the new German-speaking colony. They learned fast. Every morning Richard milked the cows, filled the large copper pots, loaded them onto his bicycle, and rode from door to door selling Strauss milk. But Nahariya had many cowsheds, and the supply of milk exceeded demand. Hilda realized that the future lay in cheese making. She studied the art of cheese making and turned her domestic kitchen into a small dairy. From professional European journals she learned how to make malodorous Limburger and milder Romadur, and she experimented with soft cheeses seasoned with pepper and paprika. She packed the 100- and 500-gram cheese parcels in wax paper stamped with a proud blue-and-white ostrich (*strauss*, in German). By 1938, she won the British high commissioner's prize for dairy products. By early 1939 she persuaded Richard to do away with the cowshed, sell the cows, and focus on the production of fine cheese and other dairy products. In the summer of 1939, when the thousand years of German Jewry came to a close, Hilda and Richard inaugurated their first dairy products facility. While European Jewry was disappearing into the great dark of the Holocaust, Hilda and Richard founded Strauss-Nahariya.

World War II propelled Nahariya forward, turning a struggling agricultural colony into a booming leisure town. Tens of thousands of British soldiers and Palestine Jews—now enjoying the wartime prosperity—were attracted to the European charm of the German-Jewish Nahariya. The beach was packed; the pension hotels were full; the cafés were bustling, serving strawberries and cream, fine bread and rolls, and imported meats. Chamber music concerts, jazz jam sessions, tango soirees, and Charleston competitions were held. Along the beach, the colorful huts of the Galei-Galil Company stood in row after row. Sailboats and rowboats headed into the Mediterranean powered by the strong arms of Nahariya beach boys. Slim girls came from Tel Aviv for their holidays, flirting by the beach huts at noon and in the swinging bars at night. While Europe was ablaze, the small European village founded by Europe's survivors on this Mediterranean shore of refuge was teeming with life. Nahariya was now one of Zionism's most famous delights.

World War II also propelled Zionist capitalism forward, turning an agricultural economy into an industrial one. The British need for an advanced logistical and technological base in the isolated Middle East made Jewish Palestine of the early 1940s a hub of private enterprise and innovation. The Strauss family was part of this process, which laid the foundation for Israel's industry and creative capitalism.

But as war broke out, tragedy struck: shortly after immigrating to Palestine, Richard's beautiful sister took her own life. Richard, too, was often depressed. He flew into rages and often sought comfort and pleasure in the arms of Nahariya's young women. Yet Hilda remained totally focused. She recognized the opportunity of the wartime boom and seized it. She was tough when negotiating with milk suppliers from the neighboring kibbutzim and aggressive in marketing her products to the flourishing cafés and overbooked pension hotels. But above all, she was

meticulous about the work ethic and the hygiene and production stan-
dards of her fledgling dairy. Throughout the 1940s, Hilda Strauss established the reputation of her company as a superior German-Jewish dairy
that produced, in Nahariya, outstanding European cheese. After the
War of Independence, Hilda replaced the Strauss ostrich with a new
and more fitting trademark: a water tower.

The 1950s brought the Strauss family an unexpected windfall: German reparations. Like other Holocaust survivors, they—and the Israeli
economy as a whole—benefited from the compensation agreement
signed in 1952 by David Ben Gurion and West Germany's chancellor,
Konrad Adenauer. Hilda and Richard invested in their dairy the deutsch-
marks they received from the Bundesrepublik Deutschland for all that
was lost in Ulm. They imported from Germany their first commercial
production equipment, as well as professional know-how. While their
young Nahariya-born daughter, Raya, stayed at home, they sent their
precocious son, Michael, to Switzerland and Germany to complete his
studies in dairy production. The German dimension of the Strauss enterprise was amplified in the 1960s, when Hilda and Richard managed
to forge a strategic alliance with a German subsidiary of the European
giant Danone. The partnership was made possible by the Strausses'
German background: if not for Hilda, Danone would not have forged
such an alliance with a small dairy in a remote country. Danone transformed the family business and reconnected Hilda to the motherland
that had rejected her a generation before. It also allowed the Strauss
family to return from the fringes of Palestine to the center of Europe,
and to remain up-to-date on European technology and business prac-
tices. In the summer of 1973, when the modern Danone-Strauss plant
opened on the Strausses' nine-dunam plot of land that the Strausses
clung to in the harsh winter of 1937, the event was not merely an industrial triumph. After three dramatic decades, the three souls who had
escaped Europe and built in Nahariya a shelter that would save them
from Europe brought Europe to Nahariya.

Michael-Peter was only two and a half years old when his parents
settled in Nahariya. As a child, he walked barefoot among the cows, and
as a teenager he sold his mother's cheese to the hotels and cafés. But
young Michael was very much a wild child raising himself. His mother
was devoted and loving, but she was caught up in business. His father

was bad-tempered and sometimes abusive. His sister was six years younger and her father's favorite. Michael received his education on the soccer field, on the basketball court, and on the beach. He spent most days and nights outdoors. The distance between himself and his parents could not have been greater. They were well educated while he could not be bothered with going to school. They were law-abiding bourgeoisie while he was a rule-flouting rebel. They were conventional and conservative while he was an iconoclast. Under the roof of European propriety, a charismatic, intuitive, and life-loving Israeli beach boy grew up who would give the Strauss dairy its Israeli dimension.

From the ages of thirteen to twenty-two Michael lived away from home: in the naval academy, in the navy, in the merchant fleet. The rough life of a sailor suited him. But after he was tamed and groomed in Switzerland and in Ulm, he returned, at the age of twenty-three, to his parents' dairy to work alongside his mother. Michael contributed chutzpah to their enterprise. He believed the sky was the limit: his mother's little dairy could conquer the young State of Israel. When the business came close to collapsing in the late 1950s, he marched into the Jerusalem office of the trade and industry minister and extracted emergency funding. When one bank created difficulties in the 1960s, he went to Tel Aviv and persuaded another bank to lend Strauss even more money. Michael used his charisma to win over partners and overcome rivals, to cajole and placate employees, managers, and sales agents. With determination and shrewdness softened by charm, Michael managed to modernize production, expand distribution, and bring Strauss products to every grocery store in Israel. But Michael's real forte was his feel for people: he could intuit people's strengths, people's weaknesses, people's needs. In the 1970s and 1980s, Michael Strauss turned the Strauss dairy into a modern company that utilized its European capabilities to give Israel what Israel wanted.

Israel is a harsh, hot land; ice cream is cold and comforting. So Israelis consume much more ice cream than North Americans and Western Europeans. Hilda Strauss realized the potential of ice cream in 1950. Although production was fraught with difficulty, she insisted that her dairy begin manufacturing it. But Michael was the one who made his mother's ice cream a national brand. He brought about the fall of the rival company Artik, bought the competitor Vitman, and forged a partnership with the Anglo-Dutch giant Unilever. Today, Strauss Ice Cream is the biggest manufacturer in Israel, with roughly half of the market share.

Israel is a bitter land; dairy desserts are sweet and soothing. So Israelis love dairy desserts. Hilda and Michael Strauss recognized the potential soon after the 1967 war. They understood that the era of ascetic Zionism, of basic white cheese and thin, yogurtlike *leben*, was over. With better times came the demand for better and richer dairy products. So they challenged the Tnuva cooperative's monopoly by offering the new Israeli customer high-quality yogurts and individual dairy desserts. In the new Danone-Strauss plant they manufactured a milk chocolate pudding called Danny, which conquered the market of the 1970s. In the 1980s and 1990s they introduced the German-inspired dark chocolate and whipped cream dessert Milky, which found its way into almost every Israeli refrigerator. Strauss became a prosperous giant, controlling the largest chunk by far of Israel's dairy desserts market.

Israel is an exciting and excitable country, so Israelis need ever-increasing excitement. The Strauss team understood that this applied to the way everything must taste. They realized that Israeli salty snacks had to be much saltier than their American counterparts, and that Israeli sweets had to be much sweeter than European ones. Chocolate had to be much more chocolaty and vanilla much more vanilla-y. There were no nuances for Israel; everything had to be fierce and aggressive, to hit the palate with flavor. The Israeli Milky, for example, had twice as much whipped cream as its German inspiration. But Israelis don't want just more, they want new. They get bored very quickly. So Strauss replaces its products much faster than its European sister companies do. To stay where it was, Strauss had to keep running. But Michael and his fellow workers loved running. They were indefatigable runners. So they took Hilda's small, solid German operation and turned it into a hyper-energetic Israeli empire.

Dr. Richard Strauss died in Nahariya in 1975. Hilda Strauss died in Germany in the summer of 1985. They left behind a son, a daughter, seven grandchildren, and the most advanced dairy products company in the Middle East. In 1997, twelve years after Hilda's death, the Strauss family purchased Elite, Israel's leading chocolate and coffee manufacturer, making Strauss-Elite the largest food and beverage group in Israel. In 2000, Strauss-Elite opened its new dairy in the Galilee. The fully automated Ahihud plant produces more than a billion cups of yogurt and dairy desserts every year. In the mid-2000s, Strauss-Elite took over several coffee companies in Eastern Europe and South America. In the late 2000s, it penetrated the American market and rebranded itself as the Strauss Group. In 2010, it opened, in Virginia, the biggest hummus manufacturing facility in the world, which now supplies over 50 percent of American demand. In 2011 the Strauss Group sales approached $2 billion, and the operating profit neared $180 million. Sales grow at close to 10 percent annually, mainly because of overseas expansion. For a while now, Strauss Group has been the fourth-largest coffee company in the world in terms of green coffee procurement—larger than Lavazza and Segafredo.

Michael Strauss greets me on the deck of his marine-blue yacht, *Lucky Me*, anchored in the Croatian fishing village of Havar. He is tall and fit. His gray hair is closely cropped, and his voice is thunderous. Even in his late seventies, he has the manner, the posture, the energy, and the mischievous look of a young sailor—hungry for life and always on the lookout for the next escapade. But during working hours, Strauss is disciplined. I find him going over emails sent from the company's headquarters a few hours earlier: quarterly reports, annual projections, analyses of the Chinese market. After offering me a glass of champagne, he makes it clear he must get back to work. Although he is semi-retired, and on his summer holiday, one must do what one must do. Only after he reads the last of the company briefs does he join me on deck to try to understand why I have come such a long way to talk to him.

"What is Israeli about Strauss?" I ask. "What is it about Israel that enables Strauss to succeed?" Michael fires back instantly: "The people. Israel has extraordinary people. Israeli human capital is absolutely unique. The challenges facing any Israeli business are enormous— a dysfunctional government, an inefficient bureaucracy, wars. Israel's permanent uncertainty is a real drawback. But what compensates for all these obstacles are the Israelis themselves. I've been around the world. There are no such people anywhere else. Israelis are exceptionally quick, creative, and audacious. They are sexy even in the way they work. They are hardworking and tireless. They are endowed with a competitive spirit—with the need to be the first at the finish line. And they are willing to do whatever it takes to be the first at the finish line. They never take no for an answer. They never accept failure or acknowledge defeat."

At noon Michael and I descend the aft stairs to the dinghy that brings us across the bay to a secluded island. It's still early in the season and almost empty: only two Russian oligarchs are enjoying the sun, accompanied by three gorgeous platinum-haired girls. Michael flirts with the pierced and tattooed barwoman who serves us a midday Chardonnay. Under the thatched roof of the inviting bar, she doesn't reject Strauss but plays his game. It's all transparent in this Adriatic resort: wealth is wealth and youth is youth and they interact.

I ask Michael if the Strauss story is the Israeli story. Michael says that though his mother was not big on words, he often sensed her deep pain: the departure from Germany, the expulsion from Europe, finding herself in a remote land whose tongue she never fully mastered. While his father took his pain to other women, his mother took her pain to the dairy. And with a strength that rose from her suffering, she made a family and founded a business. Hilda was a devoted Zionist. The trauma of the betrayal of the old homeland made her cherish her new homeland. She believed that the dairy was her way of participating in the founding of the Jewish state. As far as she was concerned, Strauss and Israel were intertwined. As Israel grew, Strauss grew. As Israel made its way through history, Strauss made its way to market. So even though Hilda was never political, and even though she never spoke Hebrew properly and never really knew the country, she *was* Israel. She embodied the need for Israel to be, the determination that Israel will be, the miraculous story that Israel is.

After we head back to the yacht and Michael goes down to his cabin for a post-Chardonnay nap, I am left alone with my thoughts. Ulm was also Albert Einstein's hometown, and Einstein was the Jewish Diaspora at its best: a combination of scientific genius and universal humanism. But Einstein's and Strauss's German-Jewish Diaspora was doomed. Einstein left for Princeton, Hilda for Nahariya. Hilda did not indulge in self-pity, but instead fought back. She realized that the task of her generation was survival. She knew her generation had to invent a new world in which their children would be able to reinvent themselves. She was never at home in this new world. Hers was a life on the cusp. But eventually her children and her grandchildren had a homeland and a home. They turned Hilda's kitchen dairy into a multinational giant employing more than fourteen thousand workers in more than fifteen countries, manufacturing hundreds of products. So now, as its owner emerges from his cabin with a sailor's smile, the glistening yacht of the son of Europe's survivors glides into the port of Dubrovnik. After some maneuvering, it finds its place among the yachts of Russian moguls, French millionaires, and British aristocrats—Europe's high and mighty.

The Richter story is a hopeful story, too. Kobi Richter was born on Christmas Eve in 1945. His father, Kalman, was a disciple of the Revisionist Zionist leader Vladimir Jabotinsky. Born in Lvov, Poland, he immigrated to Palestine in 1935, converted to Labor, worked in a potash plant in Sdom, and joined Kibbutz Ramat Yohanan in the north. His mother, Mira, was the daughter of an ultra-Orthodox family from Lvov that failed to immigrate to Palestine in time and perished in the Holocaust. Kalman was the chief welder as well as the treasurer and economic leader of Ramat Yohanan. Mira worked in the cowshed and managed the common clothing warehouse. Kalman and Mira were both strict and tough, devoted soldiers of the Zionist revolution.

Richter's first memory is of war. While the family sat in the kibbutz bomb shelter in early 1948, he put his two-year-old fingers into empty peanut shells that he imagined to be helmets. But his childhood was peaceful. By the 1950s, Ramat Yohanan was flourishing. The Holocaust was not to be mentioned, and war was a heroic memory—there was no real danger in sight. In his eyes, the kibbutz was the elite unit of Israeli society, which was the elite unit of the Jewish people, which was the elite unit of humanity. Anyone lucky enough to be the son of a kibbutz was at the apex of the apex of the apex.

Kobi Richter was gifted. At the age of four he learned to read, at the age of seven he devoured four books a week, and by the time he was ten he knew his Dickens and Hesse. At eight he learned to swim, at twelve he was the kibbutz swimming champion, at sixteen he was Israel's number 2 in mixed freestyle. At seven he learned about different screws in the welding workshop, at ten he could weld, at fifteen he built a motorcycle. In his teenage years Ramat Yohanan was paradise: there was a pool and a metals workshop and wheat fields; there were tractors, horses, and girls; duck hunting and lock picking and mushroom foraging and joyrides in cars borrowed for the night. Everything was possible.

Kobi Richter was a perceptive boy. As his bar mitzvah approached, he recognized that there was an inherent contradiction between the two values the kibbutz upheld: equality and freedom. But though he recognized the jealousy, hypocrisy, and pettiness in the commune's life, he was devoted to the kibbutz. He sang and danced in the grand socialist, national, and Jewish holidays and celebrations. When the women danced in circles and the men reenacted harvest time with plowshares in hand and the children were lifted up high, Kobi would have tears in his eyes. He identified totally with the mesmerizing secular religion of Israeli pioneerism. He felt privileged to be one of the select few who would lead his people from slavery to liberation, from weakness to might, from Shoah to resurrection.

Ramat Yohanan was not only a commune fulfilling the socialist-Zionist dream, it was a successful business. The cows in its modern dairy produced twice as much milk as the cows of the American Midwest. Its new plastics plant was one of the first of the kibbutz movement. The kibbutz also had avocado groves in which the sixteen-year-old Richter laid out an innovative irrigation system. It had cotton fields for which the seventeen-year-old Richter built a mechanical picker of his own design. Ramat Yohanan's agriculture was already industrialized, and its industry was quite sophisticated. The commune was not only the greenhouse of romantic Zionist socialism but the greenhouse of a demanding can-do ethos and impressive technological capability. When Richter joined the Israeli Air Force in 1964, he found there what he valued most: excellence, competitiveness, and high technology. He loved the challenge of seizing control of the flying machines that defied the heights and speed man was designed for. For Richter, the pilot was a modern knight, a solitary warrior battling other solitary warriors to the death. Richter loved the fight. He believed in his own capability and loved testing it daily. His sense of superiority didn't make him popular among his peers and commanders, but no one could deny his extraordinary talent. The excellent pupil, welder, swimmer, hunter, dancer, and technological prodigy became an excellent fighter pilot. Handsome, proud, and arrogant, Richter was the poster boy of the Israeli Air Force of the 1960s.

On June 5, 1967, Kobi Richter took off from Lydda airport in a French-made Ouragan bomber. Along with his comrades from Squadron 107, he headed south, flying low and maintaining absolute radio silence before turning southeast toward Egypt. Operation Moked had been rehearsed by the Israeli Air Force for years. Richter himself had rehearsed it dozens of times. The strategic idea was to get nearly all of Israel's combat aircraft in the air at once and then strike—with complete surprise and accuracy—the thirty air bases of Egypt, Syria, Jordan, and Iraq. But now, as Squadron 107 hovered over the western Negev, Richter was thrilled to see the plan become reality. Dozens of planes were in the air, some heading for Luxor, some for Amman, some for Damascus. The sky was almost blackened with the flocks of eagles about to attack. Richter felt as if mighty vectors of power were bursting out of the tiny State of Israel and were about to rattle the entire Middle East. He felt that he was part of some mythical force that had suddenly risen from the Promised Land. Every bomber was in the right location, at the right altitude, on the right course. And it all took place in absolute silence, in perfect coordination, like an extraordinary sacrament. Such an event had never happened before and would never happen again.

At 0745, Richter took his Ouragan from three hundred to three thousand feet. As the airfield of El-Arish came into view, it looked exactly as he had memorized it: the control tower, the runways, the MiG jets. Richter fired seventy-six French-made rockets at the antiaircraft battery, which ceased to exist in about thirty seconds. Then he returned for three more precision strikes, destroying three MiG-17's on the ground. Within fifteen minutes, Squadron 107 disabled the Egyptian airfield of El-Arish. Within three hours the Israeli Air Force destroyed four Arab air forces. As Richter headed home and descended over the orange groves of Rehovot, landing at Lydda airport, he knew that in its very first hours the war was already won. Israel was now a regional power, the strongest nation in the Middle East.

In 1968 Kobi Richter trained as an intercept pilot. From 1969 to 1973 he participated in a series of dogfights, shooting down eleven enemy planes. He was now one of the leading combat pilots of an air force that gave Israel air supremacy. Yet while he was still in the service he earned his Ph.D. in biology and biochemistry, and from 1979 to 1982 he did his postdoctoral research at MIT in artificial intelligence. A few years later, Colonel Richter left the air force and established his first high-tech company, Orbot, which he founded with four other graduates of the security and military system. Orbot developed an innovative automated optical inspection (AOI) system to aid in the manufacturing of printed circuit boards, with speed and resolution previously unseen in the field. In 1986, Orbot brought its first product to market. In 1989 it controlled 60 percent of the worldwide AOI market. After it merged with its Israeli rival Optrotech, Orbotech was born, which now controls nearly 80 percent of the AOI market. In the second decade of the twenty-first century, Orbotech employs more than fifteen hundred people and has an annual revenue of more than $400 million. In 1992 Richter himself resigned from the company, ready to move on to new things, though he continues to be Orbotech's biggest shareholder.

Richter founded Medinol in December 1992. He realized that the next big thing in cardiac medicine was the stent, a tiny device composed of wire mesh tubes inserted into an artery to keep it open and allow blood to flow as it should. The stents of the early 1990s were problematic—some were too rigid and difficult to insert, while others were too flexible and collapsed after insertion. What was needed was a new kind of stent that would be flexible during insertion and rigid afterward. Richter developed this new kind of stent, the rigid-flex, with the Russian tank engineer Grisha Pinchasik, who had recently immigrated to Israel. In the Richters' Ramat Hasharon kitchen, the first models of the revolutionary stent were carved from empty cottage cheese containers. Five years later—after signing a partnership and distribution agreement with Boston Scientific—Medinol sold a hundred thousand stents a month, and its annual revenues were over $200 million. By mid-1999 the tiny Jerusalem-based company controlled 35 percent of the international stent market.

What made Medinol's success even more dramatic was the unique production method Kobi Richter developed. Consequently, Medinol's after-tax profit was 86 cents on the dollar. In the late 1990s, Kobi and Yehudit Richter owned one of the most profitable companies in the world.

In 2000, a bitter legal battle erupted between the Richters and Boston Scientific, and production and distribution came to a standstill. But after five years of courtroom skirmishes, the Richters won the case. The $750 million they were awarded made the daughter of a Mengele twin who grew up in the Bizaron housing estate and the son of the soldiers of Zionism who grew up on Kibbutz Ramat Yohanan one of Israel's richest couples.

I've known Kobi for years. He is a friend. As always, I meet him in his seaside villa in the prosperous suburb of Arsuf, north of Tel Aviv. Standing in his living room, he pushes an unseen button that summons a hydraulic dumbwaiter for fine wines. He uncorks a 1964 Bourgogne and pours it into a decanter, waits awhile, then pours it into glasses. He asks me what I think of it and then tells me what I should think of it. He gives me a long lecture about Bourgogne and about the specific vineyards and winery from which this wine came, and about how local inheritance laws shaped Bourgogne's wine tradition. Then, after tasting the wine, he gives his final verdict: superb. He raises his glass in a toast to fine wines and fine books and all work that is finely done.

I ask Kobi what I asked Michael Strauss: "What is Israel's contribution to his success? What is Israeli about Orbotech and Medinol?" Richter answers that the secret is "to beat swords into plowshares"—not because it is good for peace, he says with a laugh, but because it is good for the plowshares. Beating swords is not only the sound prophecy of Isaiah and Micah, it is also a sound business plan. What made Orbotech and Medinol possible, and what made the Israeli high-tech boom a reality, were the immense resources invested over decades by the state in sophisticated military production. The military-industrial complex is for Israel what the space program was for the United States. It generates astounding human capital and develops cutting-edge technologies that eventually trickle down to the high-tech industry and push it forward. It is no accident that Orbot was founded by three pilots and two Israel Security Prize recipients. It is no accident that Medinol's breakthrough was made possible by Israel's laser and missile production technology. What the nation invested in defending itself for half a century paid off with the surprisingly bounteous dividend of the great high-tech boom.

But there is a second factor, Richter says. Orbot had a small interdisciplinary team of outstanding individuals. "We were the very best in artificial intelligence, in hardware, and in fine mechanics. This team could have done anything. That's very Israeli, too—having a small elite unit of highly qualified professionals who work together day in and day out to achieve a common goal. Medinol was a variation on the same theme; in that case one person contained within him all that the company dealt with: biology, medicine, engineering, computer science, and fine mechanics. In large American corporations, it is almost impossible to find a programmer who understands the biology of blood vessels or a doctor who understands materials engineering. So decisions are made by consensus, which is a cumbersome and imprecise process. But at Medinol, it was all integrative, just as at Orbotech it was all interdisciplinary. Time was saved, efficiency was tripled. The business enterprise functioned as a cohesive organism: focused, strong, healthy, and able to achieve the best results. In different shapes and forms this is what happens in many Israeli start-ups. Their small, unified teams have the single-mindedness, expediency, and creative drive that are scarcely found in corporate America or Europe."

The third factor was immigration, Richter says. "A million Russians came to Israel in the 1990s, among them hundreds of thousands of fantastic workers—engineers, technicians, programmers. This benefited us both at Orbotech and at Medinol. At one point, 85 percent of our employees were Russian immigrants. A Russian immigrant was both the co-inventor of the rigid-flex and co-owner of the company. This wave of immigration benefited the entire Israeli industry. The encounter between Israeli creativity and Russian thoroughness was exceptionally productive. If you ask me what made my success and the success of the Israeli high-tech revolution, my answer is fourfold: the infrastructure of the defense industry, Israeli innovation and improvisation, Russian skill, and the integration of different fields of knowledge in small, daring groups. The unique combination that enabled my companies to succeed is the very same one that saved Israel by making it a start-up nation."

As he drinks his wine, Richter tries to connect the dots. "In the twenty years that Israel was about the kibbutz, I was on a kibbutz. In the twenty years that Israel was about the military, I was in the military. In the twenty years that Israel is about high-tech, I am in high-tech. I happened to be in every nexus of Israeli advancement. My life took me from one Israeli myth to the next.

"In the kibbutz we felt like the sons of gods," Kobi says. "We were athletic and handsome and suntanned, like proud Jewish Bedouins walking barefoot in the fields and driving tractors and chasing girls. We were the new strong Jew rising from the death of the old weak Jew. We despised the Diaspora and looked down upon decadent Tel Aviv urbanites. We were the real thing, the fulfillment of the Zionist dream, the core of Israeli existence. In 1960 the myth was us and we were the myth. I was exactly what Bruno Bettelheim wrote about me when he studied our kibbutz in the 1960s: a child of a dream.

"In the air force I was Top Gun. The Arab Israeli dogfights of 1969–70 were a theater of war in which the United States and the USSR were fighting each other by proxies. So my intercept team was equipped with the very best technology America had to offer. But my team had more combat experience than the Americans did. I found myself teaching American air force intercept teams and American navy intercept teams. I was really Top Gun. It's not that I played Tom Cruise; Tom Cruise played me. Ten years after becoming a combat pilot I was one of the very best in the West. I was a world champion. Once again I found myself personifying the myth. When the kibbutz began to wane, the air force was the epitome of Israeli excellence. My peers and I were the flesh-and-blood embodiment of Israel's ability and superiority.

"But by the late 1980s," Kobi says, "the military myth was waning. Although the Israeli Air Force maintained its might, I realized that the era of absolute Israeli domination of the skies was about to end. I understood that no military power and no military victory would solve Israel's fundamental problems. But just as the second myth was crumbling, the third emerged: high-tech. First there was Scitex, then Orbotech, then another hundred new start-ups. A thousand start-ups. Tens of thousands of start-ups. There were venture capital funds, research and development centers, telecommunications, biotech, meditech, clean-tech. An astonishing geyser of innovation erupted out of this barren land. So per capita Israel has the largest number of medical-device patents in the world. We have more start-ups than France does. Every international corporation wants a subsidiary here because they all acknowledge our extraordinary creativity—all these young Israelis with all these brilliant ideas. After the kibbutz faded and the military faded, a third Israeli wave has risen. And this third wave of technological innovation is now keeping us above water. It enables us to prosper in spite of the occupation and the settlements and the decay of the state. It is the new incarnation of Israeli vitality."

The Strauss and Richter stories represent two facets of Israel's economic success story. Whereas Strauss is all about the innovations of the solid traditional Israeli industry, Richter embodies the innovations of Israel's dazzling new high-tech industry. In the 1990s and 2000s, while Israeli politics failed and the hopes for peace were dashed and an Islamic nuclear threat emerged, the Israeli economy was booming. In the twenty-first century, enterprises like those of Strauss and Richter and a thousand others have made Israel one of the most nimble economies in the West.

To understand how this came to be, I turn to Stanley Fischer. The sixty-nine-year-old economist was born in Rhodesia, educated in London, and achieved his professional renown in the United States. From 1994 until 2001, he was first deputy managing director of the International Monetary Fund. From 2002 until early 2005, he served as the vice chairman of Citigroup. For eight years (2005–13) he served as the governor of the Bank of Israel, and he became the high priest of Israel's economy. Returning to America in June 2014, Fischer was sworn in as the vice chairman of the Federal Reserve Board of Governors. In 2012, in his Herzliya home, he receives me in moccasins, tan Bermuda shorts, and a green Lacoste shirt.

As he describes the economics of contemporary Israel, Fischer prefers hard data to frothy superlatives. Sitting in a large red armchair that dwarfs his small frame, he utters the relevant figures in slow, measured, Anglo-Saxon Hebrew. In the years 2004 to 2008, Israel's average annual growth rate was 5.2 percent. While the world was in crisis in 2010–11, Israel's average annual growth rate was 4.7 percent. (In the years 2011–15, while many OECD countries suffered lackluster growth, Israel's economy grew at an average rate of 3.1 percent.) "That doesn't make Israel a Chinese tiger," he tells me, "but it is a performance far better than America's or Europe's." It is indeed an extraordinary economic accomplishment.

Fischer tells me there are four reasons for this success: reducing government spending dramatically (from 51 percent of GDP in 2002 to 42 percent in 2011, and 41 percent in 2015); reducing the national debt significantly (from 100 percent of GDP in 2002 to 75 percent in 2011, and 65 percent in 2015); maintaining a conservative and responsible financial system; and fostering the conditions required for Israeli high-tech to continue to flourish. "Israeli high-tech is truly phenomenal," he says. "It is the locomotive of Israel's growth. Because of the high-tech industry, we export as much as we import, and we attract considerable direct foreign investments. Israel has really become a start-up nation. Investment in research and development is higher than anywhere else—4.5 percent of GDP, compared with an OECD average of 2.2 percent. The ratio of start-ups to population is by far the highest in the world. The number of inventions Israelis come up with is astounding. No wonder Israel has more companies traded on the NASDAQ than Canada or Japan. No wonder that venture capital investments in Israel are larger than in Germany or France. Time after time I am amazed. There is innovation here, and there is daring, and there is exceptional ambition. Israelis are willing to take risks, and they believe nothing will stop them. So there is a unique entrepreneurial spirit in Israel. And this spirit makes the nation a powerhouse of technological ingenuity. One mustn't get carried away. We are still a small country with a small marketplace facing incredible challenges. But the high-tech revolution combined with a prudent macroeconomic policy has made Israel a hub of prosperity."

When I ask Fischer about the perils the country faces, he speaks cautiously. "We have four problems," he says. "Our education system has deteriorated, and it endangers our ability to sustain technological excellence. The employment rate among ultra-Orthodox men is only 45 percent (in 2015, it climbed to 49 percent). Most Arab women do not work. Fewer than twenty business groups control much of the local market and thus restrict competition. Right now the high-tech miracle helps to conceal these four problems that are weighing down the wider economy. But in the long term, these problems endanger Israel's ability to remain prosperous and successful."

Dan Ben David is less cautious than Fischer. I drive up from Herzliya to the Jerusalem think tank he heads to hear the economics professor say explicitly what the governor of the central bank will only hint at. "Israel's real economic miracle took place in the years 1955 to 1972," Ben David tells me. "During those years, the Israeli GDP grew twice as fast as that of Western countries, while Israel remained one of the most egalitarian nations in the West. Although it absorbed millions of immigrants and fought three wars, it succeeded in raising the standard of living of its citizens and the productivity rate of its workers. At the same time, it promoted educational excellence, social solidarity, and military might.

"But in 1973 it all went wrong. After the trauma of the Yom Kippur War, the defense budget was doubled, growth slowed, and inflation spiraled out of control. Even when inflation was vanquished in 1985, growth per capita was a third of what it had been twenty years earlier. Now the burden on the nation's economy was not defense spending but welfare benefits, which rose fivefold between 1972 and 2002. Rather than investing in human capital and essential infrastructure, Israel is transferring enormous sums of money to the poor and the ultra-Orthodox. The main reason for this is that the expanding ultra-Orthodox and Arab minorities are not fully participating in Israel's economic and social life. Whereas in its first twenty-five years Israel grew rapidly while maintaining excellence, cohesion, and social justice, in the last twenty-five years it did the exact opposite. In recent years, growth has been high, but excellence, social cohesion, and social justice have been dangerously eroded. The high-tech boom is the fruit of the long-term investment in human capital made by a previous generation. But the high-tech boom creates a shiny bubble of prosperity that conceals the fact that today we are not making a similar investment in the human capital of the future. Budgetary policy is flawed, public policy is failing, Israeli society is sick. If Israel does not change course soon, even the high-tech miracle will eventually fade away."

Ben David grew up in the United States and earned his Ph.D. from the University of Chicago. He is one of the few top-notch academic economists left in a brain-drained country that had an abundance of them only twenty years ago. As he talks to me in the spacious offices of the Taube Center, there is real angst in his eyes. "Look at this," he says, motioning me toward his desk. He talks me through a series of multicolored graphs and charts on his computer screen.

"What makes all this much worse are demographics," he says. "As you can see in these charts, over the last thirty years Israel went through a demographic revolution. During these years, the percentage of school-aged children attending ultra-Orthodox schools has risen from 4 percent to nearly 20 percent. The percentage of school-aged children attending Arab schools has risen from 20 percent to 28 percent. So today, 48 percent of all school-aged children are enrolled in either ultra-Orthodox or Arab schools. An additional 14 percent are modern Orthodox. Only 38 percent are secular. That means that by 2030, Israel's shrinking secular Jewish majority will become a minority. Israel's cultural identity will change, and so will its socioeconomic profile. Secular Israelis are the ones working, producing, and paying taxes. Once they are outnumbered, Israel will be a backward nation that will not be able to meet the challenges of the third millennium."

"What you are showing me is a national disaster in the making," I say. Ben David nods sadly. "If Israel had an effective Zionist government, it would fight this disastrous trend. It is not too late yet, but it might soon be too late. Meanwhile, successive dysfunctional Israeli governments are doing the very opposite: they reward the nonworking minorities and subsidize them and do not require them to take up modern and democratic education. As a result, nearly half of the population is not part of the national effort and does not shoulder responsibility for the nation's future. The burden on the soldiers of the productive segment of the society is unbearable. Fewer and fewer Israelis work more and more to feed nonworking Israelis. Fewer and fewer Israelis run faster and faster to carry along the Israelis who don't run at all. A flawed political system guarantees the special interests of the ultra-Orthodox, the settlers, and the megarich. But the productive middle class has been abandoned by the state. That's why this exhausted middle class is growing bitter. It feels the nation has betrayed it. It sees the Israel it loves disintegrating."

The Shmuli story is also a hopeful story. Itzik Shmuli was born in Tel Aviv in February 1980. His father was a Jaffa-born restaurant owner and his mother a Kurdistan-born nanny. The five Shmulis lived in a one-and-a-half-bedroom apartment in Ramat Gan. Although life was not easy, their home was warm. The twin boys and their young sister were showered with love.

Itzik Shmuli was a decent high school student, basketball player, and soldier. After completing military service, he worked alongside his father in their modest Tel Aviv restaurant. In 2004, he saw a television program about the homeless and hungry children in the streets of Buenos Aires. At the age of twenty-four, Shmuli got on a plane and opened an orphanage in Buenos Aires. When he returned to Israel, he studied special education at a small provincial college and was elected leader of its local students. Three years later he was the president of Israel's national student union.

On July 14, 2011, Shmuli is in New York. His friends call to tell him that something quite unusual is happening on Tel Aviv's Rothschild Boulevard. A twenty-four-year-old video editor by the name of Daphne Leef has pitched a tent in the middle of this prestigious thoroughfare as an act of protest against soaring residential rents. Within a day, hundreds have joined her. Within two days, thousands have joined her. Shmuli gets on a plane and returns to Tel Aviv to join the Rothschild protest. A few days later, he is the protest movement's responsible adult.

While many in the Leef circle lack experience and organizational skills, Shmuli has both. While many in the Leef circle are heavily influenced by Marxist and anarchist ideology, Shmuli is a sober social-democratic Zionist. He believes that in order not to lose public support, the revolt must not become sectarian or radical. He wants the movement to represent as many Israelis as possible. So he, too, pitches a tent on the boulevard. Two weeks later, Shmuli is the leader of a new Israeli generation demanding a new social order.

On July 23, 30,000 youths march in the streets of Tel Aviv, chanting a new-old slogan: "The people demand social justice." On July 30, they are 130,000 strong, on August 6, they are 300,000 strong. On September 3, 450,000 people take to the streets—6 percent of Israel's population. Shmuli is the keynote speaker at the rally held in Tel Aviv's Nation Square. "We are the new Israelis," he calls out to the 330,000 cheering demonstrators. "We love our country and we are willing to die for our country. Let us live in the country we love."

In many respects the 2011 revolt is the most impressive of all Israeli revolts. Neither the settlement nor the peace nor the Oriental Shas movements was ever able to gather so many Israelis with such enthusiasm and broad-based support. Neither settlement nor peace nor Shas united the nation in such a civilized and constructive manner. The Israeli civic uprising of 2011 is far more peaceful than Cairo's and far more effective than New York's. The young people occupying Rothschild Boulevard are generally more moderate, resourceful, and cool-headed than the ones who will occupy Wall Street later this year. Of all of the world's social-networks-to-social-protest movements, the Israeli one is the most benign. Moderate and nonviolent, it succeeds in winning the support of 80 percent of Israelis. For one summer, it unites Israelis again by giving them a sense of hope. And yet, just as the defiant wave appears, it disappears. So as I walk with Shmuli along Rothschild Boulevard in the late hours of a late autumn night, there is nothing here. There are no tents, no demonstrators, no social change. The carnival is over. It's as if it was all a sweet midsummer night's dream.

Shmuli begs to differ. "I am a marathon man," he says. "I run long distance. I know life has its rhythm, and I know revolutions don't happen overnight. From the outset, I was aware that the summer of 2011 would only be the first leg. But I do believe we will have a second and a third leg. I don't need daily demonstrations. I don't expect ongoing protest. But I really think the summer of 2011 was a tipping point. It was much larger than housing prices or food prices or the debate over the rule of the rich. The summer of 2011 was about us being a people. For the first time in my lifetime, Israelis felt they are one people, not helpless individuals, not members of rival sects. And what the Israeli people said is that they want social justice. They want the state to be reformed so it can act as an agent of change. True, right now Rothschild is quiet. Everybody went back home. But the transformation we underwent will not be taken away from us. We do not see ourselves anymore as cynical hedonists. Now our life as Israelis has meaning. This new sense of meaning is the great achievement of 2011. We love Israel again and believe in Israel and we are determined to reform it."

Shmuli fascinates me. He is slim, brown-eyed, of medium height. He has a good heart and a diffident smile. As he walks down the boulevard after midnight in jeans, T-shirt, and a backpack, young people walk up to him and high-five him and ask him not to quit. "Fight on," they tell him. "Show them, give it to them." The student leader is no intellectual and no ideologue; he is neither charismatic nor authoritative. But there is a promise in the sanity and decency that he projects. His non-macho style of leadership is inspiring. No doubt, he has a political future. He will be a member of Parliament and the young generation he represents will shape future Israeli politics. The conceptual revolution of 2011 would change the Israeli state of mind and the Israeli political landscape, so perhaps Shmuli is right in arguing for hope. I so wish he is right. Our future depends on whether the revolt of 2011 is institutionalized in a benign and constructive manner.

After Shmuli leaves, I walk by myself along the boulevard. It is back to what it was before: a pickup promenade. Boys with dogs, girls with dogs, boys with girls with dogs. So I now assemble the different pieces of the puzzle in my head—all I have learned from Strauss, Richter, Fischer, Ben David, and Shmuli. What I come up with is the following: the Israeli Labor hegemony began its decline after the 1973 war and totally disintegrated in the late 1980s. The fall of the ancien régime liberated tremendous energy. New Israeli individualism turned new Israeli capitalism into a roaring success. The free market enabled Israeli talent and initiative to burst forth and create a booming modern economy. Successive cuts in public expenditures and military spending accelerated the process. So did privatization, deregulation, and monetary liberalization. But while the private sector flourished, the public sector faltered.

An uninspired national leadership and petty politics didn't allow the state to act as a counterweight to the ills of the emerging free market. Antitrust law and enforcement were weak. Privatization was carried out in a slapdash and hurried fashion. No protective measures were taken for the middle class, the working class, and the welfare state. Public education and public health were in decline. There was no housing policy. Almost anything that was private boomed while almost anything that was public went bust. If in the 1950s Israel had too much state, in the 2000s it had no state to speak of. If half a century ago Israel hardly had capitalism, now it was all capitalism. In this setting, Michael Strauss turned a provincial dairy into an international empire, and Kobi Richter produced a billion-dollar enterprise from his unique insights. But in this setting, wealth was concentrated in the hands of a select few and social gaps expanded. Some of Israel's magnates took over much of the nation's resources and many of its assets. The underlying malaise that troubled Stanley Fischer and Dan Ben David spread and festered. The unjust regime that Itzik Shmuli stood up against took hold. The illusion that the market is a good enough substitute for the state left Israelis with no state that can represent them and serve them and promote the common good. There was no government to restrain market forces or deal with the challenges of the ultra-Orthodox minority and Arab minority. There was no political body to rein in the settlers and the rapacious rich, to represent the Israeli majority and stand for the hardworking, constructive middle class.

For a long time this cardinal problem was denied. The twenty powerful commercial groups that rule over the Israeli economy also ruled over the media and public discourse. But in recent years, a critical awareness has begun to simmer under the surface of Israeli political life. So when Daphne Leef set up camp in Rothschild Boulevard, the nation took notice. And when Itzik Shmuli led the civic uprising, the public responded. After twenty-five years of neoliberal hegemony, a new social-democratic discourse has surfaced. But it is not yet clear if the conceptual revolution of 2011 will become a political reality, whether there is a leadership and a platform that will turn what the new Israelis want into a new Israeli reality.

On both sides of Rothschild Boulevard, expensive new condominium developments and International-style buildings are illuminated from below with spotlights. Israeli affluence is still very much on display. Market forces have not waned. Along the central promenade, young men wander in torn jeans; end-of-the-night clubbers look on with chemically induced gleams in their eyes; a beautiful girl rides her fashionable bike. As dawn approaches and the boulevard empties, I try to weigh success and failure, risk and reward, hope and despair. And it seems to me now that many of our virtues and many of our flaws come from the very same source. The very same gene that makes us also endangers us.

The secret of Israeli high-tech is bucking authority, ignoring conventional wisdom, and flouting the rules of the game. The weakness of the Israeli state is bucking authority, ignoring conventional wisdom, and flouting the rules of the game. The Jewish Talmudist, the Jewish merchant, the Jewish anarchist, and the Jewish immigrant gave birth to a restless Israeli citizen. This unpredictable citizen creates an unbridled energy that doesn't allow the state to function as a sovereign body. Ben Gurion's bureaucratic tyranny harnessed this energy for half a century and founded a state. But after Ben Gurion's death in 1973, the state he forged began to disintegrate. It could no longer rule over its tribes and sects and individuals. It could no longer contain its diversified minorities and contradicting identities. The body politic stopped dealing with Israel's real challenges and stopped acting rationally. Instead of being a commando boat advancing toward its target, Israel became a captainless pleasure ship lost at sea with no compass and no sense of direction.

What happened here, on Rothschild Boulevard in the summer of 2011, was a wake-up call. Afraid of losing their nation-state, the Israelis tried to reclaim it. As a new day rises over the old Tel Aviv museum building at the end of the boulevard, where Ben Gurion called the Israeli state into being, I so wish the wake-up call will truly awaken us. It's high time. This start-up nation must restart itself. This immature political entity must grow up. Out of disintegration and despair we must rise to the challenge of the most ambitious project of all: nation rebuilding. The resurrection of the Israeli republic.

SIXTEEN

Existential Challenge, 2013

I FIRST PERCEIVED THE THREAT POSED BY IRAN IN 2002. AT THE TIME, A fierce debate was raging in America concerning whether to invade Iraq. At the time, Israel was struggling to thwart the suicide bombing offensive of the second intifada. But like a few other Israelis, I realized that the regional power America must endeavor to restrain was not Iraq but Iran. The real existential threat Israel was facing was not Palestinian but Iranian. If Iran went nuclear, the Middle East would go nuclear, the world order would collapse, and Israel's existence would be in jeopardy.

Three years later I began to write about Iran in an intensive, almost obsessive manner. But even in 2006, 2007, and 2008, few listened to me as I wrote about the whirling centrifuges enriching uranium in Iran. Only a few agreed that the Iranian nuclear challenge was the most dramatic Israel had faced since its founding. To me the task seemed clear: the international community and the State of Israel had to act swiftly so that they would not soon face the horrific dilemma of (an Iranian) bomb or (an Israeli) bombing. But both at work and at home, many regarded me as an alarmist spreading fear and anxiety for no good reason. The prominent Israelis I am surrounded by and the Israeli media I work for paid lip service to Iran but refused to grasp Iran. So did the international community and the international media. Although it was known that the Iranian threat was there—and getting closer—few acknowledged it, and still fewer tried in earnest to do what had to be done to fend it off.

The Iranian nuclear challenge has a global context. Since 1945, the international community has managed to control the proliferation of nuclear weapons in an impressive way. But if Iran goes nuclear it will bring about a nuclear globalization that might eventually endanger the post-Nagasaki miracle.

The Iranian nuclear challenge has an American context, too. After invading Iraq and after retreating from Iraq, the United States is perceived in the Middle East as a declining power. After it lost some of its old Arab allies due to the Arab awakening, America's influence in the Arab world is waning. If Washington loses the strategic battle against Tehran, it might lose whatever respect it still has in the Middle East. A nuclear Iran will become the new dominant power in a crucial part of the world and would turn it against the American Empire.

The Iranian nuclear challenge also has an Israeli context. True, Israel is said to be a nuclear power. But Israel has never taken advantage of its unique weapon. Although it is constantly threatened by its neighbors, it has never threatened to wipe them out. In the nuclear sphere, Israel has acted in an admirably responsible and restrained manner. Iran is different. Its ayatollahs seek regional hegemony and want to see Israel decimated. If they acquire the bomb they might actually use it or pass it on to others who might do so. A nuclear Iran will force Egypt, Saudi Arabia, and Turkey to go nuclear and will surround the Jewish state with an unstable multipolar nuclear system that will make its strategic positioning impossible and will turn the life of its citizens to an ongoing nightmare.

And yet, although the three contexts were known and acknowledged, both the West and Israel were dormant regarding Iran for many years. The problem was not ideological or moral but cognitive. There were no good guys and bad guys vis-à-vis the uranium enrichment facilities in Natanz and Fordow—there were only those who saw and those who were blind. In the early 2000s, it should have been crystal clear that Israel's number one mission was to do everything in its power not to reach the bomb-or-bombing juncture. But Israel failed to address the Iranian challenge seriously. The strategic establishment and the intelligence community dealt with it, but the public at large ignored it. As it had no immediate consequences and no tangible costs, the threat remained abstract and vague. It did not become part of the political debate or public discourse. It had no real place in our real lives. A mental block would not let us see Iran clearly, and it cost us a crucial decade in which Iran could have been stopped without the use of force.

The cognitive block did not blind only Israel. By 2005, all Western intelligence agencies were cognizant of the Iranian nuclear program. All Western leaders knew that Iran might endanger the future of the United States, Europe, and the world. But Western public opinion was incapable of addressing the challenge, psychologically or conceptually. Preoccupied with Iraq and Afghanistan, the Western media, academia, and intelligentsia turned their backs on the Iranian challenge. Many wouldn't hear, wouldn't see, and wouldn't comprehend. That's why the West's leaders did not have the necessary political backing needed to act decisively against Iran. Since the issue was not a tomorrow morning issue, dealing with it was glossed over and postponed. Crippling sanctions were not imposed in time. A deal with Russia, which would have put Iran under a real economic embargo, was not struck. Supreme Leader Ali Khamenei was not confronted with a credible ultimatum: (military) nuclearization or (political) survival. In the first decade of the twenty-first century, Tehran encountered a weak and distracted West that would not impede its race to the bomb.

The Israeli cognitive block and the West's cognitive block had a lot in common. Both were the outcomes of strategic success and stability. For forty years, Israelis had been leading reasonably good lives under the umbrella of Dimona, and they had begun taking for granted Israel's strategic regional monopoly. They were not fully aware of the appalling consequences of the possible end of this monopoly, or simply refused to imagine them. True, there were two Gulf wars, two Lebanon wars, and two Palestinian uprisings—but these did not threaten the existence of Israel. And as existence was not threatened, complacency increased. Israelis were no longer aware of how lucky they were and what might happen to them once the Dimona monopoly was broken.

For seven decades Americans and Europeans had been living a life of peace and plenty thanks to the safety net of Western strategic superiority. Consequently, they, too, took this superiority for granted, unaware of the fact that the appearance of a radical Islam nuclear threat would directly affect the good life of Paris, London, Berlin, and New York. True, during this period of time there was a Korean war, a Vietnam war, and the Bush wars, but apart from the Cuban missile crisis (in 1962) there was nothing that exposed the United States and Europe to a real nuclear threat. As strategic stability was not really challenged, their complacency increased. Americans and Europeans were no longer aware of how lucky they were and what might happen to them once ayatollahs or Islamist terrorists intimidated their sheltered way of life and their pursuit of happiness.

The Iranian nuclear project was like a baobab tree. In the early stages of its growth, it would have been easy to uproot. Iran was no match for Western might. But in the early stages of its growth there was no serious attempt to uproot it. Because of the gap between Iranian tenacity and Israeli and Western complacency, the Iranians had the upper hand. The United States got entangled in Iraq and Afghanistan instead of focusing on Iran. Israel dealt with settlements rather than centrifuges. Because of its internal weaknesses, Europe was paralyzed. Both the West and Israel saw the terrifying tree of a nuclear Iran grow in front of their eyes but did not fell it.

I meet Amos Yadlin in his pleasant Karmei Yosef home, east of Tel Aviv. The view from the balcony is astounding: the Tel Aviv skyline, the Mediterranean coastline, Rehovot's white urban sprawl, Hulda's gray-green vineyards, the archaeological site of Tel Gezer. Some five hundred yards from the garden fence, on Gezer's slope, are well-tended orchards where once stood the Palestinian village of Abu Shusha and the stately home in which my great-grandfather settled in the 1920s.

In 1981, Major Yadlin was one of the eight Israeli pilots who bombed Osirak, the French-built Iraqi nuclear reactor. In 2007, as chief of military intelligence, General Yadlin was the man in charge of collecting intelligence on the North Korean–built Syrian nuclear reactor in Deir ez Zor. Between 2006 and 2010, Yadlin played a central role in Israeli operations against the Iranian nuclear project. He was not the one to conceptualize the Begin Doctrine, according to which Israel will not allow any enemy nation to acquire a nuclear weapon, but he was one of its leading soldiers. Twice he managed to implement the doctrine in an extraordinary manner, while his third attempt was rather less successful. So here I sit, in a garden chair, listening closely to the round-faced, thoughtful Israeli general who, time after time, happened to be in the place where history was decided.

First Yadlin tells me about his childhood in Kibbutz Hatzerim in the Negev, where the pioneering farmers struggled to work the salt-streaked soil and eventually triumphed over it. The socialist Zionism that raised him and shaped him in the 1950s was moderate and humane; its primary goal was to conquer the desert and to make a home in the desert for the Jewish people. Then Yadlin tells me about his early years in the Israeli Air Force. He was proud in the early 1970s to belong to this most professional and efficient Israeli organization, which secured the existence of the Jewish national home. Then Yadlin tells me about the eighteen traumatic days and nights of the Yom Kippur War: seven of his fellow pilots died and five were captured, while his squadron lost seventeen of its thirty Skyhawk bombers. As war raged all around him, Yadlin learned to steel himself and regain confidence in himself. In the years of recovery that followed 1973, the IAF did the same. When Yadlin returned from training in Utah in the summer of 1980 as one of the first pilots of Israel's first F-16 squadron, both he and his peers felt a renewed sense of strength.

The 1981 mission seemed impossible: to bomb the nuclear reactor the French were building for the Iraqis on the outskirts of Baghdad. On the face of it, Baghdad was too far away and the Israeli Air Force did not have the technological capabilities required for such a mission. There was no GPS yet, no smart bombs, no airborne refueling. There was no precedent, either: no air force in the world had ever bombed a nuclear reactor. And yet, on June 7, 1981, at 1600 hours, eight state-of-the-art F-16 bombers took off over the Gulf of Eilat and crossed, at low altitude, six hundred miles of Saudi Arabia and Iraq. They covered mountains, deserts, the Euphrates Valley, the Euphrates River; plateaus, water canals, railways, houses, fields. Some Iraqi citizens, unaware of what was going on, waved to the pilots flying so low over their roofs. And then, after 103 minutes of flight, Yadlin ascended from five hundred feet to ten thousand feet in twenty seconds. He could now see the reactor's dome, and five seconds later the reactor itself was within the bomber sights. After another ten seconds the young kibbutznik pushed the button, releasing two two-thousand-pound bombs. Twenty seconds later he made a quick descent into the plumes of smoke from the erupting antiaircraft missiles, dropping to five hundred feet again, and escaped home over the darkening deserts of Iraq, Saudi Arabia, and Jordan. Sitting in the cockpit, Yadlin knew that mission impossible was accomplished. One meticulous minute over the target had removed the threat of a second Holocaust.

The 2007 mission also seemed impossible: to destroy the nuclear reactor that the North Koreans were building for the Syrians without provoking war. Yadlin will not talk to me about the details of the operation attributed to Israel by non-Israeli sources, but much has been published abroad about Operation Orchard by foreign journalists and experts.

This time the challenge was not technological but conceptual. It was not so much about the planes and the bombs, but about getting the right information and making the right decisions in time. In 2006, Meir Dagan, the head of the Israeli Institute for Intelligence and Special Operations, known as the Mossad, argued that there was no sense in investing intelligence resources in Syria, for it was a dead horse that did not threaten Israel in any way. Amos Yadlin begged to differ. He remembered that three years earlier, Israel had failed to detect the Libyan nuclear project, and he asked his lieutenants to scan all possible sources to see if any surprises were hidden anywhere. In the late summer of 2006, one of his men raised the possibility that the enormous cement structure in Deir ez Zor concealed a North Korean plutonium reactor. By autumn there was some evidence supporting this seemingly wild hypothesis. According to non-Israeli sources, Yadlin shared his concern with the prime minister, Ehud Olmert, and an American intelligence chief, who dismissed him. Both were under the influence of Dagan, who insisted that there was no Syrian reactor. But in March 2007, an intelligence breakthrough totally changed Dagan's position. According to non-Israeli sources, the head of the Mossad now demanded immediate action—before the reactor could be activated and before the Syrians realized that their great secret had been discovered. In the late spring of

2007, Yadlin's role was that of a moderator. Non-Israeli sources claim that he was the one who advised the prime minister and the chief of staff to plan a low-key operation that would not embarrass the Syrian dictator Bashar al-Assad and would enable him not to launch a full-scale retaliatory war. In a sense, the Israelis would give Assad cover to pretend that nothing had ever happened. The non-Israeli sources claimed that Yadlin's military intelligence also made the point that there was enough time to plan the highly risky air raid properly: the window of opportunity would close only in a few months' time, when the reactor might turn critical. In retrospect, Yadlin would be proven right: the precise timing and nature of Operation Orchard would achieve the two essential goals of no core, no war.

According to the American journalist and analyst David Makovsky, just after midnight on September 5, 2007, four F-16 bombers took off for the Syrian nuclear reactor from the same Yizrael Valley air force base that was used twenty-six years earlier to bomb the Iraqi reactor. In a long piece published in *The New Yorker* in 2012, Makovsky writes that the four F-16s were escorted by four F-15s that took off from the desert air force base situated close to Yadlin's childhood kibbutz, where he later served as commander. The eight Israeli planes, equipped with advanced electronic warfare devices, flew along the Mediterranean coast and along the Turkish-Syrian border. After midnight they dropped seventeen tons of explosives on the plutonium plant and flattened it.

For another seventy-two hours, tensions ran high: Would Syria respond with a devastating missile attack that would set Tel Aviv ablaze? Would a war break out that would claim the lives of thousands? Just as Yadlin predicted, an overwhelmed Syria did not react. Israeli might, deterrence, and stealth caused Syria to bow its head in defeated silence. The second implementation of the Begin Doctrine was another remarkable success. When the world failed to prevent an Arab dictatorship from going nuclear, and when the United States failed to act, Israel seized the initiative, taking its fate into its own hands. Once again, one meticulous moment hovering over the target removed the threat of a second Holocaust.

But the Iran mission is far more complex and difficult than the missions impossible of 1981 and 2007. The Iranians are much more sophisticated and cunning than the Iraqis and the Syrians. Their strategic goal is not to build a bomb quickly but to build one safely. That's why they advanced along many tracks: they built a reactor in Bushehr, a reactor in Arak, a military complex in Parchin, a uranium enriching facility in Natanz, an underground bunker in Fordow. That's why they try to do most of their work under the umbrella of international legitimacy. They are very careful not to be caught red-handed and do not provide smoking guns. They do their utmost not to take provocative steps that will so enrage the West that it will be forced to act. Just as Yadlin was being nominated to head the IDF intelligence in January 2006, the Iranians began to enrich uranium in Natanz. First they obtained a few centrifuges, then dozens, then hundreds. In early 2007, they had only a thousand centrifuges. By 2013 they had more than fifteen thousand centrifuges, some of them highly sophisticated. Accordingly, the amount of enriched uranium the Iranians piled up grew from only fifty kilograms in early 2008 to more than seven thousand kilograms in mid-2013. Although the international community (weakly) protested and although it imposed (limited) sanctions, the Iranians patiently and persistently marched on toward their goal. From his spacious office on the thirteenth floor of the IDF headquarters, General Yadlin monitored the situation as the Iranians fooled the International Atomic Energy Agency (IAEA) and fooled the UN and fooled the Western powers, inching closer and closer to their coveted atomic bomb.

Israel was late in responding to Iran's progress. In 2002, Prime Minister Ariel Sharon called on Meir Dagan of the Mossad to defuse the Iranian threat. According to non-Israeli sources, the Mossad received generous funding and carried out a series of breathtaking operations—including cyberattacks and assassinations of nuclear scientists—that achieved impressive tactical results. But Dagan's natural self-confidence turned into arrogance. In 2005 he promised his colleagues and superiors that Iran would not be able to spin even one centrifuge. Two years later, when more than a thousand centrifuges were spinning in Natanz, the IDF High Command began to worry that Dagan's approach might lead to a dead end. As the diplomatic option and the sanctions option hadn't yet yielded any concrete results, there was no other way but to consider the military option. According to non-Israeli sources, the head of intelligence, Yadlin, the air force commander, Eliezer Shkedi, and the deputy chief of staff, Dan Harel, insisted that Israel must prepare a credible military option vis-à-vis Iran. Although some senior generals objected, the chief of staff, Gabi Ashkenazi, instructed the air force to prepare an operational plan. Intelligence was gathered, and pilots trained just as they had in 1981 and 2007. The IDF prepared itself to implement the Begin Doctrine for the third time.

In November 2007, a National Intelligence Estimate (NIE), representing the consensus view of all sixteen American spy agencies, asserted that there was no conclusive evidence that Iran was indeed trying to build a nuclear weapon. After Yadlin met his American counterpart in Rome, he realized what the shocking report was all about: following the trauma of the invasion of Iraq, based on false intelligence that was manipulated by the White House, the American intelligence community was determined to prevent President George W. Bush from acting precipitously in Iran and getting America into a third war against a third Islamic nation. But after Yadlin returned to Tel Aviv and instructed his staff to assess and reassess the U.S. NIE, they came to the conclusion that it did not hold water. Four different analysis teams in the Mossad and in military intelligence asserted that the Iranians were advancing toward military nuclear capabilities and that the Americans were grossly underestimating the state of the Iranian program.

Isolation was difficult. France and Britain were the only two powers that really understood Iran. Meanwhile, China, Russia, and India were partially collaborating with Iran. Many countries in Europe were still trading with Iran. The United States was paralyzed because of its entanglement in other wars. Even within Israel the political leadership was not quite focused on Iran. The idea that Dagan could thwart Iran's progress was a widely held assumption. While in Iran centrifuges were multiplying and uranium was piling up, Israel was snoozing. Non-Israeli sources suggest that even the Shkedi-Yadlin military option was beginning to become irrelevant.

Enter Benjamin Netanyahu. When he arrived in office in April 2009, Prime Minister Netanyahu brought with him a totally new approach to Iran. As he saw it, Iran was the Nazi Germany of the twenty-first century; its combination of a nonconventional regime with nonconventional weapons was lethal. Weak and decadent, the West of the 2000s resembled in many ways the West of the 1930s. But the Jewish people would not be led again to some sort of nuclear Auschwitz. The

Jewish people now had a state, an army, and technological might. They would do whatever it took to prevent Tel Aviv from becoming a Hiroshima.

The new prime minister's great contribution to the struggle against Iran was cognitive awareness. Unlike his predecessors, Netanyahu understood Iran, internalized Iran, was totally focused on Iran. From the day he took office, he knew that his life's mission was to prevent Iran from going nuclear. To stop Iran he entered a strange coalition with Labor's Ehud Barak, who was installed as minister of defense. To stop Iran he appropriated huge funds and assigned them to intelligence gathering and to air force buildup, while holding frank talks with the leaders of the West. To stop Iran he formulated an effective Israeli military option, and time after time he prepared to use it. As he readied the IDF for action, the United States became more and more apprehensive. Several times in 2009, 2010, and 2011, Israel acted as if it was about to strike. Both in Washington and in Tel Aviv there were tense moments when it seemed as if the Middle East was on the verge of war.

Amos Yadlin and his fellow generals didn't know if Netanyahu and Barak really intended to strike or if they were playing an unprecedented game of strategic poker. The experienced pilot put his superiors to a test: he asked them to grant specific funds and authorize specific intelligence gathering that were needed only if a real strike was planned. Barak refused, but Netanyahu agreed. The IDF's top intelligence officer reached the conclusion that while the defense minister might have a hidden agenda, the prime minister meant business. Benjamin Netanyahu really believed that the fate of the Jewish people was on the line. If all else failed, he would strike, come what may.

Washington reached a similar conclusion. 2009 was wasted on a futile engagement policy, and 2010 was wasted on a failed attempt to impose UN sanctions, but by 2011 the fear of a desperate Israeli move impelled the dovish Obama administration to take nondovish steps. First the president approved cyberwarfare against Iran, then, in coordination with the Europeans, he imposed unilateral sanctions on Iran, and finally he instructed the Pentagon to prepare an effective American military option.

But while the Israeli military option proved to be a political success, within Israel all hell broke loose. Dagan refused to admit that clandestine operations and cyberwarfare had bought precious time but could not achieve the strategic target of defeating the Iranians. Chief of Staff Gabi Ashkenazi adamantly opposed the actual use of the military option he had devised. A titanic struggle evolved between Netanyahu and Barak on one side and Dagan and Ashkenazi on the other. Yuval Diskin, head of the Shin Bet national security agency, and most army generals sided with Dagan and Ashkenazi. While the prime minister and the minister of defense thought their subordinates lacked historical perspective and courage, the top army intelligence brass thought of their superiors as messianic, warmongering zealots. The fierce struggle between the two groups became personal, visceral, and ugly. To make the debate more pertinent and less personal, General Yadlin drafted a seventeen-point questionnaire designed to render decision making as rational as possible. Only if all of Yadlin's questions were answered in the affirmative would there be justification to launch an Israeli attack on Iran.

As the internal Israeli debate spiraled out of control, various doomsday scenarios were bandied about. The doves argued that an unprovoked Israeli raid would endanger the alliance with America, trigger a regional war, and elicit a missile attack on Israel that might cost the lives of thousands or even tens of thousands. The hawks argued that inaction would lead to the establishment of a multipolar nuclear system in the Middle East, to the radicalization of the region, to endless conventional wars, and possibly to the dropping of a nuclear bomb on Tel Aviv. Yadlin tried to formulate a third way. On the one hand he agreed that an Israeli bombing that would prevent an Iranian bomb was strategically justified and would not bring about Armageddon. He trusted that the Israeli military option would be effective and he believed that both Israel and the West could withstand the limited price they would have to pay. If Israel shied away from taking action just because it was deterred by a few hundred Iranian missiles and a few thousand Hezbollah rockets, it had no right and no way to survive. But on the other hand, Yadlin argued that with no international legitimacy and without American backing, an Israeli bombing would be futile. If the United States refused to complement the Israeli offensive with paralyzing sanctions, only two years would be gained at an extremely high price. The challenge was not the operation itself but the decade after the operation, Yadlin claimed. He urged Prime Minister Netanyahu not to quarrel with President Obama but to foster an intimate strategic bond with him. Only if the great American democracy and the small Israeli democracy worked shoulder to shoulder would they be able to stop the rising Shiite power.

Netanyahu ignored Yadlin's advice. He didn't make the occupation-related concessions that would win over Obama and improve Israel's international standing. Rather, he provoked Obama's anger. He turned Israel into a semipariah state. Netanyahu didn't build up legitimacy for the dramatic operation within Israel or outside Israel. When the military option yielded impressive political results, Israel's prime minister overplayed his hand. In the summer of 2012, he was perceived to be intervening in America's presidential election, and by the autumn of that year it was clear that he had missed the moment and lost whatever political leverage he had had.

Netanyahu's famous red-line speech at the UN in September 2012, in which he called for international action when Iran reaches the final stage in its nuclear program, was actually a concession speech. After realizing that he would not be able to strike before America's presidential elections, he moved the critical benchmark to 2013–14. In a sense, he put the destiny of his nation in President Obama's hands. But since that grand speech, Yadlin tells me, things have deteriorated. The time Iran needs for a surprise "breakout" that would give it a nuclear bomb has shrunk from over six months to less than three months. Soon it might shrink to one month. As we speak, Yadlin says, the Iranians are crossing Netanyahu's red line. They are approaching the point where Israel will not be able to stop them by force. Soon after, they will reach the point where even the United States will find it difficult to stop them in time. The moment of truth is nigh. If the West does not wake up soon and if America does not show determination, Israel will soon be facing the most dramatic junction. It will be forced to choose between bomb and bombing.

Yadlin believes that the surprise victory of President Hassan Rouhani in Iran's presidential elections indicates that the Netanyahu strategy was partially successful: it was the Israeli threat of 2010–11 that brought about the international pressure of 2012, which in turn brought about the Iranian political change of 2013. If the West would not budge and would tighten sanctions and put a credible military option on the table, an overall deal could be reached that would defuse the Iran crisis. But as the second-term Obama administration projects indecisiveness, the Iranians might yet have the upper hand. After being drawn again into Israel's decision-making circle, Yadlin believes that the real moment of truth will come in the last quarter of 2013 or the first quarters of 2014. If the Jewish state will be cornered, it might feel obliged to surprise and strike.

The Iranian decision is probably the most difficult decision Israel has to make in this era. In a sense, it resembles the Dimona decision. With both Dimona and Iran, the risks are mind-boggling. With both Dimona and Iran, what is needed is a unique combination of audacity, responsibility, and cunning. Israel must work with the Western powers but also stand up to them. Facing a unique challenge, the nation must mobilize all its resources and skills to produce a unique solution that a mature leadership endorses and promotes. So when I sit with Amos Yadlin, I am reminded of the engineer who ran Dimona in its critical years. The Begin Doctrine is a complement to Dimona, devised to ensure that there would be only one Dimona in the Middle East. And the challenge Yadlin and his peers faced in the 2000s was not dissimilar to the one the engineer and his colleagues faced in the 1960s. Yet there is a major difference. While building Dimona, young Israel acted in an exemplary manner, but while facing Natanz and Fordow, middle-aged Israel faltered badly. True, great deeds were accomplished thanks to intelligence and technological excellence. According to non-Israeli sources, there were incredible achievements. But the nation as such did not mobilize all its powers to contend properly with its most dramatic existential challenge.

Yadlin is an optimist. With a bitter smile he reconstructs the frustrating moments of his tenure. In Yadlin's first year, everybody still believed Dagan would solve the Iranian problem, while Yadlin shifted precious military and intelligence resources to the Iran campaign against the current. In Yadlin's second year, intelligence and military capabilities increased dramatically, but the Syrian reactor drew attention away from Iran, and the American NIE report muddied the waters. In Yadlin's third year, there was already a good intelligence picture of Iran, but by then the Iranians had gone underground in Natanz, had already dug the Fordow fuel enrichment plant, and had crossed what Israel had previously defined as the point of no return. In Yadlin's fourth year, Netanyahu reinvigorated the campaign to stop Iran, but later it turned out that the American-Israeli cyberwar strategy that Yadlin and Dagan had counted on had its limits. In the fifth year, no smoking gun was found that would persuade the international community to act decisively, and the internal debate within Israel grew ugly. But in the years after Yadlin retired—2011–13—his multiyear endeavor began to bear fruit. Inexcusably late to act, the Americans and Europeans finally imposed biting sanctions and the Iranian economy began to crumble. True, the Iranians had piled up enough enriched uranium for six or seven bombs and very much shortened the breaking-out time they needed to manufacture those bombs. But at last the earth under their feet was shaking. There was some hope that at the very last moment they would be stopped.

Perhaps it's too late. Perhaps there will be no other way but to contain Iran or stop it with force. But after a frustrating decade Yadlin wants to believe that a minute before midnight, the West is finally waking up, that the West will not forsake Israel and will not let it stand alone against the fanatical power wishing to annihilate it.

"Tell me about the Iranians," I say to Yadlin. "When you were reading the classified information coming from Tehran, what did you learn? What sort of society and what sort of regime did you see? Who are the people we are facing?"

"With the Iranians, one finds a fascinating combination of religious fanaticism and strategic prudence," says the bespectacled, solicitous retired general sitting across from me. "They are very ambitious. They regard their struggle with America and Israel as a clash of civilizations. As they see it, their civilization is the more pure and more just, and therefore it is stronger. The Judeo-Christian civilization is for them an evil imperialist civilization that is now in a state of decline. They feel genuine rage because of what the British and the Americans and the Russians did in Iran, and because of what the Zionists did in Palestine. They are totally convinced that because our civilization is spoiled and corrupt it cannot endure suffering, has no resilience, and is bound to rot. That's why they have no doubt that they will have the upper hand and eventually bring about the downfall of Israel, Europe, and America. The future is theirs, they believe. Their rising culture will topple ours.

"And yet," Yadlin goes on, "in their day-to-day conduct, these zealots act with sophistication and restraint. They are not in a hurry, they are not hasty, they make few mistakes. Rather than advance directly toward their goal and attract fire, they built a wide and steady front that is slowly approaching the goal, so at the right moment it may be conquered with a high degree of certainty. It took me approximately two years to understand this, but when I grasped what they were really doing I was deeply impressed. One cannot but have respect for the Iranians. They are deadly serious, and in their own way they are very impressive."

"Now tell me about the Israelis," I say to Yadlin. "How did we act? Were we impressive, too?"

"Our problem was that Iran is far away in every respect," he replies. "It was not at the focal point of our attention. Some Israelis thought it was not relevant for us, others thought it was too much for us to take on. Both approaches led to the same outcome: we dealt with the Palestinian terror, and we dealt with disengaging from the Gaza Palestinians, and we dealt with trying peace with the West Bank Palestinians—but we didn't deal with the Iranians. Not seriously. Not until it was quite late. At the very same time, the Americans were dealing with al-Qaeda and Afghanistan and Iraq, but not with Iran. Not seriously. Not until it was very late. So for both Israelis and Americans it was convenient to say to the Mossad, 'Take some money and solve this one for us.' The Mossad took the money but it didn't solve the problem. Only in 2007 did the IDF rise to the challenge, and only in 2009 did the Israeli national leadership rise to the challenge, and only in 2011 did the world awaken. The dramatic question is whether this awakening came too late. We don't yet know the answer."

While the summer of 2011 was a summer of protest, the summer of 2012 was one of anxiety. Early in the year, Benjamin Netanyahu and Ehud Barak signaled that for them, 2012 was the decisive year. Both argued that Iran was about to enter a "zone of immunity" that would prevent Israel from acting against it by force. If the international community would not stop it immediately, Israel would have to stop it on its own—by exercising its now-famous military option. As summer approached, tensions rose. I experienced it myself. Coming out of two private meetings with the prime minister and three private meetings with the defense minister, I felt my knees shake. Did they really mean what they were saying? Did Netanyahu really feel that President Obama was like President Roosevelt, who wouldn't bomb Auschwitz in 1944? Did Barak really think that we have only nine to twelve months left before we'll have to strike? Barak was difficult to decipher, but Netanyahu seemed absolutely sincere. He seemed convinced that he was the Churchill of the twenty-first century who must save his homeland and save the West from ultimate evil.

But Netanyahu did not act like Churchill. He did not share his dramatic perception of reality with his people and did not prepare his nation for an ultimate test. Even if he saw the Iranian challenge correctly, and even if he is a gifted, strategic poker player, he did not lay out the big picture as he should have. Under his leadership, it was not Tehran that was perceived as the threat to world peace, but Jerusalem. Because of his personal conduct, there were inconceivable gaps between the Israeli cabinet, the Israeli military, the Israeli people, and the world.

A series of interviews I conducted with some of Israel's best strategists, which I published in *Haaretz* in the summer of 2012, proved to me what I had only intuitively understood ten years ago: Iran is not a Netanyahu bogeyman; it is a real existential threat. So when the summer of anxiety came to a close without a strike, I knew that this was just a pause. The Iran crisis was not resolved, it was simply postponed. After the Palestinian front heated up again, and after Israel went into a stormy election campaign, the crucial decision was pushed back from the year 2012 to the future. But Iran is still here. Iran casts a heavy shadow over the future of Israel.

The first half of 2013 was quite extraordinary. Although by now Israelis were fully aware of the Iran dilemma and its significance, they chose to ignore it. In Israel's 2013 election campaign there was less talk of Iran than in America's presidential elections held only three months earlier. When Israel's new government was formed in the spring of 2013, Iran was not a prominent issue. By now nearly all the old players—Barak, Dagan, Ashkenazi, Diskin, Yadlin, and some prominent government ministers involved in the Iran issue—were gone, but the one player who really matters remained: Benjamin Netanyahu. In meetings with the reelected prime minister and with his new defense minister, Moshe Yaalon, and his new chief of staff, Benny Gantz, it was made clear to me that Iran was at the top of their agenda. After giving Obama a chance and after giving sanctions a chance and after giving diplomacy a chance, they actually felt that their argument was stronger than ever and that by now Israel had captured the moral high ground. They also felt that the geostrategic changes—the meltdown of Syria, the weakening of Hezbollah, the growing tensions between Sunnis and Shiites—made the doves' alarmist scenarios obsolete. If Israel were to strike, they thought, the backlash would not be apocalyptic and the Middle East would not be engulfed by the flames of regional war. So the issue was very much an American issue. Would Obama's United States have the resolve? Would post-Iraq and post-Afghanistan America use the Israeli card and the military-option card and the sanctions card and the success of Obama's assertive diplomacy and Tehran's inherent weakness to dismantle Iran's nuclear project?

On June 14, 2013, the moderate Hassan Rouhani won the Islamic Republic's presidential elections. A little over three months later, on September 23, he gave a moving speech to the UN General Assembly, seizing the hearts of quite a few American diplomats, journalists, and liberals who were captivated by his message of reconciliation. On November 24, an interim agreement was signed in Geneva, Switzerland, between Iran and the six leading world powers: the United States, the United Kingdom, France, Germany, Russia, and China (referred to as the P5+1). Less than a year and a half later, on April 2, 2015, the negotiations begun in Geneva culminated in the Lausanne declaration and understandings. Three and a half months later, on July 14, the Vienna accord was signed. The P5+1 and the Islamic Republic of Iran presented the Joint Comprehensive Plan of Action (JCPOA), intended to resolve the Iran nuclear crisis in a mutually agreed upon diplomatic manner.

So when I board a midnight flight from Ben Gurion airport to New York a few days later, I know that the thick document I'm holding in my hands is one of the most auspicious, but also one of the most potentially dangerous, I have ever seen. It will define the future of my nation, reshape the Middle East, and have far-reaching consequences for world order. Has the Obama team really saved the world? Have they managed to defuse the ayatollahs' ticking (nuclear) bomb? Will we have peace in our time?

The seemingly dry and technical JCPOA turned out to be a thriller. While my flight mates slept, I could not put down the 159 pages that might very well augur a future nuclear crisis.

Yes, there was light: the negotiating team had managed to coax the Iranians to agree to a sweeping commitment not to develop or purchase nuclear arms. More important, the team had managed to put the brakes on the old Iranian nuclear program. The reactor in Arak, the fuel enrichment plant in Natanz, the underground facility in Fordow would cease to threaten the world in the coming decade. The decline in the number of centrifuges (from 19,000 to 5,060) and in the amount of enriched uranium (from over 8,000 to 300 kilograms), and the strict monitoring program to be imposed on the already known nuclear facilities—all these were truly impressive achievements.

But there were also shadows: the Iranian negotiating team had succeeded in demolishing in its entirety the sanctions regime that had crippled their country. It had also succeeded in preventing meaningful monitoring of clandestine and as yet unknown nuclear facilities. The result? If in the future the Iranians decide to develop a secret nuclear program outside of Fordow, Natanz, and Arak, they will have a good chance of succeeding. The likelihood of being caught would not be great, and the chance that sanctions would be reimposed would be marginal. The decision whether to break out or not to break out to a nuclear bomb via a secret route would very much be an Iranian decision, encumbered by international considerations.

Then there was the darkness: in the agreement, the international community repeatedly recognizes Iran's right to develop sophisticated centrifuges. The enrichment capability of such centrifuges could be ten times that of the old centrifuges that Iran was giving up as part of the agreement—meaning that the United States and its allies were not only allowing but guaranteeing that in the future Iran would set up a much more robust and dangerous nuclear program than the previous one. In other words, in 2015 the Iranians were giving up an outdated, anachronistic, and illegal program in order to build—with international approval and consent—an innovative, powerful, and legitimate program as of 2025. The JCPOA would give us a precious gift: five to ten quiet years. But the future price of this gift would be astronomical. As soon as 2030—if not earlier—Iran would become a formidable nuclear tiger with the capability to produce dozens of nuclear bombs.

After a few hours of reading, I had to stop. The thriller had become a horror story. Not only was the content almost stupefyingly grim, so was the tone. Point in fact, in section after section, Iran's honor is upheld, while the honor of the United States and Europe is trampled. The Iranian parliament is given more respect than the American Congress is. And Iran does not express contrition or promise to change its ways— and treats its partners to the accord in an almost lordly manner.

In the quiet dimness of the jetliner, 35,000 feet aboveground, I looked at the historic document that was about to convulse the Middle East and perhaps change the course of the twenty-first century, and I shivered.

Could there have been another way? Seemingly, yes. The harsh sanctions imposed by President Obama after 2010 had caused Iran enormous harm—the country was prevented from exporting most of its oil, and its economy shrank by approximately 20 percent in five years. The collapse of oil prices during negotiations, from 107 dollars a barrel in the summer of 2014, to 45 dollars in the summer of 2015, dealt another blow, making Iran's situation dire. Had Secretary of State John Kerry not been so eager, had he not been in such a rush, he could have used Iran's desperate straits in order to accomplish different, much more amenable results. It may have also been possible to consider a John Kennedy–like walking-on-the-edge scenario, one that would not have led to war but to Iran forgoing its nuclear program.

But in a deeper sense, President Obama had no other recourse. Because of the profound trauma of the Iraq War, in the second decade of the twenty-first century the United States was not ready for a real confrontation—military or nonmilitary. Supreme Leader Ali Khamenei and President Rouhani knew this. As a result, although America was much stronger than Iran, Iran had an inherent advantage during negotiations. The scales of willpower and strategic cunning tipped toward Tehran. The Vienna accord was actually the inevitable result of President George W. Bush's historic mistake of going to war in Iraq. The JCPOA embodies the cumulative failures of the Bush administration,

the Obama administration, the Sharon government, the Olmert government, and the Netanyahu government concerning the Iran nuclear
threat. America had the capability to stop Iran, but not the will. Israel
had the will to stop Iran, but not the capability. And because the great
democracy and the frontier democracy did not succeed in forging a joint
strategic plan of action (other than an all-too-brief golden interval in
2011–12), the result was as inevitable as it was writ large. By President
Obama's thinking—the values he represents, the worldview he espouses,
and the personal convictions he brought with him to the White
House—he was right to delay by a decade dealing with the insoluble
problem of Iran's victory over the West.

During the ensuing months of public debate over the nuclear agreement, I met with everyone: President Obama, Prime Minister Netanyahu, former defense minister Ehud Barak, present defense minister
Moshe Yaalon, former Mossad chief Meir Dagan, present Mossad chief
Yossi Cohen, senior American intelligence officials, senior Israeli intelligence officials, generals, diplomats, nuclear experts. In the Oval Office
and in the West Wing, I met intelligent, coolheaded, and well-meaning
people, who were not at all naïve about Iran but were fed up with the
Middle East, loathed Arab politics, despised Israeli politics, were determined to prevent another war, and believed they had solved the nuclear
riddle and found a smart solution that would allow them to reassemble
the Iranian puzzle. At the heart of their rationale was a daring strategic
wager: that regime change in Iran would precede nuclearization; that by
lifting sanctions, bolstering reformers, empowering young Iranians,
and unshackling the economy, there would be a McDonald's in Tehran
before there would be enough fissile material in Fordow to turn Iran
into a nuclear power.

Some six thousand miles away, in the prime minister's office in Jerusalem, I found a man who was sure he had heard the thunderous clap
of history's wings and was convinced he had been ordained to prevent a
catastrophe that would divert history from its proper course. But although Netanyahu offered some salient arguments against the accord,
he could not muster a convincing overall strategy or succinctly express
his end goals. Case in point, if the Iranian threat was *the* supreme strategic threat of our time, why wasn't he more generous with the Palestinians, why did he disparage the American president, and why did he give

such a scandalously divisive speech to Congress? Why did he choose the path of irrelevancy by defining Iran as an Israeli problem and insisting that it could not be solved other than by military means?

After a week during which I met both the president and the prime minister, it occurred to me that the two leaders had divided the future between them: Obama got the next five to ten years, Netanyahu got eternity. No, Obama is not the Chamberlain that the American Right and the Israeli Right claim he is. But neither is Netanyahu the Churchill that they believe him to be. To defeat the Nazis, Churchill courted FDR and won him over. Netanyahu had done exactly the opposite.

In the end, Netanyahu wasn't willing to sacrifice what Churchill had sacrificed: the empire. The British prime minister had given up the jewels of the Crown in order to vanquish the enemy; the Israeli prime minister was unwilling to give up anything. His emotional miserliness led him to ruin. His inflated sense of greatness led him to believe that he could do everything: stop the Iranian centrifuges spinning, all the while building more settlements and mocking the man in the Oval Office. Because he did not present the Palestinians with a convincing peace initiative, he could not cultivate the international legitimacy required to face Iran. Because Netanyahu associated himself with conservative Republicans, he squandered the amity and empathy of progressive America, Europe, and many others around the world. The man who wanted to be Churchill did not know how to act like Churchill—and thus he lost the Churchillian battle he had appointed himself to lead.

The results are clear: Iran is bound to become a nuclear power. And well before that, it will become an aggressive regional player. Already, the Iranians hold sway over four Arab capitals (Beirut, Damascus, Baghdad, and occasionally Sana'a) and are becoming a Middle East hegemony that will soon be armed with sophisticated conventional weapons, and with a mighty nuclear capability in the years that follow.

While Iranian president Rouhani has succeeded in liberating Khamenei's theocracy from isolation, Netanyahu has led Israel into a dark cul-de-sac. Even when he speaks the truth, no one listens. Even when he warns against an imminent historic turn of events, no one cares. Instead of uniting the West against the threat posed by an Iran armed with a hundred atomic bombs later this century, Netanyahu has succeeded in turning many in the West against him and his country.

Rather than contributing his considerable talents toward a solution, his flaws and mistakes have become a central part of the problem. And because Netanyahu is not blind, he cannot but see the gravity of the present situation. Deep inside, he knows he has lost the battle of his life.

This is why Netanyahu went to Washington on March 3, 2015, at the height of the debate over the Iran agreement, to give an unprecedentedly inflammatory speech to a joint session of the Senate and the House of Representatives. Bibi is not stupid. He knew the controversial speech would not stop the Iran deal and would weaken Israel's position, not strengthen it. But what the prime minister saw in his mind's eye was only one thing: how history would remember him. And because he knew he could not be a Churchill of the 1940s (who averted catastrophe), he chose to be a Churchill of the 1930s (who railed against it). From this choice stemmed the need for a garish spectacle, for a speech of doom and gloom in the most dramatic theater in the world. Netanyahu's target audience was neither the president nor Congress, nor American public opinion—but future historians. Netanyahu may very well have thought to himself, *I am the man who sounded the alarm. I am the man who issued the warning. When Iran goes nuclear and the Middle East goes nuclear and world order collapses, you will remember the speech I gave on Capitol Hill in the spring of 2015. And you will realize I was right. I may not have stopped the Iranian nuclear program, but I ensured my place in history—* as a prophet of doom, as a Jeremiah, as a Churchill circa 1936.

By late summer of 2015, the Iran deal was a done deal. The president of the United States was no match for the Israeli prime minister. Obama gathered more and more support and was headed for a resounding political victory. As I observed developments in Washington, I began to wonder if there was anything that could be done to buttress the Iran agreement. I spoke to as many experts as I could in search of a third-way approach that would build upon the JCPOA—minimizing the risks it embodies and maximizing its chances of success.

One of the people with whom I spoke was Meir Dagan. When he opened the door to his modest Tel Aviv apartment, it was clear that the former Mossad chief—who died in April 2016—was ravaged by cancer. But although his physical condition was wretched, almost shrunken—having lost weight and all his hair—his mind was clear and his thinking precise. He despised Netanyahu and despised Netanyahu's military option—and he thought Netanyahu was endangering the very existence of the State of Israel. But he also thought that the Vienna agreement was a bad agreement. He thought that the Americans had rushed to sign it. And he thought they should have honored the understanding that Dagan had claimed to reach with them back in 2010: to allow the sanctions to take their course—to bring the Iranians to their knees and then dictate to them an agreement that would include full forfeiture of their nuclear ambitions.

But for some reason, Dagan said, Kerry was in a hurry. For some reason, the Americans had allowed the Iranians to one-up them—and then some. So the future, according to Dagan, was clear. Iran will cheat, he said. One hundred percent, Iran will cheat. It will wait five years in order to reap the rewards of the agreement, and then it will begin to test boundaries. After some more time passes, it might attempt—whether at a crawl or at a sprint—to achieve nuclear breakout. And when the moment of truth arrives, the JCPOA's flaws will be fully exposed: insufficient monitoring of Iran's military installations, insufficient monitoring of possible new nuclear sites. Don't forget, said the former Mossad chief, Tehran alone has hundreds of miles of subterranean tunnels. And if the regime doesn't soften—and the chances of this happening are slim, if it hardens, as Dagan predicted with a fair degree of certainty—while Tehran spends a third of the agreement's windfall on military expansion, nuclear escalation, and regional subversion, it will be very difficult to stop the hellish scenario, and it will be even more difficult to effect the optimistic scenario in which the Obama administration would like to believe.

Another intelligence hound I spoke to was Ehud Barak. In his sumptuous apartment in one of Tel Aviv's gleaming luxury towers, the former defense minister was uncharacteristically garrulous. The Vienna accord, Barak opined, proved what he had repeatedly said during the years of the great Israeli internal debate of 2009–12. Although they were never enthused, the Americans were willing to countenance preventative Israeli action. The military option was almost ready in 2010, and in 2012 it was good to go. But the army chiefs of staff, Ashkenazi and Gantz; the Mossad chiefs, Dagan and Pardo; the military intelligence chiefs Yadlin and Kochavi; and former president Peres did everything they could to prevent military action. They succeeded in whittling down the willpower of senior cabinet members (among them Defense Minister Yaalon) and cast doubt on Netanyahu's ability to act as he wanted to act. Thus, the Americans were left with no other recourse than to act on their own. At this point, Barak said, Washington could have exercised its own surgical military-technological option, which the Pentagon had developed at Obama's request. The United States could have quietly decimated Iran's nuclear program overnight without starting a war, leaving most Iranians oblivious to what had just occurred. It would have been much more like taking out Bin Laden than going to war on Saddam Hussein's Iraq. But the zeitgeist did not allow the administration to seriously weigh exploiting this impressive capability.

So, after twelve years, during which it backed Israel and isolated Iran, defining it as a pivotal opponent, the United States decided to turn Iran from part-of-the-problem into part-of-the-solution. This strategic about-face, said Barak, will have far-reaching consequences. I have no doubt, he added, that when President Obama says that Iran will not become a nuclear power, he means it. But I saw with my own eyes and heard with my own ears President Reagan promise that Pakistan would not become a nuclear power, and President Clinton promise that North Korea would not become a nuclear power. Life has its own dynamic. The Iranians will most probably honor the agreement until 2020. They won't risk their historical achievement or their newly found (relative) prosperity. But in the sixth, seventh, and eighth years of the agreement, they will start testing alternatives. They will choose a time during which the world's attention is focused on another international crisis in order to renew their sprint toward nuclear breakout. I imagine they will find a reason to expel the IAEA inspectors and dismantle the monitoring apparatus. Based on past experience, they will assume that neither the United States nor Europe has the will to confront them. So as a result of the Vienna accord, the probability that Iran will now become a rising regional power is very high, and the probability that it will become a nuclear power in the medium-to-long-term future has risen dramatically.

The third person I spoke to was my friend Amos Yadlin. Even when he was the chief of military intelligence and I was a journalist he should have been wary of, we always had a rapport. Intrinsically, we are both men of the third way. We seek the middle ground, a place to synthesize contrasting insights and incompatible facts. So when the man, who became the head of the leading research institute in Israel, the Institute for National Security Studies, agreed to meet with me for a post-agreement conversation, I was not surprised to hear him express views close to mine. As we sat down once again in his living room, Yadlin did not hesitate to hand out grades. The grade I give the Americans for the short term is a B, Yadlin said. They did not fully employ the two levers they had at their disposal—sanctions and the threat of military action—but they managed to postpone by a year or so an Iranian nuclear breakout. In contrast, their grade for the long term is an F. They failed. In fifteen years' time—maybe less—Iran will be very, very close to a bomb, with 200,000 centrifuges and five nuclear facilities like Natanz and Fordow, and ten nuclear reactors. But even worse than that, the bespectacled former general added, the agreement gives Iran legitimacy. Whatever it does, it will do with the West's approval and consent.

I understand Obama, Yadlin added; I hope that his strategic wager succeeds, that Rouhani grows stronger, that young Iranians speak up, and that the Iranian people change regimes. But because of the power and guile of the religious establishment, and because of the enormous power of the Revolutionary Guard, the probability of a peaceful, democratic, Scandinavian-like scenario is about 10 percent. The probability of a pessimistic, North Korean scenario—an open breakout or a quick crawl toward breakout in the coming years—is about 20 percent. The most likely scenario, at 70 percent, is a strategic game of patience. The Iranians won't breach the agreement egregiously, in a way that would justify American or Israeli action. They will develop all of the capabilities that the agreement allows them to develop: precise missile systems, drones, satellites, superior centrifuges. They will buy advanced weapons systems from China, from Russia, and maybe even from Europe, and they will deepen their influence in the Middle East. Then, and only then, after many of the agreement's limits-on-action expire in 2025, will they become Japan-like, with enormous nuclear capabilities, even if they don't actually make an atomic bomb. But Iran is not Japan. It will use the future power that the JCPOA gives it in order to threaten Israel, undermine the region, and endanger the most important interests of the United States and Europe.

Despite their differences and despite the bad blood among them,

Meir Dagan, Ehud Barak, and Amos Yadlin offered almost identical proposals for dealing with the aftermath of the Iran agreement. They all thought that Israel must find its way back into America's good graces. And that the United States and Israel must arrive at a mutual understanding regarding some key issues: defining what would be considered a flagrant violation of the Vienna accord; guaranteeing the necessary intelligence resources to ascertain any and every violation of the agreement in the years to come; preserving the American military option for decades to come; acting to deter Iranian expansion in the Middle East; promoting regime change in Iran; and building sophisticated and streamlined anti-missile defense systems.

In conversations I had in both Washington and Jerusalem, at the White House and at the prime minister's office, I spoke of the ideas that Dagan, Barak, Yadlin, and others had offered. As a worried Israeli citizen and a friend of the United States, I tried to convince decision makers on both sides to put behind their differences. I had no doubt that in the circumstances created by the Vienna accord, the way forward was to craft a complementary document that would not contravene the JCPOA but would actually bolster it, by forging principles and establishing mechanisms that would lessen the risk of the agreement failing and increase the chance of it succeeding. Such a parallel document would serve as a scaffold around the accord, supporting it, strengthening it, and lengthening its lifespan—at least until 2040.

At the White House, there was a certain readiness to listen to new ideas, especially if they would help reinforce Barack Obama's international legacy. I have no doubt that had Netanyahu come to the Americans with a gesture of goodwill in the summer of 2015, it would have been possible to reach the understandings required for such a complementary document. But in Jerusalem, my entreaties fell on deaf ears. Netanyahu was recalcitrant. Like the zealots of Masada, he preferred to fall on his sword in a final act of defiance as he stuck to his absolutist and destructive beliefs.

But the Iran story is much bigger than the hate-hate relationship between Obama and Netanyahu. At its core, the Iranian nuclear threat is a threat to our civilization. And it was our civilization that failed to deal with it. The Iraq War and the financial crisis of 2008 sucked all of the oxygen out of the room, leaving the West without the willpower or the cognitive focus needed to solve a problem of medium magnitude in a thorough fashion and in a timely manner. As a result, the problem grew and grew until it became unsolvable. And because of this, decision makers in the United States and Europe reached the plausible conclusion that all they could do now was delay the moment of truth, put off the day of reckoning. To buy five to ten years, until we find ourselves once again standing at the same key juncture as in 2012: either we bomb, or there will be a bomb.

The basic problem of the JCPOA is one of clocks: the Iranian technological clock was set back, putting nine more months between Tehran and the bomb, but the Western strategic response clock was set back much further, delaying America's ability to deal with a nuclearizing Iran by at least three to four years. So the same Western cultural weakness that allowed Iran to arrive at its present position will rear its head in 2020, 2025, or 2030. At that point, only if we adopt the third-way approach of truly assertive diplomacy—in the manner of John F. Kennedy—will we be able to distance ourselves from the nightmare that Netanyahu spoke so often about and Obama chose to minimize.

After bidding Amos Yadlin farewell, I look out at the ancient mound of Gezer, under which lie the ruins of more than twenty civilizations. And I look out at the spectacular Tel Aviv skyline. Tel Aviv's liberal and creative culture is like New York's: it can only survive under the defensive shield of Western strategic supremacy. But Tel Aviv is much more exposed than New York. It depends not only on Dimona, but on the fact that there is only one Dimona in the Middle East. In 1981 and 2007, Tel Aviv still had the ability to prevent others—Iraqis, Syrians—from building their own Dimonas. By doing so, it sustained not only itself, but also world peace. But in 2009–15, under Netanyahu, this was no longer the case. As time passes, the unique capability is eroding. As the world changes, the nuclear monopoly is bound to fade. Will Tel Aviv be able to retain its individualistic and hedonistic way of life in 2030? Will the Middle East of 2040 and 2050 allow the Tel Aviv culture to survive? And what will New York experience by mid-century? Can we be sure that the next 9/11 will not be nuclear?

State-of-the-art bombers are flying over the ancient mound of Gezer as I drive back to Tel Aviv, shining my headlights at the dark road ahead.

SEVENTEEN

The Millennial Challenge

ON A COLD, CRISP EVENING IN NOVEMBER 2013, MY LIFE CHANGED. THE Jewish community of Detroit had invited me to speak at its annual Jewish Book Fair just a few days before the first edition of this book was officially published. I remember every detail: walking into the brick-clad Jewish Community Center (which turned out to be one of the largest JCCs in America), stepping into a greenroom, where I received an exceptional red-carpet welcome. The lectern at the center of the large stage, the (overly) emotional speech I gave to an audience of hundreds about my book, my people, my country.

When I finished, I was graciously ushered into the lobby, where, to my utter surprise and delight, dozens of men and women were waiting for me to sign advance copies of my book. Two hours later, at a hipster bar in the middle of this resurgent, post-apocalyptic city, there appeared on my tablet screen a glowing review of *My Promised Land* by Leon Wieseltier, which would be published on the front page of *The New York Times Book Review* the following week. A half hour later, I was told that Tom Friedman had decided to dedicate a whole column in *The New York Times* to my book, in which he would urge President Obama and Prime Minister Netanyahu to read it. Then I was told that Charlie

Rose's staff had called, inviting me onto his show. Like a Technicolor Hollywood spectacle about an overnight success, everything seemed to happen within the span of one day. America opened its doors to me, and I opened my heart to America.

In the following year I crisscrossed the United States again and again. The flights I boarded almost every other day took me much farther afield than the big metropolitan centers I already knew—New York, Washington, Chicago, and Los Angeles. They brought me to Philadelphia, Atlanta, Boston, Baltimore, Miami, Charlotte, Houston, Dallas, San Antonio, New Orleans, Denver, Phoenix, Tucson, Las Vegas, San Diego, Santa Barbara, San Francisco, Sacramento, Eugene, Seattle, Sun Valley, Minneapolis, Cleveland, Columbus, Cincinnati, Kansas City, Rochester, Westchester, Jersey City, Louisville, South Bend, Omaha, and dozens more. This is how I got to know the American Jewish community—its organizations, federations, congregations, and foundations. I visited mid-city Jewish societies, suburban Jewish country clubs, and charming community centers. I met with rabbis, intellectuals, *machers*, journalists, and community leaders. I spoke in front of tens of thousands and listened to queries from thousands—and I tried to take in as much as I could. What I discovered was that the Jewish-American success story is no less impressive than the Jewish-Israeli one. While my great-grandparents, grandparents, and parents pursued the Zionist miracle of renewing Jewish sovereignty, four generations of Jewish Yanks pursued the miracle of creating, in America, the perfect diaspora.

As a young boy, I was fascinated by America. From the Rehovot of my youth, it looked like an El Dorado whose citizens were giants, their cars enormous—they even knew how to get to the moon. Even when I spent a year in Brooklyn Heights in 1969, the magic did not wane. Although by now I understood that this El Dorado wasn't really an El Dorado, I was captivated by the insight that America represented humanity's last chance—that it was the pillar of the free world. I developed a warm affection and a deep respect for Jewish America and its Conservative and Reform synagogues, which were much more appealing to me than those I knew in the Holy Land.

But only in 2014 was I exposed, without intermediaries, to the countless fascinating life stories that weave together like threads the grand tapestry of Jewish America. The fusion of Jewish culture and American democracy had produced wonders. Not only did this country allow so many Jews to realize their talents and skills—and to arrive at such extraordinary achievements in the sciences, the arts, literature, business, media, academia, film, politics, medicine, and jurisprudence—it allowed the Jewish minority to carve out an enormous, autonomous public space of a size and grandeur that had never been created before, and may never be created again. While the Jewish-Israeli community had succeeded in building—against all odds—a national entity based on sovereignty and state institutions, the Jewish community in America built a civic entity that nurtures Jewish life and preserves Jewish culture, based on voluntary institutions and communal conventions, with free will at its core. Like a sibling who comes from a faraway land and looks in awe at his brothers and sisters who have built a political universe parallel to the political universe in which he lives, I now developed not only a deep appreciation but a profound admiration for Jewish America. Rather than being apologetic for Jewish power and Jewish prowess, I thought, we should celebrate the historic achievement of the Jewish minority of North America and hold it up as a model for other minorities in the United States, Israel, and the rest of the world.

The stories were beguiling. How the Jews sailed up the Mississippi in the middle of the nineteenth century, settling in St. Paul, Minnesota, and traded in furs and alcohol, establishing the first local Jewish congregation in 1856 (they named it Har Zion—and, on a snowy winter day, I had the pleasure of speaking to hundreds of its members who had gathered in their current beautiful building, designed by the German-Jewish architect Erich Mendelsohn in 1953). Or how the Jews mined for gold in southern Nevada and invented denim there, and how a few Jewish gangsters arrived in the dusty town of Las Vegas in the 1940s and turned it into the vice-and-dice capital of America (here I spoke to a conservative, skeptical audience, who did not warm to my liberal-Zionist message). And how the Hebrew Union College was founded in Cincinnati in 1875 in order to address the growing chasm between traditional Judaism and the changing times—and erected a grand cathedral-like hall (where I was honored to speak with rabbinical students who carry the weight of the future of American Jewry on their young shoulders). And how the JTS was founded in 1886, and the AJC in 1906, and the ADL in 1913, and the UJA in 1939, and AIPAC in 1963, and J Street in 2007. How synagogues were built and orphanages founded and soup kitchens, schools, hospitals, charities, and communities organized themselves. How German-Jewish immigration changed America, followed by the mass immigration from Eastern Europe, and the twentieth-century waves of Sephardic, Russian, and Israeli immigration. I learned about the fierce feuds and schisms within communities, the (relatively few) spiritual altercations, and the (many more) mundane ones. But overall, there was a remarkably powerful movement, like an ocean wave—forward, forward. The big picture is exhilarating: a phenomenal undertaking by a small, talented, and persecuted people who found in America a safe harbor from which to go forth and build an extraordinary edifice.

Although they are widely published, the numbers are striking: of the 315 American Nobel laureates since 1950, 106 are Jewish. While they are just 2 percent of the population, more than a third of the fifty leading philanthropists in the United States are Jews. At leading universities like Harvard, Yale, Princeton—and, of course, Columbia—the number of Jewish students is remarkably high (over 15 percent). Jews are prominent members of the boards of leading museums, theaters, opera houses, hospitals, and academic institutions. From Woody Allen to Mark Zuckerberg, from Philip Roth to Jerry Seinfeld, from Alan Greenspan to Barbra Streisand, from Michael Bloomberg to Jon Stewart—Jews play a prominent role in American life. Three out of the present eight Supreme Court justices are Jewish. Since 1987, the three chairs of Federal Reserve have all been Jewish. Jews have been overwhelmingly accepted by America, and their contributions to American life have been exceptional. The pairing of Jews and America has borne fruit in almost every field.

This success is not only economic, professional, and academic, the achievements not simply material and quantifiable. My travels across the United States brought me to a beautiful minyan on the West Side of Manhattan; to a young, lively San Franciscan community; to a heady celebration, attended by thousands, at the biannual conference of the Reform movement in Orlando, Florida. Wherever I went, I found dynamic communities, high-spirited summer camps, and seminaries of profound and pathbreaking heritage. I saw Jewish leadership, community spirit, education, and renewal. There are more than 3,700 synagogues in the United States—Orthodox, Conservative, and Reform. There are over 150 federations—small, medium, and large. At most of the synagogues, federations, organizations, and community centers I visited, I saw a remarkable past and a remarkable present that filled me with enormous pride. Without planning to, without meaning to, I found myself among people whose first language is not my first language, whose country is not my country, but who are nevertheless my brethren.

But the deeper I traveled into Jewish America, the more I sensed that a dark cloud hangs over my siblings' phenomenal success. At many events, most attendants were over fifty, the predominant hair color gray. The young were missing. The hipsters, the cool kids, the trendsetters did not come. Organized Jewish life, I discovered, was impressive but older. The challenge, I realized, the existential challenge facing this perfect Diaspora is the generational divide. Broadly speaking, those over seventy have the Holocaust as their context and are religiously committed to the Jewish state and to Jewish life. Broadly speaking, those over fifty still have a strong Jewish identity and remember the young Zionist state, so even if they whine and gripe, they are unable to turn their backs on the State of Israel and its people. But those under thirty live in a different world. On the one hand, many of them still have an affinity to the country they may have traveled through on Birthright buses. On the other hand, the complexities of modern-day Israel are not especially interesting to them, or especially relevant. And organized Jewish America seems to them ponderous, disconnected, even alien. Many are baffled and perplexed by it. Many seem to be drifting away. So much so that the future of Jewish America may be in peril.

The Jewish-American future is part of this book for two reasons. The first is that 84 percent of world Jewry lives in the United States and in Israel, which means that the fate of the Jewish people will be decided in these two democracies—the big and the small. Therefore, anyone who holds dear the future of Judaism cannot ignore Israel, and cannot ignore America and its Jews.

The second reason concerns Zionism itself. As early as the first years of the Second World War, David Ben Gurion realized that the twentieth century was becoming the American century, and so he developed an American orientation for the Zionist movement. In 1948, Harry Truman's America was the first nation to recognize the State of Israel. In 1964, Lyndon Johnson's America forged a special relationship with Levi Eshkol's Israel. In 1969, Richard Nixon's America and Golda Meir's Israel turned that relationship into a full-fledged strategic alliance. Since then, Israel has been totally dependent on the United States diplomatically, defensively, and strategically, to such a degree that the evolving worldview of American millennials—both Jews and non-Jews—will very much determine the future of my nation.

The struggle for the future of the Jews and the future of Israel is taking place not only on the border of the Gaza Strip, the hills of Samaria, and the nuclear facilities of Natanz and Fordow—but on the campuses of Stanford, Berkeley, UCLA, Tufts, Brown, and Duke. That's why I felt obliged to visit these universities and many others. Having acquainted myself with the older Jewish America, in early 2015 I set out on a two-year journey to get to know young Jewish America, visiting over fifty universities.

At the radical end of the spectrum is Vassar College. The prestigious women's college, founded in 1861 near Poughkeepsie, New York (on whose board once sat its neighbor, Franklin Delano Roosevelt), became a coed school in 1969, and approximately 2,500 students now pursue their degrees there. Today, as in its past, most of its students come from affluent homes, and for a yearly tuition of over fifty thousand dollars they receive a fine, diverse education on a beautiful, pastoral campus. But in the last few years, this prosperous college has become a hotbed of extreme anti-Israeli activity, which, many concur, borders on anti-Semitism. When I arrived at Vassar on the last day of winter 2016—remnants of a heavy snowstorm still dotted the rooftops, but a bright sunshine warmed the green lawns—the first questions I asked were: What does this enchanting campus have to do with my small, tormented country? Why do these young, intelligent, and promising students have such intense feelings about what happened in the past and what is happening presently six thousand miles from here—between the Mediterranean Sea and the Jordan River?

One answer is the tribulations of the Jewish students themselves. There is no official data on how many Jews attend Vassar, but it is estimated that they make up 15 to 18 percent of the student body. Almost all of the Jewish students are liberals. Almost all of them oppose occupation, settlements, and Israel's pugnacious policies. Many feel an instinctive guilt about the resounding success of Jewish America. And about the fact that they are seen as white, rich, and privileged. Not a few of them channel these anxieties into vehement anti-Zionist postures. For them, the problem is no longer occupation or not-occupation, peace or not-peace. The problem is the very existence of Israel as a Jewish state. Other, more moderate Jews fear expressing their views openly, preferring not to defend Israel publicly—and to distance themselves from the vitriolic debate.

A second answer may derive from the frustration felt by students of color. Although Vassar is proudly liberal, committed to human rights and minority rights, on campus there are very few minorities. The number of African American students at Vassar, for example, is about 6.5 percent. The unintended exclusion of people of color creates an understandable animosity. The unrepresented—those lacking resources and an organizational infrastructure—turn a large part of their feelings of disaffection toward the represented, those with resources and a well-developed infrastructure. The result is an overwhelming identification with the Palestinians, such that many see Israel as an arrogant entity, oppressive and racist, whose behavior is reminiscent of Alabama of yore. Just as Israel became an almost internal American issue for the evangelical Right, it is now becoming an internal American issue for the radical Left. At Vassar, the tension between the two creates an atmosphere of intolerance, and sometimes a frisson of hate.

The third answer is the zeitgeist on campus. Political correctness prevents many in American academia from acknowledging that the Third World, too, is rife with acts of evil. The annihilation of hundreds of thousands in Syria, the oppression of women in Saudi Arabia, the incarceration of homosexuals in Egypt, the persecution of Christians in Gaza, and even the barbaric abominations perpetrated by the Islamic State—seem to get a pass. The legacy of Edward Said is that the intellectual, political, and moral discourse is confined to the misdeeds of the white man. Thus many in academia find it hard to see, and confront, the Middle East as it really is. They are immersed in an endless discussion of victims and victimizers, colonialists and indigenous people, the powerful and the powerless. The Iraq War exacerbated this phenomenon. The trauma it created means that any (Western) show of strength is seen as sinful, and every (Western) use of force is seen as criminal. According to this worldview, the West is always the perpetrator, the guilty party, while the inherent weakness of the non-West cleanses and absolves it of all wrongdoing.

Amid this kind of thinking, Israel doesn't stand a chance. Occupation becomes even worse than it already is when viewed through the broken mirrors of the Jewish identity crisis, interracial tensions, and political correctness run amok. The result is moral mayhem. At Vassar, there is no movement against China (Tibet) or Russia (Ukraine), but there is a fierce movement against the very legitimacy and existence of the one and only Jewish democratic state.

The small group of Jewish students I meet at Vassar's Old Laundry Building makes quite an impression. They are all J Street supporters. They all oppose Netanyahu and support the two-state solution. But in the place where they live, study, and practice politics—they seem marooned. Israel bashing is the cause du jour. Comparing Israel to apartheid South Africa is the norm. Zionism is defined as racist colonialism. As Jews, these students are seen as no more than privileged whites, with no regard or respect for their history, their rights, their past traumas, and the enlightened values they hold dear. Is this full-fledged anti-Semitism? I ask these guarded and uneasy students, who beseech me not to use their names in this book. In certain cases, they reply, it is. There is a certain venom directed at Israel—and an automatic delegitimization of anyone who supports Israel—that definitely sounds anti-Semitic, they say. Once in a while someone writes on Facebook "Fuck the Jews," and once in a while someone uses the epithet "kike." But direct, open expressions of anti-Semitism are rare. The problem, they concur, is that about half of the staff and half of the student body support BDS (Boycott, Divest, Sanction) without understanding the true meaning of BDS, or contemplating why they are calling to boycott Israel and no other nation in the world. The problem, they say, is that the one-state solution is ascendant despite the fact that no one has thought through the catastrophic consequences that one state might have. Another problem is that anyone who identifies openly as Zionist—even as an ultra-liberal Zionist—is immediately branded an oppressor, a genocide monger. And it is absolutely forbidden to talk about the Holocaust, about the fact that Jews have a traumatic history of their own. The only ethnic group that gets no respect on campus, they say, is the Jewish one.

I feel like I've been wounded, one student who tried to fight a BDS motion, tells me. I feel connected to Israel, she says, Israel is significant to me. But Israel is making it so hard for me with what it's doing in the West Bank and Gaza. On this campus, she adds, I cannot express the complexity of my thoughts and feelings. I'm silenced. To be a Jewish student at Vassar is to cry a lot. Almost every other day, I find myself in tears. Whether you call it anti-Semitism or not, we, the small group of liberal, pro-Israel students, are under siege. We are attacked, we are scorned. Even when we weep, we are ridiculed, as if our tears, our pain, are unearned, unmerited.

The real issue, another student tells me, is that the main politics on campus is the politics of race. There is a very deep sense of liberal guilt because there are so few African Americans. And somehow, she ventures, the Israeli-Palestinian conflict has become identified with white-black tension. So we, the Jewish students, even though we are liberals, are seen as the whitest of whites. As if we are members of the evil privileged group responsible for most of the injustice in the world.

When the student government held a vote on adopting the full BDS list of demands in the winter of 2016, a third student tells me, the hall was packed with nearly three hundred students, of which 80 percent were BDS supporters. The motion was carried by a wide margin. But it's not just the fact that they won an overwhelming majority, she says, and we were a tiny minority. It was the way they treated us. With such contempt, verging on verbal aggression. During the debate, I began to cry, and after the vote about a dozen Jewish students gathered together, and we all cried. It's so sad, on this progressive campus, that there is no room for our story, our truth, our feelings. And even those students who realize how outrageously we are being treated are afraid to speak up; and it's the same with many of the faculty members. They don't have the courage to stand up against it, either.

A student with sensitive eyes joins the conversation: I'm a Jew and Hispanic, he tells me. But the fact that I feel connected to my Jewishness and refuse to be anti-Israel means that I'm shunned by many minority activists on campus. Being a J Street supporter is perceived as being half fascist. Being a liberal Zionist means being a racist. And if you decide to identify yourself as an anti-occupation Israel supporter, it's just not good enough. Socially, you pay a high price, because you are shunned from progressive circles. You find yourself feeling anxious all the time. It hurts. A lot. Because no one listens to you. No one respects your identity. Even if you're half Hispanic, like me, you're seen as white, racist, utterly contemptible. When the vote on BDS took place, it was terrible. I sat there looking around me, and I began to cry. I didn't have the strength to argue, to fight back. I saw the hatred in their eyes, the verbal and emotional abuse, and I was helpless. I felt like the Jews probably felt in medieval times or in Germany of the early 1930s. I still haven't figured out how to process what I experienced that day. And I wonder, what kind of America am I living in? What do I do with my Jewishness?

Vassar is certainly at the radical end of the spectrum, but, as Freud taught us, the end of the spectrum tells us quite a lot about the spectrum as a whole. What I saw and heard during my half-day visit to this verdant campus in upstate New York was the most insipid, extreme version of what I saw and heard at other universities that had gone through traumatic BDS battles in recent years. At UCSD, I was told by students about being cyberbullied, and about being called child killers during Israeli Apartheid Week. And that the BDS victory of 2013 left the Jewish community on campus wounded, weakened, and dejected. At UCLA, I was told about the long and terrible night of the BDS vote in the spring of 2014, during which Jewish students faced outrageous accusations, bordering on blood libel, and such rancor that at dawn, after the ordeal was over, they walked out to the quad and hugged one another and began to cry. At Berkeley, I was told that BDS supporters are a rainbow coalition of minorities (among them Jews and even Israelis), while the predominantly white and Jewish-Israel supporters are seen as privileged and oblivious.

At Stanford, I was told how BDS won a surprising victory by hijacking the political agenda of this excellent technology-and-business-minded university, where Israel, the Startup Nation, should perhaps have had many admirers. At Northwestern, I walked straight into a clever, well-organized BDS campaign. The Jewish students who tried to counter the offensive were completely on their own in this losing battle, with scant support from the Jewish establishment, which did not have the proper conceptual tools and understanding to help them—or the liberal-Zionist narrative to arm them (instead they offered hard-line Israeli propaganda). At Columbia, a feminist student, the granddaughter of Holocaust survivors, told me how she felt that her safe space as a woman had been violated when a rally against sexual violence quickly became a stage for vilifying Israel. In Ann Arbor, I listened to a group of brokenhearted students describe how the battle with BDS left them bereft, struggling with their feelings toward Israel, and amplifying their doubts about their allegiance to a country that they had once seen as a victim, but is now a powerful nation abusing its force.

In American academia of the twenty-first century, I learned, there are three major transgressions: privilege, power, and particularism. Jews are accused of all three. They are perceived as powerful, privileged, and devoted to their particular ethnic clan. Every campaign against Israel on American campuses makes use of these three accusations to recruit anti-Israel supporters in order to isolate, weaken, and defeat not only Zionism, but the Jewish community itself.

Each campus is a world unto its own. And campuses, like rivers, change from year to year. But there are certain cross-campus similarities. There are certain phenomena that characterize the academic world in which the millennials are coming of age.

In the last few years, the Jewish establishment and media have been stricken by BDS anxiety. They report, discuss, analyze, and condemn the BDS vote at Vassar, the swastikas at Davis, the eviction notices found on the doors of only Jewish students' dorms on the Claremont campuses, the violent demonstration on campus in Madison, Wisconsin. In a certain sense, this anxiety is warranted. BDS is a sophisticated hate group with blatant anti-Semitic hues. In recent years, its activity on a wide range of campuses has increased significantly. But at each campus I visited, I soon learned that BDS is still a marginal, if very loud, movement. At most universities, students had never heard of it. And even on the most radical campuses, the number of people fully committed to Israel bashing is not high. What makes BDS so effective is the alliance it forms with a rainbow of minorities: African Americans, Hispanics, Filipinos, LGBT, and some feminists. The result of this brilliant, intersectional strategy is twofold: the number of supporters of BDS motions has risen from a few dozen (staunch anti-Israel activists) to a few hundred (angry, agitated minorities); meanwhile, liberal Jewish students are thrown into despair because they do not want to be seen as privileged and racist. They find themselves on the wrong side of the moral divide. BDS is not Hitler. Its power stems from its ability to take advantage of Israel's shortcomings and the shortcomings of Jewish America regarding this new young generation of college goers.

The two major problems from which BDS draws its strength are the mounting tension between Zionism and progressivism—and uninformed indifference. The tension stems from the fact that at least 85 percent of non-Orthodox Jewish students in the United States are progressive. Most were devoted to Obama, and many supported Bernie Sanders. When today's Israel is Benjamin Netanyahu's Israel and the Jewish establishment is seen (erroneously) as Sheldon Adelson's establishment, a problem arises. At Georgetown, Johns Hopkins, Columbia, and dozens of other universities, I met with thousands of students who want to admire Israel, to engage with Israel, but contend that Israel's actions prevent them from doing so. They cannot countenance the building of settlements in Yitzhar and Itamar. They cannot accept settlers in Hebron and Nablus. They are angry at the persecution of minorities and the way Israel (mis)handles the dysfunctional relationship between synagogue and state. No, they do not want to give up. In many cases, they received a good Zionist-Jewish education at home, and they had a tremendous time on Birthright. Israeli high-tech piqued their interest and Tel Aviv's nightlife bowled them over. This loud and distant land holds a place in their hearts. And many of them are sporadically experiencing something their parents never have: anti-Semitism. So Israel's attraction remains strong, and the interest in Jewish life is very much present. But the way in which the Jewish state and the Jewish establishment have been behaving over the last decade gives them pause. They are baffled and exasperated—and sometimes they choose to walk away.

Many conversations I had with these students quickly became emotional. We feel like Israel abandoned us on the battlefield, I was told at Stanford. We feel like Israel is betraying us and betraying its values, I was told at San Francisco State. We feel like the Israeli government and organized Jewish America have become rabid Republicans, I was told at

Tucson. Talk to them, I was beseeched at Tufts. Tell them what we think, I was asked at Princeton. Go to Jerusalem, go to New York, and tell the people in positions of power that they are completely detached from reality, from the values and concerns of young Jewish America.

Grave as this anger can be, a lack of anger—a shoulder-shrugging apathy—is even more worrisome. While at some highly political universities Israel is a hot topic of debate, at many others Israel is no topic at all. On a bitter winter day, I arrived at a large mid-Atlantic university. On this campus, surrounded by miles and miles of fields covered with snow, some 40,000 students go to school, 4,500 of them Jewish. Their main interests seem to be football, Greek life, dance marathons, and sex. And that's fine, especially on a campus at whose center stands a monumental, shrine-like stadium. The problem here is that despite their best efforts, Jewish organizations—such as Hillel, Chabad, and Birthright—cannot seem to recruit more than a tenth of the Jewish student body. The charming young woman accompanying me on a campus tour tells me that Judaism is very important to her, Israel is very significant. But when she tries to explain this to her three apartment-mates, they laugh. Her friends know that they are Jewish. They are even proud to be Jewish. But the Jewish aspect of their lives is almost nonexistent. Even though they grew up in Jewish upper-middle-class homes in the suburbs of Philadelphia, Detroit, and Chicago, they couldn't care less. We're losing them, she tells me. Every year, on this huge campus, we lose touch with hundreds of young Jews who cease to be Jewish.

The Hillel director at a big university in central Florida says much the same thing. Florida, he tells me, has one of the biggest concentrations of Jewish populations in the world. On his campus, 6,000 of the 60,000 students are Jewish. And the political fires are low. Pro-Palestinian activity is limited. Seemingly, everything is fine, everything works. But even on this politically dormant campus, he tells me, Israel is not cool. There is a certain, if quiet, anti-Israel vibe that is slowly getting louder. Much worse, he laments, are the apathy and ignorance exhibited by many Jewish students. Most of them come from comfortable homes in southern Florida where they weren't exposed to any significant Jewish culture or history. Some 80 percent have one parent who is not Jewish. They represent a second and third generation that is utterly lacking Jewish content. They know they are Jewish, but they have no idea what Judaism, in any of its guises, is about. Many think Israel neighbors France, and that West Bank is the name of a lake. They lack basic knowledge about Passover, Rosh Hashanah, the Sabbath. Their Hebrew is almost nonexistent. In the past decade, the number of students studying Hebrew has dropped from 350 to 120. So it isn't surprising that out of 6,000 Jewish students only 300 participate in Shabbat services at Chabad or Hillel. And it isn't surprising that only 30 out of 6,000 take advantage of Birthright to take a free trip to Israel. If this trend continues, by 2050 there won't be JCCs and there won't be federations, he warns. Half of the existing congregations will disappear. To see America's Jewish future evanesce before your very eyes, he adds sadly, you don't need to go to Columbia or Berkeley—come here, to central Florida.

On the right, many speak of BDS as the enemy at the gate. On the left, the enemy at the gate is settlements. But the truth is more complicated, and the millennial challenge is much more extensive, profound, and elusive than the Right or Left is willing to admit.

There is not one elephant in the American-Jewish room; there are five. One is that Israel's nationalist-religious policies create significant friction between enlightened American values and what is erroneously perceived as the new and ugly face of Zionism. The second is the weakening of the non-Orthodox Jewish identity in America, mirroring an overall American trend away from religion. The third is the fact that old communal conventions—those that created, defined, and preserved the American-Jewish community—are no longer compatible with the younger generation's way of life. The fourth is the guilt many young liberals feel about the Jewish success story. The fifth (and probably the biggest) is the lack of an uplifting, inspiring narrative—not one based on narrow-minded nationalism or a sense of perpetual victimhood— that would endow non-Orthodox Jewish life with renewed meaning.

What I learned in my travels is that while apathy is a major problem on the larger campuses, where the Jewish student body is quite significant, political tensions are especially prevalent at leading universities, where international awareness is high. From a pro-Israel point of view, a growing concern is that while the silent majority doesn't have particularly strong feelings regarding the Jewish state—one way or the other— a wide swath of the politically active students at many of the elite universities tends to be decidedly anti-Israel. Among the young political class, who will probably find their way to Washington one day, the critical attitude toward the Zionist enterprise is occasionally evolving into palpable hostility.

Yet all is not lost; there is still more than one reason for hope. At the University of Bloomington, Indiana, I met Jewish students whose lives may be lacking significant Jewish content, but who still choose to associate with one another by congregating at what are known as the Jewish parts of the dorms, and by pledging Jewish fraternities and sororities. Hanging out with other Jews has become the central Jewish activity for many young Jewish students. And there is a thirst for meaning, a craving to belong. In Washington, Oregon, California, and Texas, I discerned a quiet yearning for a new message, a new vision that would renew the sense of Jewish meaning. At Ann Arbor, I witnessed what a wise and warm leadership can achieve in the face of crisis. At UCLA, I saw how a smart strategy can muster a forceful response to a grim turn of events and overcome BDS supporters. Sadly, the return of anti-Semitism can also play an important part, by reminding young Jews from whence their people came, and by startling decent non-Jews, who become aware of how legitimate criticism of the State of Israel suddenly turns into an ugly, age-old hatred of the people of Israel.

But everywhere I went—Rutgers, Brown, Yale, Tufts, Dartmouth—I saw one striking phenomenon: in today's world, it is exhausting to be Jewish. There is no clear narrative, no roadmap—and Israel and organized Jewish America are no help at all. If in the past being Jewish was a given, today it is very much a matter of choice. One that has to be made consciously on an almost daily basis. If in the past it was difficult to be Jewish, today, for many American millennials, it is wearying to be Jewish. With everything else they must contend with—big issues such as environmental concerns, social injustice, and the crumbling American dream, not to mention the prospects of finding a job, paying off debt, finding a partner—who needs another headache, who wants to take on the constant emotional and intellectual struggle that is called being a Jew?

This exhaustion is apparent not just among the young. At community centers across America, the number of active members continues to decline while their age continues to rise. And some organizations and federations seem to be funded by fewer and fewer Jews, who are giving more and more money. The traditional, popular-democratic nature of the community is being replaced by (a well-intentioned and committed) oligarchy. And while the prodigiously active core continues to work tirelessly, it is surrounded by growing circles of weariness, disinterest, and detachment. After the generation that was thrilled by *Exodus* (Israel must be as good-looking and blond and blue-eyed as Paul Newman), and the generation that was captivated by *Schindler's List* (in every situation and at every point in time, we are forever victims), comes a generation that does not have a simple, clear, and attractive Hollywood story to latch onto. Something has cracked in the Jewish-American success story. The formula that produced such wonders over two hundred years seems to have stopped working.

Unexpectedly, the conversations I had with prominent, cerebral, older American Jews helped me better understand this troubling turn of events. Michael Steinhardt (financial investor, philanthropist, art collector, co-founder of Birthright) told me about the nonreligious Brooklyn neighborhood where he grew up. There, Jews were surrounded by Jews, and their frame of reference was almost always Jewish. So even when they went on to Wharton and then to Wall Street, they remained tied to the community. Michael Walzer (political theorist, historian, ethicist) told me how in the small Pennsylvania town in which he grew up, the local Jewish leader would keep an eye on community members, cajoling them to give generously, thus maintaining a remarkable system of voluntary taxation. Leon Wieseltier (intellectual, author, editor) told me that he grew up thinking that to be a Jew meant to be an aristocrat of the intellect, one who learns Hebrew, studies the Bible, reads Bialik, Tchernichovsky, and Emma Lazarus, all the while pursuing a first-class, worldly education.

Most of the young people I met at universities across America did not come from monolithic Jewish communities and are unaware of the intricate inner workings of community preservation. They knew no Hebrew, had not studied the cultural heritage of the Jewish people, its poets, philosophers, and authors. And they do not have an unconditional admiration for Israel. Furthermore, they have a choice. Every day, they can walk away. What had united their grandparents in Jewish togetherness has ceased to exist, or has become irrelevant.

It is difficult to overestimate the gravity of Israel's role in these dire developments. In a certain sense the fulminations of BDS, Zionist-progressive tensions, and the waning of Jewish identity are not new problems. In various versions, they have trailed Zionism since its inception. But at its core, the astounding success of the Jewish national movement in the twentieth century stemmed from three unspoken principles that helped it sidestep these three challenges. The first undeclared principle of Zionism was that it must always forge an intimate alliance with a benign superpower (first Great Britain, then France, then the United States). The second principle was that, with regard to the Arab-Israeli conflict, it must always seize the higher moral ground (by accepting the partition plans of 1937, 1947, and 2000). The third principle was that it must always be associated with enlightened international forces (the Left accomplished this through the kibbutzim and the Histadrut labor cooperative, and by belonging to the international socialist movement; the Right chose the Jabotinsky-esque alignment of nationalism with liberalism and human rights). But in the twenty-first century, the Zionist nation no longer adheres to any of these principles. By turning its back on progressive America, it has jeopardized its strategic alliance with the United States. By abandoning the peace process, it has lost the higher moral ground. And by forging an alliance between Tea Party Israel and its American counterpart, it has associated with reactionary forces. By doing all this, Israel is not only endangering itself, but complicating the lives of young Jews and non-Jews who want to love it but are finding it harder and harder to do so.

Yet the problem goes even deeper. Ultra-Orthodox Jews, and even modern-Orthodox Jews, do not need Israel in an existential sense. They can maintain their Jewish heritage and identity in their traditional, semi-closed communities. And with no mortal enemy on the horizon, there is no mortal danger to their future. In contrast, for non-Orthodox Jewish civilization, Israel is vital. As the forefathers of Zionism had foreseen, in order to foster significant non-Orthodox life in New York, Chicago, and Los Angeles, there must exist an enlightened Tel Aviv, and a Jewish democratic nation that can serve as a powerhouse to develop a free, modern Jewish identity that will remain relevant in centuries to come.

But over the last few decades Israel has abrogated this all-important

Zionist mission by giving itself over to fanatical forces. Paradoxically, Israel's ultra-nationalists are jeopardizing the future of the Jewish people, while the ultra-Orthodox are jeopardizing the future of the Jewish religion. By not recognizing the legitimacy and the beauty of Conservative and Reform Judaism, alongside Reconstructionist Judaism—and by turning Israel into an insular, suspicious, and chauvinistic Sparta—they preclude Jewish-American liberals from identifying with it, and are alienating from Jewish life the thousands of Jewish students I met on my travels. Purporting to be hyper-Zionist, Israel is actually hindering Zionism and endangering the Jewish future.

Jews and Israelis who think the problem is a few dozen demonstrators disrupting a speech by an Israeli ambassador are deluding themselves. Extremism on the margins is a problem, but not *the* problem. The real danger is that mainstream young America is slowly but surely turning away from Israel. Israel is not cool, Israel is not exciting. Israel is no longer seen as a young America, exuberant and intrepid, out on the frontier. And when mainstream America turns away from Israel, many young Jewish Americans find it hard to stand up for it. Given the ever-widening fissures between Jews left and right, the swelling doubts about Israel's policies, the ensuing moral fatigue—many young Jewish Americans cannot summon the motivation, the conviction, or the strength to fight for the Jewish state and the Jewish people. More so than any external threat, the internal one is the real danger facing Jewish America.

At a fashionable, farm-to-table restaurant overlooking the San Francisco Bay, a brilliant local Jewish leader tells me he is worried about the chasm between the world of his seventy-five-year-old father and that of his fifteen-year-old daughter. I'm the bridge, he says, and I'm doing everything I can to be the Golden Gate, strong and stable. But the chasm is growing wider and deeper. Sometimes I wonder if we have a future. Jewish America, he adds, lowering his voice, is like a great mother who, in her better years, fed and nurtured her young Israeli son. But the relationship is changing, the balance of power is shifting. The mother is growing older, becoming more dependent on the health, strength, and goodwill of her son. But this son is a handful, as you well know, quite a handful. And it's not at all clear that he understands how much his mother needs him.

I am far more optimistic than my dinner companion.

My travels through young America were not easy. A long stretch took place in winter, entailing many nighttime journeys—from campus to campus—on icy, treacherous roads. On many campuses, I took part not only in heartbreaking conversations, but in harsh confrontations. Sometimes I felt like a catcher in the rye, trying—at the very last moment—to pull off the ledge those children who were about to fall. More significantly, I felt like I was fighting not just for Israel of 2030, but for Jewish America of 2050. Still, as someone who comes from a country where Jewish life is a given, I was enthralled to see the engagement of young people in a place where Jewish life is not at all a given. I was impressed by the eloquence, the thoughtfulness, the intellectual honesty I encountered. The tribulations of the students I spoke to, their search for a path forward, struck a chord. The élan vital of my ancient and strange people has not dissipated.

My disconcerting visit to Vassar ended with a wide-ranging, passionate speech. This audience was very different from the welcoming one I had addressed two and a half years earlier at the Detroit JCC. It was young, critical, liberal-radical. I oppose occupation, I told them. I think the settlements are the greatest calamity Israel has ever brought upon itself. But please don't allow the present Israeli government, whose policies we all abhor, to make you give up on Israel and see it as a colonialist monster. After all, we are not really masters of the universe. We are a small, persecuted people who contributed so much to humanity, and who were treated so badly by large parts of humanity. For 1,500 years, we were white Christian Europe's ultimate other. Then we became its ultimate victim. We were not sent by imperialist forces to the other side of the world in order to loot the lands of a faraway continent. We returned to the land of our ancestors because we had no other choice. We had to save ourselves.

Did I manage to convince them? Certainly not all of them. But there was a respectful silence when I finished my speech, and a few of the students with whom I had spoken earlier, at the Old Laundry Building, came up to thank me, visibly moved. A young professor told me that he had never heard such things before at Vassar. On this campus, he added, no one I know thinks that Zionism has a liberal dimension, that Zionism has a liberal justification.

On the drive back to Manhattan, I reflected on the wistful, admirable students I had met, about Jewish America, and about Israel. We are all boat people, I thought. In our past, there occurred a catastrophe, a cataclysm, a sudden avalanche. Something from which we had to escape in order to save our souls. Some of us boarded a boat heading west, to the land of opportunity. Others boarded a boat heading east, to the Promised Land. For a hundred years, there was a sibling rivalry between the two. In the early 1930s, it seemed that those who had headed east were right, and those who had headed west were wrong. In the early 1940s, the opposite thinking took hold. But the truth is that both sides were right. Both conjured miracles in their chosen lands. In the twenty-first century, these miracles became completely dependent on each other. We would not have a life without American Jewry; American Jewry would not have a life without us. That's why it is vital that Israel be put right. That's why it is vital to effect a deep change in Jewish America. Zionism of the twenty-first century should be all about forging a new vision, writing a new narrative, creating a new spirit that will inspire Israeli millennials as much as their American counterparts. There is nothing more important. Our future depends on it.

EIGHTEEN

By the Sea

EVERY SUMMER MY FAMILY TRAVELS TO ENGLAND. PERHAPS IT'S BECAUSE our roots are there. Perhaps it's because England is the opposite of our homeland. While Israel is frenzy and constant change, England is tranquillity and continuity. As the plane descends toward Heathrow, a deep though unjustified sense of homecoming overtakes me. And as I drive my wife and three children through Somerset and Dorset, the feeling of calm deepens: we pass flocks of sheep, village pubs, ancient churches. When we reach the stone cottage we rent on the shores of South Devon, my happiness is complete. In the light rain, I stand with my wife, Timna, and my children, Tamara, Michael, and Daniel, at the edge of the white cliff across the field from our house and look out at the deep-green vales descending down to the gray-green ocean. England. There has not been a successful foreign invasion here for centuries. There has not been violence for decades. With its deep calm of solid identity, England has all that we never had and all that we may never have: peace.

Our history is more ancient, I tell my children. When we wrote the Bible, the people of this green isle were illiterate barbarians. But our history is that of "Get thee out of thy country," and our land itself is a mound, one layer of life upon another, layer upon layer of destruction. Yes, we Jews had Jerusalem when London was still a marsh. But the

English have what we can only dream of: they are born in serenity and they die in serenity. Not even world wars endanger their very existence. We, on the other hand, are always restless, for we live between great fires. We thrive between calamities. That's why we are so quick and vital and creative. That's why we are so neurotic and loud and unbearable. We dwell under the looming shadow of a smoking volcano.

England was good to my ancestors. The British Empire opened its gates to Herbert Bentwich and gave him the rights, liberties, and opportunities that Jews had not had for more than fifteen hundred years. It gave his two sons the best education the West had to offer. In the first quarter of the twentieth century it enabled hundreds of thousands of emancipated Jews to live lives of freedom and dignity under the benevolent Crown. Although these islands, too, were tainted with anti-Semitism, Jews did well in business, science, and even politics. Many of them were part of Britain's intellectual and meritocratic elites. So more than a hundred years ago, the Bentwich family went on vacations similar to ours. Some summers they spent down in Cornwall, others up in the Lake District. But mostly the Bentwiches would holiday at the family estate of Carmel Court on the Kentish coast. In their Edwardian manor, they lived as the Ramsays lived in Virginia Woolf's *To the Lighthouse;* the summer holidays of the Bentwich family could have been just like the summer holidays of the Ramsay family. As Timna takes over the kitchen of our rented cottage, and as the children plunge into the reassuring cacophonous merriment of their games, I think about my Anglo-Jewish ancestors, the Bentwiches, and about myself. What would have become of me had my great-grandfather not uprooted us from the green shores of Britain and settled us on that desolate shore of Palestine? What would have been the fate of my mother and myself and my children if Herbert Bentwich had not been overcome by an obsessive yearning for Zion?

I would like to think that I would have been a literature don at Oxford or a producer at the BBC. I would have a nice house in Hampstead and a thatched-roof cottage in West Dorset. My life would be much more relaxed and far safer than my Israeli life. I would have more leisure time for poetry and music. My children's future would not be under a cloud. But would I have had a richer inner life? Would my life's experience have been more meaningful?

Demography is vicious. When my great-grandfather enjoyed his time of leisure on the coast of Kent, Jews were 0.8 percent of the British population. Today they are less than 0.5 percent. What makes the demography even more vicious is the fact that in the latter part of the twentieth century, hundreds of thousands of Eastern European Jews immigrated to Great Britain. Many of them were ultra-Orthodox Jews whose sons and daughters now make up a third of Manchester's contemporary Jewish community and a fifth of London's contemporary Jewish community. Less than half of today's Jews are the descendants of the Anglo Jews of 1920. The disappearance rate of Herbert Bentwich's Anglo-Jewish community is staggering. In the last one hundred years, most descendants of Britain's veteran Jews have ceased to be Jewish.

The Anglo-Jewish community of the nineteenth and early twentieth centuries was remarkable. The union between Jewish talent and British culture produced outstanding poets, writers, playwrights, artists, musicians, scientists, lawyers, bankers, entrepreneurs, politicians, and revolutionaries. Jewish Britons won more than a dozen Nobel Prizes. They created legendary wealth and were prominent in every radical movement that transformed public discourse in the United Kingdom. But this creative community is shrinking fast. Low birthrates and high intermarriage rates are leading to the disappearance of non-Orthodox Jews. There appears to be a gradual loss of interest in Jewish life and Jewish identity in Britain. The descendants of Herbert Bentwich who were born in England in recent years are not Jewish, and those of my wife's English grandfather are not Jewish, either. Britain still has Rothschilds and Goldsmiths and Millibands, but in a generation or two they, too, will cease to consider themselves Jewish. So as I look out at the gray cliffs of Devon, I know that if my great-grandfather had not removed me from this coast, I myself would probably have been today only half Jewish. Tamara, Michael, and Daniel might not consider themselves Jewish at all. Our private life in Hampstead and Dorset would be full and tranquil, but the collective we belonged to would be vanishing all around us.

Yes, there is America. North America still has a vibrant non-Orthodox Jewish community. In the United States I could have been a proud liberal Jew teaching at Columbia or writing for *The New York Times*. Like the two of Herbert Bentwich's daughters who immigrated to America, I could have secured my identity there. But the demography of American Jewry is vicious, too. The numbers are controversial, but roughly speaking, in 1950, 3 percent of Americans were Jews; in 1980 it was 2.4 percent, and in 2010 approximately 2 percent. By 2050 Jews might comprise only a fraction of the population of the United States. The same comfortable circumstances that made the numbers of British non-Orthodox Jews diminish in the last fifty years will likely make the numbers of American non-Orthodox Jews diminish over the next fifty years. In the twenty-first century, the Jewish birthrate in North America is low and the intermarriage rate is high. The Jewish population is aging. More and more of the affiliated Jews are Orthodox or ultra-Orthodox or just old. Most secular young Jews have less interest in Israel or organized religion than their parents have. They are drifting away from the center of gravity of Jewish identity; they are disappearing into the non-Jewish space. Some of Herbert Bentwich's young American descendants whose parents did not keep Jewish law do not consider themselves to be Jewish anymore. Both in my secular English-Jewish family and in my secular American-Jewish family one can see the end of the line. One can imagine the last of the Jews.

So as I watch Tamara, Michael, and Daniel walk down the path toward the whitewashed fisherman's cottage that stands in solitude by the sea, I am at odds with myself. One part of me wishes that England would be home for them, that they, too, would live the enchanting life of *To the Lighthouse*. But I realize that we cannot go down this path. Over the years, our tribe could not survive on these lush green meadows. With no Holocaust and no pogroms and no overt anti-Semitism, these islands kill us softly. Enlightened Europe also kills us softly, as does democratic America. Benign Western civilization destroys non-Orthodox Judaism.

That is why Herbert Bentwich's insane journey from the shores of Kent to the shores of Jaffa was necessary. For these soft English hills and old English cottages are not for us. This continuous history and solid identity and deep tranquillity are not for us. For we are a people on the move and on the edge. This is why the concentration of non-Orthodox Jews in one place was imperative. And the one place where non-Orthodox Jews could be concentrated was the Land of Israel. So

Jaffa was inevitable. We had to save ourselves by building a Jewish national home all around Jaffa.

A few days after I return from Devon, I walk through the ancient port of Jaffa. Once it was an orange-exporting port, then an immigrants' port, then a fishing port. In recent years it has become a port of leisure. I find a large bar located in an old warehouse and sit there sipping my favorite single malt while watching the handsome young Israelis eat, drink, and make merry. I listen in on the sweet murmurs of Israel's kinetic nightlife.

Jewish demography in Israel is the mirror image of Jewish demography in the Diaspora. In 1897, approximately 50,000 Jews lived here. Now the Jewish population exceeds six million. While the number of Jews in Britain rose by less than 20 percent and the number of Jews in the United States rose by 350 percent, the number of Jews in Israel rose by more than 10,000 percent.

The contrast between Jewish demographics in the Diaspora and in Israel is astonishing. In 1897, Jews living in Palestine represented only 0.4 percent of world Jewry. In 1950 we accounted for 10.6 percent. In 1980, 25.6 percent. Now we make up almost 45 percent. The historic project that aimed to congregate most of the world's Jews in the Promised Land has had mind-boggling success. Today, the Jewish community in Israel is one of the two largest in the world. Given current trends, by 2025 the majority of the world's Jews will be Israelis.

The mass immigration of Jews to the Land of Israel in the twentieth century is Zionism's greatest triumph. It vindicated the Zionist diagnosis and gave hope to the Zionist prognosis. Zionism's other triumph was the outstanding fertility rate of the Jewish population in Israel. In 2012, America's total fertility was 2.06, Britain's was 1.9, Italy's was 1.4, and so was Germany's. By contrast, Israel's fertility was a staggering 2.65, by far the highest of all OECD countries. While Europe is aging rapidly, Israel is youthful. While the non-Orthodox Jews of the Diaspora are aging, the Jews of Israel are mating and multiplying. While half of Europeans are over forty, half of Israelis are under thirty. They invigorate our towns and cities and invigorate all I see around this bar in the port of Jaffa.

• • •

So what has happened in the Holy Land in the first century of Zionism? What was our impact here? Where have we succeeded and where have we failed? To answer this question, I leave the port of Jaffa and embark on a journey following my great-grandfather's footsteps. Unlike Herbert Bentwich, I don't stop in Mikveh Israel. From Jaffa I travel to Rishon LeZion through the Tel Aviv satellite towns that were not here in 1897: Holon, Bat Yam, Azur. En route is the absence of the Palestinian villages that were erased since 1897: Tel el-Kabir, Yazur, Bayt Dajan. The freeways have many lanes, the intersections are heavy with traffic. Between what was an orange shipping port and what was the first Jewish colony in Judea, there are no more wildflower fields, no pastures or meadows. There are no camels or flocks of sheep, no nomad Bedouins. Palestine was replaced by a great mass of housing for immigrants, endless ugly housing estates that stretch out to the south and east of Jaffa. The ten-mile route that the Thomas Cook carriages traversed on that spring morning in 1897 are now crammed full of sweaty, bustling cities.

When my great-grandfather reached Rishon LeZion in April 1897, it had approximately one hundred families, fifty houses, thirty stables, and three streets. Zionism's first colony was surrounded by 4,000 dunams of vineyards in which its farmers planted more than a million high-quality grapevines. The winery was legendary: the largest in the Middle East and one of the most sophisticated worldwide. At the top of the hill stood an impressive synagogue, and along the wide colonial boulevards rose fine colonial houses. The tiny colony founded the first all-Hebrew school in the world and the first all-Hebrew town hall in the world and Palestine's leading orchestra. Although it was still in its infancy, it was clear that Rishon LeZion had a promising future. As it impressed my great-grandfather in 1897, it impressed Dr. Herzl, who visited a year later. "May it be," the founder of Zionism wrote in Rishon LeZion, "that from this place will spring forth a blessing for our unfortunate brothers."

Indeed, from this place a blessing *has* sprung forth for our unfortunate brothers. From seventy different countries, Jews have fled to Rishon LeZion. The city's population rose from 500 in 1897 to nearly 250,000 in 2013. The fourth-largest city in Israel now has forty elementary schools, a fast-growing college, a symphony orchestra, and a booming commercial district. In the last twenty-five years alone, the number of its inhabitants rose two and a half times. Seventy-three percent of the local families own the apartments they live in, 74 percent have at least one car, 81 percent have a personal computer, and 96 percent have Internet access. On average, every family in Rishon LeZion has 2.5 mobile phones and more than 2 bedrooms. This middle-class city is also the city of middle Israel: it is neither conservative nor liberal, neither Ashkenazi nor Sephardic, neither religious nor secular. In the 2013 elections, nearly half of its votes went to centrist parties. Rishon LeZion is the typical Jewish-Israeli city of the third millennium, inhabited by hardworking immigrants and the children of immigrants who consume a lot and have many children of their own.

From the freeway I turn right to West Rishon. Until 1985 there was nothing here, only the sand dunes Herbert Bentwich saw from a distance in 1897. For nearly a hundred years nothing changed. But in the 1990s the collapse of the Soviet Union brought a million immigrants who had to be settled rapidly. Within a decade the sands were paved over, and within two decades the new West Rishon was larger in size than the old Rishon. At the age of one hundred, Zionism proved to be strong and potent. Once again it performed the miracle of something-from-nothing. Another modern Israeli city was born.

Under the blue skies stand condominium towers that were built quick and huge to answer quick and huge needs. They are efficient and commercial, but they are soulless. The streets look as if they have risen straight off a drafting table. There is a sense of affluence here, but no sense of place.

Like neighboring Rehovot, Rishon LeZion maintained its identity and character for two or three generations. After orange groves replaced the old vineyards, it became a booming citrus colony. But after 1948 came the demographic waves of the 1950s, the 1970s, and the 1990s. The local identity was erased, the unique character obliterated. By now the melting pot was not ideological but economic. And it worked, melding a mishmash of ethnicities and identities and unifying the immigrants under the roof of a gigantic mall.

Ehud Barak once defined the country as a villa in the jungle. But the real Israel is not a villa but a shopping mall: cheap, loud, intense and lively. The shopping mall embodies the Israeli condition—a desperate attempt to lead a pseudo-normal life in abnormal circumstances after an abnormal history and on the verge of an abnormal future. And West Rishon is all about its malls. Consumption is its beating heart.

I walk into Cinema City, a gaudy temple of twenty-six theaters that offer Rishon LeZion the California it wishes to be. Along the corridors stand wax figures of Superman, Batman, Charlie Chaplin, Humphrey Bogart. There is Ben and Jerry's ice cream, Domino's pizza, Coca-Cola. Youngsters wearing Diesel jeans and GAP sweatshirts and A&F jackets lug enormous vats of popcorn. Nothing remains of the initial promise of the unique beginning. And yet, seen through the prism of the horrors of the twentieth century, all that surrounds me evokes only sympathy. For Rishon LeZion is a life-saving project. Although it does not look or sound like one, it is a city of refugee rehabilitation.

From West Rishon, I travel to Ramleh. In 1897, Ramleh was an Arab town with a population of 6,000, known for its mosques, churches, inns, and markets. Its many hostels catered to pilgrims en route from Jaffa to Jerusalem. Today Ramleh is an unhappy Israeli city of 68,000: 50,000 Jews, 15,000 Muslims, 3,000 Christians. Almost all the descendants of the Muslim Arabs who lived here in 1897 were deported in 1948. The present-day Muslim population is made up mainly of Bedouins and Palestinians whose ancestors were transferred here from their villages in Israel's first years.

The Jews who inherited Ramleh are mostly immigrants, of whom nearly 30 percent arrived in the 1990s and 2000s from Uzbekistan, Kazakhstan, and Ethiopia. Many of the inhabitants of the dreary housing projects are young and poor. One third subsist on welfare benefits. On a socioeconomic scale of one to ten, Ramleh is a dismal four.

There are a few fine Palestinian houses still standing. There are several spectacular historic sites that are dilapidated and run-down. The market is lively, and there are some good ethnic restaurants around it. By the old Muslim cemetery a new mall is being built alongside a new modern quarter that is designed to attract middle-class professionals. But all in all, Ramleh is depressed and depressing. After losing its Arab identity, it never acquired a meaningful Israeli one. While Rishon LeZion gives its inhabitants the gloss of consumerism, Ramleh fails to do even that. This city never really recovered from the great cataclysm of 1948.

The Palestinians might say that when Herbert Bentwich arrived here in his Thomas Cook carriage he was carrying with him a virulent bacterium. Like the conquistadors, he wasn't aware of it, but it devastated the Palestinian immune system and Palestinian civilization, and laid waste to old Ramleh. I would not argue, but I would add that eventually the same virulent bacterium attacked the original Zionist dream, too. In 1897 it was still possible to imagine a master plan that would turn the dream into reality, but by 1950 there was no feasibility for any such plan. Need chased need. Pressure chased pressure. Danger chased danger. The naïve conquistadors were caught up in the whirlwind of the consequences of their original deed. The historic imperative that had brought them from Europe to Ramleh wreaked a havoc that no one could control. First it demolished the indigenous culture, then it demolished the pioneer culture, then it uprooted the magical orange groves of my childhood and then it created faceless Israeli cities of discontent.

I climb up the 119 steps of the white tower. The panorama of coastal Israel is overwhelming. Town abuts town, neighborhood abuts neighborhood, building abuts building, apartment abuts apartment. Almost three million human beings are squeezed into the three thousand square kilometers surrounding Tel Aviv.

Perhaps there was no other way. To maintain secular Jewish existence in the modern era, we had to congregate in one place. Today, this concentration of people is not only a necessity but the essence of Israel. For it seems we Jews need to crowd together. We need to be with one another, even to fight with one another. It is as if we cannot live by ourselves as individuals, as if we are afraid that on our own we'll vanish. So we do not acknowledge the private domain. We don't distinguish the personal from the public. We warm ourselves against the big chill together, living communally, collectively in a kibbutz, in a moshav, in a housing estate, and in this crowded concentration of population that stretches from Hadera to Gedera and from West Rishon to East Ramleh.

From Ramleh, I travel to Lydda. The train station is still located in the same stone terminal that the French built for the Turks in 1891. Where the British-Jewish pilgrims waited for the train to Jerusalem in the spring of 1897 now stand smiling Israeli soldiers carrying Israeli-made assault rifles and holding Coke cans and chocolate bars. Two ultra-Orthodox men are fervently discussing current events. A young Russian-speaking couple argue in whispers. A beautiful young Muslim girl in tight jeans and a head scarf passes by.

From the panoramic windows of my air-conditioned train car, I look out at Ramleh, Lydda, and the Plain of Judea. East of the railroad is Tel Gezer. Here stood the ancient settlement of Gezer in 3400 B.C. Here stood a rich and powerful Canaanite city in 1700 B.C. Here stood an ancient Hebrew city in the tenth-century B.C. and a nineteenth-century Palestinian village named Abu Shusha. In 1923, great-grandfather Bentwich bought a stately home here. In 1948, the IDF's Givati Brigade conquered the village of Abu Shusha, killing, expelling, and burning as it went. These days, on the mountain ridge south of Tel Gezer stands the Israeli community of Karmei Yosef, where Amos Yadlin and the grandchildren of Rehovot's orange growers live a life of affluence. Theirs is Israel triumphant: lavish homes facing the ancient somber barrow.

F-16 bombers fly overhead, preparing for yet another war. Here is another tragic triumph: when blindness finally lifted and the Palestinian villages were at last seen, the Jews acknowledged the drama they were caught in and did not recoil. They didn't panic, didn't retreat or collapse. Rather, they built an iron wall. And within this iron wall, the Jews built their nation-state. Within this wall, they revived the Hebrew language and created a vibrant Israeli culture. Within this wall, they made music and theater, art and cinema. They loved and married and bore children. They looked fate in the eye and did what they had to do and stood guard for more than one hundred years.

Along the railway are plowed fields, grapevines, and row upon row of tightly tied bales of cotton. Beyond the mountain ridge is a secret missile base.

So if I were to address some imaginary ultimate Zionist congress, what would I say? I'd probably say that the need was real. The insight was genius. The vision was impressive—ambitious but not mad. And the persistence was unique: for over a century, Zionism displayed extraordinary determination, imagination, and innovation. Its adaptability, flexibility, and resolve were outstanding. But as Zionism was late and the Holocaust preempted it, its premise of the mass immigration to this land of the Eastern European Jewish peoples turned out to be false. So was the premise regarding feeble Arab resistance. Therefore, the Zionist project did not become what it was supposed to be: a grand, well-planned engineering project like the Suez Canal or the Panama Canal or Dutch land reclamation from the sea. It did not become a grand enterprise of progress that solved in a rational manner one of humanity's ugliest problems. It did not eradicate anti-Semitism in the way that modern medicine eradicated tuberculosis and polio, or solve the problem of the Jews in the way that modern medicine solved the problem of infant mortality. Rather, Zionism became an unruly process of improvising imperfect solutions to acute challenges, addressing new needs, adjusting to new conditions and creating new realities. It reinvented itself again and again, dealing in different ways with what is basically an impossible situation. This is how Zionism wended its way through the twentieth century and this is how it shaped the land. That's why the landscape I see as the train approaches the Judean hills is that of a haphazard quilt, one patch over another, one improvised solution alongside another.

The train passes Beit Shemesh—a development town now turning ultra-Orthodox—and glides into the Soreq Gorge. On both sides of the tracks, rocky hills rise. Some slopes are bare; others are covered by a dense Zionist pine forest that hides within its thicket the ruins of some Palestinian villages.

The act of concentrating the Jews in one place was essential but dangerous. If another historic disaster were to strike here, it might be the last. The founding fathers and mothers of Zionism realized this. They knew they were leading one of the most miserable nations in the world to one of the most dangerous places in the world. That's why they were so demanding of themselves and of others. That's why they acted in such a shrewd and resourceful and disciplined manner. They knew that their mission was superhuman, as was the responsibility thrust upon them. But over the years, it was not possible to maintain such a high level of revolutionary discipline. It wasn't possible to maintain the devotion, precision, and commitment. The following generations lost the historical perspective and the sense of responsibility. They were fooled by the Zionist success story and they lost sight of the existential risk embodied in the Zionist deed. Gradually they lost the concentration and caution required of those walking a tightrope over the abyss. As resolve waned and wisdom dissipated, there was no longer a responsible adult to lead the children's crusade. A movement that got most things right in its early days has gotten almost everything wrong in recent decades.

When his train pulled into Jerusalem, Herbert Bentwich rushed from the city's old and charming train station to the most sacred Jewish site, the Western Wall (the remains of the Second Temple). When I arrive, I rush from Jerusalem's new and charmless train station to the most sacred Israeli site: Yad Vashem, the museum of the history of the Holocaust.

At the entrance I lose my breath. On the walls, ghostly images of children in black and white play violin for a tutor. Lovers in black and white glide on snow. A Jewish shtetl in black and white, a tram. Youngsters dancing in a circle. A girl hugging a doll. Two girls in black and white waving goodbye.

The museum is a triangular structure of reinforced concrete that penetrates the mountain like a bunker. On both sides of the tunnel-like main hall are dark galleries that tell the story. Christian anti-Semitism, Nazi anti-Semitism, Kristallnacht. The burning of books, the burning of synagogues, the imprisonment of humans. The racial laws, the yellow star, ghettos. Murder by hanging, murder by shooting, murder by gas. Thousands, tens of thousands, hundreds of thousands, 5.7 million. And on both sides of the triangular tunnel Zionism's ultimate arguments: Ponary, Babi Yar, Majdanek, Buchenwald, Sobibor, Bergen-Belsen, Dachau, Treblinka, Auschwitz. The unforgettable face of the Polish diplomat Jan Karski as he recalls Franklin Delano Roosevelt, who would not bomb Auschwitz in 1944. And the pale yellow map of Europe scattered with inconceivable numbers. Of the 140,000 Jews of Holland—102,000 dead. Of the 817,000 Jews of Romania—380,000 dead. Of the 825,000 Jews of Hungary—565,000 dead. Of the 3,020,000 Jews of the Soviet Union—995,000 dead. Of the 3,325,000 Jews of Poland—3,000,000 dead.

But the figure that strikes me most is the number of Jews killed at the massacre at Babi Yar. On the twenty-ninth and thirtieth of September 1941, 33,771 of the Jews of Kiev were taken to the forest, made to stand next to a ravine, and then shot by the ravine and buried in it. In the forty-eight hours of Babi Yar, more Jews were shot dead than in the first 120 years of the battle for Zion; more Jews were killed than in all of the wars of Israel. So there is a good reason for the fact that this tunnel of European devastation leads at its very end to a bright terrace overlooking the deep green of the Jerusalem mountain forests. And when I stand on the terrace of Yad Vashem I cannot help but feel proud of Israel. I was born an Israeli and I live as an Israeli and as an Israeli I shall die.

From Yad Vashem, I move on to Givat-Shaul. So that Zionism would not lose the war of 1948 and the Jews of Palestine would not end up in some Palestinian Babi Yar, Ben Gurion instructed the Haganah to go on the offensive in April of that year. He ordered the Jewish armed forces to conquer the Palestinian villages blocking the road to Jerusalem: Hulda, Deir-Muhsein, Bayt Mahsir, Saris, al-Qastal. In coordination with the Haganah, the nationalist Irgun and the Stern Gang went on their own village offensive. On April 9, 1948, at dawn, they attacked the west Jerusalem village of Deir Yassin. At least one hundred Palestinians were slaughtered. The bullet-ridden corpses were buried by a platoon of seventeen-year-olds who were sent in to clean up the mess. One of the youngsters was Herbert Bentwich's grandson, who was haunted to the end of his days by the horror he witnessed. But the State of Israel dealt with the trauma in a practical manner: in 1951 it transformed the remains of the Palestinian village of Deir Yassin into the closed psychiatric facility of Kfar Shaul.

I approach the white metal gate and ask the guard if I might enter. She refuses. So I walk along the fence, find a breach in it, and sneak in. An old Palestinian stone house is now an occupational therapy carpentry shop. Another old Palestinian stone house is an open ward. Still more Palestinian stone houses are now closed wards for those who pose a danger to themselves and others. What strikes me is the large number of religious patients. Many of the men wear white yarmulkes and many of the women cover their heads. Though here and there a modern clinic was added, all in all, the old village is still here. It's ironic that while most Palestinian villages were demolished, one of the few to remain is the one that is the central symbol of the Palestinian catastrophe. Its silent stone houses still tell the tale: what was here and what happened here when the Jews went mad.

The mountain summit of Deir Yassin is now encircled by Kablan Street and Katzenelenbogen Street, the main thoroughfares of the ultra-Orthodox neighborhood of Har Nof. Laborite Israel was reluctant to build on this tainted ridge, but New Israel had no inhibitions. The Likud and Shas coalition governments saw the potential of the real estate of Deir Yassin and capitalized on it. A few steps from the breach in the fence of Kfar Shaul where I entered stands the gaudy, monumental shrine that is Ner-Haim Yeshiva, and the gaudy, monumental shrine that is the Lev Aharon Yeshiva. Between them is the massive dormitory building of the Orot Hateshuva Yeshiva, and the grand Netivei Hatalmud Yeshiva, and the little yeshiva of Mishkan Hatorah. More than twenty yeshivas and synagogues and religious schools stand on the northern slopes of Deir Yassin, and more than twenty stand on its eastern and southern slopes. Here are tens of thousands of square meters of religious institutions whose students don't work, pay taxes, or fulfill military service. After the grand dream and the great effort and the horrific sin, what Zionism established on the land of Deir Yassin is a new ultra-Orthodox ghetto.

I travel from Deir Yassin to Israel's national site of commemoration, Mount Herzl. This is the Jewish state's Washington Monument and Lincoln Memorial and Arlington Cemetery all in one. In days past, it was the Palestinian Mount Sharafa: a few Palestinian stone houses and stone quarries scattered on west Jerusalem's imposing summit. In April 1948, an Irgun squad positioned itself here and rained machine gun fire on Deir Yassin. Sixteen months later, Theodor Herzl was buried on this very same mountain. His majestic state funeral was conceived as a symbolic marking of the end of war and the triumph of the Jewish national movement. In spite of all the obstacles it faced, the great journey that had begun in 1897 had arrived at its destination. The dream was fulfilled: Zionism reached Zion.

The architecture is dignified and restrained. Herzl's unadorned black granite grave is flat, encircled by an irregular ellipse of gardens, garden paths, and stone fences. In one corner are the graves of the Herzl family and the leaders of the Zionist movement. In another corner is the grave of Vladimir Jabotinsky, leader of the right-wing revisionists and prophet of the iron wall. In a third corner lie Israeli presidents, prime ministers, and speakers of parliament. The symbolism is clear: here, on this summit, Zionism merges with Israeliness and Israeliness subsumes Zionism. Here is the exact point where the reality of the State of Israel is derived from Herzl's vision. The symbolic site is modest and solemn. Its strength lies in its republican modesty, economy, and asceticism, in its wide gravel pathways and its sparse Mediterranean shrubbery. It is geometric and rational, with no sign of mysticism or messianism or chauvinism. There is nothing man-made here that is larger than man. Mount Herzl is an unmonumental monument.

The military cemetery is also democratic and subdued. The ranks of the fallen are not engraved on the gravestones. In almost every section, generals are buried beside corporals. There are no patriotic inscriptions praising heroism and homeland. There is no attempt to deprive the dead of their individuality. On the contrary, the small stone plaques emphasize the fact that what lies under each one of them is a human being. The simple epitaphs do not sanctify death in war but leave it as it is: final and horrific.

Mount Herzl is the Israel of my childhood. It is the social-democratic Israel of pre-1967. It is secular, egalitarian, and disciplined, both harsh and human, collective and sensitive. There is no nationalistic kitsch here, no religious kitsch. With quiet dignity it makes a statement: On the mountaintop—the visionary. Below him, his disciples. Below them, the state leaders. Below them, the soldiers. Those who toiled, those who fulfilled, those who paid the ultimate price.

Both Yad Vashem and Deir Yassin ask the same dire questions: Shall we live? Shall we overcome our past? Mount Herzl says we shall. Its preoccupation narrative claims that we shall live because we do not dwell on the past. We shall live because we successfully suppress Yad Vashem and Deir Yassin. We shall live because we are just and strong and modern. Our Israel is future-oriented. Solidarity, progress, and courage have enabled it to reign over this summit of sovereignty. Yet this benign narrative has been disintegrating since 1967. Can we renew it? Can twenty-first-century Israel reconstruct the Mount Herzl republic?

From Mount Herzl I travel to Mount Scopus. Standing where Herbert Bentwich bid farewell to the city of his longing in 1897, I ask myself the classic Israeli questions: What will be? What are our chances? Will the Jewish state survive another century? Will we still be here in 2097?

In recent years, Jerusalem has experienced something of a revival: it has more nightlife and more artistic activity and more young energy than it had at the turn of the millennium. But the capital's demography is not promising. In 1897 it had a Jewish majority of 62 percent. By 1967 it had risen to 79 percent. But over the last decades it has shrunk back to almost where it was in 1897: 63 percent. Of the children attending schools in contemporary Jerusalem, approximately 40 percent are ultra-Orthodox and more than 35 percent are Arabs. Less than a quarter of Jerusalem's youth are Jewish Zionists, and only an eighth are nonreligious Jews. It is as if secular Zionism had never happened.

True, Jerusalem is not Israel. But throughout the country, demography is turning against the Jews. Today 46 percent of all of the inhabitants of greater Israel are Palestinians. Their share of the overall population is expected to rise to 50 percent by 2020 and 55 percent by 2040. If present trends persist, the future of Zion will be non-Zionist.

To explore the challenges facing Israel I travel north: from Mount Scopus to Beit El. My great-grandfather was overwhelmed with religious emotions when he saw the supposed archaeological ruins of where Jacob is supposed to have dreamed his ladder dream. But now these remains are barely visible between the prefabricated cement walls and cement towers that Israeli occupiers erected to protect settlers traveling this road from the wrath of occupied Palestinians. From Beit El I follow my great-grandfather's route to Shilo. The remains of the Byzantine church my great-grandfather saw here lie across from an Israeli settlement surrounded by the high fences of those who chose to be masters living by their sword. Both in Beit El and in Shilo, the question is whether Israel will end occupation or whether occupation will end Israel. The same question arises all around Nablus and in the Valley of Dotan. Will the Jewish state dismantle the Jewish settlements, or will the Jewish settlements dismantle the Jewish state? There are only four paths from this junction: Israel as a criminal state that carries out ethnic cleansing in the occupied territories; Israel as an apartheid state; Israel as a binational state; or Israel as a Jewish democratic state retreating with much anguish to a border dividing the land. I still believe the Israeli majority prefers the fourth path. But this majority is not solidified or determined. Israel lacks a political force with the will required to lead the painful and risky retreat. It is also not clear whether the Israeli republic has the competence needed to evacuate settlements and divide the land. The region of Samaria that Herbert Bentwich crossed in April 1897 now looks like a monumental settlement project. So far, Zionism has not been able to summon from within the forces that will save it from itself. It is up to its neck in the calamitous reality that it created in the West Bank.

I diverge from my great-grandfather's route and head for Mount Baal Hazor. In the introduction to this book, I wrote that two factors make Israel different from any other nation: occupation and intimidation. In the twenty-first century there is no other nation that is occupying another people as we do, and there is no other nation that is intimidated as we are. Now, as an armored IDF bus takes me up to the highest summit in Samaria, I can actually see occupation and intimidation. From the radar base monitoring Israel's airspace, I think of the concentric circles of threat closing in on the Jewish state.

The external circle is the Islamic circle. Israel is a Jewish state that arouses religious animosity among many Muslims. The occupation of Jerusalem and the West Bank amplified this animosity, but it is Israel's very existence as a sovereign non-Islamic entity in a land sacred to Islam and surrounded by Islam that creates the inherent tension between the tiny Jewish nation and the vast Islamic world. For years, Israel dealt with this religious tension wisely. It forged alliances with moderate Islamic states and maintained secretive and commercial relationships with others. It created strategic partnerships and fostered mutual interest arrangements and was very careful not to turn the regional conflict into a religious one. But over the years Israel lost some of its Islamist allies as radical Islam swept to power. Jewish extremism and Islamic fanaticism fed each other. In some Islamic countries, hostility toward Israel became active. Deep currents of anti-Israel feeling are today an integral part of the political landscape in West Asia and North Africa. With massive immigration and bloodcurdling terror, Europe, too, is experiencing a new kind of challenge. At any given moment these forces could combust. Iran is the great threat, but so are some other Muslim powers.

A giant circle of a billion and a half Muslims surrounds the Jewish state
and threatens its future.

The intermediate circle is the Arab circle. Israel is a Jewish nation-
state founded in the heart of the Arab world. The Arab national movement tried to prevent the founding of Israel—and failed. The Arab
nations tried to destroy Israel—and failed. As such, the very existence of
Israel as a non-Arab nation-state in the Middle East is testimony to the
failure of Arab nationalism. When Arab nationalism was weakened
and corrupted in the last quarter of the twentieth century, it was forced
to set aside its grievances and to superficially recognize Israel. That
brought about the Israeli-Egyptian peace treaty, the Israeli-Jordanian
peace treaty, and regional stability. But the Arab awakening changes all
this. As moderate but corrupt regimes are replaced by new ones, public
tension rises and there is widespread demand for a tough line vis-à-vis
Israel. There is no great Arab-Israeli war on the horizon, but stability is
fragile. Israel now faces less Arab military might but more Arab turmoil. As the Arab nation-state (Iraq, Syria, Lebanon) is collapsing, Israel is being surrounded by failed states or extremist nations. The silver
lining is clear: there is no longer a Syrian army that can invade Galilee
and there are no Iraqi missiles aimed at Tel Aviv. Many moderate Sunni-
Arab leaders, who are terrified of Iran and Islamic extremism, now see
Israel as a strategic ally. The dark side is that young Arabs have very
little hope. The political options they have are bleak: a reactionary
monarchy, a military dictatorship, Islamic theocracy—or bloody chaos.
As the Syrian human catastrophe and the bone-chilling ascendancy of
the Islamic State have proved, new dangers are on the rise. Israel is situated in the middle of one of the world's worst neighborhoods. Peace
skates on very thin ice. Stability is fragile. A wide circle of 370 million
Arabs surrounds the Zionist state and threatens its very existence.

The third circle is the Palestinian circle. Israel is perceived by its
neighbors to be a settler's state founded on the ruins of indigenous Palestine. Many Palestinians perceive Israel as an alien, dispossessing colony that has no place in the land. The underlying wish of a great number
of Palestinians is to turn back the political movement that they blame
for shattering their society, destroying their villages, emptying their
towns, and turning most of them into refugees. As long as Israel has
overwhelming power, moderate Palestinians have to conceal their wish

and even suppress it. But moderate Palestinians are in retreat and radical Palestinians are on the rise. As Islamic fundamentalism and Arab extremism become dominant throughout the region, Palestinian pragmatism is besieged. Thus, if Israel weakens for a moment, the suppressed Palestinian wish will erupt forcefully. And as the overall number of Arab Palestinians overtakes the number of Jewish Israelis, they will be backed by real power. There is nothing more sacred to me than the Jewish democratic state. But if the present status quo continues, and Israel keeps ruling over millions of Palestinians (who make up approximately half the population of the land), we face two equally dire choices: either we grant them political rights and Israel ceases to be a Jewish state, or we continue to deny them these rights and Israel ceases to be a democracy. A status quo vis-à-vis our immediate neighbors menaces us from within. An inner circle of ten million Palestinians threatens Israel's very existence.

In recent years, the three circles of threat have merged. As Islamic forces strengthened, Palestinian and Israeli moderates weakened and the chance to reach a comprehensive peace diminished. At the same time, Israel's unilateral withdrawals from southern Lebanon and the Gaza Strip cleared the ground for terrorist organizations whose rockets and missiles rattle Israel periodically. Here is the catch: if Israel does not retreat from the West Bank, it will be politically and morally doomed, but if it does retreat, it might face an Iranian-backed and Islamic Brotherhood–inspired West Bank regime whose missiles could endanger Israel's security. The need to end occupation is greater than ever, but so are the risks.

Up until now, Zionism was very effective in defending against these three circles of threat. Wise diplomacy prevented the Islamic circle from consolidating into a politically active circle that could strangle Israel. Military might prevented the Arab circle from acquiring the ability to defeat Israel on the battlefield. Sophisticated intelligence prevented the Palestinian circle from destabilizing Israel by the use of terrorism. But pressure is mounting on Israel's iron wall. An Iranian nuclear bomb, a new wave of Arab hostility, or a Palestinian crisis might bring it down. The emergence of an irreversible one-state state may be even worse. So the challenge Israel faces in the next decade is as dramatic as the one it faced in its first decade. Atop Mount Baal Hazor it is clear that we are approaching a critical test.

From the highest summit in the West Bank I drive north to Mount Tabor. When I reach its summit, I get out of the car and walk around the Franciscan monastery and observe the valley Herbert Bentwich crossed after traveling through Samaria in 1897. At that time, not one Jewish Zionist lived here. It was all marshes, subsistence farmers, and Bedouins. But from Mount Tabor, the outcome of the hundred-year struggle is apparent: the Valley of Yizrael is mostly Jewish, but the mountains of Galilee are predominantly Arab. While Zionism won the valleys of the Holy Land, the mountains remained Palestinian. For all its efforts, Zionism did not overtake the Negev mountain or the Galilee mountain or the Central mountain. It remained a coastal phenomenon, sending long tendrils into the inner valleys. The white minarets of the villages beyond Megiddo and Nazareth make the picture clear. The vanishing Arabs are back.

The State of Israel refuses to see its Arab citizens. It has not yet found a way to integrate properly one-fifth of its population. The Arabs who were not driven away in 1948 have been oppressed by Zionism for decades. The Jewish state confiscated much of their land, trampled many of their rights, and did not accord them real equality. In recent years, oppression lessened, but it was not replaced by a genuine civil covenant that will give Arab Israelis their full rights. To this day there is no definition of the commitments of the Jewish democratic state to its Arab minority, and that of the Arab minority to the Jewish democratic state. On the one hand, there is no real equality for Arabs in Israel, but on the other hand the government does not always enforce the law in their domain and allows their towns and villages to live in partial anarchy. What emerges is a dangerous situation of lawlessness. Many Palestinian Israelis don't respect central government, but they also don't feel they belong. Their affinity to the Palestinians outside Israel and the Arabs surrounding Israel mean that their situation is fundamentally different from that of ethnic minorities in North America or Western Europe. Although they are a minority within the Jewish state, they are an integral part of the overwhelming regional majority that makes the Jews of Israel a regional minority. This complexity was never dealt with, and majority-minority relationships within Israel were never defined. For the time being, the economic benefits and the civil rights that the Palestinian Israelis do have keep the peace. Although they do not admit it publicly, they are very much aware of the fact that in many ways they are much better off than their brothers and sisters in Egypt, Jordan, and Syria. But the political bomb is ticking. As the Arab minority grows in number and confidence, it endangers the identity of Israel as a Jewish nation-state. If this crucial issue is not resolved soon, turmoil is inevitable.

I journey on, from Mount Tabor to Tiberias. The Bentwich delegation pitched its white tents south of the ancient city, on the shores of the Sea of Galilee. I drive farther south, crossing the Jordan River and reaching the southern edge of the lake. Here Degania, the world's first kibbutz, tried to combine utopia, commune life, and colonialism. A breathtaking human experiment was carried out on this lakeshore: to invent a democratic version of communism that would save the Jews.

Thirty-nine years after it was founded, Degania was attacked by an invading Syrian army: there were air raids, artillery shelling, and an armored assault. The kibbutzniks and the soldiers defending the commune stopped the tanks with antitank bazookas, rifles, and Molotov cocktails. Dozens of them were killed in the battle and were buried nearby. A small Syrian tank captured in battle stands at the gate to the kibbutz, commemorating their sacrifice.

Facing the mythological tank, I think of the mental challenge facing Israel in the twenty-first century. What enabled the defenders of Degania to fend off the Syrian army at such human cost was the conviction they had. The dream of utopia and the burgeoning reality of the commune gave them the mental strength to withstand challenges such as the war of 1948. But contemporary Israel has no utopia and no commune and only a semblance of the resolve and commitment it once had. Can we survive here without them? Can we still fight for our banal Israel as the soldiers of Degania fought for their kibbutz dream? Can our consumerist democracy hold in times of real hardship? Within the Islamic-threat circle and Arab-threat circle and the Palestinian-challenge circle and the internal-threat circle lies the fifth threat of the mental challenge. Might it be that Israel's collective psyche is no longer suited to Israel's tragic circumstances?

Herbert Bentwich crossed the Sea of Galilee by boat; I drive around the lake by car, passing Tiberias, Tabgha, Capernaum. A few miles north of the ancient fishing village where Jesus is said to have taught is the colony of Rosh Pina. In 1897 it was home to a teacher, Yitzhak Epstein, who tried to bring Jews and Arabs together, teaching their children in the same school. A decade later it was home to an agronomist, Haim Margolis Kalawariski, who was one of the first Zionist leaders to believe in peace. In the late 1920s Rosh Pina was home to a physician, Gideon Mer, who made a point of treating his malaria-stricken Arab neighbors in his clinic. But in 1937 Rosh Pina spawned the first Jewish terrorist, Shlomo Ben Yosef, hanged by the British after he tried to murder the passengers of an Arab bus climbing Mount Canaan.

The sixth threat Israel faces is the moral threat. A nation bogged down in endless warfare can be easily corrupted. It might turn fascist or militaristic or just brutal. Surprisingly, Israelis have generally upheld democratic values and institutions while being in a permanent state of war. For a long time, they have maintained a reasonably moral society. The majority respected human rights and endorsed liberal democracy. But in recent years there is growing pressure on the very core of Israeli democracy. Occupation takes its moral toll. The ultra-Orthodox and Russian minorities do not always cherish the democratic values that were previously taken for granted. The fear of the growing Arab minority breeds xenophobia and racism. Ongoing occupation, ongoing conflict, and the disintegrating code of humane Zionism are allowing dark forces to menace the nation. Semifascist ideas that attracted the right-wing fringe of the 1930s are now being endorsed by some leading politicians. Not all is dark. Israel still has a sensible middle-class center. But an evil wind is rattling the windows. In the second decade of the twenty-first century, the old liberal-nationalist Right has been replaced by a radical ultra-nationalist Right. Jewish terror has reemerged. There have been unprecedented attacks on democratic institutions such as a critical free media and the supreme court. Populism has reared its ugly head. A battle rages for Israel's soul. It is now all too apparent that one hundred years of war and fifty years of occupation have created an immense moral threat. The brutality that erupted in Rosh Pina in 1937 keeps on erupting. Israel's identity as a benign democracy is constantly being challenged.

From Rosh Pina I travel north along the Jordan River. When Herbert Bentwich rode his horse through this Hula Valley there were Arabs in it and there was a shallow lake. In 1947–1948 the Arabs were driven away, and between 1953 and 1957 the lake was drained to make way for agricultural settlement. In the decade that preceded my birth, Zionism overcame the two great obstacles it faced in this valley. With a series of military operations it eliminated the Palestinians, and with a grandiose engineering project it eliminated the lake, clearing an entire region in which it settled veteran pioneers and new immigrants, replacing a backward Palestine with a modern Israel. This dual action of Zionism succeeded in its young days by marshalling a new and powerful Hebrew identity.

Hebrew identity was revolutionary. It defined itself as a revolt against Jewish religion, Jewish Diaspora, and passive Jewish existence. It affirmed itself on the foundations of the Hebrew land, the Hebrew language, and the belief in a Hebrew future. It sanctified the Bible while dismissing postbiblical Jewish history and tradition. It cherished progress and action and a secular attitude to life. It was careful to balance its national zeal by having a universal dimension. One of its versions was socialist-nationalist and the other was liberal-nationalist, but both were anticlerical and unprovincial. Both combined collective determination with enlightenment. That is why Zionism could believe it was just and this is how it persuaded others it was just. It's a long, long road, it said, but we shall walk this road and we shall walk it singing. We shall walk it believing that it is not in years to come but here and now; believing that it is not up to God but up to us; believing in this new secular religion of doing it all with our own hands; believing in our ability to drive out the Arabs and empty the lake and move mountains.

Hebrew identity was galvanized in the first third of the twentieth century but remained dominant in the following third of the century. It was the real force that overcame the Arab uprising in 1938, the Palestinian people in 1948, and the Arab nations in 1967. It was the force that established a state and maintained it and absorbed immigration and settled the land. In some respects it was a brutal identity. It detached Israelis from the Diaspora, it cut off their Jewish roots, and it left them with no tradition or cultural continuity. In some respects, it was an artificial identity that imposed on Israelis a man-made existence based on suppression and denial. Lost were the depths and riches of the Jewish soul. But the revolutionary Hebrew identity was imperative if the Zion-

ist revolution was to prevail. It enabled the movement to execute a megalomaniacal concept that suited the Israeli condition. It granted Israel
the supremacy without which it would not have survived. And it did all
this not with solemnity but with delight. It made generations of Israelis
walk the long road they were required to walk with gaiety and optimism. We are on our way, they sang. We are on our way, hoppa hey,
hoppa hey.

In the last third of the twentieth century, Hebrew identity was
dulled. In the early years of the twenty-first century, it seems to have
disintegrated. Occupation, globalization, mass immigration, and the
rise of non-Zionist minorities have worn down the hegemony of the
Hebrews. For better or for worse, the more rigid way of life was replaced
by wild pluralism. Gone was the balance between nationalism and universalism. Gone was the secular revolt against Diaspora and religion.
Secular faith weakened, progress weakened, the collective narrative dissolved. Just as some of the brackish water of the Hula began to seep back
into the lake bed, Judaism and shtetlism and Arabism returned. Just as
the brutal deed done in this valley was partially reversed, so was the
brutal deed done to the collective psyche of the Jews. The flourishing
enterprise of Israeli self-assurance was overshadowed by existential
questions: Succeed or fail? Flourish or perish?

The pinnacle of Israel's success was in the 1950s, when this young,
faltering country succeeded, against all odds, in building a nation—and
absorbed in a very short time an immigrant population bigger than the
absorbing population. The price of this success was a Zionist-socialist-
secular oppression of individuals and minorities. These minorities (un-
derstandably) rose up in rebellion in the 1970s, 1980s, and 1990s—and
a unified society became a divided society, whose center could not hold.
In one generation Israel went from a seemingly implacable, monolithic
republic to a colorful, anarchic kaleidoscope of tribes whose various
identities are defined by their very differences. In the twenty-first century, the tribal divide, the social rift, and the loss of a sense of common
purpose are at the core of Israel's political crisis. So, the seventh threat
facing Israel is the threat of crumbling identity.

The kibbutzim I pass are like a canvas of the model Israeli landscape: tall eucalyptus trees, upright cypresses, plowed fields, and grain
silos. But behind the gates, things have changed: the common dining

halls and the nurseries are empty. The Israeliness that was once here is not really here anymore. The Hebrew culture that settled this valley and stood fast in this valley is gone. It changed form and changed character and turned into something as yet undefined. As I leave the valley behind me, I know that the question of identity is the crucial one.

At the core of the Zionist revolution was an identity revolution. Identity revolutions are tempting but dangerous. They are like gender transformations. In our case the operation seemed to succeed; the outcome was extraordinary. But the patient was not really at peace with himself and remained restless. Now it is all falling apart. Our new fierce identity is disintegrating into a multitude of identities, some of which are frail and confused. At times we do not recognize ourselves anymore. We are not sure who we really are.

Herbert Bentwich climbed from the river Jordan to the shoulder of Mount Hermon. I am more ambitious: I aim for the summit. Above the Crusader's fortress of Kalat Nimrod and above the Druze village of Majdal Shams and above the Israeli settlement of Neve Ativ and above the lower and then the upper cable cars of the ski resort, I reach the closed military base atop the Hermon. At 2,230 meters above sea level, I stand on the highest summit of the land.

Seven circles of threat: Islamic, Arabic, Palestinian, internal, mental, moral, and identity-based. By choosing this land we put ourselves at the epicenter of seven concentric circles of threat. But in the twenty-first century what is especially dangerous is that the forces that have backed us since our arrival are growing weak. The West is in relative economic and political decline. The Jews of the Diaspora are in demographic decline. The alliance of Israel with the enlightened Jews of the West is flagging. At the very same time, the Western powers' ability to maintain order in the Middle East is diminishing, as is their ability to prevent the proliferation of nuclear arms in the Third World. While Islamic fanaticism is rising in the East, there are fewer Western forces that would stand by Israel. Israeli occupation, Jewish extremism, and religious fundamentalists are undermining support for Israel among its remaining friends.

In 1967 Israel conquered Mount Hermon and built a strategically

vital military intelligence base at its summit. On October 6, 1973, Syria
conquered the base and captured its men. Two weeks later dozens of
Israelis gave their life on these steep slopes so that Israel could regain
dominance over this dominating mountain. Now the most advanced
technologies are employed in this science-fiction-like mountainous station. The Hermon high-tech fortress enables Israel to keep an eye on
Syria and beyond.

So as I observe the harsh Syrian plains beneath and the sophisticated Israeli high-tech fortress nearby, it occurs to me that Israel itself is
a fortress. Like the Crusaders, who preceded us by eight hundred years,
we live on a cliff facing east. Like the Christian knights, we depend on
our high walls and sharp swords to keep ourselves alive in a region that
wants us gone. But the strength of the modern Israeli fortress lies precisely in the fact that it does not act or feel like a fortress.

This was not always so. At first, we tried to take this land with the
water towers of utopia under which we built our red-roofed kibbutz
houses and watered the brown plowed fields of our ancient homeland.
Then, when reality struck, we took the land by establishing tower-and-
stockade settlements: prefabricated fortresses that were designed to allow
Jews to settle the land as the Arabs were viciously attacking them. For
a generation or two, Israel was pretty much tower-and-stockade. Like
the Crusaders, it led a life of religious-like devotion that was based on
ideology, modesty, and discipline. The Zionist entity lived by a rigid
code that enabled it to conquer the land, settle it, and defend it.

But in the last generation our citadel was so successful that it stopped
feeling like a citadel. Every few years we came up with a new invention:
Dimona, Mossad, air force, Shin Bet, Arrow missiles, Iron Dome. All
these inventions had a common denominator. The might created by
normalcy enabled normalcy to perpetuate itself. A free society and a
free market gave us an advantage over our adversaries. There was no
longer any need for the Crusader-like ethos of tower-and-stockade. On
the contrary. While the Crusaders needed a collective chastity to maintain their fortress, we turned liberation and individualism into our
source of power. The Israeli fort had become a nonfortified fort producing perpetual supremacy.

But times are changing. The gradual decline of the West and the
turmoil in the East are shifting the tectonic plates on either side of the

Syrian-African Rift. And on Mount Hermon this is almost visual. Old Syria is gone, Iraq is in transition, Jordan's stability is in doubt. As the mass killing of civilians and the use of chemical weapons prove, brutality is beyond comprehension. The howling winds of change that can be felt on this frontier summit are turning into a hurricane that is sweeping the Middle East. So the future of the fortress on the cliff is not clear. As I look out at the land Herbert Bentwich left behind in the end of April 1897, I wonder how long we can maintain our miraculous survival story. One more generation? Two? Three? Eventually the hand holding the sword must loosen its grip. Eventually the sword itself will rust. No nation can face the world surrounding it for over a hundred years with a jutting spear.

The second decade of the twenty-first century has seen some dramatic developments vis-à-vis the seven challenges that Israel faces. One is the New Middle East, the other is New Politics.

Some years after it excited international public opinion, the Arab Spring is still transforming the Arab world. The chain of events triggered by the Tahrir Square revolution in Egypt has had profound, long-lasting, and surprising effects. The demise of the semisecular and pseudo-modern dictatorships of Tunisia, Libya, Egypt, and Syria (and Iraq) put an end to half-century-long regimes of oppressive corruption. The disintegration of significant Arab nation-states terminates a century-long geostrategic status quo shaped by the colonial powers at the end of World War I. Arab nationalism is now giving way to tribalism. Arab modernity is deteriorating in the face of Islamic fundamentalism. As the Arab nation-state and the Arab national identity weaken, turmoil abounds. While Arab monarchies are still standing, failed states and extremist movements and torn-apart nations are replacing what were once secular and cohesive Arab republics.

Gamal Abdel Nasser's Pan-Arab dream is in tatters, Anwar Sadat's moderation has vanished, and the brutal Baath secularism of Sadam Hussein and the Hafez and Bashar Assad is gone. It is no longer clear whether countries like Iraq, Syria, Lebanon, Jordan, and Libya can sustain their national identities. The enormous forces that challenged Zionism in the twentieth century dissolved shortly after the century ended.

Obviously, these momentous changes improve Israel's short-term strategic standing. As the Jewish state proves to be the West's only reliable Middle East ally, it regains some of its old legitimacy and is perceived once again as a valuable asset. As the military gap between high-tech Israel and its blighted neighbors widens, it regains its position as the leading regional power. As the disarray in Syria, Libya, Iraq, and Egypt continues, the old threat of an all-out conventional war diminishes. The violent struggle between Sunnis and Shiites is keeping the new religious forces busy. The preoccupation of most Arabs with the internal Arab malaise temporarily neutralizes their capability to endanger Israel's existence. Some of them are actually looking to Israel to save them from radical elements that now pose an immediate threat to their future. So the vigorous Jewish national movement now seems to be much more coherent and effective than the declining Arab national movement that had been its rival for a hundred years. The declaration signed by Lord Balfour on November 2, 1917, has proven to be—thus far—much more viable than the agreement concluded by Mark Sykes and Charles François Picot on May 16, 1916, which divided up Arab land between the United Kingdom and France, thus defining the modern Arab nation states. Yes, Israel is a lonely rock in a stormy ocean. But sixty-six years after its astounding appearance, the rock seems to be far more solid than the tempestuous waters surrounding it.

And yet, in the long term, the New Middle East might prove to be even more dangerous than the old one. Now there is no hope for peace: no moderate Arab leader has the legitimacy needed to sign a new conflict-ending agreement with the Zionist entity. Now even deterrent-based stability is difficult to maintain: no Arab nation is stable enough and strong enough to guarantee quiet borders and long-term tranquility. Now the risk is growing that eventually Israel will become the Arab world's scapegoat: if political Islam fails to fulfill its promise and the masses rise up against it, the easy way out will be to turn this rage against the infidels living their outrageously prosperous and permissive life next door.

There is increasing danger that sophisticated weapons will fall into the hands of zealots who will be eager to use them against the Jewish state. In short, while the old threat of Arab military might is on the wane, the new danger is Arab chaos. The troubling scenarios are of Arab discontent and Islamic fanaticism knocking on Israel's iron gates. The combination of popular Islamic-Arab resentment from without and desperate Palestinian upheaval from within might yet prove to be explosive. Israel's ability to erect tall (technological) fences and mighty (physical) walls is formidable. As recent years have proven, up to a point, tall fences and mighty walls work. But in the future the besieged-island strategy may exhaust itself. One day the fortified rock might be struck by the angry waves of a regional tsunami.

This kind of chaos seems to be contagious. In 2015–16, it spread from the Middle East to Europe. The outcome of the European Union's inability to conduct a responsible foreign policy in Syria, Iraq, and Libya was that Syria, Iraq, and Libya came to Berlin, Brussels, and Paris. Waves of immigration of refugees and asylum seekers, who had lost all faith in the Arab world, began to undermine European order and values—and to heighten xenophobia and strengthen the far Right. The terrifyingly brutal acts of terror perpetrated by the Islamic State on European soil made things even worse. Not only in Israel's immediate vicinity, but on its mother continent, which had hitherto enjoyed years of peace and stability, there began to develop a disturbing new state of instability and insecurity. At the same time, America, too, experienced deep changes. As the presidential election campaigns of 2016 demonstrated, a separatist, isolationist worldview has taken hold among many Americans who have tired of the Middle East and tired of America's role as the world's policeman—and prefer to focus on its own internal problems. It is now clear: disorder is the new order. A weak international community, coupled with the weakness of America's foreign policy and of the European Union, mean that the regional disorder that engulfs Israel has become chronic and seemingly intractable.

In Israel, too, there have been grave instances of disorder, threatening the cherished values of liberal democracy. A sustained attack, from the radical Left, on the very legitimacy of a Jewish nation-state, and a sustained attack, from the ultra-nationalist Right, on the institutions of public order have created pressing new challenges for the beleaguered center.

The good news of this bewildering new era is that Israel is growing stronger in comparison to its neighbors. The high-tech boom, the natural gas discovered off the coast, and the resilience of its modern economy have led to groundbreaking commercial alliances with India, China, and even some Middle East players.

At the same time, and under the radar, much needed work is being done by the third sector and civic-minded individuals to address many internal fissures. While Israeli politics have gone from bad to worse, Israeli society remains rich, the economy is robust, and spirits are high, even defiant. Despite the conflict and despite a preponderance of pressing challenges, Israelis, according to international surveys, are among the happiest people in the world. The bad news is that the Middle East is growing wilder and that Israel has turned its back on it. Military and technological supremacy have allowed the new Israelis to become strangely isolationist: as they look inward, they ignore the world in which they live. The Palestinians are now the elephant in the room no one dares talk about. Neighboring Arab countries as well as the vast Islamic world are treated as if they were thousands of miles away. Dangerous geohistorical escapism and geostrategic complacency allow the nation once again to be extremely pleased with itself.

As Jews, we have never had it so good. The twentieth century was the most dramatic century in the dramatic history of the Jewish people. The first half of the century was our worst ever: we lost a third of our people, every third Jew. But the second half of the century was wondrous. In North America, we created the perfect Diaspora, while in the Land of Israel we established modern Jewish sovereignty. In Europe and in Latin America and in Australia Jews live well, too. The Jews of the twenty-first century have what their great-grandparents could only dream of: equality, freedom, prosperity, dignity. The persecuted people we were are now emancipated. The pitiable people are now proud. We acquired the ability to fulfill ourselves and live a full life. An unprecedented Jewish renaissance enabled three generations of Jews to believe they escaped Jewish fate. In America this was achieved by the remarkable project of establishing a well-organized, free, meritocratic Jewish community. In Israel, it was achieved by the remarkable success of Zionism. The Jewish national liberation movement gave the Jewish people the basic rights they had been deprived of and the life expectancy they had lost. It conquered a land and liberated a nation and carried out a revolution like no other.

Nowhere is the revolution more apparent than in the Tel Aviv port.

Here, south of the Yarkon River, the first Jewish Olympic Games—the Maccabia—were held in the spring of 1932. Within a few weeks, a sports stadium was hastily constructed in which thousands gathered to watch the hundreds of athletes that traveled to Palestine from twenty-five countries to prove that the Jew of the twentieth century was a new Jew: athletic, muscular, and strong. Here, south of the Maccabia stadium, Tel Aviv's first international exhibition, the Levant Fair, was held in the late spring of 1934. In only eight months a unique Bauhaus compound was erected in which thirty-six nations and twenty-two hundred firms showed their wares and displayed their faith in Tel Aviv's modernity. Some six hundred thousand visitors came to see the wonder: on the southern bank of the Yarkon, in the midst of the Orient, a flying camel, the symbol of the Levant Fair, attested to the architectural and commercial excellence connecting Europe to the Near East. West of the Levant Fair grounds, Zionism's first port was inaugurated in the summer of 1936. Within weeks a customs building was built, along with warehouses and a wooden pier on which the first Hebrew stevedore carried the first sack of cement into the first Hebrew port of the first Hebrew city. The thousands that assembled around him sang the hopeful national anthem, "Hatikva," with palpable emotion. Seven months later, they sang "Hatikva" again in the improvised hall in which the first concert of the Palestine Philharmonic Orchestra was held. When the antifascist maestro Arturo Toscanini conducted the sixty-five survivors of Fascism who played Brahms, Mendelssohn, and Schubert on the Tel Aviv shore, many in the audience were in tears. Two years later a former Russian revolutionary opened a monumental power station a few hundred yards to the north of the improvised hall. In only nine months the ingenious engineer Pinchas Rotenberg and his thousand men, working around the clock, managed to build the Reading power station that accelerated the electrification of the land and provided power to the fast-growing Tel Aviv. Simultaneously, north of Reading, the first runway of the first airport of the first Hebrew city was paved. In the autumn of 1938 the first international flight took off: Tel Aviv–Haifa–Beirut. In an area no larger than one square kilometer, six different events took place within six years, every one of them the stuff of legend. At the northern edge of Tel Aviv the foundations were laid for a sovereign, modern, creative, vital, and life-loving Jewish existence.

I choose to walk southward from the airport. On the promenade between the runway and the sea, a high-tech company is having a fun day out. Twenty rehelmeted men and women ride by on red-wheeled Segways. Behind them are cyclists in sleeveless shirts and Lycra shorts with determined expressions on their faces. The early morning joggers are more relaxed: married couples and male same-sex couples and female same-sex couples in their fluorescent running gear. I see willowy girls on skates, opinionated pensioners, amateur fishermen. Before me is an Israeli Central Park on the shores of the Mediterranean, a Hampstead Heath in the Middle East—with all the calm and tranquillity that only free societies can accord their citizens. There is a sense of well-being here that the Jews have not had for nearly two thousand years.

The six enterprises that were inaugurated on these few hundred acres in the 1930s laid the foundation for contemporary Tel Aviv. They all shared initiative, daring, alacrity, inventiveness, ingenuity, and a can-do spirit, but they were not of one cloth. The first two—the Maccabia and the Levant Fair—were hopeful events. We came here, we were transformed here, we triumphed. But the latter four achievements—the port, the orchestra, the power station, and the airport—were achievements born of peril. They took place under the gathering clouds of the late 1930s, between the German threat and the Arab threat, between the catastrophe expected in Europe and the war beginning in Palestine. While the first two secular miracles occurred facing an open horizon, the latter four occurred facing the pincerlike movement of cruel history closing in.

The can-do spirit and the outstanding energy that characterized Zionism from the outset took a dramatic turn in 1936. From then on, Jewish life in Palestine was an uphill battle: to mobilize faith against fate, to wrestle with fate, to act. And so, digging its harbor and playing its Mendelssohn and erecting its power station and paving its runway, Zionism was already both heroic and tragic.

The power station fascinates me. In later years ugly structures were added, but the original 1938 edifice is all austere grandeur. The Monumental International style chosen by Rotenberg's architects projects modern might. Despite all of the turmoil of the 1930s, the turbines that were about to electrify Palestine were ensconced in a shrine of progress that rose within months on the Yarkon's northern bank. But the tale of the Tel Aviv port is even more significant. Exactly a month after the Arab revolt cut off Tel Aviv from its Jaffa port lifeline, Tel Aviv constructed a wooden pier. It washed out to sea that very night, but it was replaced with a pier of solid steel. But that was not enough. Tel Aviv constructed a jetty and built more piers. Six months after it was besieged, the city sent out of its own port a first crate of oranges—to Buckingham Palace. In doing so, it articulated the Zionist mode of action against those trying to annihilate it. It responded to terror not with terror but with building. It expressed the élan vital of a young nation fighting adamantly while believing that its will to live would overcome the death surrounding it.

I stand by the cascade of warm water falling from the electricity plant to the Mediterranean. As another group of cyclists passes by, I wonder if we still have within us the fortitude that erected the Tel Aviv power station and dug the Tel Aviv port. For to face the seven circles of threat closing in on us, we need the wisdom and energy and devotion we once had. We need the initiative, daring, alacrity, inventiveness, ingenuity, and can-do spirit. As individuals, we have all of these traits of the "yes-we-can" ethos; this is why our start-ups are so remarkable and our ingenuity unique. But as a collective, we seem to have lost what we once had. This is why our nation-state is dysfunctional and our politics dire. Today ours is a free yet polarized society. So the crucial question is whether the free society that emerged here will generate enough power to withstand the external and internal threats endangering it.

Past experience is encouraging. Time after time we rose to the challenge. This pattern of overcoming threats repeated itself even in the Tel Aviv port in the first years of the twenty-first century. In 2002 a wave of terrorism rattled Israel. Dozens died every month in suicide bombings. The nation was petrified and the economy ground to a halt. But while there was blood in the streets, a new initiative was launched to renovate the historic port that had been neglected for years. Within two years the rundown warehouses were turned into a booming leisure complex: shops, cafés, restaurants, bars, nightclubs. In the very spot the Zionist spirit triumphed over the Arab revolt in the 1930s, the Israeli spirit triumphed over the second intifada nearly seventy years later. So now the challenge is to triumph over our internal weaknesses. There are some good reasons for hope. If the ultra-Orthodox community can be integrated into our modern society in the coming decades, it will bring a rush of energy resembling the one brought about by the Russian immigration of the 1990s. If the Israeli Arabs will be woven into our social and political fabric and given the equality they deserve, they might prefer what democratic Israel has to offer over what is offered by Islamist Arab nations and radical Palestinian political movements. If the windfall of offshore natural gas (which will soon make Israel energy-affluent and much richer) is properly invested, it might provide the funds needed for a real internal revolution that will revive the Israeli republic. As the elections of 2013 have proven, not all is lost in Israel. There is still sanity here and a constructive attitude and a deep wish to move forward. Anti-democratic forces might subside as more and more ultra-Orthodox, modern-Orthodox, and Russian immigrants accept the norms and ethos of the Jewish democratic state.

I cross the Yarkon River and enter the port. Although it's morning, the cafés on the wooden decks are bustling. All around me are good-looking women and men, fit girls and boys, young families and young-ish singles. They eat their continental breakfasts, organic breakfasts, Israeli breakfasts; they sip their double espressos, Camparis and champagne. I see bicycles, scooters, skateboards, prams. Bouquets of helium balloons whose colorful aluminum sheaths shine in the sun. A panto-mime performance. An impromptu accordion concert. What a cocktail: an immigrant society and a warrior society against the backdrop of the blue Mediterranean. Jewish history and Israeli present and blue skies. The genetics of pain that burst forth here into gaiety. The genetics of Torah learning that burst forth into creation. Life on the edge, at the water's edge.

I walk on the deck and pass a trendy yoga club. A slim mother walks in wearing tight designer jeans and red All-Star sneakers. Once inside, she parks the orange pram she is pushing next to a dozen other prams and joins dozens of other new mothers in postdelivery Shavasana. Here is vitality. Here is the demography of hope. An almost extinguished spe-cies renewing itself. Unlike the free societies of Europe, the Israeli free society reproduces. Ours is not about disaffection and debauchery but about warmth and family. Ours loves children and brings into a harsh world these toddlers who are crawling on the colorful mats facing the sea. As I see it, Israelis are diamonds in the rough. And Israeliness is an iridescent kaleidoscope of broken identities that come together to form a unique human phenomenon. Somehow, something quite incredible emerged in this old-new country. That is why there is an extraordinary emotional quality to our life here. That is why we are not only creative and innovative but authentic and direct and warm and genuine and sexy. That is why personal relationships here are exceptional and human contact is remarkable. After all and despite all, Israeliness is familyness. As different as they are from one another, and although they belong to rival tribes, the men and women who gathered on this shore managed to form one big, strange, loud, and diverse family.

Here are my own children approaching me: my twenty-two-year-old daughter Tamara bringing with her my nine-year-old Michael and my four-year-old Daniel. Two rowers in garish body suits are taking their boats out to sea and Daniel calls out to them. Michael waves. Tamara laughs. And as we walk back along the jetty, I suddenly realize, it is all here. The irrational project of building this port hurriedly in the wrong location and the inability to turn this shallow port into a deepwater harbor and the inability of a small artificial jetty to provide real protection from the breaking waves of winter. The whole thing should not have come to be in the first place. The project was geographically flawed and economically senseless and poorly planned. But because it captured the imagination, thousands invested capital they didn't have in Tel Aviv Port shares. And because it responded to a deep psychological need, thousands built the port of Tel Aviv. Eventually, this gush of energy created something far larger than its flaws. So although the Tel Aviv port played its intended role for only three years, it became an icon of our independence and innovation and vitality. Every generation and every wave of immigration redefines it. And now it is such a carnival. Thousands of Israelis are celebrating life. Devouring life. Michael runs ahead of me fearlessly. Daniel tries to compete with his brother. Tamara joins her young brothers. And in the golden light now flooding the port, the grandchildren of Herbert Bentwich's granddaughter run gleefully on the wooden deck. Without a care in the world. Without the burden of being Jewish. As if there was no persecution and there will be no persecution. As if there was no Holocaust and there will be no Holocaust. The land is solid under their feet. They are home.

We Israelis face a Herculean mission. To live here we will have to redefine a nation and divide a land and come up with a new Jewish Israeli narrative. We will have to restore a rundown state and unify a shredded society and groom a trustworthy civilian leadership. After ending occupation, we'll have to establish a new, firm, and legitimate iron wall on our postoccupation borders. We will have to replace Ben Gurion's first republic—and the political chaos of recent decades—with a second republic that will be a true home for all Israelis and a genuine pluralistic union. Facing the regional tide of radical Islam, Israel will have to be an island of enlightenment. Facing seven circles of threat, Israel will have to be moral, progressive, cohesive, creative, and strong. There is no other way for us but to renew what we launched here when we founded a daring project of modernity on the Yarkon estuary. The battle for our existence rages on.

After Tamara takes Michael and Daniel home, I move on to the port of Jaffa. In recent years, this port, too, was rehabilitated: galleries, restaurants, bars. A futuristic metal structure replaced the old Arab warehouses, but dozens of wooden fishing boats still bob on the quiet water behind the old jetty where Herbert Bentwich disembarked in April 1897.

We probably had to come. And when we came here, we performed wonders. For better or worse, we did the unimaginable. Our play was the most extravagant of modern plays. The drama was breathtaking. But only the end will properly put the beginning into perspective. Only when we know what has become of the protagonists will we know whether they were right or wrong, whether they overcame the tragic decree or were overcome by it.

There will be no utopia here. Israel will never be the ideal nation it set out to be, nor will it be Europe-away-from-Europe. There will be no London here, no Paris, no Vienna. But what has evolved in this land is not to be dismissed. A series of great revolts has created here a truly free society that is alive and kicking and fascinating. This free society is creative and passionate and frenzied. It gives the ones living here a unique quality of life: warmth, directness, openness. Yes, we are orphans. We have no king and no father. We have no coherent identity and no continuous past. In a sense, we have no civic culture. Our grace is the semibarbaric grace of the wild ones. It is the youthful grace of the unbound and the uncouth. We respect no past and no future and no authority. We are irreverent. We are deeply anarchic. And yet, because we are all alone in this world, we stick together. Because we are orphans, we are brothers in arms and in fate.

There was hope for peace, but there will be no peace here. Not soon. There was hope for quiet, but there will be no quiet here. Not in this generation. The foundations of the home we founded are somewhat shaky, and repeating earthquakes rattle it. So what we really have in this land is an ongoing adventure. An odyssey. The Jewish state does not resemble any other nation. What this nation has to offer is not security or well-being or peace of mind. What it has to offer is the intensity of life on the edge. The adrenaline rush of living dangerously, living lust-fully, living to the extreme. If a Vesuvius-like volcano were to erupt to-night and end our Pompeii, this is what it will petrify: a living people. People that have come from death and were surrounded by death but who nevertheless put up a spectacular spectacle of life. People who danced the dance of life to the very end.

I walk into the very same bar I walked into some weeks ago. Once again I sit by the bar and sip my single malt. I see the ancient port through the windows, and I watch people sitting in restaurants and walking into galleries and wandering about the pier. Bottom line, I think, Zionism was about regenerating Jewish vitality. The Israel tale is the tale of vitality against all odds. So the duality is mind-boggling. We are the most prosaic and prickly people one can imagine. We cannot stand puritanism or sentimentality. We do not trust high words or lofty concepts. And yet we take part daily in a phenomenal historical vision. We participate in an event far greater than ourselves. We are a ragtag cast in an epic motion picture whose plot we do not understand and can-not grasp. The script writer went mad. The director ran away. The pro-ducer went bankrupt. But we are still here, on this biblical set. The camera is still rolling. And as the camera pans out and pulls up, it sees us converging on this shore and clinging to this shore and living on this shore. Come what may.

ACKNOWLEDGMENTS

This book would not have been written if it were not for Timna Rosenheimer—my wife, my love, and my inspiration. Writing it made me an absentee husband and father for five years, yet my life partner stood by me with courage, warmth, and grace. My debt to her is eternal.

Galia Licht was my writing partner. She did much of the research and most of the initial editing, and she enlivened my writing. Whatever is worthy in this book is significantly hers.

Cindy Spiegel is the benevolent Spiegel & Grau editor who made the daring decision to trust me, believing I could actually deliver the book about Israel she thought was needed. Cindy's support and guidance led me throughout the journey, and her outstanding professionalism and sensitivity gave the raw text the shape and precision it needed.

There were two other midwives who brought this child into the world. Tina Bennett is not only my beloved agent but also my guardian angel. In her gracious manner she saw the book and me through all the obstacles and hurdles we ran into. Judy Friedgut is not only my devoted secretary but also my feet on the ground. Having the discipline and good order I lack, she worked day and night to make all this real.

My dear friend David Remnick went over the manuscript with his typical professionalism and contributed precious insights. He is the one who encouraged me to write this book, and he is the one who took care of the book graciously once written. My beloved brother-in-law Gili Rosenheimer stood by me in hard times and tough moments. So did my long-time friends Gabi Pikker and Avi Eliahu. I am deeply grateful to all three. The Natan Fund embraced the manuscript and granted it its first book prize before publication, for which I am deeply grateful. Ester Asherof did the final research, and my one and only Tamara Shavit contributed her share. It is of Tamara's future and the future of her brothers—Michael and Daniel—that I thought of constantly while writing.

My Promised Land is based on numerous interviews and discussions with hundreds of Israelis—Jews and Arabs, men and women. They all opened their homes and opened their hearts and shared their Israeli experience with me. As there were so many of them, I cannot mention all their names here, but I am deeply grateful to each and every one. The intimate and intense dialogue with my countrymen and countrywomen gave me unique insights regarding our beloved and tormented homeland whose story I tried to tell.

SOURCE NOTES

My Promised Land is not an academic work of history. Rather, it is a personal journey through contemporary and historic Israel, recounting the larger Israel saga by telling several dozen specific Israeli stories that are significant and poignant.

The chapter "At First Sight" is based on Bentwich family documents, Herbert Bentwich's own writings, some notes left by his fellow travelers, and articles describing the 1897 Maccabean pilgrimage published in the Jewish-English press and the Jewish-Hebrew press of the day.

"Into the Valley" incorporates interviews with some of Yitzhak Tabenkin's disciples and an enormous body of records and memoirs kept in the Ein Harod archives.

"Orange Grove" was inspired by numerous conversations with Rehovot's elderly orange growers, who were still alive in the late 2000s, and by the local records stored in the Rehovot archives.

The trek and seminar in "Masada" are based on interviews I conducted with Shmaryahu Gutman in 1992 and on pieces published in the spring of 1942 in Labor Movement newspapers and periodicals.

"Lydda" assembles numerous accounts of the traumatic events recounted to me in the early 1990s by Mula Cohen, Shmaryahu Gutman, Yisrael Goralnik, Gabriel Cohen, Yael Degani, Ottman Abu Hammed, and some of the other protagonists of the 1948 tragedy.

"Housing Estate" tells the life stories of Holocaust (and *farhud*) survivors I interviewed—among them Ze'ev Sternhell, Aharon Appelfeld, Aharon Barak, Louise Aynachi, Anna Spiegel, Arie Belldegrun, Yehudit Fischer, Shlomo Teicher, and some of the other residents of the Bitzaron estate.

At the core of "The Project" is a unique encounter I had in 2009 with Yosef

Tulipman, who was the director general of the Dimona nuclear reactor in the critical years 1965–73.

"Settlement" is a reconstruction of the founding of the pivotal settlement of Ofra, based on interviews with Yoel Bin Nun, Pinchas Wallerstein, Yehuda Etzion, Israel Harel, and other Ofra founders in 2009–11.

"Gaza Beach" was first published in *Haaretz* and in *The New York Review of Books* in 1991, shortly after I completed military reserve duty in the notorious detention camp.

"Peace" contains interviews with Yossi Sarid, Yossi Beilin, Avishai Margalit, Menachem Brinker, and Amos Oz (conducted in 2008–11), and an older interview with Jamal Munheir (conducted in 1993).

"J'Accuse" is first and foremost the life story of Aryeh Deri as told to me at great length by him and his mother and as described in his biography and in Israeli magazine pieces written about him over two decades.

"Sex, Drugs, and the Israeli Condition" is an updated version of a comprehensive Tel-Aviv night-life piece that I published in *Haaretz* as the previous millennium was drawing to a close.

"Up the Galilee," too, was first published in *Haaretz*, in January 2003.

"Reality Shock" embodies some of the insights I had in real time during the Second Lebanon War of 2006.

"Occupy Rothschild" is based on in-depth interviews with Michael Strauss, Kobi Richter, and Itzik Shmuli (2007–11) and on conversations with Stanley Fischer and Dan Ben David (2011).

"Existential Challenge" gives Amos Yadlin's interpretation of the Iranian saga as he described it to me in 2012–13, along with my own account of events leading to the Iran deal in the summer of 2015.

"The Millennial Challenge" reflects my impressions and insights following my extensive campus tour of the United States in 2015–16.

"By the Sea" contains a small portion of the observations I had while touring my homeland as my years-long journey was coming to an end.

Pursuing my tour of Israel, old and new, I read hundreds of books and thousands of documents that have inspired me and enriched my experience. To make sure all details are correct, oral histories were checked and double-checked against Israel's written history. The exciting process of interviewing significant individuals was interwoven with a meticulous process of data gathering and fact checking. And yet, at the end of the day, *My Promised Land* is all about people. The book I have written is the story of Israel as it is seen by individual Israelis, of whom I am one.

INDEX

PHOTOGRAPH CREDITS

PHOTO: © SHARON BAREKT

ARI SHAVIT is a leading Israeli columnist and writer. Born in Rehovot, Israel, Shavit served as a paratrooper in the IDF and studied philosophy at the Hebrew University in Jerusalem. In the 1980s he wrote for the progressive weekly *Koteret Rashit*, in the early 1990s he was chairperson of the Association for Civil Rights in Israel, and in 1995 he joined *Haaretz*, where he became one of its leading journalists. Shavit is also a leading commentator on Israeli public television. He is married, has a daughter and two sons, and lives in Kfar Shmariahu.

ABOUT THE TYPE

The text of this book was set in Janson, a typeface designed about 1690 by Nicholas Kis (1650–1702), a Hungarian living in Amsterdam, and for many years mistakenly attributed to the Dutch printer Anton Janson. In 1919, the matrices became the property of the Stempel Foundry in Frankfurt. It is an old-style book face of excellent clarity and sharpness. Janson serifs are concave and splayed; the contrast between thick and thin strokes is marked.